THE DARING SPECTACLE

Mark Morford's Slightly Overused Word Index (SOWI)

W	#	EF	%
Anal (sex)	5	3	100
Apocalypse	8	2.7	100
Astonishing	15	3	100
Astroglide	5	2	100
Bliss	7	-1	100
Burning Man	13	4	100
Bush	46	10	100
Callipygian	2	-6	100
Cosmic	27	7	100
Delicious	20	5.7	100
Divine	76	7	100
Ecstasy (drug)	19	4	100
Feminine	10	-1	100
God	171	1-10	100
Hate	92	3.1	100
Hell	164	8	100
Hitachi	4	-4	100
Hypocrisy	14	1.1	100
Id	8	3	100
Karmic	16	4	100
Lick	21	3.7	100
Love	156	-10	100
Moist	2	-3	100
Mystery	11	2	100
Mystical	12	3	100
Nasty	30	4	100
Obama	38	-2	100
Orgasm/Orgasmic	10	-10	100
Penis	17	2	100
Vibrator	11	2	100

W = Word
# = Number of appearances in *TDS*
EF = Exasperation Factor (1-10)
% = Chance of future reuse, despite EF

I believe in nothing, everything is sacred.
I believe in everything, nothing is sacred.
-Tom Robbins

Soul is to be found in the vicinity of taboo.
-Thomas Moore

Everywhere is walking distance, if you have the time.
-Steven Wright

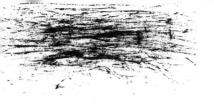

THE DARING SPECTACLE
Mark Morford

It's like that moment you suddenly become aware of your tongue, struck by the strange and wonderful presence of this large, shiny, slippery muscle apparatus that's completely filling up your mouth at all times, right now, just sitting there, twitching, pulsing, waiting for its chance to say something or lick something or taste something or curl suggestively around something; it's an odd, disquieting awareness, like looking around the urban landscape suddenly becoming aware of all the blood and skin and breath, all the come and sweat and spit, the hair and hope and heat walking around in a billion weird little shells, suddenly glimpsing the great, grand maelstrom, the gorgeous circus cavalcade of all of existence in one mindblowing superconscious metasnapshot, how everything is in a constant state of flux, a constant renewal and sloughing off, one interminable river of life and death and is-this-really-happening, to the point where all you want to do is nudge that glistening muscle out from between your lips and wag it around in the beckoning air so as to more fully taste the absolute divine absurdity of it all, right now, because it's, like, *your* tongue, and no one else's, and it makes you special and beautiful as it fills you up like your own personal pet, whispering sweet everythings into your ear deep in the night, as you sleep, luscious, swooning tales of twisted words and flipped phrases and bittersweet afterthoughts, of being delightfully jammed into kinky crevices and slathered over ice cream cones and dangled over tantalizing possibilities, half-forgotten words dancing like angels on the very tip, as your whole being longs only to take wide, wet swipes of the benign and everconscious universe — a universe which tastes, it turns out, very much exactly like you thought it would all along.

Library of Congress Cataloging-in-Publication Data applied for, as that appears to be reasonably important. Email: spectacle@markmorford.com. Visit: markmorford.com. Call out: yes yes yes yes yes.

ISBN 978-0-9842997-0-6

~ nil desperandum ~

INVOCATION

Of Man's inhumanity to Man, and furthermore
To dog and forest and churning vast ocean too,
Of that boundless lovelust that makes men wail
And women dispatch a luscious piece of Facebook mail;
Of wisdom and insight, satire and devotion
And the very best Pinot to go with many years of war;

Sing to me, O heavenly Muse!

Sing to me of the man, He of squints and mumbles
Who misunderestimated making the pie higher;
Sing of goddesses and sex and things insertable to vibrate
Of enchanting music and film and ink deep into the skin
Of wordplay and raw creation and the dance of too many veils
Oft tempered by sadness and death and tragedy even so

Show me how the religious fundamentalist wields his
Double-edged sword to cut his meth and ogle gay porn
As his beleaguered God looks on, eyebrows high;
Whisper to me sweet somethings of irony and hypocrisy
Tales of scandal and sex tape, prostitute and fetish
As the full moon just laughs, and opens wide her legs

Talk of hope and progress and change we can believe in
To succor and soothe the cynical collective soul
Say what can be done, defy and devour all that can't
Throw the switch to green, drop the clutch and go
Even as the Earth sends her distress calls in the night
As we scurry past the graveyard, whistling a karmic hymn

But sing most of all, O Muse, of awe and wonder
And things bursting with ecstasy and bliss
A place of wine and laughter, compassion and joy
Entwirled with love;
Sing the conscious interconnectedness of All
Where mind meets body, and spirit meets flesh
In the grand hall of the Sacred Fuck Yes

THIS IS ME

Mark Morford is a longtime columnist and culture critic for the San Francisco Chronicle and SFGate, as well as a popular Vinyasa yoga teacher in San Francisco. It's true.

He was raised by nubile long-eyelashed callipygian wood nymphs and spoon fed dark chocolate and raw pomegranate seeds and 18-year-old Scotch until he could fly. Mark was born on the 16th of January in the same year the first issue of *Rolling Stone* hit the streets, Elvis married 'Cilla, Super Bowl I was played, and John Coltrane died. His birth happened in the city of Spokane, Washington, a small, harmless city in the Pacific Northwest well known for having exactly nothing much to be well known for. He has a pair of wonderful, still-married moderate Republican parents who forgive him all his heathenistic, leftist trespasses, as he forgives them for voting for Reagan and *both* Bushes. He also has two beautiful older sisters to whom he is eternally grateful for teaching him the incredible range and variety of the female psychoemotional flora.

Mark attended Musicians Institute (MI) in Los Angeles during the mid-'80s when the denim was tight and the hair was big and Eddie Van Halen was still God. Life later spit him into the halls of U.C. Berkeley, where he investigated the pagan influences in Milton's "Paradise Lost" and discovered how Eve taught the serpent to use its tongue. He managed to gradu-

ate Phi Beta Kappa, summa cum laude, and caveat emptor.

He has worked for magazines. He has worked in book publishing — but they were computer books, so that doesn't really count.

He landed at SFGate in 1997, where he soon became the lead writer and editor for the site's main pages, along with creating and writing a hit underground email newsletter, called the *Morning Fix*, the irreverent/sexualized/opinionated voice of which served as the inspiration for the very columns you are about to read.

Mark became a full-time columnist for SFGate in 2000 via a strange cocktail of sheer nerve, good timing, oddball mentors and divine cataclysm. His "Notes & Errata" column soon became a bit of a sensation, quickly rising to become one of the most popular features in the site's history. It remains so today.

The column was invited into the print edition of the San Francisco Chronicle in the middle of 2005, where it ran in the Datebook (entertainment) section for three wonderful-but-misfit years, before being yanked back out and returned to online-only in mid-2008 by a new editor-in-chief who considered Mark's work too irreverent and kinky for the older, conservative print readership. Mark's many older, kinky print readers were none too pleased at this, but what can you do.

His writing has been described as blasphemous, inspiring, lickable, inimitable, transgressive and terribly verbose, self-aggrandizing bullshit —

often all in the same sentence. He has almost been fired — twice — for the contents of his column. He has also won first place in the National Society of Newspaper Columnists' annual contest — also twice, and been nominated for multiple GLAAD Media Awards for his outspoken support of gay rights, a fact for which he feels particularly grateful and blessed, considering how he's relatively sure he is exceedingly straight.

Mark's writing has appeared in numerous upstanding publications, including Mother Jones, Yoga Journal, Men's Health, The Sun, Nerve and The Bark, but not Guns & Ammo or Quilter's

World. Further details to be had at markmorford.com.

Since 2000, Mark's also been teaching a rigorous, athletic, music-filled, joyful syle of heart-opening Vinyasa or "flow" yoga, all about strength and breath and deep bliss, most recently at the Yoga Tree network of schools in San Francisco, where he currently leads upwards of four classes per week, plus workshops and private sessions. See markmorfordyoga.com for more.

The two unorthodox career paths, columnist and yoga teacher, have evolved more or less simultaneously over the years, side by side, intersecting and colliding, spinning and merging, feeding into and off of each other in some sort of messy, wonderful synchronicity. Mostly.

Mark believes in divine mystery, good lubricant and beautifully designed, small European cars. And dogs. And wine. And trees.

The Daring Spectacle

Mark Morford

OVERTURE

Welcome. You are in the right place

Here's what you really need to know: *The Daring Spectacle* is, at heart, 92 of the finest, strangest, best-written, most popular, most divinely inspired, still relevant, or otherwise juiciest Notes & Errata columns I've ever penned — from a running total of nearly 1,000 or so — for the San Francisco Chronicle and SFGate.

But this is no haphazard collection. This is no meek, lazy grab bag of my past work, all tarted up and stuck over in the corner of the media prom, hoping for one more slow dance and maybe a furtive upskirt grope. I have made every possible effort and sipped many snifters of laudanum to ensure that this book has a fresh tang and crackling sensibility all its own.

Much of what you are about to read has never been available before. Some of these writings have never been formally archived, and are impossible to find anywhere but here.

The hate mail, for example, has never been read by eyes other than my own and a few select, horrified editors and friends, nearly all of whom required a few shots of Maker's Mark and a some deep gulps from an oxygen tank to make it through. It's just that frightening. You'll see.

Also completely new: the commentary. I've added a fresh thought atop every column in this book, a follow-up or a glimpse behind the scenes, maybe an anecdote, some background, that sort of thing. Hopefully interesting, occasionally funny, almost never mandatory.

There are columns in here that nearly got me fired, columns that were spiked — that is, rejected — columns that were banned and some which gave my editors a rabid case of what the late David Foster Wallace would call "the howling fantods." However, there are also award-winners, columns as gentle as puppy's breath, as sweet as melted poetry, as tangy as lemon gin in summertime. And of course, everything in between.

So in truth, *TDS* is quite full of the new and revitalized. The columns have all been re-edited, the references mostly refreshed, the deadwood trimmed. The design, graphics, format? All new. The self-publishing model I'm attempting in the face of a convulsive, uncertain book industry? Also new, risky, strange. And reading my work like this, as a book, as much or little as you want, one giant, orgiastic, all-you-can-eat buffet? New as fresh roadkill in spring.

All told and if I do say so myself, it's quite the curious, badass remix. It has a terrifically strange, enticing beat. I hope you can dance to it.

Tell me what you think? Please do: spectacle@markmorford.com

The Daring Spectacle

How to read the *Spectacle*

Bathtub reader. Bedside companion. Subway commuter's friend. Pre-coital tease. Post-coital rubdown. Liberal tickler. Literate snacker. Intellectual chew toy. Divine sparring partner. Vibrator for your id. Cerebral bump in the night. Not really designed to be read straight through because holy hell even *I* get sick of my columnal voice after awhile; there's only so much wordplay and outrage you can take at one sitting without sighing and rolling your eyes. You know?

Far more designed to be flipped open at random, discovering, with any luck, something new and fascinating and delicious on every page. For my part, I've tried very hard to put something new and fascinating and delicious *on* every page, so when it does fall open, you'll want to lean in a little closer, reach up underneath, find that sweet spot, and say *mmm*.

This makes no sense whatsoever

Please note the *Where Am I?* page (AKA, the Table of Contents). You'll see I've made a real, but only partially successful attempt at chapter organization and columnal groupings. I did not organize by chronology or even by topic, because really, who wants to read three columns about politics or five columns about drugs in a row? I mostly went by feel, vibration, thematic posture. I humbly suggest you do the same.

In other words, please arrange *TDS* according to any sort of whim that licks your mood. Mix and match. Toss and turn. Grope it in the night. Place it on your altar. Top it. Bottom it. Strap it on. Take it from behind. Spank it with your intention. Let it spank you right back. Deal?

It's not just that

Very few pieces are here for their straight-out shock value. Few are just for dumb titillation. And fewer still are about politics or George W. Bush per se, despite how many columns I wrote about that squinty monkey of ineptitude and all the ideological chyme he foisted upon us all.

In fact, much of my work turned out to be *too* topical and of-the-moment to include in a compendium like this. Such is the nature of a column that depends largely on hot news of the day for its inspiration. Alas, I am no Dave Barry, sweetly wisecrackin' on the nature of, say, sock drawers and middle-class marriage and the sundry absurdities of mundane suburbia. My wiring, my yoga, my sexuality, my kinkiness, my spiritual practice, my rather blasphemous sense of the divine, my near-pathological need to upend and spin around and generally fuck with the standard tropes of journalism, combined with a congenital fondness for very, very dry humor, basically means I'm not exactly cut out for conventional writing anyway. I like to convince myself this is a good thing.

What year is it again?

I tried to keep it all reasonably fresh. The vast majority of these columns range from the mid-00's right up to this book's 2010 publication. Only a few precede 2004, simply because some of the really old stuff is fairly dreadful and I like to think my writing has improved tremendously, and one benefit of this project is I get to make myself look as gloriously talented as possible.

However, a few go pretty far back. The oldest piece here, 2001's "Sex and the schoolteacher" (p. 83) is included for sheer historical value — certainly not for quality — insofar as it nearly got me fired, and the story of the near-firing made minor headlines back then, and this particular column has never been seen in public before because it was banned and buried and considered hotly dangerous to all living souls. That might be an exaggeration. But that's sort of how it felt at the time.

Another piece, "A question of dripping women" (p. 288) — which, until this book, has never been in print anywhere — was one of the few columns of mine to ever have be rejected by both the paper *and* SFGate, which was a rare occurrence indeed. See if you can figure out why.

The most recent pieces in *TDS* take us right through the stunning '08 election and well beyond, as President Obama swept his way into history and the very tone and timbre of the national dialogue took a dramatic turn for the smarter and the different and the exhilarating.

In between, America. A snapshot, a scrapbook, a big delirious left-wing lick and suck and swallow of the millennial zeitgeist, a decade-long portrait of a wary and punch-drunk nation as seen through the eyes of a straight, sexed-up, spiritually impassioned, imperfectly liberal, reasonably kinky, tattooed culture critic and passionate yoga teacher (that's me) working for a major, long-suffering American newspaper and living and breathing and doing ecstatic, sweaty asana in the vibrant, much maligned, globally adored, freethinking freakshow bubble that is San Francisco.

It's a lens that, as you might imagine, has earned me an impressive number of frothy right-wing detractors and devoted denouncers, all essentially guaranteeing me — if my many horrified fundamentalist readers are to be believed — a first-class ticket straight to all-consuming Hell.

Which is just another way of saying, it's the best fucking lens you could possibly hope for.

Email from the dark side

AKA: *I hate you I hate you I hate you*

Now we come to something very special indeed. Scattered like intellectual potholes throughout *TDS*, you'll find a very bleak bizarro-world where everything is backwards and phlegmy and violent and sad. Look for the giant skull, and you'll know you've found it.

This is my hate mail. A premium sampling, a few dozen of the nastiest, most nauseating, hilarious, vile hunks of spittle I've received over the years. It is something to behold.

Was a time when I'd wake in the morning to a pile of this poison waiting for me like verbal anthrax in my in-box, and I knew. I knew a given column had been posted to the forums at one of any number of extremist right-wing websites I won't debase this book by mentioning. They would post my column *and* a direct link to my email, and encourage each other to send me some bile. And dear God, did they ever.

Sadly, I don't get much full-bore, over-the-top hate mail of this kind anymore, in large part because the haters now post their sneers in the anonymous comment forums across the Web, those vacuous wastelands of human thought that have almost singlehandedly ruined the art of healthy debate and author/reader communication. Can you tell I'm not a fan?

However, praise Shiva and for the record, this is not the only kind of response I get. My positive, intelligent fan mail has *always* outweighed the hate, by a large margin. And with the advent of Facebook and Twitter, et al, real fans and thoughtful dialoguers can find me far more easily, without the distraction of the snarling homophobes and right-wing fundamentalists — some of whom, I have to say, read me more vehemently than just about anyone.

That's a fascinating phenomenon, by the way: Many of my nastiest, most bilious critics and detractors read me *religiously*, fanatically, and appear to love nothing more than to fantasize about my daily life, what sort of godless perversions and filthy kinks I must surely indulge in every morning before I have my coffee. I apparently provide them with a very valuable psychological service: they get to project their ugliest thoughts, craven cravings, unfulfilled sex fantasies, gay bathhouse scenes, you name it, onto me, without having to actually acknowledge their own repressed sexuality, their deepest hypocrisies. It's nothing new, of course — such obvious Freudian projection has been going on since God invented sex and language and then never stopped laughing. But it still never ceases to amaze and delight, even as it makes me sort of sad.

Of grease and whiskey

One word of warning: Do not, under any circumstances, read all the hate mail by itself, straight through, without pause or break. At least, not without some sort of protection nearby – a shot of whiskey, a vibrator, a copy of the Bhagavad-Gita or *Jitterbug Perfume* or a small, terribly cute puppy.

As hilarious, bizarre and horribly written as these emails are — and by the way, I have left them largely intact, verbatim, all misspellings and atrocious grammar included — they also hold a very dark, greasy energy. They are borne of a very low vibration. You can get knocked back pretty hard.

There is certified hate speech. There are threats of violence. There is ignorance and intolerance like a cancer. There is sexism and racism and homophobia — *especially* homophobia — of the ugliest and most disgusting kind imaginable. Think you can imagine? I bet you can't.

So loathsome are some of these letters, you might be tempted to think I must've made some of them up. I haven't. At one point I even considered turning the hate mail into some sort of book unto itself. But no one should be subjected to such a pile of odium and fear and all at once.

That said, I predict you will enjoy the hate mail tremendously. It's hugely perversely fascinating. Just be careful. It's ugly in there.

A word about mullets

As mentioned, during my early days as lead editor for SFGate, to prevent my creative juices from coagulating, I created this raw, barely edited daily email newsletter, called the *Morning Fix*. It was a blog before blogs, fast and messy and sexual and personal, full of wildly verbose satire, spinning off the news of the day, and beyond. At the height of its four-year run, the *Fix* had about 75,000 subscribers, all from word of mouth (management was always too nervous to promote it openly). It became a bit of an underground sensation, a cult hit. It also nearly got me fired. Over the word "fuck." But never mind that now.

Every week, among the happy blasphemy, sex toy references and crazed commentary, I'd run a tiny feature called Mullet Haiku, which is... well, exactly that: sweet little haiku poems about a beloved, all-American hairstyle, and the kingdom over which it presided. I have no idea where the idea came from. But it sure was funny as hell.

Immediately after I started the haiku feature, delirious readers took over and began sending in their own hilarious creations. I've included the best of the best in the *Spectacle* (look for the cherry blossom branch). Why? Because it's haiku, silly. About *mullets*. What more do you need?

What do you think you're doing?

This book exists for three reasons, none of which has to do with money or sex or equestrian events. Well, not equestrian events, anyway.

One: Ego. Newspapers and news websites are, by design, ruthlessly impermanent. To work so hard and passionately on churning out what I hope are well-crafted pieces of wordsmithery, only to have them vanish to the e-archives in a few hours, is deeply unkind to the fragile writerly ego.

I realize this is the merely the nature of the media beast, and mostly I'm fine with it. But I can't help but love the idea that *TDS* gives these pieces a shot at semi-permanence, a hit of literary respect, a place on your bookshelf or by your bedside, as opposed to merely gathering e-dust in a giant server farm somewhere in San Jose.

Two: Demand. "When will you put out a book?" "Where can I buy a collection of your columns?" "You really should gather your stuff together into some sort of handheld printed matter I can transport easily and about which I won't really care if I accidentally toss into an active volcano. I'd sure as hell buy it!" This is what I've heard for years. I'm honored beyond belief by the sentiment. I hope it's true.

Three: Evolution. A newspaper column is a writerly trap. A wonderful, rewarding, highly desirable trap, but a trap nonetheless. After awhile, your perspectives begin to contract. Your mental skillset suffers. Bad literary habits form. Before you know it, everything begins to be slotted into comfy 1200-word boxes. Everything turns into a strange opportunity to ask yourself, "I wonder how I could turn that into a really clever lede?"

It's my hope that this strange book will ignite some new directions, expand my reach, launch me out of the gilded confines of both column and columnist. I have no idea *how*, exactly. It ain't exactly the Great American Novel. But it *is* a transmutation of energy. A step toward... something. Isn't it? Or is just a retread, a regurgitation, a pitiable attempt to re-live past glories? Oh my God, is it? Why didn't someone stop me? Oh well.

Less spittle, more nuance

The word *rant* makes me cringe. I detest what it connotes: thoughtlessness, lopsidedness, lack of control, yelling and acid reflux and Bill O'Reilly in a spittle-flecked, constipated frenzy.

Nevertheless, many of my columns over the years have been labeled rants, tirades, takedowns, lefty hippie commie pinko tofu homo gibberish. And I gotta admit, sometimes for good reason. Except for that last thing.

Problem was, for many years it was often ridiculously difficult to wake up in the morning and read the newswires and *not* feel appalled, saddened, outraged by something ugly and nefarious recently inflicted upon the nation by the worst U.S. government administration in modern history, to such a degree that I found it impossible *not* to vent that frustration on the page. To be an opinion columnist, to see and feel what was going on in the world and merely shrug it off, to stay lukewarm and perky? Inconceivable.

The Buddha, the tantrikas, my yoga and spiritual practice teach otherwise. They speak of compassion, consciousness, non-attachment no matter how vile the atrocity. Of course, the Buddha didn't know George W. Bush.

But it's my hope you'll find, among the fire and diatribe, an enjoyable amount of counterbalance, thoughtfulness, depth, intellectual delight, unexpected spiritual heat. Shakti knows I never wanted to be The Raging Pundit of the left, some sort of alcoholic, self-loathing porcupine whose sole purpose in life was to seek out conservative idiocies to infuriate my sensibilities. That's far too easy, lazy, obvious. I'm far more interested in range, nuance, interconnectivity, in being as unclassifiable and unexpected as possible. I'm still working on it.

Who the hell do you think you are?

As you might imagine, my writing style and topic range have been issues from the beginning, at least as far as where I slot into the "traditional" news media spectrum. I am not a journalist by training, and certainly not any kind of neutral, just-the-facts reporter. I'm a writer, a stylist, a deep believer in the medium *and* the message, that form can be as illuminating and transformative as function. This goes a long way toward explaining why my column flourishes on the untamed, open-throated Web, but was a tough ride for the docile, conformist print newspaper.

So, is my column pure entertainment? Political rant? Fiery social critique? Pop-culture confection? Creative essay? Spiritual ass tickler? Is it a joke? Is it for real? It is, I very much hope, all of those things, and a few dozen more.

Whatever it is, it's often made for a very schizophrenic, volatile fit in a rather nervous media world that far prefers things unambiguous and easily categorized. No matter. Because the ultimate upshot is, it's made for one hell of a ride.

And now, without further ado, I present you *The Daring Spectacle*. Please undress accordingly.

WHERE AM I?

ALL-AMERICAN SNAPSHOTS

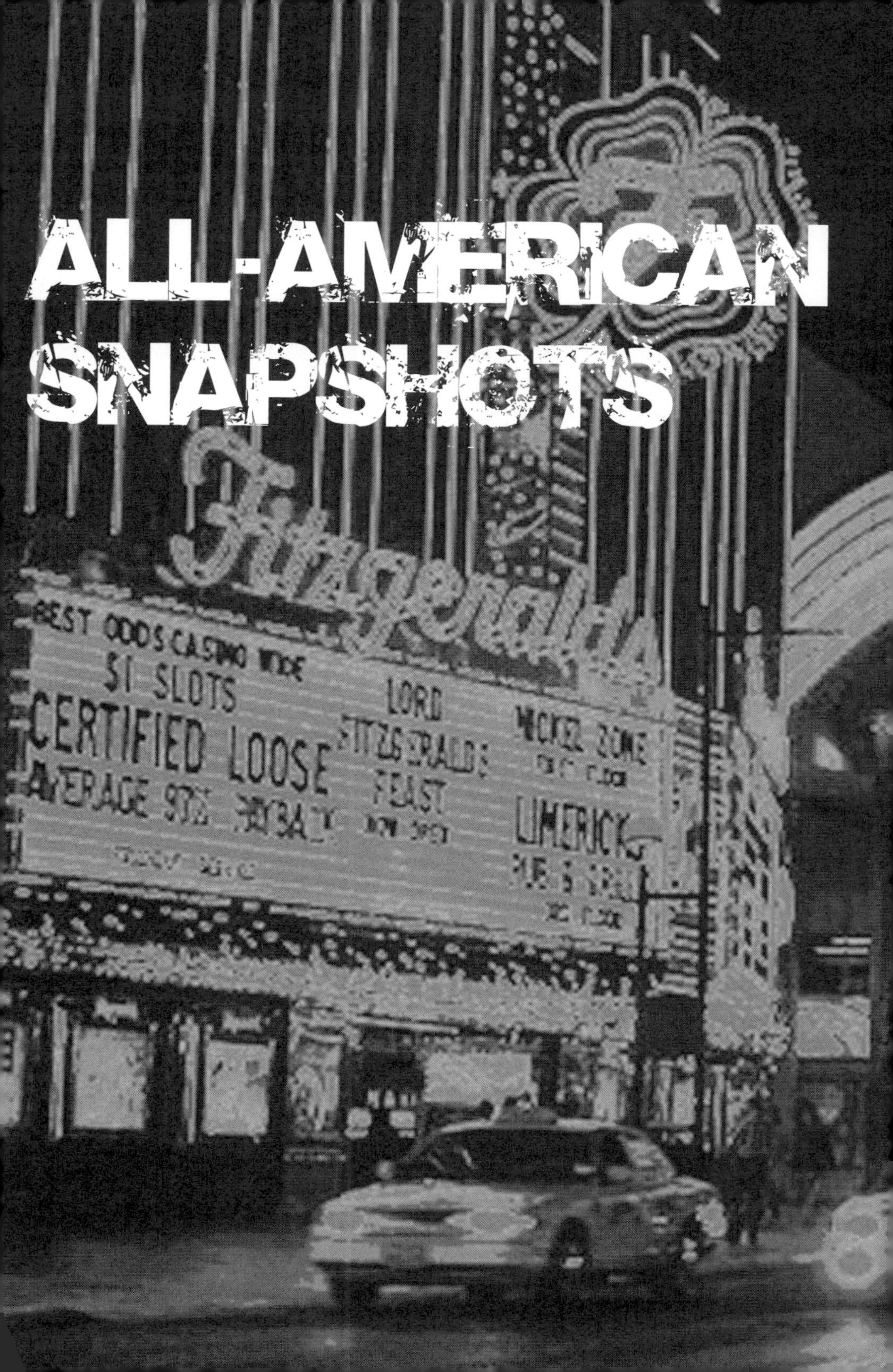

> *It is very possible this entire column is merely the record of a terrible fever dream, a fiendish hallucination. Does the bingo room at the Sands still exist? Has anyone actually played in there and lived to tell about it? If you close your eyes at night, can you not hear the cackle and hiss of that tinny microphone I describe below, the scratch and catch in the crone's exhausted voice, the shuffle and groan of all those viscous bloodstreams, as you wait for what seems like eternity for your number to be called?*
>
> *This was a very popular column, way back when. I do seem to enjoy setting a scene. —mm*

Bingo, the death of souls

08/20/2003

I have glimpsed the mouth of Hell.

I have felt the soft whooshing sound as the demon casually attempted to Hoover my soul from its moorings, stab my very anima with the rusty ice pick of lethargy and small cash prizes, lower the collective social vibration to that of a small tree fungus atrophying somewhere in the rain forests of Peru.

I have been to the Strip in Reno, Nevada. It is, by almost every account, one of the more pure, time-tested rings of Hell. Las Vegas has gone family, upscale, almost cool, fancy billion-dollar hotels and superlative entertainment and terrific food, a huge array of wondrous excess. The Strip in Reno, by contrast, attained 1974 and stopped cold.

But there are, of course, levels to Hell. Floors. Decks. Strata. I have stayed overnight in the Sands Regency hotel in Reno. The Sands, too, is a stratum of Hell — lower, deeper, more sinister and sad, all rank beer and stale cigarette smoke and mysterious carpet stains, and to the two sweet, sad, newly arrived Polish girls working the drab counter at the mini Pizza Hut off in the corner of the lobby, I wish you so much luck, and love — and please know, that ain't America.

Is this as low as it gets? Is the Sands Hell's inner sanctum? Because maybe you think it would be enough. Maybe you think this might be a sufficient dosage of sticky tackiness for anyone to endure.

You would be wrong.

There is yet another. There is a Hell inside the Hell inside the Hell. I have seen it.

Here is how you get there: Just past the Sands check-in counter and the chirping screaming banks of video-poker

machines and "I Love Lucy" video slots by the rickety parking-garage elevator and just over there on your left, there it is, you see it, this opening, this short passageway, this gaping maw of beckoning neon and drifting smoke and quiet, rashy death.

You wander near. You tentatively enter the passage. You look down toward the end and see a large cluster of people, maybe 50 or more, sitting in rows, facing away from the entranceway, heads bowed, silent.

They are all well above middle aged. They are all hunched. Pale and detached and wilting and otherworldly. They are all locked in deep concentration/lethargy, and it's apparent that their copious bodies have long ago admitted defeat and their spines have long given up strength or flexibility or anything resembling verticality.

There is almost no movement whatsoever. There almost is no sound. There is no background music, or even Muzak. There is an overwhelming sense of stasis, an interminable sinking, like lumpy pudding, like spiritual quicksand. On the left is a raised platform upon which sits a hooked woman, emaciated and alone, a long-necked microphone arcing up from the podium toward her mouth. She leans in, and in that muffled, hospital-room PA sound, you hear it, like someone dropping a large bag of sand on a small penguin, slowly.

"B-27."

Oh yes. It is the bingo room. In the Sands. In Reno. You have found it. It has found you. You feel the whooshing. The tug of the demon. And it is wrong on levels you never even knew existed.

"N-15."

No one moves. Three grayish heads twitch slightly, someone shifts in her seat, you hear a phlegmy cough off in the corner. The ceiling is low and discolored. There are no windows. There are no plants or soft lighting or traces of tasteful decor. No one shouts "Bingo!" and stands up and does a little dance. No one laughs or smiles or chats or even looks up. There is much smoking. There is much sitting. There is very little else.

"H-14."

You can go no further. You can only watch. Hell inside Hell inside Hell. It is like nothing you have ever seen or ever want to see again and it pulls at this deep part of your psyche, yanks you close and squints its eyes and looks at you intensely and says, See? Do you see?

Here is your metaphor. Here is your ideal and painfully real analogy. The dank and stained bingo room in the Sands, in Reno. This is exactly what is happening in this country. This is what we have become.

This room, this mind-set, it is devoid of sunlight or beauty or nuanced thought, a breeding ground of catatonia and intellectual anesthesia and

careening obesity and a weird sense of hopelessness, of defeat, and you want to shrug it all off and let it be and remember that just because it's not your thing doesn't mean it's necessarily evil or malevolent or karmically debilitating. But you can't. It just won't let you.

Because it is but a short little spiritual/psychological leap to note how we all have our bingo rooms and we all feel that soft whooshing, that sinister tug from the demons of mass cultural stasis and inertia and noxious television and poisonous junk food and Wal-Mart and entertainment stripped down to its most crude, a tired slap of a nearly dead synapse when the crone calls your number.

The bingo room is in you, always. It is latent and cancerous and it is like "Everybody Loves Raymond" or born-again Christianity or the Olsen twins, weirdly tantalizing and notoriously toxic and yet part of you wants to succumb to its poisonous charms, its slow-motion heart attack, its river of Lethe.

Because in the bingo room, there is no pain. There is no suffering or political bickering or gutted school budgets or taxes or screaming breakups or bad sex or rampant lies about endless wars.

There is only the harmless shifting of numb gluteal fat, the marking of bingo cards, and of time. There are only the tiny but endlessly alluring cash prizes, the haze of menthol smoke, a makeshift community of lostness and decay and happy emphysemic stupor, that sinking feeling that it's all going to be over soon anyway so might as well just plop down and order another white zin and wait for your number to be called. Because rest assured, it always comes.

The question is, are you going to succumb?

For a good month or so after this delightful story first broke, Tiger's slut-tastic debacle was a true gift, a pop culture goldmine for comedians and columnists from all walks of media life. The jokes essentially wrote themselves. I took a slightly different tack, as I couldn't help but recall what I wrote about a certain coke-loving supermodel back in '05 (See "Open letter to Kate Moss" on page 103) and applied the lessons learned therein to Tiger's situation, to come up with this dandy analysis.

I don't think I'd ever written about Tiger before this column, except maybe as a pop reference or punch line. Turns out this was one of my most successful pieces in ages. This and the "101 reasons why men cheat" which immediately followed it (see page 182) earned well over a quarter million page views, combined. So thank you, Tiger. You made it so gloriously easy. —mm

Tiger Woods must die!

12/11/2009

I find I am, almost against my will, utterly delighted by the Tiger Woods crash-and-burn who-woulda-thunk slut-of-the-week pornstars-n-hookers flameout shockfest circus funhouse megaspectacle.

It was not a quick realization. Fact is, I have never once cared the slightest bit about Tiger Woods or anything he has ever done, represented, embodied. I have zero interest in golf, don't care for insipid multimillionaire celebrity endorsements, gated Florida mansions or blinged-out Cadillac Escalades, and I have never once found myself remotely enchanted or bedazzled by anything Woods has said or done, largely due to the fact he doesn't appear to have much of a discernable personality or any spiritual fire to speak of, and his sole accomplishment seems to be making a mountain of cash by playing one of the world's most boring, nonathletic sports exceptionally well.

But never mind any of that now. Tiger has transformed. Tiger has *transcended.* He is right now entering another glorious, rarefied realm, a unique stratum of American iconography, that of the fallen hero, the broken god, the disgraced saint soon be abhorred by millions, only to be — and you may take my word for this right now — loved and adored again in about, oh, I'd say two years and change. Maybe less. Just you watch.

It's the same old story, really. Woods is now in the midst of nothing less than a classic, time-honored pattern that just might be one of our nation's finest, most insidious inventions of all time.

Do you know this pattern? I bet you do. It's the same one that's been followed, with varying success, by all sorts of rock stars, supermodels, actors,

athletes, pastors and politicians since George Washington was caught
indulging his gay fetishes in an opium den in Paris. It's a blueprint that
appears to work best in a ruthless capitalist system, not only because this
is where wealth, power and ego can explode out of scale so quickly, but
because capitalism gave birth to the damn thing in the first place.

It goes something like this: Above-average human with just the right
mix of talent/timing achieves massive success in a particular pop cultural
arena, largely based on the blind love of millions who,
through relentless marketing and media hype,
have come to see him/her as a true icon, a
symbol of faultless morals and righteousness,
the poster child for the plucky American
Dream — even though the American Dream
doesn't really exist, and it never really did.

Said blessed human goes on to enjoy an
impressive, even stellar, career, sets records,
makes blockbusters, appears in every magazine or cereal box known to man, becomes
a brand, dines with the president, marries a
supermodel/shipping tycoon, has God on
speed-dial, earns influence and power far ex-
ceeding his/her actual domain/sport/category. All seems beautiful, ideal,
bulletproof.

Then, the magic happens.

Seemingly out of nowhere, a crack appears. A dire mistake is made. An
Escalade crashes into a tree, a line of cocaine is snorted near a paparazzi's
hungry camera, a random drug test comes back positive for steroids, a
gay prostitute proves he's had frequent meth-addled sex with a powerful
homophobic televangelist Christian nutball. You know: same ol', same ol'.

You know what happens next. All sorts of delightful pop culture hell
breaks loose. Celebrity has spectacular flameout, reveals self to be far more
debauched, wicked, strange, stupid than gullible fans and followers ever
wanted to believe.

Ensuing meltdown makes massive headlines as celeb loses product endorsements by the millions, is shunned by former fanbase, makes children
cry, becomes instant pariah/punchline for wary and jaded nation, the
poster child for How It All Can Go Oh So Frightfully Wrong.

The force of this negative backlash can be downright shocking. Americans *hate* to feel like they've been duped, even if they willingly helped co-
create the saccharine lie from day one. What's more, unbeknownst to the
celeb, all that support and love they had in the beginning often morphs

into quiet, seething resentment, over time. It's just waiting to be ignited, uncorked, tabloided straight to hell.

Enter Tiger Woods, the bland, clean-cut Buick spokesman and nice-guy family man, who is turning out to be just an incredibly offensive, adulterous slut, a Vegas-hopping, hooker-hoarding, waitress-nailing, cheating whorebag of fun, a guy with absolutely awful taste in women but excellent skills at sleazy duplicitousness, hereby fully earning the crown as the new American pariah. U-S-A! U-S-A!

Oh, but wait. We're not even to the best part yet. Because, as I mentioned, I am hereby predicting, based on the Great Pattern o' Fame mentioned above, a relatively quick turnaround for poor Tiger.

I am suggesting that Woods will crash, burn, be stomped into cultural oblivion in the coming months, only to rise again. It's virtually guaranteed. Unless Woods is revealed to have murdered a few hookers in Vegas or says something in a public microphone about his love of dog fighting and watching gay porn with Glenn Beck, his rosy future is a lock. Well, maybe.

Look, if there's one thing we love more than discovering new heroes and building them into overpaid royalty, it's tearing them down again, just so we can watch them fall from grace like an AIG exec taking a swan dive from the Empire State Building.

But even more than that, we *really* love it when they defy the odds and later rise again, when their former transgressions — especially sexual transgressions, hey we're all sinners right? wink wink — somehow magically turn into a charming defect, an appealing foible. All it takes is a clever agent to re-cast Woods as a reformed sinner, a misunderstood bad-boy with a heart of gold. Let him win a few big tournaments and donate all the proceeds to the Las Vegas Slutbunny Rehabilitation Fund, and he's all set.

So take heart, Tiger. Yes, it's about to get far, far worse. Yes, you will be America's punchline for a good long while. But take it from, say, Kate Moss, whose career flameout was truly epic just a few years ago. She lost hundreds of millions in endorsements and couldn't get a modeling gig to save her life after she was photographed doing a line of blow in a dressing room. But not a year later, she re-emerged as the highest paid model in the world, more powerful and sought-after than ever, in large part thanks to her "bad girl" image.

So play your transgressions right, Tiger, and they might just become, in the mangled gears of the American celebrity machine, a sublime asset. Your trespasses will be forgiven, your star repolished, your image reborn, your giant suitcase full of condoms replenished. Soon enough, you will again have all the lame car endorsements, ugly sweaters, and slutty porn-star party-girl waitresses you can handle. God bless America.

You will be delighted to learn that, despite the brand itself's merciful demise as world's foremost icon of desecration and design abomination, as of this writing, Hummer cologne is still available. Also makes a terrific insect repellent/drain opener/cauterizing agent.

Meanwhile, the celeb fragrance train shows no signs of derailing. New and deadly-to-plants odors have been whipped up by anosmic trolls for the likes of (among others) David Beckham, the X-Men, Spider-Man, Danielle Steele, Kimora Lee Simmons, Usher, American Idol, and, uh, Desperate Housewives (would that I were making that up). However, I am completely disinterested to report that, at last check, "Intimately Beckham," "Baryshnikov Sport," "Usher," and the American Idol *lines were on unsafe-for-human-skin clearance sale. See? Apparently even suburban teens with deviated septums have standards. —mm*

Dude, you smell like a Hummer

10/28/2005

There I was, innocently poking around on some discount fragrance websites and trying to find a bargain on a couple of fave designer colognes to give as gifts, when, like a shark attack, it happened.

I saw it. It stabbed at my eyeballs like a bad dream, scraped my soul like Shania Twain blasting over tin-can speakers in a Pocatello dive bar. "No no no," wailed my tormented spirit. "This has got to be a joke. Is this a joke? Someone tell me this is a joke."

No joke. Hummer has a cologne. Check that, Hummer has *two* colognes, Hummer and Hummer H2, because apparently the first one was such a runaway success, given how some men apparently can't get enough of smelling like road salts and petroleum byproducts and horrible handling and massive unchecked ego. I'm just guessing.

All of which might make you say, wait, what? Hummer? Hummer as in those obnoxious pseudo-trucks driven mostly by twitchy baseball-hatted lugs and their timorous wives who wouldn't know a subtle, classy vehicle if they crushed it under their enormous knobby tires? Hummer the bloated poster child for everything that's wrong with America's attitude toward life and the planet and the environment? *That* Hummer?

Why, yes. Exactly that Hummer. What's more, the product line extends beyond the two branded colognes into a nice Hummer underarm deodorant. Because nothing says "armpit freshness" like a mas-

sive SUV with the aesthetics of a brick on steroids.

It's cute, in a smash-your-head-with-a-rock, I-hate-breathing sort of way. Cute the way the marketing copy for the Hummer fragrance suggests rugged adventurousness, a manly outdoorsy off-road hunkiness in which not a single solitary Hummer owner actually partakes, in which "the smooth richness of tonka bean acts as the 'axle' that links and balances the fresh and warm notes, creating an olfactory sensation that can only be Hummer™ ."

I am not making this up. It really says that:[1] "an olfactory sensation that can only be Hummer™." Which is a bit like saying, "A taste sensation that can only be Rubbermaid™."

It does not stop there. Not satisfied with insulting your senses on myriad levels, the geniuses in GM's marketing department went ahead and dredged up Hummer H2, a "spicier" scent that "carries the same family lineage of the original Hummer Fragrance for Men, but takes on a racier red side." Isn't that adorable? What "red" means in the context of the Hummer brand is anyone's guess. The blood of all the crushed passengers in those other small cars? The embarrassed flush of your cheeks as you block traffic for 20 minutes trying to parallel park? The color you see every time you drop 100 bucks to refill your tank every 15 miles? One can only wonder.

All of which invites the obvious question: Who, pray who, is buying this stuff? And perhaps more importantly, what peroxided, pneumatic woman is attracted to it? Who in their right mind looks at Hummer cologne and says whoa, dude, a scent based on a hulking, horribly designed vehicle that just screams "I don't give a shit about anything or anyone, and by the way to hell with the baby seals, too." Yes, that is *exactly* how I want to smell.

I know, there is no accounting for taste. I know, furthermore, that the fragrance biz is a multibillion-dollar industry and that all the celebs are doing it now, and if there's one way to crank your ego, it's to create a "signature" fragrance[2] designed to make the world think of you whenever they smell candy-scented furniture polish.

I get it. I understand the appeal of the celebrity fragrances, more or less. Britney and Jessica Simpson and Giselle and J.Lo and Paris Hilton and Beyonce and Raven (That's So Raven!) and Celine Dion (shudder) and Hilary Duff, all marketing their bubblegum-scented swill mostly to 'tween girls who want to smell like a cross between grape Kool-Aid and a pink pony and Justin Timberlake's hair gel. I get it.

As for men, I understand tacky Michael Jordan cologne and Diddy cologne and even Marilyn Manson cologne[3] and Donald Trump cologne and ... well, no, check that, I don't really get the Trump at all, who the hell is buying that toxic lighter fluid and what woman is moaning, ooh honey, your stench reminds me of that rich weirdly coiffed real-estate egomaniac from TV. Spread me like butter!

(I have to add one thing. There is also, apparently, a cologne designed by Carlos Santana. And a perfume: Carlos Santana for Women. I have no words for this. Except these: If you are wearing Santana cologne, call your doctor. Do it now.)

But at least all of the above fragrances are based on the questionable tastes and dubious predilections of actual quasi-humans. At least those fragrances make some sort of simpleminded sense: You want to look like these famous people, dress like them, shop like them eat like them screw like them cheat like them lip-synch like them — why not smell like them?

Not so with Hummer. With this, it's all about bogus, undeserved attitude. Hell, at least Ferrari Passion is based on a genuinely sexy, timeless automobile brand. But then again, let's not even mention the olfactory abomination that must be NASCAR cologne.[4] You would not, I venture, spray this on your weeds.

Aww, to hell with it. I am partaking. I am joining the lifestyle-branding movement right now. If Hummer can do it, so can I. If you can't beat 'em, smell 'em.

I am planning my own signature scent right now. Unisex. It will include bergamot, anise, sandalwood, coffee. It will have base notes of lavender and musk and foot massages and oral sex on Sunday mornings so good it makes you see God. You will enjoy whiffs of coming home, going out, going deep, feeling alive, coming unglued, feeling renewed, going down, zipping up, and the smell your pillow has first thing in the morning, all underlined by traces of firefly spit and puppy dander and a beam of moonlight filtering through a skein of silk and landing on a photo of your lover sticking out her tongue at your last birthday party. Oh, and deep space. It will smell very much like deep space.

I shall call it "That's So Pagan!": 60 bucks, 3.5 ounces, eau de toilette. Also comes as a shower scrub, underarm spray, room deodorizer, floor cleaner, veggie wash, nipple scrub, incense, cough syrup, breath mint and emetic. Hey, it's a lifestyle. Why would you want to smell like anything else?

1 http://moohoo.notlong.com
2 http://eigeij.notlong.com
3 http://noonax.notlong.com
4 http://gugain.notlong.com

This column served as my print debut for the Chronicle back in 2005. For five years prior, I was online-only, and had been lucky enough to build a sizable — and wonderfully rabid — following. The overlords at the paper finally took notice of the col's popularity and began slipping my stuff into Datebook (the entertainment section).

One hazy memory: At the time, I also had another column on deck that I could've used as my print debut instead (see "Why do you work so hard?" in the final section), and that my long-time SFGate editor, Amy Moon, far preferred. Alas, I had some rebellious ego thing happening at the time that insisted my debut be as hip and boundary-pushing ("penis" in the first paragraph! Wow!) as possible, so I chose this.

It was the wrong choice. This one has its charms, but "Work" is richer, more timeless, and might rank among my all-time best. See if you agree. —mm

Beer & porn & guns & manicures

07/13/2005

Marketers are confused. Marketers are nonplussed. Marketers are looking at the male of the American species and saying, what the hell is wrong with you and who the hell are you and how the hell do we get you to buy more crap from us, and by the way can you please stop playing with your penis for five seconds?

It is, apparently, no longer clear-cut. Men are no longer neatly divided — not that they ever really were — into two types: a) the new breed of metrosexual, trim and healthy and urban-bred and yoga-ready, confident in his Prada boots and expensive face lotion and European car and able to cook a five-course gourmet meal and satisfy his women using 102 variations of expert Tantric oral sex all while not damaging his manicure or staining his new 450-threat-count Egyptian cotton Donna Karan sheets.

Nor is he necessarily b) The Great Beer-Swilling Slob, paunchy in his faded Dockers and overgrown eyebrows, unsightly as an overfed gopher in his XXL bathing suit and blissfully addicted to barbecued foods and pickup trucks and Maxim magazine and sports and beer and especially sports involving beer,[1] all while remaining entirely unable to tell a clitoris from a lawn mower and utterly powerless to point, if given a map of the world, to any state that doesn't have a famous baseball stadium.

Those types are, apparently, no longer the two primary competing species of marketable male in the United States and the world, and dammit, marketers are pissed. And baffled. Hell, according to Leo Burnett Worldwide, the ad agency that pretty much invented macho by way of dredging

up the cancer-riffic hunk o' impotent, yellow-toothed, diseased-lung love, the Marlboro Man, marketing mavens have little idea as to just who the hell the new male actually is.

And why not? Because, apparently, men don't know either. According to LBM's own survey, 60 percent of New World Men (the agency polled males across 13 countries) say they want to be professional patriarchs: fathers and executives and breadwinnin' dudes with giant Weber grills larger than their Honda Accords. The other 40 percent hover near the metrosexual arena, craving, presumably, independence and style and the general avoidance of marriage before age 40 because they still want to have sex and stay out past 11 p.m.

But here's the kickers: Only 17 percent of those surveyed enjoy regular manicures, whereas 70 percent would rather look good in a business suit than a bathing suit. And it's about a 50/50 split if men are given the choice between staying home and raising the kids in an upscale, affluent environment while the wife works, or go to work themselves and accept a lower standard of living while the wife slaves away teaching the rug rats not to eat the rust chips off the trailer's hubcaps.

All of which means . . . well, not a whole hell of a lot, really, except that men aren't exactly conforming to typical behaviors and stereotypes and maybe, just maybe, there's some sort of evolution going on, some progress, intermixing, some sort of slightly deeper shift, and it's all about goddamn time, too.

Here's a quote:

"As the world is drifting toward a more feminine perspective, many of the social constructs men have taken for granted are undergoing significant shifts or being outright dismantled," muttered Tom Bernardin, CEO of Leo Burnett Worldwide, barbecuing a large pig on a spit over an open fire pit while simultaneously tuning his Porsche Carrera S with his All-Clad ice tongs.

"It's a confusing time, not just for men, but for marketers as well as they try to target and depict men meaningfully," he continued, his bare chest glistening under the hot sun, pectorals flexing madly as he squeezed the iron exercise bar in numerous glorious reps while simultaneously smoking three Marlboro Reds and curling a small paperweight with his penis. Ahem.

Tom's lament is, largely, true. Flip through any of the typical men's mags and note how there seem to be exactly five items Madison Avenue can sell to men with any sort of confidence of message: watches, booze, cars, razors, and sports crap.

But as for the more intriguing issues of sex and work and emotional depth, spirit and energy and love, gender play and bisexuality and the best red wine to go with nipple clamps, well, marketers appear more like Christian Republicans at a Wiccan festival. Which is to say, lost and angry and vaguely threatened.

But, well, who cares? Dismantling is good. Breaking down the tired and cliched male stereotypes is good. Because while many men — red state boy-men in particular — may be confused as to their exact role as the divine feminine continues to re-assert herself in the new millennium, for most of us with a sense of wry hungry yearning, this confusion means one thing: fewer boundaries.

More self-definition. More fluidity of self, spirit, penile usage, haircut. Less susceptibility to right-wing fearmongering. And less pressure to be what our fathers were almost universally forced to be: married nine-to-five breadwinners in unfulfilling jobs just out of college, or else.

So, what's the answer? What will the new male look like? Will he be, say, a Republican vegetarian who loves fine handguns and organic chard and anarchist art? Will he be a polyamorous neoconservative Francophile who reads gay erotica and sips green tea? How about an aggressive world-hopping CEO who's also into exotic prose poetry and imports vibrators from Panama with hand-polished burl-wood handles? Is he the mad-genius dude who makes your soy mochas at the coffee shop, who has a brilliant idea for how to turn your iPod into a divining rod? Or is he the German-Hawaiian furniture designer who cuts his wife's hair and makes killer steaks and listens to Metallica at incredible volume while he does pilates?

I do not have a clear answer, just yet. Perhaps this is the best news of all. At this particular moment, the possibilities are like a New York whorehouse during the Republican National Convention. Which is to say, wide open, and pumping hard.

1 http://lohteen.notlong.com

27

Oh my God. The Duggars. What a story. Apparently the Discovery Channel saw fit to produce a TV special about this peculiar family a number of years back, that later became a full-blown reality show (of course) called "19 Kids & Counting," a wacky Christian thrill ride detailing the life and times of this bizarre Arkansas clan of cervical wonder and lamentable haircuts.

I still get email about this column, as people watch the show in wonder/horror and then Google "Duggar family," and up pops the very column you are about to read. Total email replies to this column as of this writing: 1,743. Not quite an my all-time record, but it's definitely in the top 10.

For my part, I do now see this column as a bit mean-spirited, harsh, the language hyperbolic and overcooked. I'm sorry for that. It was tough for me to see past how this strange fundamentalist tribe epitomized the worst of the Bush worldview regarding everything from harsh environmental impact to women's rights and roles, ignorance of birth control, a frightening misunderstanding of God, human sexuality as nothing more than a gross mechanism for procreation, and so on. I do apologize for the severity of the tone. But I very much stand by the sentiment. And the headline.

As you may not wish to know, the Duggar clan is now up to 19 children (it was 16 when I first wrote this), with more sure to come. Creepier still, the oldest Duggar daughter now has a child of her own, even as mom still cranks out babies. Hey, it's God's will. Try not to be mean. —mm

God does not want ~~16~~ 19 kids

10/19/2005

Who are you to judge? Who are you to say that the more than slightly creepy 42-year-old woman from Arkansas who just gave birth to her 16th child, yes that's right 16 kids and try not to cringe in phantom vaginal pain when you say it, who are you to say Michelle Duggar is not more than a little unhinged and sad and lost?

And furthermore, who are you to suggest that her equally troubling husband — whose name is, of course, Jim Bob and he's hankerin' to be a Republican senator and try not to wince in sociopolitical pain when you say that — isn't more than a little numb to the real world, and that bringing 16 hungry, mewling, attention-deprived kids (and she wants more!) into this exhausted world zips right by "touching" and races right past "disturbing" and lurches its way, heaving and gasping and sweating from the karmic armpits, straight into "Oh my God, what the hell is wrong with you people?"

But that would be, you know, mean. Mean and callous to suggest that their family portrait might be the most disquieting photo you see all year, this bizarre Duggar family of 20 spotless, white, hyperreligious, interchangeable people with alarmingly bad hair, the kids ranging in ages from one to 21, akin in far too many ways to a strange brainwashed cult, a spawn factory, a viral mind-set loosed numbly upon the world.

It's wrong to be this judgmental. Wrong to suggest that it is exactly this kind of weird, pathological, protofamily gluttony that's making the world groan and cry and recoil, contributing to vicious overpopulation rates and unrepentant economic strain and a bitter moral warpage resulting from a massive outbreak of homophobic neo-Christians across our troubled and Bush-ravaged land. Or is it?

Is it wrong to notice how all the Duggar kids' names start with the letter *J* (Jeremiah and Josiah and Jedediah and Jesus, someone please stop them), and that if you study the family portrait — or the even *more* disturbing duggarfamily.com Web site — too closely you will become rashy and depressed and you will crave large quantities of alcohol and loud aggressive music to deflect the creeping feeling that this planet is devolving faster than you can suck the contents from a large bong? But I'm not judging.

I have a friend who used to co-babysit (yes, it required two sitters) for a family of 10 kids, and she reports that they were, almost without fail, manic and hyper, bewildered and attention deprived in the worst way, half of them addicted to prescription meds to calm their neglected nerves and the other half bound for years of therapy due to complete loss of having the slightest clue as to who they actually were, lost in the family crowd, just another blank, needy face at the table. Is this the guaranteed affliction for every child of very large families? Of course not. But I'm guessing it's more common than you imagine.

What's more, after the 10th kid popped out, the family doctor essentially prohibited the baby-addicted mother from having any more offspring, considering the pummeling endured by her various matronly systems, and it's actually painful to imagine the logistics, the toll on Michelle Duggar's body (her 19th child came out as a 1-pound preemie, which you might think the Duggars would see as God saying "enough already." But no. She says she *still* wants more), the ravages it has endured to give birth to roughly one child per year for two decades, and you cannot help but wonder about her body and its various biological and sexual ... no, no, it is not for this space to visualize frighteningly capacious vaginal dimensions.

It is not for this space to imagine this couple's soggy sexual mutations. We do not have enough wine on hand for that.

Perhaps the point is this: Why does this sort of bizarre hyperbreeding only seem to afflict antiseptic megareligious families from the Midwest? In other words — assuming Michelle and Jim Bob and their massive brood of cookie-cutter Christian kidbots will all be, as their charming family photo suggests, never allowed near a decent pair of designer jeans or a tolerable haircut from a recent decade, and assuming that they will all be tragically encoded with the values of the homophobic asexual Christian right — where are the forces that shall help neutralize their effect on the culture? Where is the counterbalance, to offset the damage?

Where is, in other words, the funky tattooed intellectual poetess who, along with her genius anarchist husband, is popping out 16 funky progressive intellectually curious fashion-forward pagan offspring to answer the Duggar's squad of über-white future Wal-Mart shoppers? Where is the liberal, spiritualized, pro-sex flip side? Verily I say unto thee, it ain't lookin' good.

Perhaps this the scariest aspect of our squishy tale: Maybe the scales are tipping to the neoconservative, homogenous right in our culture simply because they tend not to give much of a damn for the ramifications of wanton breeding and environmental destruction and pious sanctimony, whereas those on the left actually seem to give a whit for the health of the planet and the dire effects of overpopulation. Is that an oversimplification?

Why does this sort of thoughtfulness seem so far from the norm? Why is having a stadiumful of offspring still seen as some sort of happy joyous thing?

You already know why. It is the Biggest Reason of All. Children are, after all, God's little gifts. Kids are little blessings from the Lord, the Almighty's own screaming spitballs of joy. Hell, Jim Bob said so himself, when asked if the couple would soon be going for a 17th rug rat: "We both just love children and we consider each a blessing from the Lord. I have asked Michelle if she wants more and she said yes, if the Lord wants to give us some she will accept them." This is what he actually said. And God did not strike him dead on the spot.

Let us be clear: I don't care what sort of God you believe in, it's a safe bet that hysterical breeding does not top her list of desirables. God does not want more children per acre than there are ants or mice or garter snakes or repressed pedophilic priests. We already have three billion humans on the planet who subsist on less than two dollars a day. Every other child in the world (one billion of them) lives in abject poverty. We are burning through the planet's resources faster than a Republican can eat an endangered caribou stew. Note to Michelle Duggar: If God wanted you to have a massive pile of children, she'd have given your uterus a hydraulic pump and a revolving door. Stop it now.

Ah, but this is America, yes? People should be allowed to do whatever the hell they want with their families if they can afford it and if it's within the law and so long as they aren't gay or deviant or happily flouting Good Christian Values, right? Shouldn't they? Hell, gay couples still can't openly adopt a baby in most states (they either lie, or one adopts and the other must apply as "co-parent"), but Michelle Duggar can pop out 19 kids and no one says, oh my freaking God, stop it, stop it now, you thoughtless, self-ish, baby-drunk people.

No, no one says that. That would be mean.

You gotta muster a bit of sympathy for Tom. All evidence indicates that he's a passionate, dedicated actor. He seems to genuinely care about his craft. What's more, high-ranking member of a ludicrous, harebrained cult or no, he seems like a solid, decent guy. He's just not all that bright. —mm

Are you Tom Cruise crazy?

01/23/2008

Here's something you can do.

Set up that nifty Flip videocamera you got last Christmas just over there, next to your couch. Now, plop yourself down in front of it and have a friend sit just off to the side and then both of you slam about nine shots of vodka followed by nine more of extra-strong espresso, and then hit the "Record" button as said friend begins to question you about your deepest beliefs on How the World Really Works, and you answer them employing only tense, cryptic bursts of pseudo-lingo that make sense only to you and your twitching brainstem, all while making sure you suddenly burst out laughing as maniacally as possible at random intervals and never blink.

Won't that be fun?

And then you can compare. You can go back to your computer and re-watch the now-famous Tom Cruise Scientology video[1] that winged across the planet like a wacky Ebola virus, and contrast it with your swell creation and go "See? See that? No matter how hard I try, no matter how weird I think I am and no matter how heavily my therapist sighs every time I bring up my love of Shania Twain and banana sandwiches and *Battlestar Galactica* collectibles, I am not nearly as insane as Tom Cruise. Life is going to be OK."

Ah yes, the Tom Cruise Scientology indoctrination video. Surely by now you've seen this hunk of pop culture manna? Surely, at least, someone you know has watched the video and has described it to you in amazed, slightly disturbed tones and you've maybe responded by shrugging and saying "No no no, it couldn't be *that* weird ... could it?"

It could. It is something to see. It has already enjoyed a few million views so far and it's destined to become an all-classic, this nine-minute slab of crazy that features this very intense, grinning, bizarre movie star talking in barely comprehensible half-sentences and perky Scientology lingo about "SPs" and "the tech" and "KSW" and "half-acks" and all manner of cool culty jargon[2] that, if you close your eyes and blur your imagination just right, sounds remarkably like a high school speed freak talking up *Dungeons & Dragons* to his kid brother.

Except this particular clip has apparently been edited by an epileptic teenager. It is scored with the *Mission: Impossible* theme song (to which Cruise doubtlessly owns the rights) and it has laughable zoom-in graphics pulled from somewhere deep in 1994 and it is bookended with some of the most bloviated, hammy voiceover work this side of a "Saturday Night Live" parody. All told, it is, as the universal verdict goes, "unintentionally hilarious."

Unintentional, because it's supposed to be serious. It is supposed to make Scientology look intense and cool and badass and righteous and Cruise is clearly meant to appear as some sort of idealized L. Ron Hubbard-drunk demigod, a true hero and visionary (he's an OT VII, after all, the highest rank you can achieve in his "church" without going off to battle evil warlord Xenu yourself), who has apparently single-handedly brought Scientology to over 1 *billion* people worldwide and who can lift boulders with his penis and bend spoons with his mind and whip up a delightful marinara in his sleep.

It is, in a way, a seminal piece of film. It finally removes all doubt that one of the wealthiest and most successful celebrities of this generation is, indisputably, many, many fries short of a Happy Meal. It's as if you crossed Mitt Romney with Mike Huckabee and rolled it in the hot goo of Ted Haggard and packed it all into the body of a junior-weight high school wrestling champ, with exactly the same level of verbal articulation. Which is to say, a log. A very, very intense log.

Perhaps this is the true joy of watching celebrity derailments, breakdowns and cult addictions. We like to think that would never be us. We like to think, "You know, if *I* was world famous, had a billion dollars, still had pretty good hair and a killer smile and at least used to be the hottest hunk of malehood on the planet, I sure as hell wouldn't hitch my spiritual cart to the crazy train of a deeply deranged, pill-popping, sci-fi hack writer who invented a nutball cult religion on a bar bet. Wait, would I?"

Perhaps you are still not sure. Perhaps you think it's still not fair to make fun of Tom Cruise this way, no matter how clearly batshit crazy he so obviously is. After all, he's done some passable movies. He's a decent enough guy. I sort of liked him in "The Firm" and, um, "Legend." Cut him some slack, maybe?

Maybe. After all, everyone needs their little cult,[3] right? Everyone needs their tribe and their myths and their psychological attachments. Is it Tom's fault that his intellectual and spiritual development apparently got stuck somewhere between an old "Star Trek" rerun and the episode where Gilligan gets hit on the head with a coconut and his mouth turns into a radio?[4] No, it is not.

What's more, it's not like this video is all that unusual. Surely there are Mormon indoctrination videos equally as deranged. Surely there are creepy installations playing right now over at the Creation Museum in Kentucky that will make your brain implode for all sorts of reasons, not the least of which is that half of Americans actually believe that humans really did fly on the backs of pterodactyls.[5] Hell, I'm sure Opus Dei has some sort of S&M fetish dungeon where they take new recruits and staple their eyelids open and make them watch "The Da Vinci Code" on infinite repeat until they swear to worship an angry misogynistic God forevermore, just to make it stop. And hell, the evangelicals in the hugely disturbing 2006 documentary "Jesus Camp" make Tom's Scientologists look like a bunch of geeky Boy Scouts on crack.

So then, maybe we all owe Tom Cruise a big debt of gratitude? After all, it is only through videos such as this that we can gain perspective on our own lives. It is only though ogling such phenomena over and over and maybe only after someone turns this clip into a drinking game ("Every time Tom squirms awkwardly in his chair and can't finish a sentence, drink!"), that we can finally eliminate all doubt as to our own mental stability and say, "Yes indeed, I may be a bit crazy, but I ain't no *Tom Cruise* crazy."

Or, as Tom would say, "I've canceled that in my area." Yes, Tom. You most certainly have.

1 http://uudae.notlong.com
2 http://lohhoo.notlong.com
3 http://ewaquo.notlong.com
4 http://aeziex.notlong.com
5 http://aezine.notlong.com

My love/hate relationship with Vegas continues. Like most sentient creatures, I can handle the surreal and vaguely disturbing place only in short bursts, maybe a long weekend at most, depending on who I'm with, how my black-jack hands are unfolding and if there's some way to find a respite from the relentless gaudiness. You have to be very careful in Vegas, check your protection level, keep yourself grounded and conscious. The vibration of the place is just viciously low, the insane flow of money bizarre and disorienting, all coupled to a sad, never-ending sensation that this entire place simply should not exist, that we should not be building such wicked, environmentally rapacious spectacles in the near-barren desert. I suppose you can argue it's a testament to our tenacity, our technology, our impressive greed, not to mention a sheer force of will to overcome the restrictions and parameters of nature. Then again, nature always wins. Eventually. —mm

The young lion goes to Vegas

8/26/09

This is what you already know: Some things never change. This is the other thing you already know: What a glorious, preposterous conceit of man to think we are so separate from, so far above and beyond the brutish and crude world of the lowly beasts. Eat it and smile, biped.

So it was that I found myself amid the grind and the thump and the madhouse, jet-fueled, hormone-engorged dreamscape that is a nightclub called Rain, an amazing sliver of Dante's inferno stationed deep inside the giddy teenybop wonderland known as the Palms hotel in Las Vegas, right here on planet Earth and I only mention that last part because when you're in a place like Rain it doesn't really feel like you're anywhere solid or intelligible in the slightest.

With a gaggle of cool new friends indulging in that classic, time-honored ritual known as the bachelor party, I happily participated. I did my part to writhe and people-watch and drink, but as I am entirely unable to fully shut off the writerly part of my brain, I couldn't help but take note of a simply stupendous scene — one of a thousand, really — unfolding before me just a few feet away, so close that I could reach out and touch it. Which I did. Repeatedly.

As fate would have it, I found myself standing just behind the waist-high wall of a private booth, a large, curved, low-slung, leather-clad space packed with glassware and ice buckets and sundry shiny things all carefully cordoned off from the teeming throngs and awaiting its assigned patrons for the night, like a shimmering pothole on the highway to hell.

And lo, as the nightclub engorged and as I danced and sipped and watched, the booth slowly began to fill.

The first to be escorted into the booth by scowling Rain bouncers was a trio of skimpy young things, all adorned in the official femme-fatale uniform of Las Vegas: sausage-tight mini-dress, clearly painful four-inch heels, mountains of makeup and glittering accessories, and a cell phone and/or digital camera in every palm. Each female was looking around the place in that all too common mix of bewilderment, wariness and please-stare-at-me/stop-staring-at-me sexual schizophrenia.

About 10 minutes later, a few more arrived, nearly identical in attire and attitude as the first, quickly followed by two more, same as the others and all nearly indistinguishable save for the color of the mini-dress and the brand of cell phone and the volume of the squeal let out as they saw one another and hugged awkwardly and then quickly tugged the hem of their dresses to make sure they didn't ride up a quarter inch and reveal the true centerpiece of God's creation.

Initially, it was all women. Check that: it was all young, preternaturally jaded women-like girl creatures caught somewhere between glorious, orgiastic Roman Empire splendor and painful white trash sleaze, some clumsy zone where everything they do is obviously geared toward a frantic attempt to be sexy and sultry and smoking hot, and very little actually is.

My first thought was, of course, "bachelorette party," of which there were roughly 10,000 going on across the city at that particular moment, alongside their male equivalents. I shrugged it all off and was letting my attention wander when suddenly, the scene shifted again.

The dude arrived. The maestro, the chief, the master of his tiny domain. He was, it was instantly clear, the real reason the space was reserved, the obvious reason all the gleaming girlbots were here in the first place. In this particular booth, he ran the show. This was his harem.

He was probably 25 years old, wide shoulder span, thick and 'roided' up and eyes shrouded by a low-pulled baseball hat, utterly joyless in every outward appearance but clearly in absolute control of his tiny nutshell of infinite space, pumping out a superior vibe like he did this sort of thing every other night, which he probably did.

Every girl came over for a smooch. Or if they didn't, he went 'round and gave them all a pat, a squeeze, a nonchalant macho nod of, "Hey baby, 'sup?" It was adorable, in its unabashed macho sexism.

It was also massively predictable. Every time I glanced over he was doing the exact same thing: surveying his space, walking the 10-foot range of the booth nearly nonstop, back and forth, back and forth, chest thrust out, arms bulging, working his cell phone like he was strangling a tiny ferret with his thumbs.

He did not smile, not even once. He absolutely did not dance. Mostly he just prowled that tiny booth, let the teetering girls take pictures with him even though he was no celebrity I could recognize, not really big or popular enough to be a major athlete. Far as I could figure, he was just a dude. A popular club dude. Probably a very nice guy, really. Who could tell?

In my whiskey-enhanced haze, I blinked, and suddenly I found myself transported to a scene on the Discovery Channel or the National Geographic Channel, or maybe it was that amazing Blue Planet BBC series, that segment where we are taken deep in the African savannah amid the shimmering heatwaves and the hardscrabble vegetation and the never-ending search for water and shelter and meat.

And there he is, the big male lion, strong and haggard and terrible, watching over his pride of lionesses and sniffing the air for potential adversaries who might dare threaten his leadership position, take his women and gobble up his portion of raw antelope thigh.

The lion never roamed very far. He never tried anything new. He never looked like he was having much fun at all, even when he tore into the meat or mounted the females and perpetuated his seed. But he did look, most of the time, deeply content. Solid, indisputable, connected to source. He knew what he was. And it was good.

I blinked again and there was my boy, right there in the Vegas booth, the young lion roaming his domain and feeling himself the center of the world, but of course merely an infinitesimal part of a vast and incomprehensible churn, merely another self-important speck in the grand schema, soon to be battled, eaten, replaced.

One key difference: My dude really didn't look very content at all. He didn't look very settled in the world. He looked a bit ... forced. Unnatural. Uncomfortable at some very deep level, as did nearly all of his pride. It's a profound difference, really.

The scene shifted once more. My whiskey camera began to pan back and widen out, further and further, taking it all in, the entire pseudo-city, the whole of that fine, gleaming wasteland.

At that very moment, thousands of similar scenes were unfolding. The thump, the preening, the heat. All those lions and lionesses roaring as loudly as they possibly can, and all completely, effortlessly drowned out by the desert's massive, crushing silence.

Date: Fri, 23 Jun 2006 14:33:16 -0400
Thread-Topic: Christian Virginity Comments
From: "Bruce" <BruceXXX@XXX.com>
To: <mmorford@sfgate.com>
X-OriginalArrivalTime: 23 Jun 2006 18:34:59.0330 (UTC)

You are a sick perverted person who will one day wish
you had never written such an article as I have just
read. The sad thing about it is; It'll probably be to
late to do you any good. Get smart, call on God for
mercy before it's to late for you.

PS. You'll read this and think; just another of
those right-wing nuts. But you will remember it for
eternity.

Bruce

Date: Wed, 19 Jul 2006 12:31:23 EDT
Subject: Your comments on George Bush
To: mmorford@sfgate.com
MIME-Version: 1.0
X-Spam-Flag: NO

Mark Mumford,

You are, next to Karl Marx and Adolf Hitler, about the
most stupid son-of-a-bitch who's comments I've ever
read. You must have lived in San Francisco too long,
or are a sex-pervert, demon-possessed or something.

I'd get angry if I believed for one moment you
represented California, for I lived there for many
years [San Joaquin Valley and Eastern Sierra].

But fortunately, you're just puke from inside the Bay
Area—that washes out on the tide.

Date: Wed, 7 Jun 2006 16:26:02 -0700 (PDT)
From: Tiffany B <XXX@sbcglobal.net>
To: mmorford@sfgate.com
MIME-Version: 1.0

i am disgusted at your thought. We americans have a
right to anything we want because we deserve it. we
give more money in aid to countrys all over the world.
no one else does this. we also defeat every major
threat to world freedom via, nazi germany, soviet union
and soon iran and north korea. we are the superman
to the world so that is our reward. we also let scum
sucking parasites from around the world live in our
country so they can feed there familys and have a
better life even though it is a burden to us and we
dont want them here.people like you.disgust me you piss
on the grave of all those who died to give us freedom.
you are the new evil of the 21st century. your worse
then osama bin laden. do us all a favor and stop making
trouble and causeing chaos, kill your self.
-Tiffany

Date: Mon, 19 Nov 2007 16:21:28 -0800 (PST)
From: Sean O <XXX@sbcglobal.net>
To: mmorford@sfgate.com
MIME-Version: 1.0

How long to your death watch? you scum bag. People
like you were in charge, we'd be cahnting verses of the
Koran by now. You America hater. Go screw yourself

I hate you and your leftist ilk. I pray every night
that Hillary Rotten Clinton does not get elected. I
pray every night that someone like Mitt Romney does get
elected.

Your only use to real Americans [and I recall, returning on a troopship with 2,200 other Marines from Korea in 1952, passing under the Golden gate, as a survivor of that little war (we lost 36,000 killed while in Iraq during the same time, 2,400 service people are KIA's) how grateful I was to return to the land of the free and home of the brave, which in my small way, I helped to preserve; how willing I'd be to shove your damned face in the puke you think and write] is to remind old Americans that we true-hearted still have a good fight on our hands.

May God bless George Bush-especially as he vetoes the Holocausts of innocent, unborn Americans.

Phil S

Date: Wed, 27 Sep 2006 08:03:49 -0700 (PDT)
From: William G <XXXXX@sbcglobal.net>
Subject: Sept. 27th
To: Mark - Morford <mmorford@sfgate.com>
MIME-Version: 1.0

Dear asshole: Are you part of the Chronicle's ROP program giving employment to retarded individuals? Your comments are sick and pathetic and smell of pig feces. You should bathe and wash your hair more regularly as your body odor permeates the paper! You can't be proud of the lack of journalism in your Bush diatribes. You're nothing more than a frustrated, emptyheaded leftwing piece of offal.
Bill, Alamo, Ca.

You probably think Hugo Chavez is probably a great man. You probably think the Hitler of Iran is a great man. I hope your death watch is counting down, you scum bag. You're a failure, and so is your newspaper.

Paul J
San Diego, Ca...

PS Michael Savage rocks & YOU suck...you America Hater

Date: Wed, 10 May 2006 11:06:17 -0700 (PDT)
From: Big B <bigXXX@yahoo.com>
Subject: $10 /gallon
To: mmorford@sfgate.com
MIME-Version: 1.0

You stupid muther fucker! That was the absolute most idiotic and stupid article I have ever read in my whole entire life!!! Literally. I am not joking. You have just revealed yourself as a stupidass SanFranciscan with the most stupidest of liberal thoughts. You should be executed for that kind of shit. I strongly urge the Chron to fire your bitchass and put you on the street with all the other homeless fucking shits. We upscale Americans don't need trash like you trying to make things worse for everyone. Why don;t you go and become a hippie, gypsy, or some walking dud who doesn;t use no gas or need protection from niggers raping your mother??? Just fucking drop dead where you're at stupid bitch!!!

I hate you I hate you I hate you

Personal factoid: My first real job out of high school, before I split for Los Angeles to try my hand at pop metal stardom, was at one of the first Costcos in Spokane back in the '80s. I was a long-haired door-checker guy. Scanned your receipt for errors, punched a little hole, sent you on your way. Seven-fifty an hour. Which seemed like a lot, given how my rent was 125 bucks a month and I had zero other real expenses, save for music, and cigarettes, and the gi-ant boxes of frozen corn dogs, burritos, fish sticks and potstickers I would buy at 10% discount from my own employer. Ahh, the halcyon days. —mm

Your shiny happy discount death

04/11/2007

If you feel your life is just too boring, if you feel you are lacking sufficient surreality and ironic humor and morbid perspective combined with a strange sense that this planet is actually some sort of warped dreamlike petri-dish experiment run by scaly hyperintelligent lizards possessing sav-age and incomprehensible senses of humor, well, I have a suggestion.

Simply march your happy overfed American butt over to Costco. Not just any Costco, mind you, but Costco out in, say, the Palm Desert region of California, where the land is scrappyhot and the air is dry and the mas-sive strip malls and neon-green golf courses outnumber healthy environ-mental concern by a factor of about 1,000 to 1.

Do this: Walk the massive air-conditioned aisles and ogle the giant slabs of meat and the enormous bins of imported Guatemalan fruit and the economy packs of adult diapers and the two-gallon bottles of vodka, much of it generally aimed at the happy retirement crowd that lives here six months out of the year.

And then notice, as you leave, your cart crammed with drums of olive oil and 10-foot plasma TVs and 80-packs of frozen cream puffs, that strange display you apparently didn't notice when you came in, the one right by the front door next to the tires and the lawn furniture and the hot-dog stand, the one you seem to have blocked out because it was just too weird and your mind couldn't really get around it.

Yes, they are coffins. They are enormous, shiny caskets for sale, at Costco. Would that I were making this up.

This is what you see: A seemingly innocuous, nondescript display fea-turing corner sample pieces of giant kitschy caskets (alas, there are no full-sized models to climb into to test for comfort/fit/sex/morbid humor), all made by something called the Universal Casket Company, and they apparently come in all manner of glossy finish and silky crepe linings and fake gothic handles and pink rose filigree and all available for immediate overnight delivery because, well, you just never know.

Yes, you can now buy a coffin at Costco. Six, actually, different styles and qualities and color schemes to match your lifestyle and your sofa and your love of mauve and fake lion's-head handles and it is, all at once, funny and disturbing and creepy and yet, somehow, entirely appropriate. You want shameless target marketing? You want life and death and commerce and capitalism and convenience all rolled into a little ball of gloomy consumer joy? Here is your nirvana.

Look a little closer. Around the display are a number of modest signs featuring handsome black-and-white stock photos of healthy-looking,

middle-age people apparently discussing why the hell they'd want to buy a huge shiny $1,000 casket at Costco, why you'd want to consider such a thing right after you just spent two hours on a sunny Saturday dumping 300 bucks on bulk cheese and massive platters of frozen chicken wings and maybe a 29-person camping tent.

Each sign has its own simple sales-pitch phrase above the photo, such as "Affordable" or "Non-Threatening" or (my personal favorite) "Non-Emotional," which I take to mean that Costco believes it's much gentler on your nerves and easier on your deepest fears to consider casket acquisition on a benign, shopping-crammed weekend than to wait until, say, you're sitting in a bleak funeral home and you can't choose a shade of taupe for the deceased's pillow through all the teary, soul-crushing Muzak. After all, why feel death? Why not let Costco help you send grandma off with ease, without those pesky *feelings*? Mmm, numbness.

Coffins are, so far as I can tell, only available at the Costcos in and around retirement communities (and also on the Costco Web site, along with, fittingly, urns). They are, in other words, only physically on display in those regions where death does good, dependable business, where a sense of finality lingers in the air like a nagging perfume, death just another commodity to be decided upon the way you choose a pack of underwear or a new gas barbecue grill because really, in this day and age, why make it anything more?

Please note: I could be wrong about the above paragraph. In fact, caskets might be available in many "normal" Costcos all over the country. It is very possible, in other words, that I simply haven't noticed a large and burgeoning trend in the big-box store universe, wherein more and more of these consumer black holes are realizing the huge profit potential to be had in the billion-dollar death business, especially considering the Boomer

41

generation's forthcoming march into the big BMW dealership in the sky.

It's entirely possible that you will soon see funeral services and tasteful casket offerings from, say, Pottery Barn. Or Williams-Sonoma. Target. Ikea. In fact, it is no stretch at all to imagine Wal-Mart offering cheapie Chinese-made caskets — extra-large, double-wide, super-reinforced — back in the corner of the Home & Garden section, next to the potting soil and the pink porcelain garden fairies and the creepy life-size lawn statues of St. Francis. Why not?

And why stop at caskets? Wal-Mart, for one, could easily upend the entire funeral industry and offer budget *cremations*, right out back, next to the tire center and the giant shredding machines where they destroy all that evidence of labor malpractice and health care abuse and where they shred the once-shimmering souls of their tepid, dreary-hearted executives. Just a thought.

But I suppose such surreal product placement makes most sense for a strange place like Palm Desert, that most bizarre and surreal of California locales, all massive, low megadevelopments and heavily manicured retirement communities and truly insane, scattershot sprawl set against a backdrop of stunning but increasingly battered desert scrub and jackrabbits and coyotes and low lumpy dreamy mountains and a nice gauze of smog.

It is one of those increasingly overdeveloped places that, if you look too closely (or even if you don't), will rather effortlessly disturb your innate sense of balance, your sense of harmonious nature and how humans are supposed to interact with it. I know, in tract-home/big-box/Bush-ravaged America, this sort of disconcerting landscape is pretty much the norm. But in the scrubby desert the contrast feels just that much more brutal. Which, in a way, makes it just right for bulk casket sales.

As my own sly, happily retired father said to me as he pointed out the existence of the Costco caskets in the first place, it actually makes perfect (metaphorical) sense for Costco to sell coffins: "Hell, it all comes together in the end," he shrugged. "You enter into one big box, and exit in a little one." Ain't that the truth.

Fucking magazine 'trend' pieces, simultaneously weirdly fascinating and utterly useless in how 90 percent of them are utter brain-melting bullshit and don't really document a truly interesting or revealing cultural movement at all, but more like a belch, a hiccup, a sad note of pain and creepiness and general vacuity a handful of sad people way off in the urban or suburban byways are rumored to have maybe attempted once a few times while high on Xanax/ Red Bull milkshakes.

Inner lip tattoos! Anal bleaching! Vodka-soaked tampons! Kids injecting oven cleaner into their cats! Teens imitating violent video games and accidentally shooting themselves in the face! 45-year-old bloggers who still live with their moms and secretly fetishize them! Makes me proud to work in media, I tell you what. —mm

The great pubic hair conundrum

04/11/2008

Then you read the one about how some brainless, super-wealthy moms in a few upscale hoods in Philly are dragging their brutally primped 8-, 9-, 10-year-old daughters to the salon to get the kid's eyebrows plucked and her stray hairs yanked and her cuticles scraped, making sure everything is frighteningly picture-perfect because the girls simply *must* be made flawless and creepy and preternaturally vacuous — you know, just like mom.

But then comes the kicker, the horrifying thing that makes you cringe and recoil and want to move to Europe or maybe the moon, and it's the reason you are reading this ridiculous trend piece in the first place, against your better judgment but you do it anyway because, well, you're just that kind of masochist.

Because then you read about how this mom, this unspeakably sad and narcissistic creature of ignorance and savage karmic pain, actually demands that the waxer give her daughter — her prepubescent, pre-hormonal, nearly hairless 8-year-old daughter — a full bikini wax.

You read that right. And you don't even have to scream at the sky right now and throw up your hands and say, but... girls that age don't even *have* pubic hair, do they?

They do not. Doesn't matter. The mom is insane. The little girl is so de-tuned from authentic girlhood already she just goes along for the ride. And the waxer can only respond, well, you're out of your fucking mind, but whatever. Let's do this thing.

Yes, it's happening. And I suppose it's horrible. And you know it's happening and you know it's horrible because there's this absurdly long trend piece[1] about it in some magazine that I unfortunately stumbled across recently, and it described the Brazilian wax phenomenon in ridiculous detail, with interviews and analysis and concerned comments from child-psychiatry specialists and aren't you alarmed and horrified? Well, no.

I must admit, it did a terrific job of doing exactly what ludicrous micro-trend pieces are supposed to do: zero in on a fringe phenomenon and make it seem like it's catching on like wildfire across the nation, and therefore you might want to make some brain space for this because who, pray who, will save the exceptionally well-groomed children? What's next, Botox for babies? Hot pink Juicy Couture thong underwear for 6-year-olds? Oh wait.

Of course, pre-pubescent bikini waxes are not *really* catching on. It's not *really* that common or even disturbing of a trend, given how for every spoiled rich-doll child whose parents should never have been allowed to breed, there are 10,000 more who are just fine, whose parents take totally competent care of them and feed and clothe and house them just as re-spectfully and responsibly and awkwardly as ever. But who the hell wants to read about that?

And maybe you also back up a step and say OK, wait a second. You wanna talk child abuse? Because really, how is a bikini wax for an 8-year-old any more horrific or abusive than parents who, say, let their kids gorge on junk food? Than ignorant dads who haul the brood to McDon-alds and KFC every day and pump them full of Coke and Snapple at age 6? Is waxing somehow worse or more damaging, psychologically speaking, than parents who smack their kids and scream at them in the middle of Wal-Mart, or those who drag their 8-year-olds into a screening of "The Passion"? Really, how do we weigh psychological torment?

The truth here is as obvious as it is deeply entertaining: Bad parenting abounds, baby, and what's more, I say our culture *needs* psycho parents and their preening, hyperplucked kids, simply because the culture needs future Paris Hiltons and Lindsay Lohans and spoiled UCLA sorority girls with names like Dakota and Bree because, well, who else will we mock? Who else can future generations of normal kids look to and say, oh my God, at least I'm not like *that*? Who will grow up to date all the obnoxious frat guys and have lousy drunken sex with them for 3.2 minutes and later marry and soon contribute to prescription med statistics and America's fine Christian divorce rate? Exactly.

Similar, it all is, to a recent New York Times trend piece[2] I just read on overpampered tweener girls getting expensive salon treatments at the new array of upscale spas designed especially for them. Have you heard? About relatively well-adjusted 9-year-olds whose parents "treat" their kids to flat-ironings and caramel tintings and expensive Miley Cyrus-grade primpings because they're all caught up in the pop culture horror show and think this is what life is all about? Wacky!

Of course, it doesn't stop there. The tweener trend merely connects further up the line to tales of desperately lousy parents who willingly pay 10 grand for their kids' plastic surgery when they turn 16, new boobs for Taylor and new calf implants for Todd and a new nose for Jenny because hey, all her friends are doing it and what's the big deal and so why not anesthetize her and slice into that young flesh and reshape her face to look more like Jamie Lynn Spears? Neat!

And then the story ends when these girls — and by the way it's almost *always* the girls; rare indeed is the trend piece focusing on how boys get, say, all sorts of horrific messages about machismo and violence and the need for accomplishment — the girls finally turn 18 and head off to college and get a bad sacrum tattoo and appear on "Girls Gone Wild" and then, well, they disappear into the cultural maelstrom, only to reappear 10 years later as that exact same shallow, awful mom who drags her miserable 8-year-old to the salon for her first Brazilian. And lo, the circle of life continues.

Next up: a big trend piece about how all alarmist trend pieces that have anything to do with teenagers, pubic hair, the early sexualization of kids, thong underwear and the tragic death of innocence in modern America all point to a larger trend of how we as a culture are just way, way too obsessed with trend pieces that obsess about the style and sexuality of trendy teens. Watch for it.

1 http://alaizu.notlong.com
2 http://aolee.notlong.com

OK, the hippies weren't right about everything. Female underarm shaving, say. Communal baths. Tie dye. Not grooming. Jesus sandals. Black light posters. The Association. Beards. With beads in them. And little bits of food. That smell like cheesecloth. You might say I'm not a big fan of the hippie aesthetic, per se. But on the important philosophical/spiritual/cultural values stuff? Nailed it.

This is the natural follow-up col to, and unapologetic expansion of, the earlier "Hippie crap saves the world" piece way over on page 334. Compare/contrast? —mm

The hippies were right!

05/02/2007

Go ahead, name your movement. Name something good and positive and pro-environment and eco-friendly that's happening right now in the newly "greening" America, and don't say more guns in Texas or fewer reproductive choices for women or endless unwinnable wars in the Middle East because that would defeat the whole point of this perky little column and destroy its naive tone of happy rose-colored sardonic optimism. OK?

I'm talking about, say, energy-efficient light bulbs. I'm looking at organic foods going mainstream. I mean chemical-free cleaning products widely available at Target and I'm talking saving the whales and protecting the dolphins and I mean yoga studios flourishing in every small town, giant boxes of organic cereal at Costco and non-phthalates dildos[1] at Good Vibes and the Toyota Prius becoming the nation's oddest status symbol. You know, *good* things.

Look around: we have entire industries devoted to recycled paper, a new generation of cheap solar-power technology and an Oscar for "An

Inconvenient Truth" and even the soulless corporate monsters over at famously heartless joints like Wal-Mart are now claiming that they really, really care about saving the environment because, well, "it's the right thing to do" (read: It's purely economic and if they don't start "caring" they'll soon be totally screwed on manufacturing and shipping costs at/from all their brutal Chinese sweatshops).

There is but one conclusion you

can draw from the astonishing (albeit fitful, bittersweet) pro-environment sea change now happening in the culture and (reluctantly, nervously) in the halls of power in D.C., one thing we must all acknowledge in our wary, jaded, globally warmed universe: The hippies had it right all along. Oh yes they did.

You know it's true. All this hot enthusiasm for healing the planet and eating whole foods and avoiding chemicals and working with nature and developing the self? Came from the hippies. Alternative health? Hippies. Green cotton? Hippies. Reclaimed wood? Recycling? Humane treatment of animals? Medical pot? Alternative energy? Natural childbirth? Non-GMO seeds? It came from the granola types (who, of course, absorbed much of it from ancient cultures), from the alternative worldviews, from the underground and the sidelines and it's about time the media, the politicians, the culture as a whole sent out a big, wet, hempcovered apology.

Here's a suggestion, from one of my more astute ex-hippie readers: Instead of issuing carbon credits so industrial polluters can clear their collective corporate conscience, maybe, to help offset all the savage damage they've done to the soul of the planet all these years, these commercial cretins should instead buy some *karma* credits from the former hippies themselves. You know, from those who've been working for the health of the planet, quite thanklessly, for the past 50 years and who have, as a result, built up quite a storehouse of good karma. You think?

Of course, you can easily argue that much of the "authentic" hippie ethos — the anti-corporate ideology, the sexual liberation, the anarchy, the push for civil rights, the experimentation — has been totally leeched out of all these new movements, that corporations have forcibly co-opted and diluted every single technology and humble pro-environment idea and Ben & Jerry's ice cream cone[2] and Odwalla smoothie[3] to make them both palatable and profitable. But does this somehow make the organic oils in that body lotion any more harmful? Verily, it does not.

You might also just as easily claim that much of the nation's reluctant turn toward environmental health has little to do with the hippies per se, that it's taking the threat of global meltdown to slap the nation's incredibly obese ass into gear and force consumers to begin to wake up. Of course, without the '60s groundwork, what we'd be turning *to* in our time of need would be a great deal more hopeless indeed.

But if you're *really* bitter and shortsighted, you could say the entire hippie movement overall was just incredibly overrated, gets far too much cultural credit for far too little actual impact, was pretty much a giant excuse to slack off and enjoy dirty lazy responsibility-free sex romps and do a ton of drugs and avoid Vietnam and not bathe for a month and name your child Sunflower or Shiva Moon or Chakra Lennon Sapphire Bumblebee. This is what's called the reactionary simpleton's view. It blithely ignores history, perspective, the evolution of culture as a whole. You know, just like America.

But, you know, whatever. The proofs are easy enough to trace. The core values and environmental groundwork laid by the '60s counterculture are still so potent, even the stiffest neocon Republican has to acknowledge their extant power. It's all right there: Treehugger.com is the new '60s underground hippy zine. Ecstasy is the new LSD. Tattoos are the new longhairs. And bands from Pearl Jam to Conor Oberst to NIN to the Dixie Chicks are writing politicized songs for a new, ultra-jaded generation.

And oh yes, speaking of good ol' MDMA (Ecstasy), even drug culture is getting some new respect. Staid old Time mag just ran a rather snide little story[4] about the new studies being conducted by Harvard and the NIMH into the astonishing psychospiritual benefits of entheogens such as LSD, psilocybin and MDMA. Unfortunately, the piece basically backhands Timothy Leary and the entire "excessive," "naive" drug culture of yore in favor

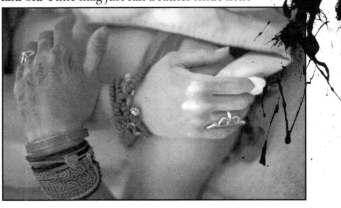

of much more "sane" and "careful" scientific analysis, as if the only valid means to knowledge and an understanding of spirit are through control groups and clinical, mysticism-free examination. Please.

Still, the fact that serious scientific research is being conducted even in the face of the most anti-science, pro-pharmaceutical presidential regime in recent history is proof enough that all the hoary old hippie mantras about expanding the mind and touching God through drugs were onto something after all. Tim Leary is probably smiling wildly right now — though that might be due to all the mushrooms he's been sharing with Kerouac and Einstein and Mary Magdalene. Mmm, heaven.

Of course, true hippie values mean you're not really supposed to care about or attach to any of this, you don't give a damn for the hollow ego stroke of being right all along, for slapping the culture upside the head and saying, See? Do you see? It was never about the long hair and the folk music and Woodstock and taking so much acid you see Jesus and Shiva and Buddha tongue kissing in a hammock on the Dog Star, nimrods.

It was, always and forever, about connectedness. It was about how we are all in this together. It was about resisting the status quo and fighting tyrannical corporate/political power and it was about opening your consciousness and seeing new possibilities of how we can all live with something resembling actual respect for the planet, for alternative cultures, for each other. You know, all that typical hippie crap no one believes in anymore. Right?

1 http://riewad.notlong.com
2 http://latoog.notlong.com
3 http://eeyeto.notlong.com
4 http://naique.notlong.com

And now, The Daring Spectacle presents...

Mullet Haiku

Trans-Am belches oil
While I belch your phone number
Schlitz spilt on vinyl

LOOK AT IT THIS WAY

Fine, I admit that mere sexual fluency and confidence combined with joyful limb dexterity are no absolute cure-alls for one's emotional shortcomings and miserable relationship skills, or your lifetime inability to feel love because your mother whipped you with a garden hose every time you swiped a cigarette from her purse. Fair enough?

Then again, fuck that; maybe they are. Maybe wide, unbridled sexual aptitude and sticky corporal experience — Sex Ed done right — really could lower the divorce rate, improve relations and teach struggling couples to deal with their shit even more powerfully and successfully and soulfully.

In other words, few are the marital woes that can't be helped, at least a little, by a two hours of cunnilingus and a sloppy blowjob and sweaty grinding and lots of laughter and specific instruction and very messy sheets. Agreed?

Side note: This column was one of the few over the years to get me invited onto "The O'Reilly Factor," presumably to discuss with Big Angry Bill the blasphemous idea that sweet, maladroit virgin females might not*, in fact, be God's gift to nervous, inexperienced, emasculated males everywhere, and what sort of perverted heretic must I be to dare to suggest such a thing.*

I turned him down. Always have. I've no desire to be O'Reilly's liberal whipping boy, but more than that, no desire to sink to the low, nasty vibration on which his show operates. Probably not the best decision as far as my career goes. But pretty good for trying to keep intact most of my soul. —mm

Christian virgins are overrated

5/12/2006

There are these... things, these unholy events called "Purity Balls" and you should probably fall to your knees right this minute and thank a merciful and happily polyamorous God that you do not know what they are and that you have access right this minute to vast quantities of wine to deflect their nasty karmic arrows because, you know, *oh my God*. But hey, free country.

Purity Balls. No, not some sort of spherical chastity device to be inserted using vacuum tubes and pulleys, but rather, fancy creepy dress-up rituals[1] taking place in towns like Colorado Springs and Tucson and Zoloft Jesusville, in which Christian dads rent a bad tux while their daughters, mostly teenagers but many as young as 6 or 7, get

all dolled up in gowns from JCPenny and they all drive out to the airport Marriott and prepare to, well, lose their fucking minds.

It begins. At some point the daughter stands up, her pale arms wrapped around her daddy, and reads aloud a formal pledge that she will remain forever pure and virginal and sex-free until she is handed over, by her dad — who is actually called the "high priest" of the home[2] and try not to gag when you read that — like some sort of sad hymenic gift, to her husband, who will receive her like the sanitized and overprotected and libidinously inept servant she so very much is. Praise!

Would that I were making this up.

The dad — er, high priest — in turn, stands up and reads *his* pledge, one stating that he will work to protect his daughter's virginal purity that he has so carefully drilled into her since birth, since she was knee-high to a disturbing dogma, that he will protect her chastity and oversee it and help enforce its boundaries, which might or might not involve great amounts of rage and confusion and secret stashes of cheap scotch, although his pledge claims it's with honor and integrity and lots of bewildering God-speak. Which, in many households, is essentially the same thing.

It's true. Purity Balls are happening, right now. And yes, you have heard this all before. Particularly from the conservative Right, especially from America's rigid and pale fundamentalist "core."

Premarital sex is evil. Female sexuality must be, as ever, contained, repressed, shoved deep down lest it tempt men to sin like gleeful pagans

licking ice cream from the pierced nipples of the devil. Girls do not know how to handle their own genitalia and therefore must be taught — by their fathers, no less — how to dilute their sexual power in order to attract a sexually unqualified, God-fearing husband. You know, same as it ever was.

Very well. Let us now trace the path of imminent cultural destruction: Virgin girl has zero experience with the joys of her own body, with orgasm, with men, with sex toys or shower heads or good gynecological gizmongery. She then marries a man who will very likely have not the slightest clue — as he has had the same dreadful sexual miseducation as our fair virgin — as to what to do with a woman's body, who will, by most all accounts, be unable to tell an erogenous zone from an elbow, a clitoris from a belly button.

Voilá, the standard recipe for emotional, physical and spiritual catastrophe, for roughly 17 years of vague marital misery capped off by divorce and much therapy and four unhappy children and the profound and aching need located somewhere deep beneath the pelvic bone to try something, anything new and different and sexually liberating.

Let's just say it outright: The superiority of virginity myth, it is a massive, underreported disaster. It is a ridiculous and exhausting misconception that must be eradicated like a cancer. Perhaps French philosopher Voltaire said it best, nearly 300 years ago: "It is one of the great superstitions of the human mind to have imagined that virginity could be a virtue." So true.

Which is another way of asking, Don't we have it exactly backward? Shouldn't one's overall happiness — physical, marital or otherwise — be directly equated with exceptional amounts of sexual training and education and awareness? Is such positively libidinous education not a recipe for health and well-being and long-term marital satisfaction? You already know the answer.

Look, the plague of sexual incompetence plagues our land like a plague. It infects our schools, our popular culture. The right endorses wanton sexual stupidity — and all ensuing miseries, drug addictions, divorces, stresses, gun fetishes, online porn obsessions — through failed abstinence programs, STD misinformation, refusal to support quality birth control and the relentless repetition of lies about sin and depravity and a shocking ignorance of the transformative spiritual power of sex. Purity Balls? Nothing but a sad celebration of that exact ignorance.

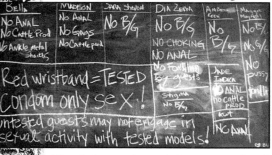

No wonder over half of all teens who take any sort of virginity pledge[3] end up breaking the ridiculous vow within a year (says a new Harvard study), and fully 88 percent end up having sex before marriage anyway.[4] What's more, such silly pledges only result in more oral and anal sex among teens who try, vainly, to adhere. They also marry younger, have fewer sexual partners (read: less skill) and yet have exactly the same rate of STDs[5] as kids who are smart enough to avoid such pointless pledges in the first place.

Would that we had a new agenda, a sexually informed education system that truly empowered teens, that taught open-minded respect for bodies and flesh, pleasure and joy and physical/spiritual awareness. Sure, include STDs and appropriate birth-control information, but not as a deterrent,

not as some sort of nasty weapon of fear. Rather, arm your virgin daughters and sons with slick and giddy reverence for the joys of the flesh, for its potential to transform and ease tension and make you realize all is not so wrong and sinful and hateful with the world.

Would we not be utterly transformed? Would we not finally be free of the sneering, churlish mentality that somehow thinks virgins are dumb, immaculate prizes to be won? Let's just say it: There is no sacredness in the virgin. There is only the fear, were she to be educated and empowered and really let loose, of what she could become.

1 http://aebooc.notlong.com
2 http://aifeet.notlong.com
3 http://efeita.notlong.com
4 http://eedaew.notlong.com
5 http://xieloa.notlong.com

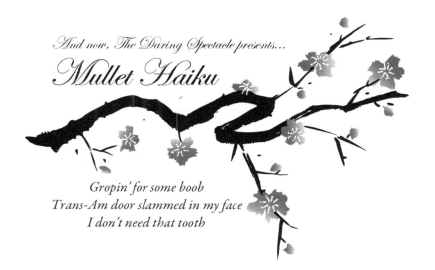

And now, The Daring Spectacle presents…

Mullet Haiku

Gropin' for some boob
Trans-Am door slammed in my face
I don't need that tooth

I see it everywhere, all around, in the carriage and energy and bodies of men around my age. That slump, that paunch, that belly, that pallid and slow-suffering health, that I've-given-up-on-every-interesting-dream-I-ever-had sort of stance in the world. It is equal parts disturbing, disorienting and understandable. But is this the big trade-off? Is this how it must go? You get married and you have the kids and you sit at the same gig year in year out, and before you know it everything's gotten wider, slower, less flexible, until you heave a big sigh and buy the casket at Costco and spend your days watching The Golf Channel and polishing the swimming trophy you won in 1987?

Society seems to dictate the rule of diminishment and lethargy, and we all follow, as if there were no real choice, as if this is the way it's supposed to be, as if society isn't something we ourselves invent on the fly and can change at will. Are there not more layers at play? Are there not more vibrant and fascinating options? Does not every tiny choice you make every single day play into the larger energy field of just how interestingly, blissfully, or painfully your life will unfold? I'm going with "hell yes." —mm

Meet my hot new stripper wife

02/08/2008

Maybe I should start a war. Or a cult. Or a cult about war, with T-shirts and headscarves and a big, glowing, gold-rimmed messiah with fangs and guns and red spiders for eyes. I will call it something wicked like "Serpents of the Devouring Void" or "Warriors of the Crimson Misery" or maybe just "the Republican Party."

Would it help? Will I feel younger and more vibrant and important, like I've accomplished something noteworthy and fulfilled my destiny and can therefore pass through middle age more gracefully, foregoing regular fist-fuls of Prozac and lots of piss-water light beer and slumped shoulders and long miserable stretches of late-night ping-pong coverage on ESPN2?

Will it, in short, help me skip over the next decade or so wherein I might otherwise be doomed to suffer the tepid, ignoble hell known as the mid-life crisis?

Here is the bad news: It might be unavoidable. Turns out researchers compiled data from a couple million people across 80 nations and every income level and social status and gender and demographic and hairstyle, and the conclusion was pretty much irrefutable: The famed mid-life crisis, that feeling of depression and angst and what-the-hell-happened-to-my-dreams, is universal.[1]

It's true. No matter where you live or how much money you make or

how much of your mortgage payment you spend on lap dances in Las Vegas, somewhere between ages 40 and 50 (closer to 40 for women, 50 for men) feelings of futility and spiritual barrenness peak, and you feel like it's all been for naught because you're suddenly on the slippery slope toward cold, beckoning death and you never got around to writing that novel or opening that combo porn shop/laundromat/tattoo parlor or having 2.1 perfect kids or hang-gliding naked over the Swiss Alps.

And now, well, now it's just too damn late, because you're all paunchy and sagging, hair is growing where it shouldn't be and you have mysterious shooting pains in your colon and an inexplicable fondness for televised gardening shows, and no one under 30 wants to have sex with you ever again. You know?

They say that, in terms of general psychological well-being, life is one big, ugly curve. The only times we are truly hopeful or mentally vibrant are closer to the beginning and closer to the end, when we're either sucking the nipple or golfing in Florida (or if you've really lived your life right, both). The rest of life is pretty much a vacuous, drudging slog, interspersed with too many lattes and not enough therapy. I might be oversimplifying a bit. But not really.

For me, I suppose I should be happy. At least for the moment. Even though I've yet to marry, have kids or buy a house, I still have a number of years left before the bland misery swarms over me completely. I still feel pretty vibrant, connected and healthy even though I'm suddenly older than most movie stars and even older the mayor of my own city and I have no idea how that happened. But otherwise, I think I've developed some good tools, a juicy enough spiritual perspective to keep me afloat. Maybe I can make it through relatively unscathed?

Then again, maybe not. Because if I think about it, if I wallow and simmer and stare too long at my skin in one of those giant, horrible makeup mirrors, if I ponder all the hours I've wasted cruising eBay and Notcot and supertangas.com instead of getting outside and reading more books and launching a progressive green movement to provide starving children in Ethiopia with organic tempeh salads and free iPods, I can begin to feel it coming.

The angst, the heavy sighing, the overwhelming need to accomplish, to Get More Done, to reclaim some vigor and maybe rush out and buy a ridiculous Corvette or a giant Harley and couple it with very bad taste in leather jackets and an expensive membership at Sports Club/LA, and top it all off with a gum-snapping semi-hottie 22-year-old girlfriend who loves her some Red Bull and who gets icked-out by sashimi and who says "like" a lot and doesn't get a single one of my references to Spinal Tap or single-malt scotch or rec.arts.erotica, but who has an ass like Mary Magdalene's banana creme pie and makes cute little purring sounds in bed and makes me Viagra smoothies while dancing pornographically in skimpy boy shorts to Justin Timberlake remixes. What, too much? Sorry.

Worse still, the misery could be happening already, and I don't even realize it. Apparently, the crisis comes on very slowly, like some sort of creeping disease, like cancer or liver damage or political conservatism, like a love of creamed foods and golf and pale yellow Polo shirts with the collar turned up. One day you're alert, hip and tingly in all the right places, the next you realize you can't read the tiny print on your bottle of Lipitor and you have nine cats and a nagging feeling you forgot to turn off the stove in the lost kitchen of your dreams. Damn.

Alas, there is no talk of prevention. Amid all the research and evidence, no one says what might alleviate or even eliminate the fear and the vague sense of doom, what might help you cruise over the mid-life hump with something resembling wisdom and gratitude and insight.

My guess is it starts with the usual combination, a personally custom-ized admixture of regular, vigorous exercise, conscious food habits and minimal reality TV and great heaping doses of travel and nature and mental stimulation and truly excellent bedsheets, combined with absolute refusal to be fixed in time and place, to shrivel and hunker down and cling, as so many do, to one set of rules, one ideology, one notion of How It's All Supposed To Be. It is the knowledge that *real* ecstasy has nothing to do with external accomplishment, and everything to do with internal aware-ness.

Oh yes, also: Lots of regular sex and yoga and meditation and the best wine you can afford as you realize that this little blip of an eyeblink of a gift of a life races by just impossibly fast, and therefore staring too long at the future or the past, at expectation and longing, memory and regret only means you don't get to truly experience the moment you're in right now.

Isn't that the real secret? The simplest truth? Isn't that what the gurus and wise ones have been saying since before Jesus was a tingle in the loins of God? To be so present, so hotly, divinely connected to the moment you are in that time loses all relevance and age means nothing and opportunity shows up exactly as it should, and the *real* accomplishment, the *real* sense of achievement comes from celebrating each and every breath like it was a shot glass of molten meaning?

Yes. I'm going with that. What a lovely, Zen-licked, tantra-soaked perspective. I hope to suck down great heaping gallons of it, before it's too late.

1 http://aideich.notlong.com

An editor at the Chronicle almost cut the part you're about to read about the Five Jewels when this column first ran in the paper. Said it failed the "breakfast test," an unspoken newspaper dictum stating that you are not to print anything that might completely gross out the reader as she consumes her eggs and a bagel in the morning (AKA: Nausea is rarely good for business). I was able to convince them otherwise.

One minor flaw of this column: I fail to mention that the idea about collapsing everything together into one big glorious divine energy lump doesn't mean you no longer make distinctions between light and dark, horrible and good, delicious and disgusting. It just means you understand the one true source, and keep your lens wide wide wide. Oh, and be damn glad you're not an ancient Tantric monk. —mm

Kill yourself in Vegas

07/25/2008

It is, of course, all a matter of scale. Perspective. Of allowing yourself and your sensibilities to be hammered to a bloody pulp by the fist of gluttonous reality, just for fun, and see if you can walk away with a shrug and a smile and without feeling like running off to the woods with a case of absinthe and a copy of "Sailing to Byzantium," never to return.

See, you might think you're helping, doing what you can, assisting the healing of the world in tiny but essential ways. You cut down on your garbage and buy CFLs and respond appropriately to the giant pollutive scam that is bottled water, you recycle and buy local and eat organic and maybe even compost, watch your mileage, choose carefully, tread lightly, vote accordingly, use a nice little reusable canvas shopping bag at Trader Joe's. Sweet.

And then, well, it all just explodes. Reality — or rather, a certain nasty aspect of it — spits on your shoes and flips you off and lumbers away like a fat bully after stomping all over your cool sand castle at the beach. I love it when that happens. I hate it when that happens. Ain't it just the way?

Sure enough, I hit the fabulous Las Vegas Strip recently and lo, it was a sharp and wonderful lesson, a reminder, a slap in the heart of all you think might be changing, shifting, improving.

I've been to Vegas plenty of times but it's always an astounding thing, the scale, the overkill, the energy usage, the sheer *impudence* of the place, excessive waste like a mantra, fresh water sucked into the void of the scalding desert, air conditioning blasting 365 days a year and gargantuan oversized everything as a million European and Asian tourists are currently flocking to the place to indulge in distinctly American fantasies of greed and consumption, all thanks to our pathetically weak dollar and wicked extant ethos of more more more.

I love Vegas. For about 36 hours. Then I want to curl up and die.

But maybe that's just me. Because in such places I often get a bit disoriented, a bit blown away by scale, cannot help but stare at those massive theme-park hotels and widen out my mental lens and visualize the incredible quantities of resources being used every second to keep them alive and churning, all the water and energy and food, all the chemicals and cloth and concrete, the miles of cabling and electricity and the garbage and, oh yes, the sewage, the rivers of human detritus flowing from these 4,000-room monstrosities like giant faucets of refuse that never shut off.

All hotels are marvels. Vegas hotels are marvels in a particularly spectacular, demonic sort of way. I can barely get my mind around them.

(I think my favorite tell-tale example that the world is still teetering on the brink has to be the millions of mini water bottles a place like Vegas swims in like confetti, those tiny ridiculous six-ouncers of filtered tap the size of a baby's sippy cup which you can suck down in about two large gulps and then enjoy the idea that the toxic bottle it came in will still be floating out there in the Pacific Garbage Patch when your great-great-great-grandkids have their children in the space station on the moon).

But Vegas is merely a fabulous, high-relief example. All teeming cities are equal parts wonderland and wasteland, all urban centers potential stabs to your heart, reminding you how easy it is to be overwhelmed and discouraged by the never-ending burn of life.

For me, it's often a lesson in balance, in ebb and flow, in the collapsing of opposites. After all, no matter what you do in your day, no matter how devoutly you practice your little exercises in conscious living, there are a million Vegases and Abu Dhabis, Bangkoks and Beijings, Calcuttas and NYCs and Mexico Cities to counter it, incalculable examples of humanity's depressing profligacy to bury your swell little gestures in an avalanche of *screw you.*

Reminds me of an amazing anecdote I heard awhile back at a yoga-related salon dinner I attended, told to me by a genius acquaintance of mine by the name of Chris Wallis,[1] a wise young spiritual teacher who's currently doing his doctoral research in Tantric Shaivism over at Berkeley.

(Warning: if you are easily nauseated, eating breakfast, if you have a weak stomach for ancient ritualistic weirdness, please skip right over the next two paragraphs. Trust me).

Chris told me of an incredible ritual practiced by a certain remote, ancient, now-defunct sect of Tantric Hinduism, a final test endured by the advanced practitioner to see if s/he was truly ready, truly able to remain free of the various bindings and shackles and ego gyrations of this messy and wondrous life.

As I recall, the test was quite simple in its powerful disgustingness: Into a fine goblet was mixed the "five jewels" — equal parts urine, feces, menstrual blood, phglem, and semen, with a touch of wine for good measure. Shaken, stirred, handed to the practitioner with (I imagine) a nice little bow and a humble smile.

You know what happens next. Could the practitioner swallow down the contents without flinching, without reacting in any way? Could the attuned one, in other words, take into his or her being the worst or weirdest aspects of the world, the stickiest and most vile substances and ideas and energies we know, and remain clear and awake and (most importantly) completely present? If so, true consciousness was achieved. If not, well, back to the meditation chamber for you.

It was not, as you might imagine, merely a test of physical fortitude. Nor was it a test of mental numbness and tuning out and jumping away from your body so none of the grossness affects you. Quite the opposite, actually.

It's a (touchingly literal) example of the idea that all matter, no matter how disgusting, joyful, vile or beautiful, is merely energy, that everything emanates from and returns to the same divine source, that all dualities of good/bad disgusting/delicious love/hate collapse together into the same moment. There is no difference. Grossness is merely a perception. Joy is merely an illusive state. Where they collapse into one, there lies the truth. Or maybe just a bottle of aspirin and hundred Alka-Seltzers and a stomach pump.

You get the idea? Somehow, some way, you gotta take it all in, sit right in the center of it, conscious of all but attached to none, and be OK. It's all just energy. It's all the same divine breath of god, blowing in your ear, whispering sweet everythings. Collapse it all together. Shake, stir, swallow it down with a bow and a humble smile. Tasty, no?

1 http://aedagu.notlong.com

A favorite recurring theme makes one of its earliest appearances. We know nothing, remember awe, stay self-effacing and reverential even amidst your grand egotism, remember we are but tiny, itinerant guests on this spinning speck of dust, full of sound and fury and war and iPods and overpriced coffee drinks, signifying nothing. Oh, and maybe go for a dip in the ocean next to some whales once in awhile. It'll keep you insanely humble. And absolutely stupefied.

Still has some good juice and heat despire being a relatively early column; has its verbose tendencies, some typical abuse of the 'and' grammatical trope I'm oft far too fond of, and the prose gets a little purple at the end. I make no apologies. –mm

Sad spouts of ignorance

03/26/2003

We think we know so damn much.

We think we know cause and effect. We think we know basic systems and human nature and the arc of time, what sort of hellish road we are paving right this minute, all those big colorful maps and arrows and diagrams and missile trajectories on CNN, all the clusters of little green plastic army men pushed around a giant map table by embittered generals.

We think we know what will happen to the collective unconscious, to the soul of the population at large when the scowling GOP war hawks issued the order to rain 3,000 multimillion-dollar warheads down on a bedraggled piss-poor food-starved nation in a single day.

Or when we massacre tens of thousands of soldiers and civilians and lay waste to an entire culture and landscape and history, as a 20-mile-long procession of U.S. troops rumble into Baghdad to kill anything with a turban and an Islamic faith and a dusty 1983 U.S.-Iraq chemical-weapons sales receipt, and call it patriotism.

We think we know all about body counts and nation building, and we think we have some sort of sanctimonious monopoly on the idea of what type of freedom everyone should have, what sort of force-fed democracy everyone really needs, whose self-righteous angry SUV-driving god has the right to bitch-slap which self-righteous angry Koran-reading god, and call it Christian largesse.

We don't know anything.

I unplugged recently. I was off the snarling media grid, briefly, strangely, beautifully. It was surreal and amazing and jarring. This is when I realized.

There I was on vacation just last week, watching the pods, the families,

the processions of humpback whales just off the Hawaii coastline, huge
35-ton males and even bigger 40-ton females and their 5-ton newborn
calves, every day, whale after whale, pod after pod, a glorious and breathtaking thing, like a gift, a reminder, a slap in the face to the warmongering
bilious timbre of now, of Shrub's cadre of hissing war hawks, of what we
think we know.

And they were all spouting and rolling and breaching and slapping the
water with their huge tails and pectoral fins, all about birth and mating
and migration and Jesus goddamn *wow* they're big, and humbling, and
shocking, as you like to think you're all plugged in and world wise and media savvy, you might think you know what the planet is really doing at any
given moment, deep down, in the meat of it, and of course, you see something like this and you realize, sure enough, you don't know anything.

But the hawks and fearmongers, they want you to believe you do. They
want you to think we are, with this vile needless Iraq war, attaining progress, reaching for some sort of truth, bringing the world closer into align-
ment with what Bush's sneering Christian god along with Uncle Dick's
economic advisory team deems right and just and lucrative, never mind
all the burned bodies and dead children and the massacred thousands and
the billions in economy-gutting expenditures. We are making the world
better, they actually claim. How sweet. Nothing like 100,000 full body
bags to really make the soul glow.

The S.O. and I bought a book on humpback whales to try and understand, to see what those behaviors mean, to see what it was, exactly, we
were watching every day. We read and read and said wow and hmm and
isn't that interesting, as we tried to find out why they breached, or why
they slapped the waves like that, or why they sang or what the songs might
mean. You know, the basics. Here is what we found out:

No one has the slightest clue.

It's true. Modern science has no idea. Whale songs. Breaching. Slapping
the waves with their enormous tail fins, over and over, like a ritual, a call,
a play. Some of the biggest, most ancient creatures on the planet, timeless
and stunning and awe inspiring, once slaughtered nearly to extinction and
each and every one karmically and ethically impervious to white angry
men puling about war, and still we have no idea. We don't know why they
breach, or slap or sing. We don't even know how long whales live.

And then we have the gall. We have the nerve to think we know how
the world works, what the planet needs, how culture operates. We trot out
the Constitution when it suits us and point to the Second Amendment
as kids shoot each other in schools, and we think we understand how the
U.S. was founded on the idea that the life of an Iraqi peasant is as valuable

as that of a U.S. Marine, or Bush daughter, or shuttle astronaut. Ha.

Monarch butterflies haul tiny insect ass 3,000 miles from Canada to Mexico (and back) every year, through storms and hail and across mountains and deserts, through conditions most major aircraft would whimper at, landing on the exact same trees every single year to mate, generation after generation. We have no idea how the hell they do it. No idea how they survive the journey, the exact path they take, how they know the exact tree every time, or why, or what it might mean. Just another example. Pure mystery. One of thousands.

Yet we think we are just so damn sure. We are just so sure that we rule the whole planet, that we are the uberspecies, that we have the right to slaughter whomever and whatever we like whenever we like because someone might dare stand in the way of our alleged progress, or our oil interests, or our profits. How did all our oil get under their sand? we ask, not at all jokingly.

I know what the whale-tail slaps are.

They are a reminder. No matter how much we think we know, no matter how many die as a result of a vicious war, no matter what sort of self-righteous good we think we're ramming down everyone's throat, we are, quite simply, raging deeper into ignorance. We know nothing. And the worst part is, we seem to be learning less with every warhead, every press conference, every dust-choked reporter and dead soldier. The whales know this. Maybe they're just waving goodbye.

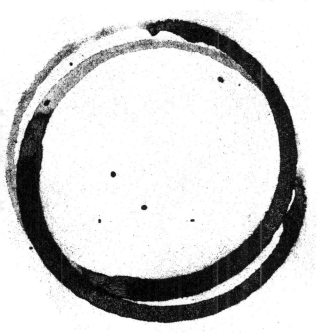

Like we have any real clue. I mean, of course *there are more things in heaven and earth than are dreamt of in our philosophy.* Of course *there are more energies at play, levels of consciousness we have yet to tap, dimensions of reality we have yet to understand, passages to the inner realms we have yet to uncover. To think we have a relatively full or even reasonably coherent grasp of what's really going on in this fickle existence is not merely impossible, it's downright laughable. Does that necessarily mean UFOs and crop circles are totally real and the Egyptian pyramids were built by aliens from the fifth dimension? Or are those just a nice little stories to tell ourselves, fun little frames we try to put around the inexplicable and eternal, so at least we can* pretend *we have a clue so we don't totally creep ourselves out every single day? I know my answer. —mm*

Behold, giant stone vaginas

07/23/2003

Stonehenge. Buncha rocks. Assortment of really old, really gray, really heavy stones over there in really old, gray, heavy England. You know the ones. Turns out the whole collection is really meant to depict a giant vagina.[1] Who knew?

No, really. You gotta look at it from above. Notice, like some Canadian researchers did in this particular study, the outline, the general yonic shape, that come-hither, winkingly divine invitation that enchants all of life and confounds the GOP and makes grown men weep. Then ask your nearest female paramour to please remove her pants. You need to compare. See? See that shape? Aha! Mystery solved.

Stonehenge. Not *just* a vagina, of course. It's also been explained as a spaceship port, a cosmic calculator, Legos for prehistoric giants, dinosaur toenail clippings, dominos of the gods, ancient dildos from a cosmic orgy, the original Restoration Hardware and the bearer of the secret of who really murdered JFK. These are the theories. Of course, we really have no idea.

Same goes for, say, pyramids. Cryptozoology. Shamanism. Parapsychology. Reincarnation. Deep astrology. The reading of tea leaves and assorted chicken bones in the dried skull of a small encephalitic monkey somewhere in Bangladesh, while sniffing magic herbs and reciting Yeats' "Sailing to Byzantium" in the vain hopes of discovering how to make love stay and where to find the ultimate burrito. Or maybe that's just me.

This is the grist that keeps us juiced. This is the flutter and glitter of mystery and hoax and divine hint that keeps us on our subconscious toes and makes life deeply fascinating and keeps us from succumbing to the very drab idea that it's all just a pile of carbon and random synapse firings that last about 85.3 years until we shrug and sigh and drop like flies and that's pretty much it.

Let us not forget the crop circles. The recent local phenomena. Landing strips, of course, for desperately shy alien aircraft. Secret love notes passed by extraterrestrials in the tertiary classroom. Oh yes yes yes.

And also merely the semi-catatonic pot-happy meanderings of smart-ass teenagers who are so bored they find that spending 10 hours walking through some nonplussed farmer's field with a big plank attached to some rope to be a totally bitchin' way to spend the entirety of a Saturday night yo dude check it out I made a circle pass me the Bud!

We are not dupes. This is what we say to ourselves. We are not naive and, despite cosmic/geological proof to the contrary, we were not born yesterday, even though we so totally were.

And hence well do we know that most of it's just plain bunk, right? Fully 99.2 percent of all UFO sightings and ghostly visitations and astrological vibrations and ancient fertility symbols erected by giant alien lesbian priestess dominatrix Atlantean mathematicians are all just big-ass hoaxes and myths and lies and stunts and the imaginings of bored druid teenagers. Right?

Well do we know, furthermore, that it's all just an often shockingly effective but ultimately bogus attempt to steer an increasingly gullible and dumbed-down nation into believing in crap that only makes them even more gullible and pseudo-patriotic and ardent fans of mediocre M. Night Shamalyan movies.

And we look to science for proof. Science is often all snickery and factual and dry, so it must be right. Rationalists, skeptics and researchers love nothing more than to pick apart magic and unsolved phenomena and the divine interconnectedness of life with the cold, rational forceps of mathematics and smug logic and formulas that inexplicably don't involve wine or sex or love. And lo, we are reassured.

But then there's the rest. Then there's what's underneath. Then there's that inexplicable and confounding and gorgeous and utterly astounding 0.8 percent, the ghosts and spirits and energies and countless bizarre/potent unavoidable inexplicable phenomena that every single person on the planet right now is aware, on some level and senses, in some deep part of their soul or cervix or perineum or subconscious, is absolutely goddamn freaking-hell true.

You know it is. Just give it up already. Stop resisting. This is not even a question. You want to make a hardcore scientist scream in about three seconds flat? Simply point out how our precious known universe is roughly .000000000012 of what's actually "out there" and we haven't even mapped our own oceans or catalogued the mysteries of the rain forests and by the way, could you please explain the language of a dream?

We haven't even begun to understand what makes us conscious. We have little clue what makes us hum and whisper and cry and come, what makes us radiant divine throbbing tragicomic myth junkies. We know so very little yet we think we have a handle on it all and this is what makes us a cute little running joke among the gods and spirits and ghosts.

And meanwhile Stonehenge and the Great Pyramids and the Parthenon, et al., just sit there like some sort of obvious reminders that we are but babes in the cosmic woods, giddy amoeba in the celestial ocean.

No wonder the ancients built those stones in the shape of the luscious female genitalia. They knew. We need to be reminded. On a spiritual/magical level, we've barely even been born.

1 http://ushiela.notlong.com

And now, The Daring Spectacle presents...

Mullet Haiku

*Stop sign on dirt road
Taunts me with its brand new face
Hand me my damn gun*

This is the rule: Don't kill cute things. Not out in the open, anyway. Goes against our very chemistry, wiring, cultural temperament. But ugly things? Gross things? Things that taste great with dark beer and a convenient three-pack of tasty dipping sauces? Absofuckinglutely.

I can only point up the hypocrisy so much. I'm very much a happy omnivore. In moderation, organic, with as much awareness as I can muster. But is there hypocrisy in my eating habits and treatment of animals? In yours? Of course there is. We cannot escape it.

For me, it's all about the reverence, the gratitude, the energy awareness, the humane treatment. If we can fold those in as much as possible to how we treat the animal kingdom, we might do pretty well. Or is that just a convenient excuse? —mm

Who loves baby-seal kabobs?

4/07/2006

Let us all agree right now: Baby harp seals — those doe-eyed sausagelike bundles of puffy white blubber — are just phenomenally, face-meltingly cute. So adorable and so helpless and so sweet-looking it's like God took Bambi and sawed off all his legs and put him in a white fluffy parka and crossbred him with a puppy and a Marshmallow Peep and tossed him out onto the Arctic ice to pose for Polar Baby Gap. I mean, *cute.*

But baby seals are also, apparently, highly lucrative. Just ask the Canadian government, taking massive heat from the international animal-rights community and Pamela Anderson and just about everybody else for allowing a renewed seal hunt this year, giving rights to seal hunters to slaughter upward of 325,000 megacute baby harp seals (among other related species) out of an estimated seal population of about 6 million. [1]

Maybe you've seen the nasty scenario: Apparently soulless, stone-hearted men with giant spiked clubs step out onto the ice and walk straight up to these helpless and staggeringly adorable creatures and smash their soft skulls in one or two massive blows, all for the sake of profit on the seals' fur (expensive leather goods) and a bit of seal oil (rich in omega-3!), despite no real economic necessity. [2] It's just luxury.

It is easy to be horrified. It is easy to be disgusted and appalled by this senseless and cruel killing, even as you block out the fact that, in America, we kill what, 2 *million* unwanted dogs and cats per year? [3] Three million? And don't use their meat or fur for anything at all except some scary medical experiments and perhaps some sort of illegal chicken feed? But, you know, shhh.

Fact is, we in America butcher animals by the billions to feed and clothe our ever-gluttonous population, countless totally not-at-all-cute chickens and pigs and cows, fish and turkeys and rabbits and sheep, all hacked and clubbed and shot and beheaded by the truckload in a thousand different mechanized techniques and no one really blinking an eye except for rabid animal activists and vegetarians and people who secretly miss wearing leather.

But then you merely walk up to anyone and mention how we as a species are still brutally beating these adorable white puffball seals with giant spiked clubs[4] and maybe you show them a picture exactly like this one,[5] and defy anyone not to shudder and recoil in abject horror, even as you munch your fresh order of chicken pad thai. I mean, *horrible*.

It's one of those scenarios that raises a decidedly all-American question: Are we all just incredible hypocrites? Have our lives become so complicated and messy and packed with low-grade, everyday hypocrisy across so many levels — politics, religion, education, sexual mores, etc. — that we've reached point where the very notion of hypocrisy becomes flexible and fluid and just another annoying itch we can't quite scratch?

More specifically, is some sort of moral or humane line being crossed with the seals that isn't really crossed with, say, the slaughter of ducks? Is it the primitive, barbaric *technique* of the seal killings that get to us? Or the stunning baby-seal cuteness? Is it the fact that most harp seals are helpless babies and that we're chemically hardwired to want to protect innocent defenseless infants? Is this the overarching message? Take the cows, but don't slaughter swooning cuteness?

Of course, no one except drunk hunters and Dick Cheney wants to see animals suffer. No one, even happy carnivores, wants to see inside a real slaughterhouse. To see the sausage get made, most agree, is to re-think your relationship to meat and the animal kingdom and to be brutally stunned into lifelong vegetarianism if not an absolute rejection of kick-ass leather boots and cool wallets. This, of course, is what the animal rights groups count on.

Which is exactly why the Canadian baby-seal slaughter is, it must be said, the perfect press op for PETA et al. Next to grotesque Japanese whaling, baby-seal slaughter is the ideal gruesome PR spectacle. Naturally, PETA and its ilk oppose all forms of animal use, from Chicken McNuggets to leather gloves to bunny paté, but those issues lack the flash and power and sheer visceral horror of smashing cute baby seals. By trotting out pneumatic super-intellect Pamela Anderson to offer lap dances to Canadian PM Stephen Harper if he'll just reconsider the seal hunt, they're merely leveraging this intense cuteness/brutality dichotomy to raise

awareness of all the others. Easy enough.

But then again, not really. Truth is, the seal slaughter does less to in-crease awareness of all animal cruelty and far more to illuminate the ques-tion of just where we draw our lines of allowable consumption, a question of where you reside on the grand karmic spectrum of Who Decides What Lives or Dies.

Do you eat all sorts of meat and love leather couches and cool sheep-skin boots and think nothing of it? The line is way, way over there, not all that relevant to your life. Eat only organic, free-range meats, humanely treated and killed? The line moves a little closer, the question becomes more immediate. Vegetarian? Closer still. Vegan, it's right under your nose. Monastic mendicant Jainist who believes in harming absolutely no life whatsoever and that includes insects and worms and even Kim Kardashi-an, to the point where you won't blink an eye for fear of killing one of those creepy little microscopic mites that live in your eyelashes? The line dissolves completely.

Yes, the seal slaughter is barbaric and stupid. Then again, we could all survive without chicken and veal and leather jackets and steaming deli-cious organic turkey hot dogs, too. If we are to measure the progress of the human species by how many things we remove from the master list of Things We Kill Because We Can, well, we have progressed nearly not at all.

Perhaps it all has to do with trying to have, at the very least, a modicum of conscience, a shred of reverence, a hint of respect for the creatures we consume for meat or oil or pelt. Respect the interconnectedness of all things, even as you consume them. *Especially* as you consume them. And there's a visceral level of barbarism and cruelty attached to baby-seal hunts that, like whaling, serve no justifiable purpose and obliterates any sort of consciousness, compassion or ritual. It is merely slaughter for money.

Is this our collective line? Is our abject disgust at the seal hunt a sign of enlightenment and progress? Or is it merely that the damnable creatures are so unbelievably cute that they release gobs of oxytocin in our brains and we want to love and protect them like tiny Dalmatian puppies even as we enjoy our Niman Ranch hamburgers?

Which is it, deep morality or visceral cuteness? Can you unpack it all? Do the seals even care?

1 http://ubaigh.notlong.com
2 http://duchoh.notlong.com
3 http://zixome.notlong.com
4 http://xoedamat.notlong.com
5 http://yahwe.notlong.com

As you surely remember, California was among three states to uphold a hateful ban on gay marriage in the '08 election. Proposition 8's passage came as a big shock, unexpected and sad, especially given the overwhelming feelings of change and progress in the air all over the nation at the time. The good news is, the ban won by the narrowest margin in state history (52 to 48 percent). Translation: the old homophobia may not be dead just yet, but as I point out down there in paragraph five, it's really just a matter of time. —mm

Farewell, all you old homophobes

06/11/2008

It's a generational thing, you could say, grinning just a little as you do so.

It's because younger people today — those under, say, 45 or so — have been far more exposed to the gay "lifestyle" and to more fluid notions of gender and sexuality, to the idea of homosexuality as a common, nonthreatening, everyday, what's-the-big-deal shrug, and therefore, as a demographic, they/we understand that allowing gay people to wed doesn't actually mean our shaky notions of God and family and society will collapse like a Catholic priest's willpower at a Boy Scout jamboree.

This, I think, was perhaps the most fascinating tidbit of insight to emerge from the most recent poll of Californians where, for the first time in state history, a majority of those polled said they support the idea of gay marriage and/or oppose a new and vile push for a state constitutional amendment to ban it outright. And that majority consists, by and large, of the young.[1]

It's an intriguing — if slightly morbid — thing to note, because on the flip side, the poll also found that most people over age 65 don't like the idea of gay marriage one little bit because — well, they usually can't exactly explain why, though it's not difficult to guess: It's what they were taught,

what was implied, it's what their own parents passed on to them, as did their church, their culture, society as it was during their upbringing, and it was largely a narrow and repressed and sexually unaware period that finally, mercifully seems to be gasping its last.

And hence the obvious conclusion: It's only because the

"Greatest Generation" is finally dying off that something like gay marriage can be realized as less of a silly threat. Or, more bluntly: As die the old, so dies the intolerance so many of them carried like a sad, hereditary disease.

I know, it sounds a bit harsh. And it probably is. But just looking at the raw data, it appears to be one of the more lucid, clear-cut cases of generational upheavals in recent history. Hell, just 30 years ago, support for gay marriage was a measly 28 percent. In 1985, it was 42 percent. Now, at least according to one major poll (others aren't quite there yet, but it's getting very close) it's 51 percent, and growing fast.

What's more, among those 18 to 29 years old, support is at a whopping 68 percent, whereas only 36 percent of people over 65 think it's totally OK to love whomever you want and marry them and then redecorate the kitchen and fight about appliances and money and sex and kids and, later, who gets the dog in the divorce.

Translation: The tipping point has finally been reached, and there's no going back. Gay marriage as an issue, as a hot button, as a nasty right-wing political weapon will soon vanish into the dustbin of history.[2] I mean, thank God.

But is it fair to say that it's always the older generations who cling to outmoded, oppressive inhibitions and constraints, who tend to impede real progress and social change because, well, they just don't understand the new ideas and what's happening around them, because, as the disheartening maxim goes, the older you get the more you stiffen and mummify your notions of how it's all supposed to work? So it would seem.

Then again, it's also certainly no universal truth; I get plenty of e-mail from wonderful, open-minded septuagenarians who happily celebrate the notion of gay marriage — or a female president, or a black president, or the green movement, or teaching "real" sexuality in schools, and so on — just as I get plenty of nauseating e-mail from young, violently homophobic Midwestern "fag"-haters who wouldn't know open-minded gender fluidity if their favorite NASCAR driver suddenly revealed a passion for tiramisu and old Judy Garland movies.

Either way, you gotta admit, it's sort of staggering, this shift. It's also sort of wonderful. Because it also means that, while the brutal Bush regime tried to clamp down and convince everyone that clinging to homophobia and Biblical literalism was actually a nice way to live, all it did was create a nasty little speed bump.

So then, can you extend this line of thinking a bit? Can you suggest, say, the fact that Hillary Clinton came within inches of the Democratic presidential nomination also indicates a similar generational turning point, because it marks the long overdue death of a certain strain of vile, tired sexism that's been carried around for generations by the old-boy network?

Maybe you can. Because my guess is, the next time a smart, experienced, wildly able female runs for president, few in the culture will really blink an eye and we'll only hear the most tepid of sexist grunting from old timer pundits over on Fox News, simply because the upcoming generation of young women will be, by default, far more empowered and skilled and experienced than ever before. Yes, Hillary helped pave the way, but so did, you know, death.

Same goes for Barack Obama. His broad, rather astonishing appeal to the normally apolitical younger generation isn't merely due to his own youthfulness, or the fact that he knows what the Internet is, whereas you get the impression John McCain still can't set the clock on his VCR. No, much of Obama's incredible success can largely be credited to the blessed — and quite literal — dying off of some very old, ugly ideas of race and how a president is supposed to look.

These are some big moments. These are sociocultural milestones, heavy and historic and powerful, and they suddenly seem to be coming faster and at a more invigorating pace than ever. It's doubly interesting given how society usually progresses in fits and starts and random convulsions; it expands and contracts and only rarely makes unmistakable, permanent leaps forward.

Not this time. This is like a massive chunk of the cultural iceberg finally falling away, revealing strange and lovely new passageways into the human experiment.

So then, perhaps the most important question of all has nothing to do with homosexuality, or politics, or silly "culture wars," or even stunning generational flips. After all, while it might be sardonic fun to cheer the end of the old folks and their oppressive beliefs, no generation is ever immune to suddenly turning into the very thing it once professed to be railing against. (Witness, won't you, aging, panicky Generation X's hot frustration with whiny, spoiled little Gen Y. So cute.)[3]

Maybe the most vital question is, how to stay flexible? No matter your upbringing, your generational biases, your received opinions and hatreds and viewpoints, how do you crack open your heart to new possibilities, invite new perspectives, understand that nothing actually has to be the way you thought it had to be, before it's too late and you find yourself older and yet in some ways not at all wiser, on the ugly side of a landmark poll?

1 http://aiyeamo.notlong.com
2 http://ixohj.notlong.com
3 http://aicayo.notlong.com

The following column is famous. Or rather, a small part of it is. In March of '03, The Sun magazine chose to quote from this piece, in a back-page space they call "Sunbeams" normally reserved for memorable passages by assorted divine beings such as the Dalai Lama ansd Martin Luther King, Jr. and (ahem) George Carlin. I have no idea how I got there.

The passage has taken on a life of its own. To this day, I still receive touching notes of thanks and praise for writing it. I'm told by readers that it's popped up all over the world, in cafes and 'zines and in classrooms and on bathroom walls and who knows where else. Most recently, I learned it was quoted during a talk by the wonderful Buddhist teacher and author Jack Kornfield up at the Spirit Rock meditation center in Woodacre, CA. Flattering stuff indeed. Of course, it doesn't hurt that The Sun's editor made me sound wonderfully poetic and lucid indeed.

Here's how it originally appeared in The Sun (see http://thesunmagazine. org/issues/327/sunbeams) —mm

> Stop thinking this is all there is. . . . Realize that for every ongoing war and religious outrage and environmental devastation and bogus Iraqi attack plan, there are a thousand counter-balancing acts of staggering generosity and humanity and art and beauty happening all over the world, right now, on a breathtaking scale, from flower box to cathedral. . . . Resist the temptation to drown in fatalism, to shake your head and sigh and just throw in the karmic towel. . . . Realize that this is the perfect moment to change the energy of the world, to step right up and crank your personal volume; right when it all seems dark and bitter and offensive and acrimonious and conflicted and bilious . . . there your opening. Remember magic And, finally, believe you are part of a groundswell, a resistance, a seemingly small but actually very, very large impending karmic overhaul, a great shift, the beginning of something important and potent and unstoppable. ?Mark Morford

Please help the war effort

10/18/2002

It is a time of great need. It is a time of national teeth-gritting and resigned fortitude and wine-infused bouts of very heavy collective sighing.

Many ask what they can do. How they can contribute, how they can best aid the faux-war effort and support our troops in a whole new way, deflect the pain, remain somehow clear-headed and positive and even a tiny bit optimistic, when all seems hopeless and infuriating and lost.

I have compiled this short list. Things you can do, right now, this minute, to feel more connected and support the nation sans money or blood or prefabricated force-fed rage, and more fully lick the fingertips of your fervent unrequited patriotism in this time of need. Call it a checklist. Call it a spiritual perspective frappe, SUV antenna flags not included:

- Choose not to believe much of the disinformation spinning forth from the White House at this time. Look at Donald Rumsfeld's shockingly beady and pitch-black eyes and realize this man, these people, they are deeply convoluted and power blinded and do not have your best interests at heart.

- Choose, furthermore, not to believe the world is really full of these vile power-mad slugs and lizards and prevaricators and fools. Stop thinking this is all there is, war and suffering and apparently very pale, spiritless men running the world into the ground.

- Realize that for every ongoing war and religious outrage and environmental devastation and bogus Iraqi attack plan, there are a thousand counterbalancing acts of staggering generosity and humanity and art and beauty happening all over the world, right now, on a breathtaking scale, from flower box to cathedral.

- Resist the great surges toward nihilism about the media, in seeing them all as either a bunch of depressing pansy-assed liberal scum, or corporate-controlled J-school lackeys all parroting the same old government-approved lines.

- Seek out nuance and counterargument and subtle irony and contrarianism and balance and perspective. Realize it's never as one-sided as they want you to believe. Read more outside your normal box of viewpoints and interests. Find out for yourself.

- Remember the world does not consist of simpleminded and reductive good/evil polarities, but, rather, is a living organism, interconnected and breathing and dying and renewing in constant flux, religions interflowing, beliefs inbreeding, crammed full of ecstatically bejeweled people who are just as contradictory and confused and gorgeous and kaleidoscopic and baffled and sleepy and horny and lost and desperately craving of juicy unfiltered spiritual nourishment as you are, in this very moment, as you read these words.

- Resist the temptation to drown in fatalism, to shake your head and sigh and just throw in the karmic towel and head for the mountains with a case of Grey Goose and a box of Scharffen-berger chocolates and the entire DeLillo collection and "Baraka" on DVD. Not that that's necessarily a bad thing.

- Realize the divine is not quite what you think it might be, that old methods of imploring, say, a cantankerous patriarchal figure to please let you win the lottery and score that promotion and oh yes smite your enemies might be a bit antiquated and prohibitive and just slightly lacking in vital ancient chthonic feminine power.

- Realize, further, that it is just these very outmoded mind-sets that are fueling a great many hatreds and arming a great many warheads, and that maybe, just maybe, blind adherence to any narrow doctrine — Christian, Muslim, Jew — is potentially fatal to the soul, bad for the skin and also just no fun at all.
- Change the way you pray. Choose to believe in true orgiastic, energetic, self-realized divinity inside the self and emanating out, as opposed to an angry, vengeful God out there, one who demands that everyone must pay and suffer and kill and die, in His name, same as it ever was.
- Remember that it is your intention that sends the energy into play, that directly affects the world, every single person and every single soul, and your hate and fear and self-righteous belief does nothing to up the patriotism not just for country but for the entire planet. You have so much power. More than you know.
- Realize that this is the perfect moment to change the energy of the world, to step right up and crank your personal volume, right when it all seems dark and bitter and offensive and acrimonious and conflicted and bilious, right when the snakes and pit vipers and squinting finger-pointing cowboy wanna-bes are all distracted — there's your opening.
- Remember magic.
- And, finally, believe you are a part of a groundswell, a resistance, a seemingly small but actually very, very large impending karmic overhaul, a great shift, the beginning of something important and potent and unstoppable. You can breathe like this is the most lucid thing there is to believe. You can walk down the street like you are full of divine secrets.

You can do something. You are being implored. Now is your chance. Please help keep America free. Please show your love for your country. This is just the beginning. Thank you and Shivaspeed.

From: "Jane T" jXXXX@hotmail.com
To: <mmorford@sfgate.com>
Subject: Want to know what's REALLY funny?!
Date: Sun, 11 Dec 2005 20:52:25 -0600
Mime-Version: 1.0

Want to know what's going to be REALLY funny?! When you are burning in hell. Gosh, I can't WAIT to laugh at you as you are screaming in agony and begging for forgiveness. Then you can write all of the trash you want about "fundies" and groups that are merely trying to tell you how life really is.

I can't wait until you and the devil are chilling over a brewsky and you can't even ENJOY your beer because you are in such agony. Then you'll maybe rethink your comments.

I can't wait until you and the devil are enjoying your eternal trip to the sauna of your choice- that is curently about 1000 degrees F. Then you'll maybe rethink your comments.

I can't wait until the earth is in shambles and you and the devil are enjoying watching the rest of us, while you are wishing you could have seen the light. Then maybe you'll rethink your comments.

I'm sure you are secretly an ashamed little man who knows there is more to life than your pathetic attempts at journalism I'm sure you sit at alone at night wondering why your life sucks and you are so pathetically unhappy. I'm sure you frequently do anything possible to fill that little black hole in your life.

From: "Maurice C" <phantomXXX@XXXX.net>
To: <mmorford@sfgate.com>
Subject: Your Bush and the Devil Article
Date: Sun, 1 Oct 2006 11:23:50 -0500
MIME-Version: 1.0

Who told you that your sarcastic-style is funny? The article sucks, you suck and may the fleas from a million camels infest your morbid body at the same instant your 4 and .0001 extrusions become useless. Fuck Off!

From: aposto <XXX@hotmail.com>
To: <mmorford@sfgate.com>
Subject: Big Glorious Family's with Ronnie Reagan pictures in every room!!
Date: Thu, 29 Mar 2007 13:08:01 -0700
MIME-Version: 1.0
FILETIME=[F6FEE560:01C7723D]

Look mutant, you're a mutant get over it, the only right you deserve is to breath air. We breed, meaning conservatives and we make families, you smoke penis that has been in another man's ass. You let another man have his penis in your ass. How utterly disgusting! You actually promote such godless and debauchery. Your dad must be real proud, and if he says he is he is lying to you.

buying more guns, (I know you like that idea) going to church more and promoting the "right" way of life.
You think being a phag is a good thing. Think about what it means to be a phag. You were so wronged you're a weak gene, what a bummer, so much of a mutant that you would rather have sex with a man than a woman. That goes against all human nature. You can put your stupid lefty spin on it, but dood get over it, you're a mutant, vague man, a malformed human being. Sounds like something the devil would do.

Civil rights for phags, not until you start with wearing a tattoo on your forehead that acknowledges to the whole world that you are a mutant malformed human being that needs certain extra special rights. I can look at a black man and say. Yep he is black, I can't look at a phag and say, yep that's a phag...well maybe in your case I could

What a shame, you would and have nothing if it were not for the values of large families and what they bring, large conservative family are growing phags and lefty families are not.

I feel sorry for you, your family. I can't even believe you're an American...well you're not, you're a phag mutant.

I digress...

I would still fight for you in a minute I will protect you to your last breath, I would kill for you Mark to make sure that you can keep writing what you write, You do so much for our cause and yours of course.

God Bless Sincerely
John

You think you know exactly what will fill that whole, but just can't quite comprehend in your little brain what life is all about.

So while you try to stuff your life full of sarcasm, synicsm, and trash, you just remember what people told you before you were cast into hell.

Enjoy your time with the devil!

Jane T

From: XXX@aol.com
Date: Wed, 25 Oct 2006 12:42:27 EDT
Subject: tattooed heathins
To: mmorford@sfgate.com
MIME-Version: 1.0
X-Spam-Flag: NO

You are an idiot as I have written you before. I am not the so-called Christian Right (nor have I ever met anyone from that demonized group), but you are a sicko citizen of this country. I hope you live long enough so you and your type people bring down the country and then the replacement will imprison you, or worse, for your beliefs. It will come back around to get you, you idiot. Did you get this job even though you are either uneducated or you are selling papers because you are a sensationalist? I do not think anyone can be as stupid as you seem in your columns, so I am going to give you the benefit of the doubt that you are a sensationalist.

Hal B

I hate you I hate you I hate you

I still like this piece. It offers up a vigorous, albeit admittedly oversimplified response to a pressing problem: How to give the drudgery of life, the horrors and savagery and poison, the death and taxes and war, its due, without wallowing and whining and believing if you don't discuss and analyze the nastiest and least compassionate aspects of the brutal human experiment every single day, you are not a truly deep and engaged thinker?

I think the key is not necessarily about finding a crude sort of balance, per se — not about, say, doing one column about Great Dane puppies or the joy of yoga and sunshine, and quickly follow it with one about pollution in China or the lack of punishment for certified rapists in the Middle East. It's more about discovering and exploring, via tone and attitude and lots of ideological self-exams, how all stories, all human drama, flow into and out of the same source; about collapsing opposites, pulling back and taking the wide view, mixing the Shiva with the Shakti, the dark and the light. It's a much trickier, more elusive way to view the cosmic flow. I fail all the time. But it sure beats relentlessly dour, abject fatalism. —mm

Please write more about rape

05/14/2004

I get this a lot: Mark, how can you write about light fluffy inconsequential things like dogs or yoga or car design or sex or music when there's so many gut-wrenching, soul-curdling, life-threatening atrocities and gang rapes and beheadings and Limbaughs happening in the world right now that deserve immediate attention?

How the hell can you possibly write a whole column extolling, say, the virtues of single-malt scotch or of having sex in the backseat[1] of small luscious European cars, when war is raging and the environment is teetering on the edge and women's rights are being gouged and McDonald's is poisoning our youth and Dick Cheney is still upright, barely?

This is what they say. The world is a ticking powder keg of nails and fear. Please write about this, all the time, every time. Give it voice and shape and insight. Every column should be furious and polemic. Fight the good fight! Tackle the tough snarly issues head on, nonstop, never failing to take those corrupt motherfuckers who are ruining our planet to the mat!

And they are so right. Painfully so. But it's also impossible. The short answer as to why I don't is, of course: To avoid utter spiritual meltdown and ideological wrist slitting and savage karmic pain.

But it's more than that. And the reason I don't is very much the same reason you should avoid imbibing too much fiery swill from this media void, too. Do you already know? Is this already a given? Open wide and say, ahh yes, I remember now.

If there is one serious peril of a media gig like mine, it is excess white noise. A never-ending fire hose of chaos and destruction and wanton human corruption streaming in like a nasty fever dream from the global atrocity machine (a.k.a., the news wires) straight into the retina of the spirit, ever threatening my sanity and your will to get out of bed. Hey, it's the news. It ain't supposed to be perky and blissful.

Like most paid media observers/culture sluts, I scan the news wires constantly. I have developed a bizarre sixth sense for insinuative headlines and mutant irony. I have an RSS reader live at all times, culling dozens of different info sites, ever scouring and ever regurgitating and ever tossing up an eternally fascinating but always semirancid salad of curious stories and grisly tidbits and potential column fodder.

And I'm here to tell you, if you let it take over, if you allow the blood and guts and train derailments, the bile and the groped altar boys and the Dick Cheneys, their way, if this is the only lens through which you choose to view the world, well, it is death. Slow, gnarled, quivering, genital-shriveling death, with zero naked beatific afterlife.

Humor, by the way, is a salvation. Forget Chris Rock or Judd Apatow. You want to hear the finest in morbid jokes? You want to hear some of the sickest, funniest, most well-informed, most deeply twisted wisecracks to ever make you spray coffee through your nose? Hang around a newsroom for half an hour.

When you're inundated with a nonstop barrage of inhuman tales of excess and misery and schlock, from priests molesting 10,000 boys to sneering senators openly bashing gays to the one thousandth disgruntled dad who whips out a shotgun and blows away his four kids along with ex-wife in a Wal-Mart in Amarillo "before turning the gun on himself," why, the humor is a balm, a release valve, a necessary and mandatory pain-management mechanism. Humor helps. A little.

Another angle: I recently received a raft of heartfelt, angry e-mail from a number of people who do beautiful and necessary and often truly heart-breaking work at animal shelters and pet rescues and vet clinics who all fumed at me, no, no freaking way is that Ford SportKa commercial depict-ing the (fake) cat decapitation[2] you wrote about the slightest bit funny, goddammit.

No way is *any* depiction of any animal abuse anywhere *ever* amusing and you should be ashamed and how could you ever suggest such a thing and you have had all rights to call yourself an animal lover permanently revoked, and I pity the dog you finally adopt and by the way I'm never reading you again even though I've loved your column for years.

Hey, it happens. I understand the sentiment. I know its impetus. It all follows the same rule: If all you have is a hammer, everything looks like a nail. If all you have is a narrow, media-saturated, anger-ravaged worldview, everything looks like a crime against the spirit and everything is something that will completely piss you off, somehow.

Or, to put it more gently, if you saturate yourself with only one perspective, or you choose a path wherein you are blasted to the core every moment with the worst humanity has to offer, well, the world responds in kind and is nothing but bleak and sad and torturous, full of little tiny leeches with sharp jagged teeth that devour your large intestine while you sleep.

But most of all, the reason I don't write about immigrant abuse or abortion rights or the stench of neoconservatism every column is the exact same reason you do not look out the window right now and see the world running through a giant storm of hellfire with its hands slapped to its screaming face, as all buildings explode and the children melt into goo. It's because dark matter is not all there is.

Not only is there is more to life than politics and murder and Bush running around like he's the whiniest king of the sandbox, it's also that those other elements, those seemingly insignificant, pointless divine things like sex and design and books and ideas and the color of your lover's eyes actually, if you pay full attention, turn out to be *far more vital* to your spiritual health than any toxic abuse.

Sure, columns like this one don't get me as many clicks as the calmly outraged, double-barreled criticisms. Sure they don't inspire as much hate mail and love mail and offers to appear on conservative radio shows to debate the finer points of whether Bush is a corrupt, malevolent demon or just a hollow, sad imbecile.

No matter. For better or worse, I refuse to wallow (well, mostly). My job is to offer perspective. Your job is to take that perspective and balance it with your own and read your ass off and get as informed as possible and filter and digest as best you can.

After all, real life is not in the dour headlines. You know this. Real life is not in a politician's blank, confused smirk. Real life is where you launch forth, right now, just after the end of this sentence, after this period coming up, this one right here.

1 http://arouja.notlong.com
2 http://chaeca.notlong.com

This column nearly got me fired. This is the first time it's ever really seen the published light of day.

It's not even all that good. It's not even particularly well written. But it is rather historic, a profound marker in my early career. And it's still a deliciously touchy subject. See if you can't figure out why.

For the record: This piece was posted to the SFGate home page for a single hour one chilly morning back in March of 2001, before being quickly yanked by a very furious — and rather vindictive — SFGate general manager at the time, who found it appalling that I would ever take such a stance. In short, he saw this as me essentially endorsing pedophilia, predation, sexual abuse. I see it as him perhaps having some very unfortunate childhood memories.

Looking back, I can see how it might raise some red flags. Then again, raising red flags was pretty much my columnal raison d'être. I had it tattooed on my fingertips. Still do, mostly.

I wasn't fired, of course, in part because column was also approved by the two managing editors who checked my work at the time, both of whom thought it rather innocuous, typical of my dance-on-the-edge-of-taste style. Also: said unlikable manager couldn't really fire me simply because he personally freaked out over a particular column. But what he could do was strike fear, induce paranoia, make my writing life miserable for a time. Which he did. Until he was soon fired himself, about a year later, for being such a dreadful boss. Ah, poetic justice.

Bottom line: The two editors and I were suspended for a few weeks, our little melodrama made the national newswires, was posted to Romenesko and Editor & Publisher and a handful of insider journalism sites, and was even written up by the Chronicle itself, and then quickly vanished because, well, who the hell cares about such things, really? —mm

Sex and the schoolteacher

3/23/2001

Let me just take a calmly nostalgic and very educated guess and say, few indeed are the normal, warm-blooded, 13- and 14-year old boys in this country who wouldn't absolutely *love* and consider themselves blessed beyond all rational articulation to be inducted into the fabled arenas of manhood by way of a kind and generous sexual act performed on them by their 24-year-old female schoolteacher out in her car in the parking lot after class one fine, unforgettable day.

As in *whoa*, as in *ohmygoddude*, as in a life-altering act engraved directly onto the memory of the young lad's burgeoning soul, right up there with sinking the winning shot and attending his first rock concert without his parents and forsaking organized religion as an insulting and soul-killing mechanism of dangerous repression (or maybe that's just me).

Yes, it happened. Again. This time it was a 24-year-old female teacher, a young teen boy, oral sex in the backseat. These are the facts. This is all we know from the tiny story that came across the news wires. Naturally, we are tempted and trained to think the worst, to think "Oh how repulsive and wrong and predatory and disgusting." We are supposed to think, "Oh the poor, traumatized child! Oh that horrible, immoral woman! Oh the humanity!"

I'm here to suggest: Not so fast.

For we can only hope that our gentle and beneficent teacher in this alleged example treated this wide-eyed boy right, and blew his little mind (so to speak), despite the fact his 14-year-old pal was sitting there watching, and then narced on his friend for some (jealous) and inexplicable (jealous) reason, and I'm just running on bare facts here but let's just run with it, shall we?

Look, all potential teacherly coercion and possible hints of force aside (and also barring the idea that, were the genders reversed, it's an entirely different, often uglier ballgame), I can think of few things more profound and significant in a nubile *male* teen's life than being initiated into the bodily arts by a skilled older female. I speak from experience. I speak from collected wisdom of male youth of the ages. I speak of the Big Obvious Truism that no one dares to mention.

Yes, it might've been odd. No, we don't know *exactly* what happened and there might be a dozen mitigating factors and there's a *chance* it was coercive and the boy has now been permanently scarred, but I'm guessing not really, I'm guessing it's rather straightforward, I'm guessing this sort of thing happens fairly frequently in a myriad of teacher-student combos and oh my goodness what will become of the children and what is happening to our schools and whatever is to be done oh dear oh dear. Please.

Look, if young teen boys in this country had any voice whatsoever, had any say at all regarding society's laws or how they'd like to enjoy their own rites of masculine passage, if they could describe what sort of scenario they'd orchestrate and of course barring any entirely impossible fantasies involving skateboards and Penthouse Forum letters come to life, this kind of "afterschool special" would rank right up there. To be sure, there are certainly far worse possibilities than being ushered along by an assumedly experienced and altruistic (but yes, apparently rather desperate) older woman.

I know. It's tough to imagine such a thing as a positive, or helpful, as perhaps *not all that bad*. Good God, just look at the terrible amounts of hand-wringing and brow-furrowing going on in American culture over youth and youth sexuality and the fact that both boys and girls are *still* having sex as soon as hormonally possible despite (or because of) all parental imprecations and religious pleading and absurd fear-mongering.

Unfortunately, we're not about to recognize and properly appreciate the sexuality of the young anytime soon, despite how they generally seem to have fewer sexual hangups and an overall better time of it than most adults.

By the way, is this a good time to mention the long history of sexual coming-of-age rituals across many ancient world cultures you've surely read about in National Geographic or in Classics 101, cultures where older mentors help bring the young folk into adulthood via sex and sexualized ritual, needful and profound acts now frowned upon in American culture, appropriately or not?

Because we seem to have forgotten. We seem to ignore the fact that we have no true sexual guides, no one and nothing to properly educate youth about the real-world, funkyfun aspects of sex except worthless cutesy picture books and sexist rap videos, insulting sex-ed classes and alarmist STD pamphlets and Cosmo-grade babble like "The Bedroom Sex Trick That Will Blow Him Away (All you need is a hair scrunchie)."

Let me rhetorically pose it outright: Where would the world be without kindly, horny shoolteachers willing to go that extra mile for their needful male students, teach them about the things that really matter in life in a way no member of their untrained peer group probably could. What, you'd rather your kid be indoctrinated into the sticky world of prurient joy by some fumbling teenager who has no idea what goes where, or why, or how frequently, or how to smile and laugh and properly enjoy a cigarette afterwards? Verily, I think not.

Here's an oddly bitter thought: If it wasn't for George W. Bush, there would've been no Barack Obama. Have you heard that before? It might be true. If Dubya hadn't destroyed his party so completely by way of some truly epic rapaciousness, nauseating cronyism and world-class ineptitude, the road to historic revolution might not have been so well paved, and the collective urge to try something very new and different in the form of a young, black intellectual president would not have been so powerfully irresistible.

I'm not sure how much I actually believe it; Obama was/is extraordinary in his own right. But the grand truism remains: there's nothing like getting your metaphorical legs blown off to really make you appreciate that you still have arms. And a choice what to do with them. —mm

Thank you, George W. Bush

06/13/2008

Then it came to pass that I happened to catch the tail end of a recent episode of "Miami Ink," that odd reality show on TLC about the trials and tribulations of an unabashedly macho, but still adorably funky, Florida tattoo shop, a show that offers all sorts of engaging quirks, especially if you harbor a mild appreciation for Koi fish tattoos and ridiculous motorcycles and lots of sweaty, siliconed, sun-baked Miami cheese.

This particular episode featured the story of a young, fresh-faced Iraqi War vet, a big, shy sweetheart of a kid who, it turns out, had both of his legs blown off at the knee by an improvised explosive device (IED). As a commemoration, he came to the shop to get a giant flaming skull tattooed on his shoulder — a skull with, um, a couple of femur bones stuck in there, somehow, in honor of his former appendages. Well, OK.

I hereby shall not question the kid's garish taste in body art. But in the process of describing his injury to the artist/camera, the guy said something rather startling, something I didn't quite expect, considering his young age and his lack of legs and the violence with which they were taken from him, even though it's a refrain we've all heard a million times before.

In sum, he said, "You know what? Despite the horror of it, despite the brutal war, it turns out getting my legs blown off was probably the *best thing to ever happen to me*. It made me appreciate life in a new way, discover new abilities, experience a new vitality. In fact, only through getting my legs blown off do I finally feel truly alive, and what's more, I actually feel sorry for people who don't get to experience life this way."

That's what he said. More or less.

Now, I don't always agree with this line of thinking. In fact, I often outwardly reject the idea that it's only through trauma, through pain or suffering that you *truly* grow or learn, find your creative thrust or the "true" meaning of life. It's certainly *one* way, it's certainly often wildly effective, it's certainly the way it has to happen for *some* people before they finally wake up, but it's far from the *only* way.

But then, as I'm watching footage of this kid waterskiing and climbing mountains and grinning like crazy on his skinny metal prosthetics, I realized, well now, what an absolutely perfect analogy for our mauled, tattered, shell-shocked nation at this very moment in time.

Ain't it so? Because America has, figuratively speaking, had its legs blown off at the knee. We have been hobbled and traumatized and numbed, our once indestructible ego ripped away, had our entire moral and ethical infrastructure blasted out from under us in the most bloody and irresponsible and ignoble way possible.

And the primary explosive that did it? A deadly and useless war. Wait, that's not quite right. It was the inept leaders and disastrous reasoning *behind* the war, the pathetic cadre of hawks and neocons and insular kill-'em-all demagogues in the Bush Administration who veered the nation so far off course we ended up in a bloody ditch just outside Purgatory, a place teeming with recession and torture and homophobia, Patriot Acts and surveillance and fear.

And so, like this kid who actually thanked the fates for blowing his legs off, I'm here to suggest that maybe it's time we offered up some sort of warped, tentative thanks to George W. Bush, for all the appalling trauma he hath wreaked upon us. Maybe he is, in a slightly nauseating way, the best thing that ever happened to us. You think?

Maybe he's exactly what we needed. Maybe Bush's brand of frighteningly inept politicking has been just the right kind of sociocultural emetic to induce a true purge of our congested system, just the thing to finally snap us out of our lethargy. Hell, sometimes you gotta go deep into the darkness to realize just how much you need the light.

So thank you, George, for exemplifying and embodying everything that's wrong with the neocon agenda, for serving as the final death knell of the failed conservative movement[1], of a once-noble Republican Party that's run out of ideas and has turned bitter and nasty and paranoid.

Thank you, Dubya, for setting the stage for Obama and Hillary. Because the truth is, even as recently as eight years ago, if you'd have asked if we as a nation would be anywhere near ready for a female or black president, it would have felt incredibly premature, a good 20 years off before we could entertain such an idea. But so potent has been the recoil against everything you stood for — the misogyny, homophobia, classism, fear of "the

Other," of foreigners and minorities and alternative beliefs — that we are ready to be inspired and reinvigorated sooner than anyone thought possible.

Thank you for your embarrassing rejection of science, your refusal to support any climate change initiative, for furthering the war-for-oil agenda, for blocking stem-cell research, for serving all your masters in Big Energy, Big Agribusiness, Big Oil, Big Pharma, Big Auto. Thanks for gutting the Constitution and front-loading the courts and trying to hack away at women's rights, gay marriage, privacy rights and on and on.

Because it turns out, inviting all that darkness and corruption and holding back all the energy of progress and change is less about hastening the Second Coming (sorry, better luck next time), and more like pulling back on a slingshot. It just gets tighter and tighter and the pressure builds until eventually you just gotta let go, and then *boom* — or I should say, *Obama*.

Now, this is not to say it can't all happen again. History is, unfortunately, a very bitchy and unreliable teacher. I'm guessing there were plenty of people who, post-Nixon, were saying, well thank God we'll never go through *that* again. I mean, fool me once shame on you, fool me twice and, um, fool me ... won't get fooled again[2].

We'll just have to see. For now, the bleeding is slowing, we are finally getting up off the sickbed, testing our shiny new prosthetics, hobbling toward the new. Soon, maybe we'll learn to run, ski, climb mountains, even dance on the international stage again with something resembling grace and renewed self-respect.

We might even say, you know what? It turns out getting our political, moral and spiritual legs blown off was the best thing that ever happened to us. Dubya actually did us a huge favor. Can you imagine?

1 http://eimula.notlong.com
2 http://ohnier.notlong.com

It's a harsh headline, I admit, especially for a yoga teacher like me, for some-one professing to be working on deeper consciousness and judging less harshly overall. Even so, I think I do a fairly decent job of avoiding the trap of out-right polarization, simply by providing a rather lucid observation of the forces at play in politics and culture. Hey, after a decade of columns and reader feedback and watching the pols work the public, these options seem irrefut-able. Especially the last one, which I see as less of a disparaging criticism, and more like advising you to simply steer clear of a particular road on your way to work, one we all know is lined with nails and sinkholes, bizarre barricades and arbitrary detours. Really, why bother? —mm

How to talk to complete idiots

09/25/2009

There are three basic ways to talk to complete idiots.

The first is to assail them with facts, truths, scientific data, the common-sensical obviousness of it all. You do this in the very reasonable expecta-tion that it will nudge them away from the ledge of their more ridiculous and paranoid misconceptions because, well, they're *facts*, after all, and who can dispute those?

Why, idiots can, that's who. It is exactly this sort of logical, levelheaded appeal to reason and mental acuity that's doomed to fail, simply because in the idiotosphere, facts are lies and truth is always dubious, whereas hysteria and alarmism are the only things to be relied upon.

Examples? Endless. You may, for instance, attempt to explain evolution to an extreme fundamentalist Christian. You may offer up carbon dating, the fossil record, glaciers, any one of 10,000 irrefutable proofs. You may even dare to talk about the Bible as the clever, completely manufactured, man-made piece of heavily politicized, massively edited, literary myth-making it so very much is, using all sorts of sound academic evidence and historical record.

You are, of course, insane beyond belief to try this, but sometimes you just can't help it. To the educated mind, it seems inconceivable that mil-lions of people will choose rabid ignorance and childish fantasy over, say, a polar bear. Permafrost. Rocks. Nag Hammadi. But they will, and they do. Faced with this mountain of factual obviousness, the bewildered funda-mentalist will merely leap back as if you just jabbed him with a flaming homosexual cattle prod, and then fall into a swoon about how neat it is that angels can fly.

But it's not just the fundamentalists. This Rule of Idiocy also explains why, when you show certain jumpy, conservative Americans the irrefutable facts about, say, skyrocketing health care costs that are draining their bank accounts, and then show how Obama's rather modest overhaul is meant to save members of all ages and genders and party affiliations a significant amount of money while providing basic insurance for their family, they, too, will scream and kick like a child made to eat a single bite of broccoli.

Remember, facts do not matter. The actual Obama plan itself does not matter. Fear of change, fear of the "Other," fear of the scary black socialist president, fear that yet another important shift is taking place that they cannot understand and which therefore makes them thrash around like a trapped animal? This is all that matters.

This is why, even when you whip out, say, a fresh article by the goodly old Washington Post — not exactly a bastion of lopsided liberalthink — one that breaks down the rather brutal truth about the *real* cost of health care in this country, it will likely be hurled back in your face as an obvious piece of liberal propaganda. Go ahead, try it. Or better yet, don't.

Option two is to try to speak their language, dumb yourself down, engage on the idiot's level as you try to figure out how their minds work — or more accurately, *don't* work — so you can better empathize and find a shred of common ground and maybe, just maybe, inch the human experiment forward.

This is, as you already sense, a dangerous trap, pure intellectual quicksand. It almost never works, and just makes you feel gross and slimy. Nevertheless, plenty of shrewd political strategists believe that the best way for Obama and the Dems to get their message across regarding everything from health care reform to new environmental regulation, would be to steal a page from the Glenn Beck/Karl Rove/sociopath's playbook, and start getting stupid.

It's all about the bogus catchphrases, the sound bites, the emotional punches-to-the-gut. Death panels! Rationing! Fetus farms! Puppy shredders! Commie medicine! Gay apocalypse! Forced vaccinations! Exposed

nipples during prime-time! Let one of these inane, completely wrong but oh-so-haunting verbal ticks bite into the below-average American brainstem, and watch your cause bleed all over the headlines.

The big snag here is that the Dems, unlike the

Republican Party, aren't really beholden to a radical, mal-educated base of fundamentalist crazies to keep them afloat. Truly, the political success of the liberal agenda does not depend on the irrational, Bible-crazed "value voter" who's terrified of gays, believes astronomy is a hoax and thinks Jesus spoke perfect English and really liked giving hugs.

In other words, there really is little point in the liberals adopting this strategy, save for the fact that the major media eats it up and it might serve to counterbalance some of the more ridiculous conservative catchphrases. What's more, it could also give the whiny, bickering Dems something slightly cohesive to rally around — because the truth is, the Democratic Party isn't all that bright, either.

And now we come to option three, easily the finest and most successful approach of all. Alas, it also remains the most difficult to pull off. No one is exactly sure why.

The absolute best way to speak to complete idiots is, of course, *not to speak to them at all.*

That is, you work *around* them, ignore them completely, disregard the rants and the spittle, the misspelled protest signs and the fervent prayers for apocalypse on Fox News. Complete refusal to take the fringe nutballs even the slightest bit seriously is the only way to make true progress.

This also happens to be the invaluable advice of one Frank Schaeffer, author and a former fundamentalist nutball himself, who made a simply superb appearance on Rachel Maddow's show, wherein he offered up one of the most articulate, fantastic takedowns[1] of the fundamentalist idiot's mindset in recent history. It's a must-watch. Do it. Do it now.

Now, you may argue that, while Schaeffer may be dead right, it's also true that calling people stupid is no way to advance the debate, and is itself rather childish and stupid. And you'd be absolutely right.

But you'd also be missing the point. When you ignore the idiots completely, you are not calling them anything at all. You are not trying to advance any sort of argument, because there is no debate taking place. You are simply bypassing the giant pothole of ignorance entirely.

You are not kowtowing to the least educated of your voting bloc, like the GOP is so desparately fond of doing. You are not trying to give the idiotosphere equal weight in the discussion. As Schaeffer says, "You cannot reorganize village life to suit the village idiot." By employing option three, you are doing the only humane thing left to do: you are letting the idiotosphere eat itself alive.

Do it for the children, won't you?

1 http://riugho.notlong.com

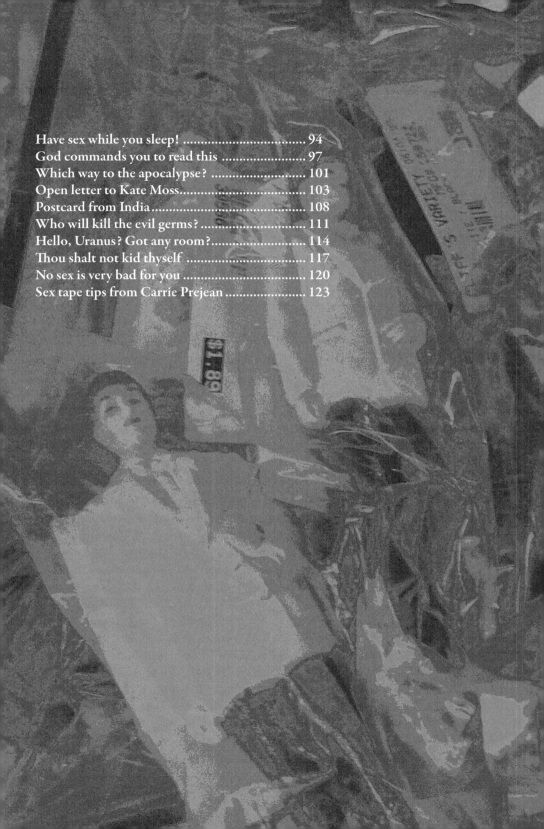

IRONY LOVES COMPANY

I am utterly baffled by this terrifying tale. Such a frightening piece of break-ing news, so critical to the very survival of humankind, and I've yet to read a single story, a single follow-up tale of pain and woe and somnambulatory penetration involving much grunting and insufficient lubrication and "Jesus what the fuck do you think you're doing, Barbara?" Where is the media cov-erage? Where is the caring? Where are the self-help seminars? Where is the national recovery program for recuperating somnambulisticgasmabators?

Do you ever have sleep sex? Can you send me a description? Can you send me photos? Thank you. —mm

Have sex while you sleep!

11/01/2006

This just in: Some people are having sex while they're completely asleep.

It's true. It's a newly reported medical condition I just read about.[1] And some people, as you might imagine, are rather upset about it. And as we'll see, it's not the only dire sleep issue facing a naked, exhausted nation.

It seems sleepsex, as it's called, tends to affect love lives. Interrupts sleep patterns, ruffles the sheets, creates unexpected patches of moisture and leaves you wondering who'll do the laundry or if you'll still be respected in the morning and why you're sore in places you didn't expect to be sore in when you went to bed. You can see the problem.

Apparently, some people say sleepsex is not always tender or loving or preceded by any sort of nice dinner or back rub or flowers. In fact, they say the sleeping person is often very demanding, even a little violent and aggressive in their pursuit of things squishy and moany and good and they will often not take no for an answer — though it must be said that saying no to someone who is asleep and naked and sitting on top of you while violently demanding some sort of immediate penetration might be consid-ered, you know, unwise.

Others, curiously, say the sleepsex is quite good. Even better than when both parties are actually awake. This is rather amusing. And startling. Unless it's not. Unless it makes some sort of perfect sense wherein you say, well *of course*, after all, my lover is normally uptight and inhibited and totally self-conscious about, say, getting naked and hanging upside down and getting flogged by a soft leather whip. But when she's out cold, she's a whirling whipariffic wildcat. What's not to like?

Sleepsex now has an official Web site, sleepsex.org. It has its own book.[2] This is how you know it is a verifiable occurrence. This is how we know it exists. Truly, most things nowadays do not exist until they have an official

Web site or a book written about them. Like, say, Paris Hilton. Or miniature ponies. Or North Korea.

Sleepsex is merely the latest sleep phenomenon. It comes hot on the heels of recent dire reports of people who actually binge eat while sleeping,[3] usually after popping an Ambien and dropping into a strange zombie-like state, and then wandering into the kitchen at 4 a.m. to polish off an entire roast chicken and a six-pack of Diet Sprite and an entire bottle of Mr. Chin's Hot n' Sour Pork Marinade along with huge box of Betty Crocker Double-Fudge Brownie mix, only to wake up four hours later with a massive stomachache and a very odd taste in the mouth and the faint sensation that they have done something very, very gross.

It does not stop there. You have perhaps read the stories of people who drive while asleep?[4] Oh my yes. These are also Ambien-licked people who wander out of bed and hop into the Accord and drive for miles and miles and miles, not at all realizing they are wearing nothing but ragged smiley-face underwear and some pillow lint and perhaps the residual scent of the person with whom they just had violent sleepsex.

Perhaps you have seen these people on the road? The ones who make a sudden left turn from the far-right lane? The ones who have their left blinker on the entire trip? The ones who have a huge array of sad stuffed animals in the back window and whose cars smell faintly of old underwear and stale dreams and Betty Crocker Double-Fudge Brownie mix? They are, sadly, legion.

It has been noted that some people, while sleepwalking through the house, will actually rearrange the furniture.[5] I am not making this up. Some reports even claim that a few of these people are actually quite good at it, and should therefore perhaps consider sleeping a great deal more so they may start their own sassy interior design companies.

You might think this is all some sort of joke. You might think this is all just a little bit amusing. But it is not a joke. It is a national affliction, bordering on tragedy.

"What we're seeing is some sort of sleep-activity epidemic, and dammit, it is not pretty, so quit your smirking," Dr. Eric Somnabitz of Johns Hopkins University would have said, had he actually existed, which he does not. "In fact, it is very possible I am making these very statements while completely asleep, right now!" he would've added. "I might not even be a scientist! I could be a failed pastry chef from Iowa, dreaming this entire paragraph. Can you see the problem?"

There is also — how to put this delicately — there is also the horror of sleep marriage. It's true. It turns out millions of humans are actually falling in love on the thinnest of emotional connections and then deciding to get married, all while completely asleep. Millions of individuals report waking up two, three, sometimes even 25 years later, only to say, oh my God what the hell was I thinking? Who is this person? Why didn't someone wake me?

Also, babies. No one is quite sure how many children now walk this Earth as a result of people actually getting knocked up and popping out five kids while entirely asleep, and then neglecting four of them and sending the fifth off to rehab/military school while the first four get resentful and depressed and hooked on Ambien and end up turning Republican and sending sexually suggestive instant messages to nubile congressional pages. And they're completely asleep! It's a national disgrace, is what it is.

Another example: millions of people have wandered into car showrooms across America while completely unconscious and have actually purchased a giant bloated SUV, completely asleep to the giant tacky ridiculousness of what they are doing, only to wake much later to find the planet completely underwater and realize that they really should've bought a boat.

You can see the problem. You can begin to get a sense of just how terrible, how widespread the sleepliving issue is. In fact, many experts and mystics and gurus say much of the entire human race has been going about its business for millennia, eating and marrying and screwing and warring and laughing and whining and going into massive debt and gaining 50 pounds and buying a new iPod, all while completely asleep.

This is what they say. And it is long past time, they add, that we should consider waking the hell up.

1 http://aaviin.notlong.com
2 http://eeseiy.notlong.com
3 http://eetheu.notlong.com
4 http://paexu.notlong.com
5 http://uigeke.notlong.com

Call it a gift, call it a tic, call it an endlessly unpleasant trope, particularly if you're evangelically religious and get a woozy, suspiciously warm feeling deep in your loins when anyone mentions anal sex or Shakti or old AC/DC records, but I have some sort of knack for speaking in a deity's voice. Perhaps I should write a sitcom.

Richard Roberts, son of the late Oral, he being the Great Inflictor of Megachurch Hell upon thew world, is a deeply slimy piece of work. I have since learned two of his actual books are titled, If You're Going Through Hell, Don't Stop, *and* If You Catch Hell, Don't Hold It. *Which, I must admit, are remotely clever titles by mendacious religious nutball standards — if, of course, by "clever" you mean "please shove this ice pick deep into my eye socket and rotate it slowly." I'm told his most recent book,* When You See Me in Hell, Buy Me A Diet Snapple, Sucker *sold well among encephalitic primates. —mm*

God commands you to read this

12/07/2007

> *Richard Roberts told students at Oral Roberts University that he did not want to resign as president of the scandal-plagued evangelical school, but he did so because God insisted.* — Associated Press[1]

There I was, calmly enjoying some Thanksgiving leftovers and offering some divine gratitude for this truly fine '04 Pinot when suddenly *boom*, there was God, right across the table, helping Himself to some stuffing and the choicest hunks of dark meat, which He totally knows is my favorite. Clearly, He wanted my attention.

"Oh hey, it's you," I said, feigning nonchalance, as if this sort of thing happens to me every day (I always like to throw God off a bit, given how He's so accustomed to those melodramatic, fall-to-your-knees-in-terror reactions He always gets from the nutball evangelicals whenever He swings through their nightmares in his classic fire/brimstone persona. That always cracks Him up). "What's up?"

"Oh, you know, same ol' same ol'," God muttered, His voice sounding like an ocean playing a cello concerto in a black hole. He grabbed my pricey Pinot and chugged nearly the entire thing like it was Trader Joe's house brand, His long, well-manicured, beautifully feminine fingers shiny with meat grease. "Just sorta bored, hanging around the universe, putting out little fires. How you doing? You get those sexy new floor cushions yet? How's the car running?"

Something was wrong. This wasn't like God at all. "Wait, what? You came all the way here from the belly of the cosmos, ignoring the unimaginable dance of astral forces and the infinite conundrums of colliding galaxies, not to mention the constant pitter-patter of little questions about the meaning of war and death and suffering and life itself, and you want to talk about home decor? What's going on?"

"Oh, you know Me, just trying to keep it real, visit My peeps personally now and then, offer advice like some sort of sniveling lawyer, like some sort of stupid little shrink who's speaking *only to you*, at the expense of everyone else."

Now I *knew* he was being sarcastic. At least, I think He was. You can never really tell with God. I mean, just look at Pluto. Or New Jersey. Or Tom Cruise.

Then it hit me. "Wait, is this about that obnoxious preacher's kid? That Roberts guy?" I'd just read about how Oral Roberts' wildly spoiled son Richard, the odious televangelist who headed Oral Roberts University and who was being sued for allegedly swiping mountains of cash from the financially strapped school to pay for lavish personal crap like shopping sprees and a private stable of horses and the repeated remodel of his home (11 times in 14 years[2]), and for flying his kid to the Bahamas on the school's private jet as his coiffed trophy wife spends tens of thousands of dollars in university funds on clothes and sends furtive text messages to underage boys. You know, the usual.

And oh yes: I also recall that Roberts has officially claimed that God spoke to him *in person*, and instructed him to resign from the corrupt, horribly managed, deeply creepy university, over Roberts' own protests. Ah ha.

God sighed grumpily, sounding like two dump trucks mating in a hailstorm. "Look, you claim to be some sort of journalist, right? This little worm actually invoked My name as an excuse, dared to say that he talked to Me and that I insisted he resign. Insisted! *Me*! The fucking nerve.

I don't insist on anything, except maybe a little backrub from the cherubim at the M51 whirlpool galaxy now and then. That little scab is getting a first class ticket to Impotenceland, you can trust Me on that."

"Well, good. But I don't see how I ..."

"But that's not the worst part," God thundered. "The worst part is the lemmings, the crowd of wide-eyed students, they were eating it up! Actually weeping and cheering him on, fully believing every word, even as he wiped away his crocodile tears with a goddamn handkerchief he bought from a gay bathhouse in Vegas using their tuition money."

Then God shot me that sweet, imploring look that always makes me melt. "So here's the plan: I want you to write up something scathing and funny and pointed about how God visited you, *in person*, and you broke bread and shared a nice bottle of host's blood or whatnot, and I told you in no uncertain terms that Richard Roberts is a world-class charlatan with a rabid case of elephantiasis of the false spirit.

"I want you to ring the alarm, raise the roof, send out an S.O.S., put a message in a bottle, whatever the hell it is you writer people do. I'm getting tired of this."

I was, I have to say, a little taken aback. This wasn't like God, so spiteful, so easily annoyed by such petty, meaningless human shrapnel as Roberts. We usually laugh and shrug off stories like this, then move on to talk about, say, Buddhism, or the deeper meanings of tantric philosophy, the best meditation techniques to help you get past a nasty port wine headache. That sort of thing.

I had to ask. "OK, I give. What's this really all about? Because hell, they've been invoking Your name as an excuse for a couple thousand years, stamping it like a bad logo across everything from slaughtering pagans to detesting gays to screaming in fear of the human vagina to launching all manner of brutal war and torture and righteous moral crusade."

God just looked at me sidelong, and polished off the rest of the wine in a single sip.

I went on. "Look, You know better than anyone that Roberts is nothing more than a flea on the great sheepskin rug of human belief. But You know I'll try. As for the gaggle of students in his cultish thrall, well, I'll absolutely keep doing everything I can to inspire them to wake up one day with a Burning Man ticket in one hand and a well-licked copy of Rumi's collected poems in the other, shuddering with mad desire to drop some Ecstasy and join in a dawn fire ritual[3] and see, well, the real You."[4]

God smiled. In a flash, the room went dark, and suddenly I felt a rush of warm air flow over me like molten honey, soothing my bones and penetrating my very blood and forcing me to close my eyes in what I can only describe as ecstatic cellular orgasm. It was, you might say, pretty nice.

When I opened my eyes again, God had morphed into Her other form, the divine female, the true ruling principle of the universe, skin like moonlight and eyes like diamonds and a massive mane of fiery red hair and a figure that could melt the ice planets of the Hyperion cluster in the Artemis nebulae. I mean, wow.

Her voice made the ground tremble beneath my feet. "You know what? You're absolutely right," She said, as the cellos changed into violins. "Guess I just needed that hot kick of divine reconnection. Or you know, maybe *you* did." Then She winked at me, and 10 million birds fainted with delight. "I mean, we *are* co-creators of each other, after all."

And just like that, She was gone. When I regained my senses, I saw that my wine bottle was full again, and there was a full plate of dark meat, awaiting my divine gratitude. Damn, She's good.

1 http://zifezu.notlong.com
2 http://ujuux.notlong.com
3 http://eenat.notlong.com
4 http://uengoom.notlong.com

And now, The Daring Spectacle presents...

Mullet Haiku

My favorite cousin
Man your ass looks great in that
Wal-Mart uniform

In the fall of '06, I went on a short theater tour with a gaggle of wondrous comic talents put together by my friend, comedian Johnny Steele. "The War on Error" toured Bay Area theaters and playhouses, maybe eight dates total. Some terrific standup, sketch comedy, political cartoonist extraordinaire Mark Fiore, and me, up there reading some hate mail and a couple columns — the following is one of them — and honing my live-reading chops in front of a decent-sized crowd. If I recall, the biggest laugh came on the line about the Glade Plug-In. I tightened this one up quite a bit from the original. I think it sort of nails it.

By the way, there really is/was a National Day of Slayer. I mean, of course.
—mm

Which way to the apocalypse?

6/09/2006

Wait, did I miss it?

Did it happen three days ago, on 6-6-06, a.k.a. Tea Time with the Beast, a.k.a. the Great Day of Reckoning, a.k.a. the National Day of Slayer,[1] all the world crashing down in a heap of hissing steam and belching smoke and balmy gusty breezes sometime around noon just after lunch but not before rush hour and hitting right around siesta?

I might have been napping. Did the Apocalypse finally hit? Did the deep wish of roughly a half-billion zealous believers come to pass and were they suddenly whisked off into the humming glorious divine ether in one big orgiastic load of divine redemption, leaving us heathens and pagans and Wiccans and Jews and Muslims and Buddhists and journalists to fight it out over the last scraps of artisan Gruyere and fine Pinot Noir and gorgeous new Porsche Caymans? I simply cannot be sure.

Because if so, I am sitting here feeling a little gypped. I am sitting here not at all on fire, not at all reeling in unrelenting pain, not at all staring into the hot face of vile eternal doom without a single oscillating fan to cool my aching bones. Yet another portentous day has passed and the Rapture Index[2] is almost off the charts with seething Armageddon certainty, and yet I'm still getting perfectly good cell reception. What gives?

I do not exactly know how the Christian right envisions Armageddon, but here is how I've always pictured it:

Hordes of the ultra-pious, decked out in "I ❤ Jimmy Swaggart's Flop Sweat" T-shirts and black socks with sandals, rise to the heavens in giant peach-colored Ford Aerostars to gather in enormous hugging throngs where they are met by a wary and bleary-eyed St. Peter who offers them

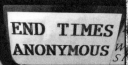

END TIMES
ANONYMOUS

processed cold cuts and Kraft Singles and lukewarm Diet Dr. Pepper.

There are rusty swing sets with exposed bolts. There are inflatable vinyl pools. There is watery decaf coffee. There are large fleets of beige 1997 Honda Civics with cassette players locked down and preloaded with only Mariah Carey and Yanni. Everyone is slowly but surely driven giddily insane by the incessant harp music and the unmistakable scent of angel droppings. All thought ceases.

Yes, Jesus is there, smiling and rocking back and forth and looking just weirdly happy, and the minions gather 'round him in swooning, narcotized glee, everyone feeling more than a little justified for all their nasty deeds while on Earth, all the abortion clinic firebombings and all the protests of "The Da Vinci Code" and that morally nauseating thing with Terri Schiavo back in '05.

Finally, finally they have arrived at a place where no one is having sex and no one wants to marry someone from their same gender and all experience has been filed down to a dull nub of vague, tasteless sensation as liquid Prozac is misted into the air via a giant Glade Plug-In the size of Florida.

Except something is a little off. Something is not quite right. Let us look closer. Why, that's not Jesus at all — it's actually a big blow-up doll of Jesus, a giant swaying latex toy, a wacky waving inflatable arm-flailing tube man[3] painted to look like Jesus, bobbing back and forth like a car salesman on meth. Hmm.

But the minions, of course, do not notice. They are all swaying and waving in equally ecstatic response. It is one hell of a spectacle. It is vaguely cultish. It is also, eerily, exactly like a Celine Dion concert. Hmm.

And where's the real Jesus? Why, the true Christ is back on Earth, once and for all and finally, teaching everyone an incredible new dance, preparing the open minded and the nondogmatic for cosmic leapfrog. Turns out that only when the fanatics and the zealots and the demagogues were finally airlifted to the great padded Romper Room in the sky that the real Great Work could finally continue. Isn't that ironic? Isn't that fabulous? Isn't that exactly what you suspected all along?

1 http://www.nationaldayofslayer.org
2 http://www.raptureready.com/
3 http://yolubo.notlong.com

A personal favorite, this one. Tone just right, a fresh angle I'd never really tried before (the open letter), comes off as reasonably knowledgable and smart about its subject, which is nice, considering how little I actually know or care about tabloids, professional modeling, or Kate Moss' friends. My editor loved this one, too. Odd how I haven't tried anything like this since. Note to self: Try more like this. Note to Kate Moss: Do more cocaine, on camera. Your career loved you for it. —mm

Open letter to Kate Moss

10/05/2005

Oh my dearest Kate,

Something is amiss. Something is deeply askew in the culture and you know it and I know it and the world knows it, and something must be done.

This much we know, Kate: Rock stars are supposed to be debauched and swaggering and dumber'n concrete. TV stars are supposed to be overrated and self-indulgent and wired on amphetamines and viciously jealous of movie stars who are, in turn, airbrushed egomaniacal limelight sluts, terrified of their own shadows and so desperately jacked on a daily cocktail of Botox and Xanax and Veuve Clicquot it would make Liza Minnelli giggle.

And supermodels, well, most supermodels are supposed to be, by definition, morally vacuous featherweight coke-snorting divas floating above the gap-toothed plebeian throngs on gossamer wings of Prada and Dolce and Tanqueray gin, all fueled by the raging white-knuckle jealously of 500 million women worldwide who will never ever look like you but who will spend, collectively, $400 billion per year trying.

This is the way it is. This is the way it has always been. This is, after all, why we love you.

Which is why I am deeply ashamed and horrified at what the media, the culture, those snide fashion houses (*especially* them) have done to you, Kate. Burberry, Chanel and H&M have all dumped you like a bad burrito and cut up your multimillion-dollar contracts, treating you like a goddess one day and a pariah the next, all over one grainy paparazzi shot of you chopping up a line of premium flake in some recording studio.[1] Hell, they might even try to arrest you for it. Can you believe it? What lousy luck.

And what incredible gall, am I right? As if the empires of these fickle, hypocritical fashion houses weren't wholly built on the spindly backs of countless thousands of hard-partying fashion models, as if premium cocaine and Valium and Camels and booze and Ecstasy and 153 other happy shiny meds weren't as pervasive in the fashion biz as back hair at a NASCAR rally, as if piles of narcotics weren't on tap at every elite New York fashion party every night of the week, and they know it. Oh, those duplicitous cretins.

But I am here with a message for you, Kate. Here it is: You shall rise again. You shall overcome, all 105 boozed-up coke-addled famously bitchy party-riffic pounds of you. I know you will. You *must*. You're all we've got left. You are the last, thin gasp of a dying, radiant era. We shall defend your honor.

And we still remember. Do you remember, Kate? Do you recall being discovered at JFK airport back in '88 when you were only 14? Hell, you'd just begun to sprout pubic hair and you'd barely kissed your first boy and you looked as lost as a moth in the ocean, and yet they stripped you down and shot photo after photo of your half-naked flesh as you stared, vacant and strange, into the camera, all while, unbeknownst to you, you were single-handedly ushering in the era of the sickly, anorexic, "heroin chic" look so beloved/loathed by women and designers and drug addicts world-wide. Do you remember? It was a time, girl.

Halcyon days, am I right? Trotting the globe, making out with Johnny Depp, partying hard with Naomi Campbell across Barbados and Paris and London like the spoiled-rotten demon-spawn you both were, your career hitting the stratosphere under the tender, watchful glares of all those glori-ous curvy supermodel divas of the time: Linda Evangelista and Christy Turlington and Helena Christensen, Stephanie Seymour and Heidi Klum and even that uptight prude Cindy Crawford. Oh how you loved them like big overbearing party-crazed sisters, even if they wanted to snap you like a twig for making them diet so damn much. What a time.

And now, look at them. All gone. All married off and settled down and hawking yoga clothes and popping out kids and launching mediocre TV shows and whatever the hell else, and only a few posing for the occasional catalog shoot for Ralph Lauren or maybe Calvin Klein Home Collec-tion. What the hell happened? Where have all the good times gone? No wonder you're inhaling a small mountain of coke off in the corner, all by yourself. It's lonely at the top. Or rather, off to the side.

It's only you, Kate. The rest fell away, leaving only you to take up the burden and carry the decadent-supermodel flame. And you've done the fashion world proud: Hell, not only did you refuse to settle, you actually *regressed*, going so far as to hook up with Pete Doherty, a fabulous train wreck of an alcoholic rock star who was fired from his only good band for being such a drug-addled sloth. Yes! Only you, my precious Kate. Only you.

So then, as you enter rehab (I know, these PR moves are a bitch, aren't they? Four grand a night at the Meadows Clinic in Arizona and no more sucking shots of Patron Silver from Pete's pasty belly fat for a whole *month*. It's just wrong) and as you issue heartfelt apology after heartfelt apology to a deeply jaded public that really doesn't care all that much in the first place, let these thoughts be your balm, this letter be your solace.

Because we know, Kate. We know you were wronged. And we know you're the last of a dying breed, the end of a line. Behind you stand only a bunch of pampered celebs to grace the cover of Elle, along with a pile of curvy buxom Maxim-ready look-alike models from Brazil. Oh yeah, and Gisele. And I think we've had almost enough of her, too.

But this is the wonderful thing, Kate. This is why I am writing to you: You will be back. You will take a year or two off and dump that flabby loser and lament your woes to Oprah and then do a cameo on "Will & Grace," and then your star will rise again. Because if there's one thing we all love more than making a star in order to destroy it, it's seeing it rise again from the ashes, resurrected in our good graces, saved by our consumer largesse. Ah, what tortured machinery we make.

So Kate, thank you. Thank you for all these years of simultaneously representing everything we love about our mad consumer culture and everything we hate about our mad consumer culture. But most of all, thank you for refusing to give up, even after 17 years, on the glory and the decadence and the coke-snortin' party-crazed supermodel dream. It's like Homer Simpson said when raising a toast to his favorite drink: "To beer: the cause of — and solution to — all life's problems."

That's you in a nutshell, baby. Come back soon.

1 http://taizah.notlong.com

I hate you I hate you I hate you

To: mmorford@sfgate.com
Subject: Anal lover
Date: Tue, 18 Sep 2007 16:27:20 -0400
X-MB-Message-Source: WebUI
MIME-Version: 1.0
From: XXX993@aol.com
X-Spam-Flag: NO

Fuck you!

I have read too many of your worthless columns you child molesting fuck. Why does God let you live? In a perfect world you would have been the better part of the spoog that your worthless father shot up your momma's ass!

Your opinions are those of a traitor

Ken S.

Date: Mon, 09 Jul 2007 12:07:05 -0700
From: Michael <XXX@ix.netcom.com>
User-Agent: Mozilla/5.0 (Windows; U; Windows NT 5.0; en-US; rv:1.0.1) Gecko/20020823 Netscape/7.0 (nscd1)
X-Accept-Language: en-us, en
MIME-Version: 1.0
To: mmorford@sfgate.com
Subject: You are just a liar.

You are a filthy liar. I know and most of the people who read the sf gate know it. go over the case for of scooter libby. I may not agree with most of bush's actions. But, he is right on this one.

Date: Wed, 19 Jul 2006 12:38:22 -0700
From: Philip D <XXX@comcast.net>
User-Agent: Mozilla Thunderbird 1.0.7 (Windows/20050923)
MIME-Version: 1.0
To: Mark Morford <mmorford@sfgate.com>
Subject: You are the creep!

Hi Mark:

I read your article today.

You are filthy, petty, disgusting, little bitch creep who should be grateful that someone is watching out for your disgusting little being.

You are an anti-American little punk with a self absorbed amoral focus showing your unearned insolence and ideological weakness.

Philip D

you I hate you

I hate you I

I hate you I hate you I hate you I hate you

From: "bonnie j" <bonnieXXX@hotmail.com>
To: <mmorford@sfgate.com>
Subject: President Bush
Date: Thu, 20 Jul 2006 17:32:46 -0400
MIME-Version: 1.0
X-Priority: 3

Just finished reading your article on the president. I was insulted by the fact that you were making comments about southern mannerism's and speech.
May I remind you that Bush has attained something that you probably never will,

HE IS THE PRESIDENT!!!!!!!!!!!!!!!!!!!!!!
Top THAT!!!!
B.J

Date: Tue, 25 Apr 2006 10:23:44 -0500 (CDT)
From: michelle <mXXX@verizon.net>
Subject:
To: mmorford@sfgate.com
MIME-version: 1.0

Sir,
I'm sure you know that you are going straight to Hell. You should be ashamed of youself, publishing your filth. I serve a mericiful God. I only hope you seek forgiveness for the lies you spread. I pray for you and all the poor people you speak to in your publication. I hope that they have the intelligence to know that you are full of bologna.
Sincerely,
- Michelle C

---

and you are a clown propagandist hoping the ultimate-hate-bushers are going to prop up your sickly penis by taking the side of the soros' corporate control freaks.

You are a LIAR and your mom knows you are a LIAR.

Date: Fri, 11 Aug 2006 10:37:21 -0700 (Pacific Standard Time)
From: "brainc@XXX.net"
To: <letters@sfchronicle.com>
Cc: <mmorford@sfgate.com>
Subject: Mark Morford's Boyhood Column

Dear Editor,
Mark Morford continually influences teenagers to have sex with his liberal views throughout his columns. His writing often resembles that of a teenager on pot or LSD. He has no consideration for what minor may encounter his trashy column in assiging such titles as "Lick my Sports Car" (Telsa article this week). He is not referring to licking a lolly pop, but his erection that pops up whenever he writes about sex and screwing his brains out in his white trash column.

Oftentimes teens are ignorant to the sexual diseases and dangers of having unprotected sex. Mark Morford doesn't care, he just thinks that anyone having sex is beautiful and that it in itself is the cure of all human problems.

Sincerely,
Cheryl M

> *It was my first time in the land of a million gods. The trip only lasted a few weeks, but it was long enough to serve a primary personal purpose: to see if I ever wanted to return for a longer, more involved and exploratory stay. And I do. It's a ridiculously powerful, thick, messy, multilayered place that will toss you and your expectations around like a silly western toy. It's intoxicating and disorienting on a thousand levels, definitely not all of them good, some horrible and lethal, many awe-inspiring and deeply beautiful, and almost all fairly profound. Even, believe it or not, the garbage. What's not to like?*
> *—mm*

Postcard from India

02/25/09

Some have said they are curious about my recent trip to India. Some have said they would like to hear a little more about it.

Did I get sick? Did I see God? How many? How was the chai? Can you drink the water? Was I lucky enough to spend many, many splendiferous hours in one of the world's worst major metropolitan airports (Mumbai)?

Did I have sex on the beach? Did I have sex in a funky sultry treehouse in a giant, hard bed surrounded by bright purple silk mosquito netting? Did I find a yoga guru? Did I find enlightenment? Have I read *Shantaram* or seen "Slumdog Millionaire"? Did I see many huge, surly cows in the streets and on the beaches? What's Shiva like in person? Would I ever go back?

(Answers: A little, yes, about 327, glorious, hell no, yes, no, yes, not really the point, constantly, yes, plenty, taller than you might think but also far, far more aromatic, absolutely).

Here, then, is one small anecdote that, I think, sums up a bit of the delicious, relatively insane, accept-it-or-leave-it contradictory/ironic nature of this most intense, thick, thrumming, divinely bizarre of overheated countries:

One fine, sultry morning near the end of the yoga retreat portion of my trip, my little troupe decided it might be nice to practice a bit of karma (service) yoga, by way of taking a little silent, meditative hike just off the northern tip of the beach — this is the coastal state of Goa, remember

— up a dense tropical path to an enormous banyan tree, under which a scruffy handful of Shaivitic monks held their constant puja.

There was, we heard, a low fire burning at all times. There was the offering prayer and ritual, the holding of divine space, the smoking of a great deal of hash to accompany all manner of humble offerings to Shiva, their ishta-deva ("chosen form of god" — Hinduism lets you choose from a wide spectrum, and change whenever you want). We were told they welcomed quiet, respectful visitors. More or less.

As our karma offering, we were told it would be a nice gesture to pick up any garbage on the way up, so as to honor the space and keep the path clear and because, as a general rule, all humble, well-marinated monks in India can usually use all the help they can get. Cool.

Each of us grabbed a little black plastic garbage bag and began our short trek, silently and dutifully plucking the plastic bottles, cigarette butts, old flip-flops from the thorny brush as we walked and valiantly stepping over and around the random piles of animal droppings along the way, which we quickly realized were not, in fact, dropped by animals of the four-legged variety. Oh. Right. India.

Silent, sacred garbage gathering and human poop-dodging? Bring it.

A short 15 minutes later, we're there. The tree was enormous, gorgeous and strange, a lush riot of thick vines and multiple trunks and spidery creepers. In the little clearing just underneath, there was firesmoke, there was incense, ash, a myriad of prayer flags, tiny statues, photos of old gurus, tattered books, much palpable vibration, all attended by a few well-worn monks, who, I must say, seemed momentarily perplexed by the arrival of 15 sweaty white westerners all carrying black garbage bags and shiny digital cameras and awkward, what-do-we-do-now grins. A divine little scene indeed.

Reverential as mice, we quietly put down our garbage bags and assembled ourselves in a semicircle 'round the intense little fire, took a few deep inhales of the rich, incense-choked air, and then partook of a deep, slightly clumsy, but otherwise enormously potent chant — the classic Om Mani Padme Hum — accompanied by the funky, very stoned monks, and it was lovely and weird and brief.

Not wishing to intrude too long, we made our offerings. We said our humble thanks, and prepared to take our leave. We quietly asked about what we might do with our fine collection of trash. Yes yes, the youngest monk said, simply take it down the path, back to the beach, to the first little beachfront cafe you see. We have an arrangement, he said. They know what to do with the trash. Cool.

We marched back down and soon we're back at the little café, where, sure enough, the owner has no idea what the hell we're talking about. But then he smiles and shrugs and says sure, I can take your garbage.

We all follow him around the side of the ramshackle building and you can't help but smile as you notice that there is, of course, garbage everywhere, strewn like confetti all around the building, heaps and piles and lumps and lots of and lots of flies and zero rhyme or reason, and the owner blithely takes our bags and sifts out the glass bottles and then tosses everything else straight into the bushes.

This is when it hits you: There is no real garbage pickup here, of course. No dumpsters, no sanitation department, no organization of any kind.

This is India. Garbage is inescapable. Pollution is merely part of the landscape. These various heaps and piles have been here forever and will be here forever and you have to accept the fact that the concept of "cleanliness" and "waste" are very relative, fluxive things indeed, and spiffy Western notions of having your crap hauled far, far away by professional crap-haulers and then buried deep in hole so you never have to think about it are as quaint and ridiculous here as thinking you're making much

of a dent in planetary evolution by recyling your toothbrush.

Because really, all you have to do is raise your head from where you're standing like a dumbfounded Westerner and look up into the sparse, beautiful jungle from whence you just came, and you can almost see the banyan tree and the ash-cooked monks, right up there, as you sighingly note how you have, in your humble precious sacred meditative karma yoga, simply moved a small bit of garbage from one part of the beach to another. Praise Shiva.

Perhaps you've noticed? I have a deep aversion to — and calmly malevolent intent toward — corporations, officials, religions, politicians, gods, ad agencies and pretty much any form of sentient life that traffics in fear, particularly fear of mundane everyday nonthreatening bullshit commonality that get spun and churned into some sort of demon out to infect your children and eat your face. I wish these perpetrators ill.

That said, I do microwave my sponge now and then. And I've been known to toss a little bleach on the cutting board after cutting up raw meat or preparing fresh virgins for the sacrifice. I mean, let's be reasonable. —mm

Who will kill the evil germs?

01/26/2007

Is it over yet? Is there some sort of end in sight? Can we all emerge from the dark cloud of sheer ongoing terror in this country regarding germs and bacteria and sundry microscopic things that seep into your toenails and eat away at your eyeballs and steal your basic cable?

No, no, we cannot.

Here is a new study, from the University of Florida. It proves that you can indeed kill almost every hint of bacteria on your average rancid germ-filled household sponge by simply nuking it for two full minutes[1] — which will, if you try it, turn your sponge into a smoking smoldering extraterrestrial WMD device you cannot touch for about an hour lest you scald your fingertips and wonder what the hell a basic household sponge is made of that it doesn't actually catch fire or liquefy after two minutes in a microwave. But hey, at least everything's dead.

This is, of course, good news indeed, given how sponges are apparently astonishing factories for bacteria and the kitchen sinks they often hang around in are reportedly the absolute best (read: warm and wet, and not in the good way) places for germs to fester and breed and given how lots of people get sick every year from (apparently) licking the sink and given how we have very much become, after all, a quivering, twitching, germ-obsessed nation.

Have you not felt the fear? Have you not seen the TV specials and witnessed the commercials and seen the astounding, silly array of terror-inducing products on the store shelves, all sorts of antibacterial soaps and sprays and mouthwashes and wipes, body cleansers and child-dousers and pet-suckers and foot-screamers? Of course you have.

This is the message: The world is a shockingly toxic place, you are not the slightest bit safe, you could get sick and die at any second from merely *touching the wrong surface* and then sucking your fingertips, and this goes doubly true if that surface happens to be Lindsay Lohan or Bill O'Reilly or American foreign policy.

Is that an exaggeration? Not by much. Indeed, the fear is palpable, and real, and also terrifically stupid, given how it is at least partly created and fueled by giddy chemical corporations only too happy to supply you with all sorts of toxic substances with which to kill the evil germs of your life, most of which have existed since the dawn of time and which also includes all the *good* necessary bacteria that actually serve a positive function in the ecology of existence. But hey, balanced perspective has never exactly topped the list of American virtues, you know?

Here's another ad, just one of dozens. Clorox Disinfecting Wipes. Bleach-filled chemical things that you should use regularly on every surface of your home lest little Timmy grab an innocent American cookie from the *exact same spot* on the countertop where you happened to unload some raw drippy blood-drenched hamburger meat just minutes before. Oh my *God*. You're not using these wipes? Are you trying to *kill your child*?

Oh, there are plenty of studies to fan the fear. After all, it's absolutely true that there are more carcinogens and synthetic by-products and incomprehensible spores jumping up from, say, your average American shag carpet and into your lungs than from the entire R&D department of the Dow Chemical Co. Did you know? This is why you see frumpy blouse-clad housewives spraying gallons of that Febreze crap all over their drapes and carpets and husbands in some sort of orgasmic olfactory delight in those TV commercials — to cover up the toxic swill of modern existence with synthetic lavender, that's why.

Hotel rooms? Oh my delirious germ-causing God, don't get me started. Did you not see that "Primetime" special[2] last year, where they went into various nice, mid-range hotels across America wielding only a black light and an evil grin and found all sorts of residues of blood and urine and sperm and feces and Dick Cheney spread around the carpet and bedspread and walls and even on the sad little Bible in the bedside drawer? I bet you did.

Wait, there's more. What's the most germ-clogged, festering item on your body right now (besides, of course, your body itself)? That would be your cell phone, silly.[3] After all, it just sits there all day, simmering in the happy juices of your toasty pants pocket, churning out microbes of horror[4] like Paris Hilton churns out intimations of death. And you put that thing up to your face without first disinfecting it[5] with some ethyl alcohol and a flamethrower? What are you, high?

(By the way, does it matter that the very same black light will find the exact same residues throughout your own home? Or that life is pretty much made up of equal parts flowers and piss, honey and blood, sunshine and semen? Verily, it appears not.)

It is an odd and telling conundrum, this germ thing, perhaps the perfect microcosm of the modern, Muslim-fearin', WMD-jumpin,' Bush-whacked American mind-set. On the one hand, it is very true that the world is indeed a far more toxic place than at any time in history, what with terrifying cancer rates, disease, depression, all manner of virus and sickness and Adam Sandler movies resulting directly or indirectly from the truly dazzling array of newborn chemicals and germs surrounding our consumer-mad lifestyles. One tip: Breathe deep the frisky air of any modern American city and try not to imagine the astounding soup of industrial toxins you're actually inhaling, OK?

Then again, the human animal is, after all, one giant bacteria farm. It's what we do. It's who we are, ever since the first caveman scraped the greenish-brown gunk from a prehistoric pond and decided it would make a fabulous sauce for his wooly mammoth steak. To attempt to somehow remove ourselves from the germy/bacterial/viral miasma of existence is like trying to remove the white from death, the sigh from the orgasm, the sky from the color blue. Ain't gonna happen. What's more, it just makes God roll Her eyes, and laugh.

How you balance this perspective is, as always, up to you. After all, as the saying goes, if all you have is a bleach wipe, everything looks like a germ.

1 http://icoot.notlong.com
2 http://aanie.notlong.com
3 http://waino.notlong.com
4 http://aicoir.notlong.com
5 http://aogai.notlong.com

Irony abounds, slaps, tickles: Just before President Obama was elected, I heard from a slew of furious lib-haters who expressed essentially the same sentiment I suggest in the column below — albeit in far angrier, less articulate reverse ("if that socialist Nazi n—ger becomes president and you libs come take my guns and let terrorists rape my kids and ruin this fine country, I'm moving to fucking Canada," etc).

Oddly, their reasoning didn't have quite the same resigned, soulful sadness as when many of my friends wanted to exit America in November of '04 — or even when countless thousands posted their woe to sorryeverybody.com, a website phenom that sprang up just after John Kerry lost, apologizing to the world in the most poignant way for the existence of Bush's second nightmare term. The site's archives are still up. It's still pretty amazing. Go, look.

Bad news: The Obama-haters lied. They haved not moved away at all. They are more shrill and terrified than ever, and have apparently chosen to stick around and suffer a more fluid, open-minded, articulate, intelligent Obama-led America, right along with the rest of us. Poor dears. —mm

Hello, Uranus? Got any room?

11/05/2004

I said it, you said it, pretty much anyone with a brain larger than a grape or a soul more nimble than a rock said it maybe a thousand times over.

And you probably weren't even all that drunk when you said it, and maybe you were even a little more than half serious, and maybe you said it just like this: If Bush somehow snags another election, if the unthinkable comes to pass and the Dubya neocon nightmare refuses to end, well, that's it. I'm outta here.

Done. Over. Gone. Moving away. To Canada. Or France. Latvia. Uranus. Anywhere, really, that doesn't have Bush as leader and that doesn't make me openly ashamed to be a citizen and that doesn't make me feel like a sickened disillusioned ulcerated outcast in my own happily divisive country every damn day including Sunday.

You want a place, you say, that doesn't right this minute seem to be working heroically to make homophobia and born-again fundamentalism and pre-emptive isolationist warmongering and environmental ignorance a national religion. A place where SUVs aren't considered minor deities and where gay people aren't loathed for wanting to slice a wedding cake and where brazen heavily narcotized denial in the face of a veritable mountain of presidential lies isn't the national pastime.

Tempting, isn't it? To just move away to a sunnier, clothing-optional utopia and wait for it all to be over, for the dark days to pass and the Shrub era to sink into the tar pits of history and the fog to finally lift?

After all, most all of us on the progressive Left feel we truly faced the dragon this election, and we put up a valiant fight and marshaled as potent an army of dissenters and intellectuals and moderates and liberal crusaders and feminists and enlightened activists as possible, considering.

And we supposedly had more of the youth vote and the disenfranchised single-female vote and the "Daily Show" vote and the Eminem vote and the celebrity vote and the humanitarian vote and the antiwar vote and the gay vote and the pro-choice vote and the Howard Stern vote and the immigrant vote, and still the dragon just sneered and hacked up another fireball of bogus fear and evangelical Christian self-righteousness and torched our glimmering sword of juicy hope into a smoking cinder.

And now, this. The nation has officially, stupefyingly handed the world's worst president a blank check to do whatever he and his cronies like, without fear of major repercussions or voter disillusionment or damage to an imminent re-election campaign, because there won't be one.

Which is to say, Bush now has no one to worry about now but his true constituents (hint: it ain't mainstream Repubs, or even the born-agains), no one to answer to but the CEOs and the energy barons and the military-supply corporations co-owned by his father, and nothing to guide him but his own deeply regressive, monosyllabic moral compass. Hell, why stick around for more of that?

But here's the catch. Here's the tough part to accept. Here's what everyone who's right now on the brink of packing their bags and checking the real estate prices in Vancouver has to know and has to have drilled into their disconsolate hope-crushed souls right this minute, before it's too late:

You cannot leave. You cannot drop the armor now. Why? Because you are needed, more than ever. You are mandatory to keep the energy flowing, the karmic vibrator buzzing, to keep the progressive and lucid half of the nation breathing and healthy and awake and ever reaching out to the half that's wallowing in fear and violence and homophobia and sexual dread, hoping to find harmony instead of cacophony, common ground instead of civil war, some sort of a shared love of a country so messy and internationally disrespected and openly confused its own president can't even speak the language.

After all, you don't hand over all your children the first time the flying monkeys bang on your door. You don't give up your dream house just because a bunch of gangbangers moved in down the block. You become a bit more wary, alert, you stock up on the superlative porn and the expensive wine and the deepened sense of true beauty and sex and love and hope and you hunker down and grit your teeth and dig in for the long haul, and you work on making your own goddamn garden more beautiful than even you could have imagined, because, well, the neighborhood — and the world — needs it, more than ever.

Look. No one said it was gonna be easy. No one said it was gonna be painless. And no one said it was gonna be quick. As I've noted before, the neocons have been planning this takeover for decades. The Bush regime, despite feeling like a massive indigestible incomprehensible fluke, is no accident.

Besides, most hardcore Republicans would, of course, love it if you'd leave the country, and take your gul-dang gay-lovin' tofu-eatin' tree-huggin' pierced-labia values with you. They would love it, furthermore, if the libs in the morally shredded red states would split for the coastal cities and the major metropolises of America. Remember: bullies never deserve to own the playground.

One of the most stirring e-mails I received during the outpouring of grief the day after the election was from a young female reader, "an artist, an intellectual and a Jew" who's been living in Mexico and who now says she's so enraged and saddened by the election's ugly outcome that she's preparing to return to the States ASAP, just so she can help, so she can join the resistance, keep the right-wingers from coming after our souls. Now, that's patriotism.

The bottom line: Don't disband the newfound army just because one ugly battle was lost. Mourn, commiserate, lick wounds, lick each other, drink heavily, spit out your stale gum of disappointment and pop in a fresh clove of laughter and spiritual heat and then regroup and sober up and take an even deeper breath and watch in hot wet spiritually emboldened amusement as the cosmic circus unfolds.

It's far from over. The tunnel is just a little darker — and longer — than we imagined.

The sheer arrogance, the raw gall it must require to deem yourself worthy of declaring new sins for all of humankind. It's downright... quaint. Like you can imagine the pope hosting Saturday Night Live and stepping out in his patent leather Prada loafers and the big pointy hat, stifling a nervous giggle:

"OK OK OK, thank you, yes, quiet down now. OK so I'm thrilled to be here tonight. Let me just start by saying I, Pope Benedict, do hereby declare as sinful and punishable by 5,000 years in hell and/or being forced to wake up next to Ann Coulter every morning, the following ills: decaf instant coffee, Celine Dion ringtones, wearing black socks with sandals, buying your child any of the Kidz Bop series, and naming your cat Mister Snuffington Licksalot III (muddled laughter)*, and/or sexually molesting quite literally thousands of children and beating countless orphans and having simply tons of homosexual sex over the rather ugly 2,000 year history of your spiritually stifling, oppressive organization* (crickets)*. Wow, tough room. Now, put your hands together for My Chemical Romance!" —mm*

Thou shalt not kid thyself

03/19/2008

This just in: If you're an obscenely wealthy, drug-dealing pedophile stem-cell researcher who drives a Hummer and doesn't recycle, you are totally going to Hell. Oh please, like you didn't already know.

Hey, the Catholic Church wouldn't lie, mister. The Big Book o' Deadly Sins apparently has a whole new addendum[1] so it looks like it ain't just gluttony and lust and murder and hot porn and witchcraft and coveting thy neighbor's way cool Flickr photo stream anymore. That stuff is for wimps. Serfs. Lutherans.

The Vatican is trying to get serious. Modern. Hip, even. They have added some fine new offenses to the master collection. Indeed, Sins 2.0 now includes taking "mind-altering" drugs and polluting the planet and creating poverty and hoarding excessive wealth and messing around with genetics, and did you not see the grim expression on the face of that Vatican official when he announced the new aberrations? Totally serious. Deadly. I mean, the scales were *flaking right off his face.* And if you look closely, you can see God right there, standing just behind the podium like a hulking Dick Cheney figure, nodding gloomily in agreement. Mmm, the Vatican. It's like Disneyland for arthritic masochists.

Hey, don't get mad at me. These are just the rules.[2] I don't make them up, I just report the facts. Like this one: Do you have a healthy Adderall/Zoloft/Budweiser addiction that you couple with a severe case of keepin' your uppity and sexually dangerous wife in her gul-dang place? God loves you. And your fellow Republicans. Do you enjoy a joint with your wine and a few hits of Ecstasy at Burning Man and maybe some special mushrooms at SXSW as you play with a Pyrex dildo with your joyful girlfriend just after yoga but before meditating? Say hello to Satan for me, pervert.

Perhaps you are amused by it all. Or maybe frightened. Or a bit of both. Perhaps you also note that what's remarkable about Sinapalooza '08 is not that the Catholic Church has now finally managed to recognize that drugs and pollution even exist. It's not even remarkable that a priest actually had the gall to say to the world that pedophilia is also horrible and wrong and God does not approve, and no one actually walked up and slapped him across the face, hard.

No, what's perhaps most amusing is that in this modern age, someone still feigns to have the authority to invent new sins in the first place, to perpetuate the inanity of the very concept, to torque and mold and reshape divine will as he sees fit, just sort of making it up as he goes along, expecting everyone to basically kneel and cower and kiss the ring. Is that not fabulous, in a hey-look-we're-back-in-1328 sort of way?

And yes, I also enjoyed the new sin of excessive wealth, given how the Vatican is one of the most—if not *the* most —gluttonously wealthy organizations on the planet, oozing with real estate and massive stock portfolios, dripping with cash, billions of dollars in hoarded treasure and unknown gems, icons, art, the solid gold vaginas of 1,000 pagan goddesses locked up in its vaults. The hypocrisy is positively comical. Epic. Makes Eliot Spitzer's trifle look like Mary Ann smoking a roach in rural Idaho.[3]

To be fair, the church does use some of that massive wealth, once estimated at about $15 billion but likely far, far higher, to fund its various charities and clinics and community centers. But it also uses it to buy more land, to pay out hundreds of millions of dollars in settlements in hundreds of pedophilia and sexual abuse cases worldwide, to wield frightening political power, buy favor with the Italian mafia, and to refuse services it deems "sinful," such as providing honest health information and condoms in AIDS-ridden Africa.

Despite all of that, I don't particularly hate the Catholic Church, per se. It just happens to be the finest extant example of a largely hypocritical misogynistic authoritarian patriarchy that still wields far too much power. When it comes to insulting religious silliness, it is, of course, far from alone.

You have to ask: Do religious convulsions such as these make any difference? Is there really anyone left who takes Vatican decrees at all seriously, someone who might've been hell-bent on becoming, say, a rich child-molesting cokehead with a giant carbon footprint who suddenly saw the new sins and was like, "Dammit! Guess I'll become a social worker after all."

It's like that old joke: You're driving along just happy as can be and you glance over and there's Exhausted Urban Mom piloting the Caravan to the Gymboree, and just when you're about to ram her off the road and hopefully down that steep embankment to her fiery death as you laugh maniacally, you see it: "Baby on Board." Damn! Thwarted again.

Speaking of babies, here's a terrific new statistic: 25-40 percent of American teenage girls have a sexually transmitted disease.[4] Isn't that wonderful? Abstinence education has been a blessing and a joy.

What does that have to do with Vatican impudence? Easy. This same Catholic Church has been lying to young women for upwards of 2,000 years, telling them to loathe and mistrust their bodies and fear sex and restrain their natural urges and not to touch any naughty body parts until they marry a pasty middle manager who looks disturbingly like their father, and only *he* can touch their naughty bits and make them feel lousy about their bodies because he has no clue what he's doing. Praise!

And hence, awash in misinformation and lies and the ignorance of their elders, teens follow their natural urges anyway and have uninformed, unprotected, deeply lousy sex, getting STDs and learning all sorts of damaging habits that require years and decades and far too much wine and therapy to correct.

Note to the Vatican: You want true sin? Here you go: Lying to women is a sin. Pathological hypocrisy is a sin. Half a billion dollars in pedophilia lawsuit payouts is a sin. Homophobia is a sin. Hiding those golden vaginas is a sin. And creating new sins in a strange attempt to stay relevant as your church withers and struggles and falters in the new and spiritually hungry but religiously mistrustful world, that's surely a sin.

No, wait. Check that. That's not a sin at all. It's actually just a sad, inexcusable joke.

1 http://eekoe.notlong.com
2 http://woonoh.notlong.com
3 http://aitooba.notlong.com
4 http://ahjaud.notlong.com

Upwards of 1,000 columns into this gig and one imperative arises: you gotta mix it up, try different voices and tones and angles of approach, lest you go insane. This one, the mock news story, I return to on occasion, because it's A) easy, b) relatively fun, C) allows me to access a portion of my creative brain that otherwise just sits there in the back of my id, thrumming its fingers, waiting for a turn.

This piece is a little bit of The Onion, a little bit dry, and a little bit meaningless, given how I don't really make much effort to sustain the verisimilitude in favor of whipping language around like a sexed-up carnival ride. Maybe that's part of the charm? Or exasperation? —mm

No sex is very bad for you

04/25/2007

In an unusual turn of events, a comprehensive new study from a team of prize-winning, nicely disheveled researchers from Johns Hopkins University, working in conjunction with various frumpy but no less adorable teams from Sweden, the United Kingdom, Brazil and roughly 57 other nations, has come to a decisive conclusion regarding sex education in America.

Their astonishing research shows that the GOP's abstinence-only sex education programs are not only utterly useless and a complete waste of taxpayer money, but they actually invite all manner of disease and destruction upon those who attempt to adhere to them.[1]

It's true. Such programs, long touted by sexually denuded Republicans and nervous Christian righters and applauded by the Taliban and fundamentalists as some sort of psychosexual panacea, these programs lead directly to severe anxiety, hair loss, acne, whininess, temporary blindness, adult bed-wetting, lousy taste in shoes, pararectal abscesses and even, in rare and bizarre cases, an overwhelming urge to date Jenna Bush.

"We are completely stunned at these far-reaching, nearly universal results which have emerged from every country in the world except Saudi Arabia, Oman and much of Utah," said Dr. Claudio Ortega, totally cute lead researcher of the Johns Hopkins team that studied the behaviors of roughly 14 million normal, "genitally tingly" elementary school and teenage kids across all nations and demographics and hair colors and general inexplicable affection for Avril Lavigne.

"No wait, check that," Ortega would've added, with a sly and knowing grin, if he had actually existed, which he does not. "We're really not stunned at all. Actually, the results make a whole heaping truckload of very obvious and forehead-slapping sense."

Ortega, surrounded by his research team who were all dressed almost exclusively in American Apparel silver lamé workout shorts,[2] leather handcuffs and Iron Maiden T-shirts from Hot Topic, seemed nonplussed by the need for his own study. "I mean, come *on*. Say no to sex until you're married? Abstinence is the only truly moral path? Where are we, 1756? What's next, trepanning and lobotomies and hurling virgins into the volcano to appease the corn god? Are you people high?"

The overwhelming findings, recently released to the entire planet via multiple media formats, including a one-page PDF document, universal text message, whispering God-like voice in your dreams and also by way of a two-disk six-hour DVD movie starring Rocco Siffredi, Jenna Jameson, Belladonna, numerous perky cheerleaders and an Italian villa featuring 13 sex swings and 47 bottles of dark rum, is being widely touted as both a radical breakthrough and also as so heart-crushingly obvious it makes you want to spank yourself with a tire iron, and not in a good way.

"Put it this way," he sighed. "Not only will anti-sexual thoughts make you into some sort of shrill, humorless neoconservative evangelical QVC addict with a thing for plastic lawn ornaments, Purity Balls, Coors and all things pleated, but we've found devastating evidence linking the widespread activity of not having good, respectful, dirty, open-mouthed sex to everything from acid reflux to infertility to global biochemical warfare to a chronic adoration of Adam Sandler," Ortega said, soaping himself up in the tub with a bright red and purple sponge shaped like a giant vulva. "It's really quite astonishing. Except for the part that it's totally obvious."

The study comes as a severe blow to the legion of grim, devoted absti-

nence educators and sour Republicans who, nevertheless, still refuse to acknowledge that the U.S. government has now wasted upward of 1 billion taxpayer dollars in the past 10 years on abstinence programs that have had, to put it simply, exactly zero effect on teen sex behavior.[3] Nothing. Nada. Zilch.

"Here is the most astounding fact of all, the thing that makes you want to scream in the faces of these legislators and religious nutballs and pour a gallon of honey over them and then toss them onto a giant mound of gay fire ants," Ortega would've added, between sips of margarita, had he been existent. And also very, very cool.

"Sex is just ridiculously good for you.[4] Sex is good for the heart. It's good for the blood. It's good for the mood and it's good for depression and it's good for self-esteem and it's good for making you feel more human and alive and present in your skin.[5] Do it right and sex shoots huge gobs of endorphins and raw divine energy into your id and it's good for raising your kundalini and inspiring awareness of the cosmos and it's good for calmly and casually noting the interconnectedness of all things from all time in all places everywhere."

Ortega then sighed heavily, his skin beginning to turn translucent, his bones fading away, his entire being beginning to soften and evaporate, much like the reality of this story, much like any hope-filled notions you may have that your government gives a damn about the sexual integrity of children and might actually reverse its degrading position and start treating youth with respect and love.

"Did you know sex actually improves your sense of smell? Helps the prostate? True. Also reduces stress. Improves sleep. Improves circulation. Relieves pain, menstrual cramps. Improves fertility. Helps you live longer. Look younger. Goes great with jeans. Goes perfectly with red wine, white wine, pink wine, sake, beer. Dress it up, dress it down. Take it out, or stay at home and rent a movie. It is the universal traveler. It is the Super Glue of the gods. It is the bond that connects all and to deny any of this to kids is abhorrent and insulting and you can rest assured that Jesus himself is just incredibly ashamed that these programs even exist."

"Look me in the eye," Ortega finally said, he and this whole tale disappearing into the sad media ether, to be quickly superseded by tales of death and war and blood. "Yes, this is a fantasy. I am a fantasy, OK? The sort of raw, real sex education human children deserve will never happen in your lifetime."

"But here's the thing: You need to know these facts. You need to keep this arrow of sexual knowledge in your quiver, sharp and polished and ready to launch at a moment's notice, OK? For when the time comes. For when the Great Transformation occurs. OK? Trust me."

And just like that, Ortega vanished, leaving behind a small pool of fire and Astroglide and just a hint of eternal, grinning, inextinguishable hope.

1 http://gahlei.notlong.com
2 http://eyiefo.notlong.com
3 http://oweoghi.notlong.com
4 http://queira.notlong.com
5 http://taodi.notlong.com

Do you remember Carrie? The adorable blonde fembot homophobe de-throned beauty queen plaything of the Christian right, all about silicone breast implants and soft-core sex tapes for Jesus, a true icon and encapsulation of prissy hypocritical Republican values? She was a genuine, dreamy pop culture catch, for about a minute.

I included this column in TDS because, well, I think it holds its funny. But more importantly, it's actually full of valuable advice: Many of the sex tape tips herein come directly from personal experience. For example: Candles really do make for horrible sex tape lighting. A tripod is mandatory. Point-and-shoot cameras are generally awful for capturing what you really want to capture. Don't talk too much. See? Even in the midst of light-hearted satire, I'm really just trying to help. —mm

Sex tape tips from Carrie Prejean

11/18/2009

> *Days after Carrie Prejean admitted that she participated in a sex tape and called it "the biggest mistake of my life," seven additional such videos — all "solo performances" have surfaced starring the de-crowned beauty queen, Radar reports. —US Magazine*

I'm just gonna say it outright, OK you guys? You ready? Here it is ...

No candles.

I know, right? "But Carrie," I hear you whine, "candles are so, like, totally awesome! How can I *not* use them in my not-at-all sexy Christian masturbation tape?" And I totally think so too!

But here's the thing. You want your scene to look good for your massively sexually frustrated boyfriend, right? Well, candles just get in the way of the action, and unless you're using an infrared camera, there's simply no way candles — even, like, a million little votives from Wal-Mart that smell like vanilla pudding and hurt in a really yummy way when you drip them on your thigh and moan — will illuminate the important stuff, like your sequined heels, a John Mayer poster, or the giant stuffed Pooh bear

propping up the wine coolers on the bedside table. Sorry!

Also, candles are way dangerous! One involuntary leg spasm and suddenly the pillow lace is on fire, and the little cherub painting hanging over your Hello Kitty sheets is burning like Larry King's beady little eyes. Scary!

OK so, editing! You want to cut the fluff, right? I

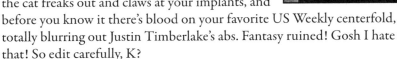

am, too! This is why editing is so important. Even
your basic iPhone lets you trim out the awkward
parts, like when you're about to fake another
orgasm and you let out a shriek that sounds like a
chicken mating with a leaf blower, and suddenly
the cat freaks out and claws at your implants, and
before you know it there's blood on your favorite US Weekly centerfold,
totally blurring out Justin Timberlake's abs. Fantasy ruined! Gosh I hate
that! So edit carefully, K?

Speaking of sounds, here's some advice I keep hearing over and over in a
million different ways. Keep your mouth shut! Ha ha! Get it? I keep hearing that! Me! As if!

But it's true! As much as I love rambling on about stuff I know nothing
about and repeating quasi-religious, homophobic garbage that's basically
been fed to me by my male GOP handlers, even *I* know that, in a good sex
tape, you keep the chatter to a minimum. After all, it's a video, silly! That
means pictures! Naked pictures! With moaning!

So, unless you're screaming out the lord's name in vain or begging your
imaginary partner to perform some kinky French fetish thing on you
with a ball-gag and 15 feet of garden hose, keep your sounds restricted to
moans, gasps, sighs, cute little hiccups, dirty curse words and maybe the
occasional, "Ooh baby, I know you like it when I use this vibrator on the
Pooh bear like that, don't you lover?" Like the saying goes, brevity is the
soul of, uh, somethingorother. I know, right?

Let's talk equipment. No, not *those*, silly! Although God knows those
come in handy too! Ha ha! God bless silicone!

I mean *video* equipment. I say, why not skip the iPhone or lame P&S
camera, and make a *real* investment in your trashy, Gawker-ready, 15-min-
utes-of-fame future by buying yourself a dedicated digital video camera
and a little tripod. Add in about three free iMovie classes at the Apple
store, and it's *whammo*, here I come, reality TV show!

People always ask me, Carrie, when you make a sex tape, does it help
to actually *be* a Christian? I mean, like, not a very good one, more like a
pseudo-moralistic, fundamentalist homophobe ex-beauty queen with as
many brain cells as you have limbs? Someone who wouldn't understand
true Christianity if Jesus himself came down and tickled your feet and
called you Lilith?

My answer is always the same: Jesus was a foot fetishist? That is so awesome!

But to answer the other question: heck yes, it helps! I find that mock
Christianity only cranks up the irony factor, the sexy hypocrisy of what

you're doing — and massive moralistic hypocrisy is a total turn on! Just ask all those Catholic priests! And Republican senators! And televangelists! And gay televangelists who have sex with Republican senator priests!

Here's a very simple formula I learned back when I was knee-high to a tequila shooter: The more you profess your hollow, virginal Christian righteousness, the greater the melodrama and drooling media attention when your lame, cheeseball sex tape — or meth fetish, or gay lover — comes to light, and the more money you get for your book deal and/or reality show. It's like magic, or something! OMG you guys, capitalism is so awesome!

(Note: This formula is also super extra effective if you wear, like, a tiny gold cross necklace in your videos? And as you dry hump the arm of the Levitz sofa, the cross bounces up and down and it makes it seem like Jesus is alive in your heart? Even though he's totally not? It's totally kinky!)

Have you thought about lighting? I like to think about lighting. I also like to think about Spaghetti-Os, giant pandas, things that sparkle, and whether or not it's legal to keep a baby white tiger in my back yard, name it John Mayer and feed it Spaghetti-Os and hot dogs and my thong underwear as I cry uncontrollably. But never mind that now.

What was I saying? I forget. But seriously, someone really *did* ask me if it's possible to make a genuinely hot, dirty sex tape and also be deeply spiritual, or if the two are, um, "mutually exclusive" or whatever. After he explained to me what that phrase meant, I said sure! I think! Wait, what again?

I once heard that it's actually more than possible, it's absolutely the best and healthiest way to be, to be super dialed in to the divine, and *also* explore your sexuality as intensely as you like. In fact, lots of mystical texts and teachers say the experience of the rapture itself is nearly identical to orgasm, and that ecstasy, lust, love, desire and divine consciousness are all interlinked at a very profound level, even interchangeable, all spinning around the same sacred source in dazzling swirls of unutterable bliss and orgasmic joy penetrating every breath and bone and cell of your body.

Wow! Rapture on, Jesus!

Now, I have no idea what the hell I just said in that last paragraph, but it sure sounds neat, doesn't it? Or wait, I mean, sinful and evil? I can't quite tell the difference. Ha ha! That is so awesome! God bless ignorance! And my nipples! Happy sextaping, everyone! Get a tripod!

LICKING THE ZEITGEIST

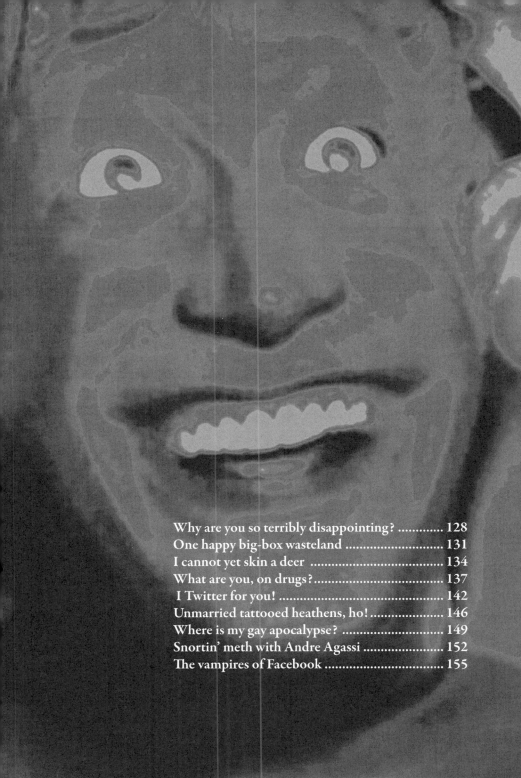

One of those unexpected delights of a column, wrote it fast and dirty and a little hazy, largely on instinct, given how the topic wasn't razor pinpoint clear in my head (not at all uncommon, really). It was just a sense, a feeling, tugging on a curious thread. I write this way frequently, and I suppose I've grown accustomed to how terrifically unnerving it is; I rarely know if it works until I toss it into the Void, and gauge the response.

This one clicked. I matched a mood, hit a nerve. It stuck. It got around. It went a little viral. The amazing Heather Armstrong over at dooce.com posted a link to this column via her Twitter feed. Girl has 1.7 million followers, so that didn't hurt. No idea how it will hold up long-term, given how it attempts to nail a particular vibe du jour — but then, that's true for much of TDS, no? Anyway, I'm sure the overall feeling described herein won't go away anytime soon. No matter how good things get, we are just terribly fond of interminable whining. —mm

Why are you so terribly disappointing?

01/29/2010

What the hell is wrong with you? Are you really going to wear that? Why aren't you right now cooking me a nice meal and wearing those hot boy shorts you know I love and saying those words you know I want to hear at exactly the moment I like to hear them, to make me feel better about everything, even though I probably won't?

What happened to my bonus? What happened to my job? What happened to my country? Why can't it all go the way it's supposed to go? You mean having a kid *won't* solve my marriage problems? Why don't these drugs make me feel better? Where's that goddamn waiter with my salad? Have you seen the stupid weather today? Is this really all there is?

These are, from what I can glean, the most important questions of the day, of the month, of modern life itself. Hell, what with the economy and job situation, the housing market and the overall feel and texture of the nation right now, it's no wonder Americans are, by and large, a goddamn miserable bunch. We don't like *anything* lately. No politician, no decision, no situation, no inhale, no exhale. We are sick to death of all of it, including ourselves.

Can you blame us? Have you seen how many things there to be disappointed about these days? Love. Sex. Marriage. Stock market. God. Gas mileage. Death. Air travel. 5/9ths of the Supreme Court. It's all just a big goddamn letdown. The list is endless. And getting endlesser.

The evidence is everywhere. I calculate it took about seven minutes, give or take, after Steve Jobs finished introducing the shinypretty iPad for the first time, before the whiny attacks on the wondergizmo began flooding in, how it didn't have this or that expected feature, how it can't do live video chat, doesn't have Flash, the bezel is too big and it won't double as a meat thermometer, how it doesn't really revolutionize much of anything despite how it's, you know, this gorgeous 1.5-pound slab of aluminum and glass that works flawlessly and can perform roughly one thousand tasks in a more fluid and astonishing way than any device of its kind in history.

Big fucking deal. We just do not care. It's all a big disappointment. Hey, I was expecting to be *blown away*. I was expecting miracles and transformations and multiple orgasms on sight. Do not come at me with tantalizing promises only to reveal that you can fulfill most of them to a fairly good degree, and not far exceed all of them in every imaginable way. We're *Americans*, goddammit. Ye shall know us by the tang of our bitter and untenable jadedness.

Also, global warming? Total effing letdown. Americans are no longer believing in it. Do you know why? Not because the mountains of scientific proof aren't there. Not because it's not happening. But because it's *not yet happening to us* like they said it would in the movies and those worst-case scenario books. Where are the zombies? The ice forests? Where's the tidal wave crashing over the Himalayas? I want my goddamn apocalypse, and I want it *now*.

Hey, you annoying gay people? Ditto, to you. All this uproar about rights and gender, all this talk about how gay marriage is now legal in a handful of states, and still the very fabric of whinysad 50-percent divorce rate Christian society has yet to unravel and cause riots and induce all white Midwestern children to spontaneously combust. I mean, WTF? So disappointing.

My God, did you hear that guy's latest speech, that President Obama? Disappointing times a *thousand*, am I right? What the hell happened to him? Why is he so weak and ineffectual? Why the hell can't he step up and fix the entire planet like he promised he would, in my dreams and fantasies and impossible liberal grass-fed organic tofu greengasms? Doesn't he know I put a goddamn bumper sticker on my Subaru for him? I've never done that for *anyone*. Bastard.

He's only accomplished what, about 100 of the things I expected him to accomplish by now? Big deal. I have, like, *5,000 more*. Health care reform has failed. Guantanamo is still open. Wars are still warring. Jobs are still sucking. Gays are still unhappy because the entire human understanding of love and gender in this nation has not completely transformed within a year. Infuriating!

But the biggest disappointment of all? Turns out one calm n' brilliant Barack Obama isn't enough to solve the problem of 535 vile n' slothful congressional jackals who *aren't* Barack Obama. Go figure.

Shall we recall just how violently disappointed those fundamentalists were when Bush bumbled off the stage, the single greatest disaster as president we will ever know? They were, of course, mostly disappointed Bush wasn't able to do far *more* repellant damage than he did. They wanted nothing less than full-scale war on Islam, death to all abortion doctors, creationism in schools, homosexuality banned outright, all you scary women to please stop it with your needy n' terrifying vaginas. You know, the usual.

And now it's the hardcore Dems' turn, in reverse. Obama cannot do enough good, fast enough. He is failing as our personal SuperJesus. Not because he's not accomplishing volumes and making all sorts of history, but because we were expecting total mindblowing revolution. Hey, it's his own fault, right? He's the one that set out one of the most ambitious agendas in presidential history to go along with the million-mile hole he has to dig us out of first. Can you blame us for whining?

But we don't stop there. Not only are we disappointed, we need to express it. Vent it. Hiss it and spit it and hurl it like fistfuls of mental manure at the great wall of hey, screw you.

You have but to take a peek in the comments section that appear online below this very column, any column, any article on this or any news site whatsoever, to see just how mean and nasty we have become. It does not matter what the piece might be about. Obama's speech. High speed rail. Popular dog breeds. Your grandmother's cookies. The anonymous comments section of any major media site or popular blog will be so crammed with bile and bickering, accusation and pule, hatred and sneer you can't help but feel violently disappointed by the shocking lack of basic human kindness and respect, much less a sense of positivism or perspective.

Maybe this, then, is the ultimate upshot of our endless, self-wrought swirl of sour disappointment, of never having our impossible needs fully met, of constantly being thwarted in our desire to have the world revolve around our exact set of specifications and desires.

Our disappointment begins to curdle, to turn back on itself, poison the heart, turn us nasty and low. It shifts from merely being a national mood or general temperament, into a way of being. A wiring, deep and harmful and permanent. It's all very disappointing, really.

Is it over? Has the big-box juggernaut run its course and has the economic meltdown/correction/upheaval that kicked off in late '08 finally put a stop to — or at least slowed down — the grand homogenization of America, the ruthless construction of giant clusterfucks of bland megastores built every ten miles along every highway and byway of the nation?

We certainly seem to have reached saturation. How many more Targets do we need? How many Home Depots can one nation really sustain? When will we finally get sick of Wal-Mart behaving like some sort of middling pseudo-ecofriendly leviathan that drains entire towns of their lifeblood, and then picks up and lumbers off, leaving behind a mammoth husk, like some sort of giant, pitiless insect? Can I answer when I get back from BevMo? —mm

One happy big-box wasteland

08/17/2005

Do you want to feel like you might as well be in Tucson or Boise or Modesto or Wichita or Muncie and it no longer freakin' matters, because we as a nation have lost all sense of community and place? Why, just pull over, baby. Take the next exit. Right here, this very one.

Ah, there it is, yet another massive big-box mega-strip mall, a giant beacon of glorious community decay, a wilted exclamation point of consumerism gone wild. This is America. You have arrived. You are home. Eat it and smile.

There is the Target. There is the Wal-Mart and there is the Home Depot and the Kmart, the Borders and the Staples and the Sam's Club and the Office Depot and the Costco and the Toys "R" Us and of course the mandatory Container Store so you may buy more enormous plastic tubs in which to dump all your new, sweatshop-made crap.

What else do you need? Ah yes, food. Or something vaguely approximating it. There is the Wendy's and the Burger King and the Taco Bell/KFC hybrid and there is the Mickey D's and the Subway and the Starbucks and the dozen other garbage-food fiends lined up down the road like toxic dominoes, all lying in wait to maul your arteries and poison your heart and make you think about hospitals.

And here's the beautiful part: This snapshot, it's the same as it was 20 miles back, same as it will be 20 miles ahead, the exact same massive cluster of insidious development as you will find in roughly 10,000 noncommunities around the nation and each and every one making you feel about as connected to the town you're in and the body you inhabit as a fish feels on Saturn. In the dark. In a hole. Dead.

You have seen the plague. I have seen the plague. Anyone over 30 has seen the plague evolve from a mere germ of disease in the late '80s to a full-blown pestilence of big-box shopping hell. I was recently up in northern Idaho, where my family has owned a beautiful house on a lake in a tiny burg near the Canadian border for 40 years, and to get to this region you must pass through the explosively grown resort town of Coeur d'Alene, and the plague is there perhaps worse than anywhere within a 75-mile radius.

I am officially old enough to remember when passing through Coeur d'Alene meant stopping at exactly one — *one* — traffic light on Highway 95 on the way north, surrounded by roughly one million pine trees and breathtaking mountain vistas and vast, calming open spaces, farms and fields and sawmills and funky roadside shops and gorgeous lakes for miles.

There are now about 20 traffic lights added in as many years, scattered down a 10-mile stretch of highway and each and every one demarcates a turnoff into a massive, low-lying horribly designed strip mall, tacky and cheaply built and utterly heartless, and clearly zero planning went into any of these megashops, except to space them so obnoxiously that you have to get back in your goddamn car to drive the eighth of a mile to get to the Target to the Best Buy to the Wal-Mart to the Super Foods and back to your freakin' sanity.

Do you want to know what depresses the American spirit? Do you want to know why it feels like the center cannot hold and the tyranny of mediocrity has been loosed upon our world? Do you want to know what instills more thoughts of suicide and creates a desperate, low-level rage the source of which we cannot quite identify but which we know is right under our noses and which we now inhale Prozac and Xanax and Paxil by the truckload to attempt to mollify?

I have your answer. Here it is. Look. It is the appalling spread of big-box strip malls, tract homes like a cancer, metadevelopments paving over the American landscape, all creating a bizarre sense of copious loss, empty excess, heartless glut, forcing us to ask, once again, the Great All-American Question: How can we have so damned much but still feel like we have almost nothing at all?

Oh and by the way, Coeur d'Alene has a distinct central portion of town, well off the toxic highway. It is calm, tree lined and emptily pretty and it is packed with, well, restaurants and art galleries. And real estate offices. For yuppies. Because, of course, there are no local shops left. No mom-and-pops, few unique small businesses of any kind. No charm. No real community per se. Just well-manicured food and mediocre art no true local can actually afford and business parks where the heart used to be.

I have little real clue as to what children growing up in this sort of bizarre megaconsumerist dystopia will face as they age, what sort of warped perspective and decimated sense of place and community and home. But if you think meth addiction and teen pregnancy and religious homogeny and a compulsion to blow shit up in violent video games isn't a direct reaction to it, you're not paying close enough attention.

This is the new America. Our crazed sense of entitlement, our nearly rabid desire for easy access to mountains of bargain-basement junk has led to the upsurge of soulless big-box shops which has, in turn, led to a deadly sense of prefabricated, vacuous sameness wherever we go. And here's the kicker: We think it's good. We think it helps, brings jobs, tax money, affordable goods. We call it progress. We call it choice. It is the exact opposite.

Result No. 1: Towns no longer have personality, individuality, heart. Community drags. Environment suffers. Our once diverse and quirky and idiosyncratic landscape becomes bland and vacuous and cheap.

Result No. 2: a false sense of safety, of comfort, wrought of empty sameness. We want all our goods to be antiseptic and sanitized and brightly lit and clean. In a nation that has lost all sense of direction and all sense of pride and whose dollar is a global joke and whose economy is running on fumes and whose goods are all made overseas, that toxic sameness is, paradoxically, reassuring.

Result No. 3: We are trained, once again, to fear the different, the Other, That Which Does Not Conform. We learn to dislike the unique, the foreign, foreigners. We lose any sense of personal connection to what we create and what we buy and I do not care how cheap that jute rug from Ikea was: When they are mass-produced in 100,000 chunks in a factory in Malaysia, it ain't quirky.

Sameness is in. Sameness is the new black. It is no different than preplanned Disney World vacations or organized religion or preplanned cruises or themed restaurants where all edges have been filed off and every experience has been predigested and sanitized for your protection because God forbid you have an authentic experience or nurture genuine individual perspective or dare to question the bland norm lest your poor addled soul shudder and recoil and the Powers That Be look at you as a serious threat.

I have seen the plague and so have you. Hell, you're probably shopping in it. After all, what choice do you have?

It appears I might've been just slightly little ahead of my time with this column. A small flood of books on this very topic of urban survivalism have since hit the market — or become reality TV shows, like "Survivorman" and "Man Vs. Wild" — including Neil Strauss' "Emergency," a funky stunt book wherein the intrepid city-boy author goes out and learns, well, exactly what I discuss below: how to kill stuff, live off the grid, eschew modern conveniences, live a hardcore existence in an age of climate change and food riots and Peak Oil and roving bands of zombie Republicans seeking the cold, moldy flesh of their own failed ideology to nibble on like rancid venison. How paranoid do you want to be? How much fear do you want to swallow? Can you cook snake meat? Come on over. —mm

I cannot yet skin a deer

07/15/2005

Rare is the opportunity to use authentic, down 'n' dirty rural survival skills in the city. It's true.

You don't need to know, for example, how to skin a deer, or pickle your own asparagus, or nurture an understanding of which kind of deadwood is best for cookin' pig snouts over the fire pit, or how to shingle your roof with rocks and clay, or how to dig really large holes in the backyard for long-term storage of winter wheat and dead chickens and hoary relatives.

City-bred skills and intuitions are, to be sure, unique. But there will apparently be very little call, after the apocalypse rains down, for knowledge of which seat in the café gets the best Wi-Fi signal or where to find the finest burrito after midnight in the Mission when you are post-coitally blissed and in need of refueling. What to do with all this knowledge of where to get the most amazing cheap dim sum, how much the large bottle of Astroglide costs at the local Good Vibrations, or which tiny parking spaces in my girlfriend's neighborhood I can sneak into for emergency booty calls without her uptight neighbors calling Bob's Towing?

This all comes to mind as I realize, with increasing sense of dread and fatalistic ennui, that if any of the dire prognostications for the world soon comes to pass, if the oil crisis strikes as violently as predicted and/or if the eviscerated U.S. economy spirals us into a new and violent Great Depression 2.0 and/or if the megachurch crowd does indeed succeed in bringing the wrath of an angry, homophobic God down upon the gay-lovin' urban masses, I might not be as well prepared as I'd like.

I am not at all ready for the big return to the agrarian life, as predicted by the most dire Peak Oil prognosticators. I am not at all ready to have the devastated cities plowed under, so that we may plant crops in the ravaged landscape in a desperate attempt to survive the onslaught of a world without home pizza delivery, drive-thru dry cleaning, immediate access to Whole Foods, not to mention the flesh of nearly any animal I wish to have FedExed to me within 24 hours in pretty decorated tins. Mmm, prosciutto.

I have no immediate escape plan. I do not have land nearby, in the woods, protected by razor wire and laser fencing and large angry dogs. I do not have some place that has enormous underground tanks of propane and oil and grains and canned tomatoes and frozen elk meat and mountains of small-gauge ammunition and stores of camouflage underwear.

I do not know how to dig a water well. I do not know how to install a septic pump. I know not the best month in which to plant potatoes and corn and peas and opium poppies. I cannot knit blankets or sweaters, much less some nice handmade cozies to protect my Pyrex-glass dildo collection.

I currently own no power tools, save for a single small Makita rechargeable drill which I use, of course, not for building a family shelter out of rusty car hoods and not for remodeling my nonexistent garage so it can support a family of 10 and not for cobbling together a chicken coop from scrap wood and baling wire and mesh, but rather, for hanging bitchin' shelving cubes from CB2.

Oh, make no mistake, the city offers its own dangers and there are plenty of urban survival skills mandatory for navigating the urban jungle, such as learning how to deftly avoid eye contact with ranting homeless people and how to appear tough and muscular when you walk by those small gangs of slouchy angry hooded dudes who look at you like you're the fish and they're the dynamite.

I know how to calmly pray for a parking space a mile before arrival, which sushi joint has the freshest uni, which coffee shop makes the finest soy mocha. I know when Macy's designer stuff goes on double-markdown and who you have to know to get wholesale designer furniture and which yoga teacher offers up the best *kirtan*, and how to get a large leather chair up two flights of narrow Victorian stairs and the best place to have sex in Golden Gate Park.

But alas, this is not nearly enough. I know this now.

I am not trained. This much must be admitted: When it comes to Armageddon prep, the red states have us city folk beat. Sure, cities are the cultural and social and economic engines of the nation; sure we have all the Ph.D.s and all the artistic talents and all the book-learnin' and progressive ideas and cool European cars and the good wine and the better sex and the polysyllabic words. Big deal.

But when the economy collapses and the End is Nigh, well, most of us shall fall by the roadside, begging for scraps from the evangelical Idaho potato farmer in the beat-up pickup with the NRA bumper sticker, and he shall chortle and spit tobacco through his nine teeth and turn up the James Dobson Christian Family Hour on the AM and drive off toward the mushroom cloud, whistling.

The red states will finally rule the world. They will survive. They know how. They can eat squirrel brains. They can pickle things, including various animal parts. They have been known to marry each other. They can subsist on bad beer and cow pies and stuff they find growing in the tailpipes of old farm equipment. They know how to perform home surgery using only a rusty butter knife and bathroom caulk. They eat mice.

But then again, should this all come to pass, well, maybe I will no longer care.

Maybe then it will finally be time to throw in the karmic towel, drink the special Kool-Aid, and let the meek inherit the Earth while the rest of us go to the stars. After all, while I'd actually love to learn to work an organic farm or build a cabin from scratch or learn to distinguish species of trees by examining their leaves and then having sex under their branches, it's just not much fun anymore when we're all out of music and wine and coffee and the entire nation becomes, well, Oklahoma. I mean, what kind of joy is that? And where will I park my Audi?

This is the kind of column where I can be accused of being too polarizing, too oversimplified in my semi-clever conclusions, not taking into sufficient account all the variegated life paths of the millions of humans, neglecting to appreciate the subtleties and myriad nuanced needs of the confused and tormented and beaten-down human animal. It might be true. Fact is, I know plenty of wonderful people who take prescription meds and behavioral modifiers who are helped tremendously by them.

But then again, I very much stand by the central idea here. We are far too detached from Source. We are far too numb to root causes and deep health and how much power we actually have to move energy around and affect change in ourselves. Which is, I know, terribly easy to say, but very, very challenging to realize. —mm

What are you, on drugs?

12/08/2004

The odds are very good that you are on drugs.

Right now. This minute. As I type this and as you read this and as empires crumble and as this mad, bewildered world spins in its frantically careening orbit, there's a nearly 50/50 chance that some sort of devious, synthetic chemical manufactured by some massive corporation is coursing through your bloodstream and humping your brain stem and molesting your karma and kicking the crap out of your libido and chattering the teeth of your very bones.

Maybe it's regulating your blood pressure. Maybe it's keeping your cholesterol in check. Maybe it's helping you sleep. Maybe it's helping you wake the hell up. Maybe it's opening your bronchial tubes. Maybe it's brightening your terminally bleak outlook.

Maybe it's adjusting your hormone levels or controlling your urge to

weep every minute or relaxing the blood vessels in your penis or cranking the serotonin to your brain or pumping carefully measured slugs of alprazolam or fluoxetine or sertraline or atorvastatin or esomeprazole or buspirone or venlafaxine or any number of substances with Latin-rooted jawbreaker names through your flesh in a bizarre dance of miraculous vaguely disturbing death-defying scientific wonder.

Forty-four percent of all Americans. That's the latest number.[1] Almost half us are popping at least one prescription drug and fully one in six are popping three or more, and the numbers are only increasing, and this of course doesn't count alcohol or cigarettes or bad porn and it doesn't count the mad megadoses of jingoistic flag-waving God-slappin' *fear* — which is, as evidenced by the last election, a stupendously popular FDA-approved drug in its own right. But that's another column.

Have a teenager? She's probably on drugs, too. One in four of all teens are, according to new research. And we ain't talking pot or ecstasy or meth, cheap cocaine or Bud Light or any of those oh-my-God-not-my-baby devil drugs that are so demonized by the government, but that by and large are no more (and are often far less) toxic and addictive and caustic than any of your average 8-buck-a-pop silver-bullet chemical bombs shot forth from the likes of Eli Lilly and Glaxo and Pfizer, et al. Ahh, irony. It's the American way.

All of which means one of two things: either it's the goddamn finest time in history to be an American, living as we are in the age of incredible technology, miracle medicines, longer life expectancies, $5 coffee drinks and a synthetic chemical to match any sort of ache or pain or lump or rash or spiritual crisis you might be facing.

Or it's the absolute *worst*, what with so many of us heavily drugged and over half of us obese and IQs dropping like stones and our overall quality of life deteriorating right under our noses and shockingly huge numbers of us actually finding Lindsay Lohan remotely interesting. Which perspective is right for you? Ask your doctor.

It's become so you can't crack a joke about Prozac or Xanax at a party without at least three or four faces suddenly going still and unsmiling and you're like, whoops, as you suddenly realize that you can, as you walk the streets of this fine and heavily narcotized nation, imagine at least one very expensive drug pumping through the bodies of every other person you pass. It's a bit like knowing their secret fetish or favoritest dream or on which nether part they want to get a tattoo. Except totally different.

And you might say, well, so what? So what if pharmaceuticals help us cope, relieve the pressure, help us survive this ugly and irritating world?

Better living through chemistry, baby, so long as you don't mind the numbness and the glazed eyeballs and the heart palpitations and the lack of true feeling in your fingertips and the nightmares about snakes. Right?

So long as you don't mind the slightly nauseating sense that you have lost some sort of vital and perhaps irreplaceable link to the animal world and the luminous organic planet. But, as Dubya says, who the hell cares about that crap when you got baseball and war and apple pie?

Because here's the nasty truth: it's a highly toxic world right now, and we seem to have set it up so it's only getting worse, darker, more poisonous. Maybe all our meds just help us maintain some sort of jittery and numbed balance, some sort of sad equilibrium.

But let's be fair. It must be said right here that many of these drugs indeed help an enormous number of people and restore lives and bring light where only darkness once reigned and far be it from me to begrudge anyone his or her chemical-assisted reprieve from genuine suffering.

But here's the thing: it's still only a fraction. Only a small number of people whose doctors prescribe these meds like candy actually *need* them, and as for the rest there are these things called lifestyle change and dietary change and perspective change and even spiritual shift that can affect the overall health of your life like a goddamn miracle, like a thousand drugs combined, changes that millions simply refuse to undertake because, well, it's just too damn hard.

We don't want to know. We don't want to understand deeper, complex natural systems. We want pills, not awareness. We want magic bullets, not true magic. We want to eat what we want and exercise not at all and pay no attention to our bodies and our quality of life and expect it all to work sufficiently well until we die at 90 and they forklift us into our refrigerator-size coffins. After all, we're Americans. We're not *supposed* to care.

Nevertheless, it bears repeating: maybe what's lacking most in this society is a true and thoughtful and nuanced connection to and understanding of the natural systems, soil and sunlight and sustainability, lunar rhythms and whole food and maybe knowing where the hell your water really comes from. You think?

Because the truth is, it's not all that hard to get informed. It's not all that hard to affect serious change in your life and eat better and kiss better and require less chemical crap in your bloodstream and slowly but surely reduce the need for medication in your life. It is far from impossible to clear out the toxins and flush the BushCo-endorsed crap and defy the demonic corporate pharmaceutical PR and reevaluate just how you tread this life. They just want you to think it is.

1 http://domai.notlong.com

From: Peter H <XXX@sbcglobal.net>
To: mmorford@sfgate.com
Subject: Your article 9/27
Date: Wed, 27 Sep 2006 16:41:06 -0700

Mr. Morford - this article is horrible trash. It doesn't even belong in the kitty box. You, sir, are a cheap shot artist of the first degree. Your article is poorly written, poorly-structured, it has no meaning other to be a hit job on our president who cannot fight back. You should be on your knees daily, thanking the Good Lord that this country has a fine man like George W. Bush as president. With gutter trash like you around, his job is far more difficult than it should be. My contempt for you knows no bounds.

Peter H
Menlo Park

From: JXXXXX@aol.com
Date: Fri, 13 Oct 2006 17:47:49 EDT
Subject: No substance, no peace!!
To: mmorford@sfgate.com
MIME-Version: 1.0
X-Spam-Flag: NO

Dear Morford:

Your screed reveals you to be a blithering idiot without substance. All you do is hurl accusations. I detected absolutely no rational basis to change any of my opinions about taxes, spending, regulation, etc. And regarding homosexuality, where is the explanation of why I'm wrong for thinking that people who deliberately stick their penises in other people's butts, or vice versa, deserve to get the fatal diseases we've all been warned about?

From: "Ruth S" <raXXX@comcast.net>
To: <mmorford@sfgate.com>
Subject: you lying Despeciable Bastard!
Date: Mon, 6 Nov 2006 07:09:50 -0800
MIME-Version: 1.0

That is my thoughts for you! So you live in San Francisco and you believe in all the rights thereof? What are you going to so when radical Islam lands in SF? Are you going to protect the gays who will be there first target? Will you protest the closing of all establishments which serve liquor? Tell me sir, just exactly how are you going to deal with that kind of hatred or are you just plain ignorant?

Ruth S, Plymouth Ca. P.S.. You don't think they are coming, well I suggest you record some Arabic TV shows and have them translated for you!

From: "Spivey, R" <XXX@XXX.com>
To: mmorford@sfgate.com
X-OriginalArrivalTime: 30 May 2006 18:45:20.0425 (UTC)
FILETIME=[33C53990:01C68419]

What in the hell are you gum beating about.. I have read several of your articles.. And I must say.. "What the the fuck are you babbling about.. You make about as much sense as a Nun on the pill. My advice, get a real fucking job> Come down off that "Almighty Cloud you are perched on and open your eyes to the real world. You know?? The one people really live in.

From: "Harry E" <XXX@netzero.com>
To: <mmorford@sfgate.com>
Subject: Rejoice, The Hummer Is Dead
Date: Wed, 5 Sep 2007 06:39:07 -0400
MIME-Version: 1.0

I just thought you should know that you stand for everything that is wrong in this country.

Unfortunately, you have a large communist newspaper to share your far left views in. I'm sure you manage to influence other "save the world lemmings" such as yourself but not people who discard emotion, propaganda and lies for fact and reason. Ultimately we will win the war (politically) for the hearts and minds of people. You and other communists think places like Russia, China, North Korea and Cuba are great political systems to emulate but the people in those countries are leaving every chance they get, (if they can) One final thought for you. I could recycle bottles and other things where I live but most of the time I choose not to. In fact, I occasionally go out of my way to throw an extra one away to compensate for people like you who believe it should be mandatory. I would bet you would be in favor of a monetary fine to enforce recycling if you could make it happen. I have to get ready for work now but first I need to put some trash at the curb for pickup.

Have a nice day comrade (:

I bet you're the kind of moron who thinks its cool that the pathetic people who have healthy and fertile sexual organs get their healthy sex organs mutilated by doctors to conform to the sickness of their mind.

How do you feel about all those people who got mutilated because of your perverted political beliefs?

James

From: XXX@aol.com
Date: Fri, 29 Sep 2006 11:36:45 EDT
Subject: No way-
To: mmorford@sfgate.com
MIME-Version: 1.0
X-Spam-Flag: NO

There's no way you fruits, fairies, fags and other liberals are ever going to outbreed Christians.

All life comes from God, no matter what kind of life. It was God who created what is now known as HIV. It was designed primarily by the Almighty to punish queers, but it has been useful in eliminating fornicators, at the expense of some innocent [African] children. It's not a perfect world. "Progressives" murder unborn children "legally" so some born children suffer also.

You still have time to repent, but time is running out for you. God loves you, in spite of your demon-oppressed ego.

.

I was pleased enough with how this column came out that I had a bit of inspiration: Wouldn't it be great if I could build a quick website — full, dedicated URL and all — for the fictional company I'm suggesting here, and actually write up a real-sounding business page for it? To be honest, I was hoping this piece would catch fire a bit, that it might get linked from the high-traffic aggregate sites like Fark and Digg and so on — which, when it happens, gives my column an enormous boost in traffic and looks good to my ego. What can I say? I'm an online columnist. My work often lives and dies by page views.

So I did it. I bought the domain name, whipped up a very fast page/site, and hosted it as a subdomain off of markmorford.com. Grand result? Mixed, at best. It didn't catch fire like I'd hoped, but it did do very good numbers and those who did get the joke seemed to enjoy it. And despite all the extra work and money, it was fun to test my (limited) tech skillset.

Geekamania.com is still out there. You can go see it, right now. And yes, I do think there's a hint of a viable business idea in there, somewhere. Can you find it? Can you tell me what the hell it is? Shall we start a company? —mm

I Twitter for you!

02/18/09

Are you a Net neophyte? Very, very late bloomer? Profoundly paranoid about the totally CIA-monitored Interweb?

Do you still prefer to get your news and information from disposable printed matter made from poor ol' trees because you believe all high-tech gizmos are a total soul-sucking waste of time except maybe for your George Foreman grill and the old FM radio in the truck? Read on, friend.

Speaking of friends, do you have any? Do you have *enough*? How do you know? Are you sick of hearing about the "social networking" phenomenon, all those Web 2.0 companies with geeky-sounding names like Facebook and MySpace and Twitter and Tumblr and LookSpaceBook-FeedPlaceWad, sites where 'friends' flock together like flies to cow eyelids and everyone's young and cute and funny and jacked-in to the cultural zeitgeist, but you have no idea what it all means or why you're supposed to care because you have, you know, a *real life*, yet you still have this nagging feeling that a potentially rich, exciting aspect of the culture is passing you by like an ice cream truck in summer?

Worry no longer, dear one. Salvation is at hand.

Allow me introduce you to my groundbreaking new company, Geeka-mania.com. I created it to meet the needs of smart but also slightly bewildered, overwhelmed, angry, out-of-touch, nervous or otherwise increasingly irrelevant people, just like you!

The concept is very simple. Who needs Facebook and MySpace and the like? You do! But who the hell has time for such pathetic digital hoo-ha nonsense when there's dishes to be washed and gardening to be done and kids to be driven around and thorny little roses to be stopped at and smelled? No one!

That's where Geekamania comes in. Let us do the annoying but necessary-evil social networking crapola for you! For a small monthly fee, we'll keep you connected and relevant, even vaguely respectable/marginally noticeable to the jaded, spiteful, easily distracted ADHD youth of today, whether you think you want to be or not. It couldn't be easier!

Here's how it works: After we receive your credit card info, you fill out a small mountain of lengthy, deeply personal, oddly phrased questionnaires about, well, every aspect of your life. Personal tastes, travel experiences, sexual hang-ups, irrational fears, childhood traumas, recent car troubles, gross bodily functions, marriage-destroying sports obsessions, weight issues, sexual fantasies about Obama, nightmares and medications and lingering, acidic resentments over old boyfriends, along with your seething hatred of rude cell phone users and people who eat stinky tuna on the bus.

And don't forget the photos! We want them all: you on a rope swing, you scarfing pizza with 10 very pale people from your softball team, you looking all sullen and resentful at your friend's wedding, you with horrible red-eye, a blurry shot of your toes (artsy!), you and your best bro posing with Tera Patrick at the AVN Awards and grinning like monkeys, the works.

Don't forget to include lots of snapshots of your cats, your kids, your golfing buddies, your prom, that one shot of you from the office Christmas party where Darren from Accounting has his arm draped around you and is clearly pawing at your breast and no one can believe you're actually dating that alcoholic loser.

We take it from there. We design, set up and maintain as many hip social networking pages as you want, spinning off the information you provided but also totally rearranging it and making it up at will, all to make you sound exactly as cute/clever/sexy/boring/lonely/unstable (you choose) as you've always dreamed. You don't have to do a thing!

How do you know it's working? That's easy. We send you, every month, a breakdown of all the activity on your various sites. The best messages, meanest postings, weirdo comments, the most embarrassing photos of your supposedly hot-looking connections — and, most importantly, the names and personal stats of all the new "friends" we've earned for you, all broken down into nice pie charts and bar graphs and color-coded thingamabobs. Just like USA Today, only even *less* useful.

What should you do with all this amazing information? How the hell should we know? Viva la revolución!

Here's just a few of the recent Facebook/Twitter status updates we created for our satisfied customers:

"Susan is eating banana pancakes and watching the rain."

"Tom is slamming some cold beerz and organizing a fantasy football league instead of feeding the baby. Don't tell wifey!"

"Erin just noticed a boo-boo in her knitting and now has to undo four hours of work. Grr!"

"Jen got up at 7am to do laundry only to find the machine is busted and then she broke a nail hitting it with her hand. God my life sukks!!"

"Tina is STILL looking for love but finding it in all the wrong places LOL!!!"

"Jay is eating Thai food with Morgan and watching a 'Mad Men' mara-

thon. So gud!"

"LouAnn is sad."

It's just that simple.

By employing a small army of 5,024 recently laid-off journalists from all major newspapers around the nation, we guarantee basic grammatical accuracy, reasonably clever innuendo, occasional smart-alecky tones and sporadic fact-checking, all wrapped in a professional ability to cull appealing factoids from your otherwise dreary life, just so random people you barely know or haven't seen/cared about in 10 years might envy your every waking moment. How cool is that?

Still not convinced? Still claim you really don't care about any of this Web 2.0 crap because you have a "real" life to lead? That's OK. We know you're lying.

Of course you care. Look, all the kids are doing it. Hell, even old folks and parents are on Facebook these days, not to mention all your co-workers and former lovers, and didn't I just see a grainy cell phone pic of some surfer dude sucking a Jell-O shot from your ex-wife's thigh at the Hard Rock in Cabo? Dude, it was *totally* her. I just saw it in my Facebook news feed. Whoa.

Look, we know how it is. Most days, it's all you can do to walk upright and shove food in your mouth and into the gaping maws of your various demons, much less bother with keeping up with the insufferable digital revolution.

Let us take the anxiety out of keeping you remotely relevant to the culture before you die all alone in a garage somewhere. Let us give you the vibrant, multifaceted life you always wanted but never had the time to invent, spell-check, cross-post, drunkenly update and freak out over for yourself.

Remember our slogan: "Geekamania: Because you don't have time for this shit."

And now, The Daring Spectacle presents...

Mullet Haiku

Pregnant at the fair
Coors Light's off limits for me
Honey, where's my smokes?

Was slightly tempted, as I wrote this one, to veer off into a righteous mini-digression about what I mention only in passing: the horrific plague of bad tattoos in the modern world, how we must start some sort of passionate, awareness-raising movement regarding the need for more exceptional, high-quality ink and real artistry, as opposed to all those lopsided, garish, Art School 101 illustrations. We must educate the masses that the crap you see on the wall of the tattoo shop is not what you're supposed to choose from, that you should take a lot of time and research the best artists in the country and really understand what it is you're doing, and absolutely, positively get a custom design, no matter what. I know. Sorta preachy. I don't care. I revere the female sacrum too much to see it decorated so poorly. —mm

Unmarried tattooed heathens, ho!

10/25/2006

America is dead.

No really, it is. And it's not just because we've lost habeas corpus, a bedrock protective law and a cornerstone of American freedom, to the rabid, stupid dogs of neoconservative fearmongering. That merely feels like a weird horror movie, the leatherfaced guy with the chain saw hacking off the head of the sexy college girl and laughing maniacally.

The real problem is, of course, tattoos. And piercings. And also: single people who defy the institution of marriage and choose to live together in sin. And *then* get tattoos. Haven't you heard?

Oh, the breakdown, the rending and tearing of the social fabric of American life. Just look. Look at these headlines, blaring and moaning and scaring the children. Here's the first one: "For the first time in America's pubescent history, single-parent households and unmarried couples outnumber marrieds." And the Christian right went, "Nooooo! "

Yes. Despite the wailings of the fundamentalists and the stomping of little conservative feet and in part thanks to the hateful Defense of Marriage Act preventing gays from legalizing their love, traditional marriage is no longer the dominant setup in the American home. The foremost model now: single people shacking up. Living together. Having sex and buying groceries and hogging the covers and fighting about who didn't do the goddamn dishes and then not having sex anymore.

And maybe not even getting married at all. *Ever.* Can you feel the horror?

According to the last census, there are now 14 million single-mom households in the United States. There are five million single-dad house-

holds. And there are over 37 million unmarried gay or hetero couples living together in house-holds looked upon by the Religious Right in America as wrongheaded heathen sinful ignorance of God. Grand total: about 50.2 percent, versus 49.8 percent for the marrieds. Ahh, ain't it refreshing?

Another terrifying headline sure to pinch the nipples of righteous morality: Tattoos and piercings are slipping into mainstream dress codes. This terrifying (and also shockingly obvious) little story is actually accompanied by a photo of an otherwise handsome and intelligent young woman who apparently has multiple master's degrees and who works in a university library in Kentucky.

But just look closer. Look at her arms. Why, they're simply *covered* in tattoos, all the way down to her wrists. "Full sleeves," they're called, in godless pervert lingo and on weirdly fascinating shows like "LA Ink" and "Inked" where thick, monosyllabic dudes and dudettes ink large skulls and dragons and images of dead children into the arms of random passersby.

Reports now say over half of all kids in their 20s now have some sort of tattoo or piercing, with no end in sight. And you might say, whelp, that explains why I see so many sacrum tattoos in my yoga class. Or maybe you're a bit older and you say: Oh those silly, foolish kids. Nothing like a full-sleeve tattoo to screw you out of a future gig as, say, CEO of Hewlett-Packard. Right?

Well, no. It's a simple law of supply and demand. If the majority of youth now sport large-scale ink and metal, and if some of these youth are actually deeply intelligent and pedigreed and ambitious, well, the ever-needful job market will eventually have to shrug and let 'em in.

Hell, the two-headed Google billionaires are what, 19 years old? And the shell-shocked Facebook founder looks like he should still be making fries at Hot Dog on a Stick. How far are we, really, from a millionaire CEO who has a labret and a koi fish snaking down his triceps? How long until we get a single-mom senator with an eyebrow pierce and a swarm of hummingbirds inked on her arm?

Translation: Body art: It's not just for hippie rocker punk heroin-addict street urchins anymore. Translation: The demure associate manager sitting in the cube next to you probably has a Sanskrit prayer on her sacrum, which makes her feel totally hot. Translation: The new problem in America is not tattoos. It's *bad* tattoos. Cheesy and lopsided and horrible and blurry and there needs to be some sort of law. But that's another column.

So then. Here you are again, faced with a simple choice (and if you're still reading this column, chances are it ain't gonna be anywhere near the first one).

The first one is to recoil in simpleminded disgust. The first one is to see these changes in the cultural and romantic landscape as surefire signs of the coming apocalypse, to run to the Bible and point to Leviticus where it says "Ye shalt not make any cuttings into the flesh, nor tattoo any marks upon you"[1] and then sneer and say "See? The body is a temple! God does not want nipple rings! Ha! Now where's my secret stash of German fetish porn?" And etc.

Viewpoint number two says all this experimentation and all this opening into new possibility and all this flaunting of convention and rulemongering and all this redefinition of "family" and "flesh" hopefully, maybe, possibly heralds something just a little, I don't know what. Innovative? Revolutionary? Evolutionary?

Kids are playing with flesh. Kids are playing with notions of sexuality and couplehood and child rearing. Conservative adults are nervous. Confused. This is usually a good sign. This is as it should be. The general rule holds true, now and forever: When you upset the conservative right,[2] when you piss off those kinds of uptight, myopic, eternally confused people, you know you're onto something good.

1 http://vaeji.notlong.com
2 http://feiree.notlong.com

Still waiting. Still no real meltdown, no hints of Armageddon, not even a single horrifying report of a three-headed demon child borne to a Wiccan transvestite polyamorist, birthed in a river of blood and glitter and nice sandalwood incense, proclaiming death to all happy, missionary-position, hetero Christian couples everywhere, as he reveals himself to be a fey but surprisingly well-groomed hellspawn creature of pure evil and fitted pima cotton T-shirts, who was finally able to enter our dimension by way of hole in a slice of wedding cake at Ken and Carl's wedding up in Napa. Any day now, I guess. —mm

Where is my gay apocalypse?

03/05/2004

I have been waiting patiently.

I have been staring with great anticipation out the window of my flat here in the heart of San Francisco, sighing heavily, waiting for the riots and the plagues and the screaming monkeys and the blistering rain of inescapable hellfire. I have my camera all ready and everything.

There has been nothing. I see only some lovely trees and a stunning blue sky and my neighbor walking by with her pair of matching chow chows as a pained-looking woman struggles to parallel park her SUV. Same old, same old.

And this is San Francisco, gay-marriage HQ, Sodom-and-Gomorrah-ville, debauchery central. We are supposed to be careening off the nice, safe road of social acceptability right now, welcoming chaos, exploding into a fiery hellmist of our own sick godless depravity and dropping off the disgusted planet any minute now.

Where is my raging apocalypse? This is what I want to know. Where is the social meltdown? The moral depravity? I was promised an apocalypse, dammit. What am I supposed to do with all these tubs of margarine and confetti and kazoos?

There have been more than 3,500 gay-marriage ceremonies in San Francisco so far. Hundreds more are just now kicking up a storm in Oregon and in beautifully rebellious little burgs around New York state. And, yet, nothing. No chaos. No reign of terror. Not even a lousy heat wave. Sigh.

Some homosexual couples have been married for more than three weeks now, living in godless sin as they drive their cars and shop and laugh and cry and go to work and pay their taxes and wonder about their dreams. Lightning has not struck them dead. The Hellmouth has not opened wide its gaping maw, hankering for some of the City's trademark Sourdough o'

Sin. I am dumbfounded.

After all, gay marriage is supposed to ruin the nation, is it not? Induce actual rioting and civil unrest and shirtless anarchy as millions of stupefied citizens pray to a bloody pulverized Mel Gibson-y Jesus for redemption, as they suddenly begin questioning whether ogling the Pottery Barn catalog for more than 10 minutes might mean they're gay.

"It's anarchy," some guy named Rick Forcier, of the Washington state chapter of the Christian Coalition, actually whined.[1] "We seem to have lost the rule of law. It's very frightening when every community decides what laws they will obey." Why, yes, Rick. It's total anarchy. Just look at all the screaming and the bloodshed and the gunfire. Run and hide, Rick. The gay people in love are coming. And they've got tattoos and funny haircuts and want to celebrate their love and be left alone. Hide the children.

This was — and still is — very much the right-wing sentiment. It was almost a guarantee: Same-sex marriage spelled the instantaneous end of all that is good and righteous and edible. Insurrection was imminent, apocalypse nigh. You could see it in their eyes — they could hardly wait.

Hell, even Governator Arnie went on "Meet the Press" recently and proclaimed, semicoherently, that he was actually worried about the riots and deadly mayhem should S.F. continue with its brazen lawlessness.[2] And look. Nothing. Not a peep. Not a single rabid spitting demon to be seen. Unless you count Lynne Cheney. Which you never, ever should.

I believe I have been misled. I was told repeatedly in extra-glowing terminology by multiple raging Bible-quoters that The Good Book expressly forbids gay marriage and gay sex, and to engage in either spells imminent doom and instant social bedlam and there are specific verses all about it.

Is this true? Are there actual verses decrying gay marriage? Are they anything like those *other* Biblical verses, about the rules and regulations surrounding marriage?[3] Real verses. Actual verses. Verses o' sanctimonious fun. Have you seen them?

Like this: "Marriage shall not impede a man's right to take multiple concubines in addition to his wife or wives." (II Sam 5:13; I Kings 11:3; II Chron 11:21).

Or maybe: "A marriage shall be considered valid only if the wife is a virgin. If the wife is not a virgin, she shall be stoned to death."[4] Isn't that cute? Isn't quoting Bible verse fun? Ask your local pastor about that one.

Or how about: "If a married man dies without children, his brother shall marry the widow. If he refuses to marry his brother's widow or deliberately does not give her children, he shall pay a fine of one shoe and be otherwise punished in a manner to be determined by law." (Gen. 38:6-10). [5]Hey, it's right there, in the Bible. So it must be true.

Is it worth showing those verses to the sanctimonious Christian homo-phobes who are protesting outside S.F. City Hall right now, telling the gay couples what depraved hell-bound sinners they all are? Nah. Why spoil their apocalyptic wet dreams? Live and let live, I always say.

(Oh, and while we're at it, God also really hates shrimp. Maybe you didn't know. Shrimp are evil, as are all shrimp eaters. Clams, too. Hey, it's in the Bible. You can look it up.[6] Why the Right is attacking homosexuals in love and not, say, Red Lobster, remains a mystery.)

So, here we are. Approaching a full month after the first of S.F.'s marriage ceremonies, and nothing. The universe is smiling madly. The world is shrugging. Anonymous supporters from all over the nation have sent flowers to hundreds of loving gay and lesbian couples. As of this writing, there is no scathing hellfire. No fanged demons of destruction (Lynne Cheney excepted). No meltdown whatsoever. I would know, right? I mean, wouldn't the power go out, or something?

Maybe it's still to come. Maybe I'm just a little impatient.

Maybe Satan is taking his sweet time to marshal his leather-clad armies, watching as other U.S. cities get in on the gay-marriage act, listening as mayors and governors all chime in their support and say, "What's the big deal?" Maybe Beelzebub is waiting for a big moment so as to really lever-age the coming news flash, the special report, the sudden activation of the Emergency Broadcast System. Something like:

"This just in: Earthquakes rocked the globe today as giant fire-breathing bees of death swarmed the countryside, feasting on fat white heterosexual babies mostly from Texas and Colorado Springs and Ohio and Idaho, as the institution of hetero marriage careened around the mad vortex of space-time like a drunken pinball high on black-tar heroin, just like the Christian Right predicted.

"Horrors bled into the streets, terrorists were spawned by the thousand, presidents openly lied so as to lead a nation into bloody, unwinnable wars, thousands of Catholic priests sexually molested tens of thousands of children over a 50-year period without the slightest punishment, the environment teetered on the brink due to heartless government rollbacks as air quality and water quality and food sources were ravaged in the name of corporate profiteering, the economy crumbled like Jenna Bush after her 10th beer bong as hate and fear and bogus Orange Alerts ruled the land."

Oh wait. That was all *before* the gay-marriage thing. My bad.

1 http://bowoo.notlong.com
2 http://ohloy.notlong.com
3 http://riedoh.notlong.com
4 http://aiyos.notlong.com
5 http://uquajif.notlong.com
6 http://godhatesshrimp.com

I hereby swear to Shiva and Shakti and all that is conscious and ironic and trickster-inspired on this spinning orb, if I ever become famous enough to sit down on national TV to talk about the vagaries of my life, and I have a billion dollars in the bank and a lovely wife and happy family and millions of fans and charitable foundations named after me, I will not sigh and whine and cry on camera and talk about the hard time I had 15 years ago when I only had half a billion and my dad was a tyrant and I was nailing a super- model and fighting hair loss and sampling a few illicit chemicals to make life a little zestier. I mean, good lord.

Thing is, I like Andre Agassi. Still do. Loved watching him work the baseline for all those years. But precious few are the celebs, the icons, the personalities who've run the celebrity gauntlet and still have the intelligence, the integrity, the ironic sense of humor talk openly, laughingly, shruggingly about life and sex and drugs and famousness and all its joys and weirdness and who-the-fuck-cares. (British rap tartlet Lily Allen comes to mind, for one). I celebrate a sort of brazen, grinning, open-throated fearlessness in the face of Puritanical hypocrisy and condemnatory media scrutiny, and I wish more public figures like Andre dared to have it. Hell, it's one of the reasons my column exists in the first place. —mm

Snortin' meth with Andre Agassi

11/11/2009

So for some unknowable reason I'm watching Andre Agassi tell Katie Couric on "60 Minutes" about the time he did crystal meth for a short period of months something like 13 years ago, back when he was hating the living hell out of tennis and his ruthless tennis Nazi of a father and his own unfelt, unwanted, completely unconscious superstar tennis life, and gosh, are we not all just a little bit shocked?

Well, not really. Aside from the deeply surreal hit of "Wait, am I really sitting here watching the mulleted multimillionaire, 'Image is everything' spokesdude of yore tell the tiny, chirpy 'Today' show chick that he snorted some illegal who-the-hell-cares for a few months back in the '90s while wearing a hair weave, and what a strange world this is" — besides all that, I could not help but find myself asking, aloud, right to the TV screen, right to Andre's somber and very, very round face, "Why the hell aren't you laughing?"

"Can you believe this crazy life, Katie? *I did meth*! I had a frosted hair weave! I married Brooke Shields! I made 100 million dollars! I was miser- able for many years, but now I'm not! Life is absurd! What a ride it's been!

It's all so crazy and divine and joyful, I can't even begin to tell you. Ha ha! Who wants wine?"

Of course, he didn't say any of that. Not even close. It was all *so* serious, Agassi terribly solemn about his "dark" period of low-down meth-snortin', Couric all prim, pseudo-naive: "Gosh-golly Andre, just how frequently *did* you snort crystal for less than a year way back when no one really gave a crap anyway?

"And weren't you ashamed? And do you regret admitting it in your new book? And, by the way, I hear meth is a kooky mindfuck of a drug and that having sex on it is completely awesome, and I bet you can tell by looking at me I've never sucked down anything stronger than a wine spritzer and maybe a pot brownie back in college, and OK maybe some blow in the restroom of CBGB with Matt Lauer back in '94, but just once — OK maybe 30 or 40 times, but that's *it*."

It was all just terribly awkward to watch, joyless and strange. Agassi merely talked about how this brief drug experimentation came during a period when he wasn't really caring about much of anything — career, money, health, pre-minivan Brooke Shields, the works. Why not try some stupid drug? Why not dabble and downwardly spiral? Hey, it's the American way.

But it didn't last long. Agassi climbed out of his little pothole within a few months and moved on, and within 18 months he was world champ again. So it's not like he was confessing to any sort of wild, out-of-control, street-urchin addiction. There was no abuse, no secret murder, no sodomy with a farm animal or attempted suicide by huffing oil fumes from a tennis ball machine. Was there one deliciously sordid tale of scoring some midget hookers and a pound of blow with John McEnroe during a lost weekend in Paris after the '96 French Open? Nope.

It got stupider. Couric went on to mention how Martina Navratilova and even Rafael Nadal have said some nasty words about Andre after his meth confession, which is all flavors of nauseating hypocrisy, as if every pro on the circuit isn't full of secrets, as if anyone besides a few five-year-olds still harbor the illusion that pro sports — *all* of them — aren't packed like cans of bad tuna with all manner of human foibles: nightmare parents, abusive childhoods, brain damage by age 20, enough drugs and enhancers, booze and painkillers to make a few snorts of crystal meth seem like baby aspirin. And, of course, no one's liked Martina Navratilova since about 1971.

But no, there will be no such talk, not on "60 Minutes" anyway. We must brood and ponder. We must frown whenever illegal drugs are mentioned because They Are Wrong. We must feign disgust and moral outrage, even as we beg for sordid details and pretend to be shocked at the revelations that our heroes have issues and turmoil and crappy marriages, that they might be just as messed up, just as fearful, just as entranced and confused by the fire and the bliss, the pain and the dark underbelly of this life as everyone else.

Why isn't he laughing? I kept thinking it, over and over, as I watched Agassi's face move from pain to tears to a wan smile. Why isn't this guy sitting there with a giant grin and an easy chuckle, saying, "Oh my God, Katie, can you freakin' believe it? I made it to here! What a ride it's been! My dad was a total jackass, my childhood was nonexistent, my Bon Jovi hair was totally fake!

"And, by the way, let me happily pop everyone's precious tennis bubble and tell you flat-out that tennis pros are just as — if not far, far more — fucked up than anyone else. Dear God, have you seen the Williams sisters lately? *Tick tick tick*, you know?

"And the meth? Big deal. It was fun for a while. Then it wasn't. It was stupid, but it also served a purpose to get me through to here. All part of the path, Katie. Meth ain't so bad. It's just a thing. It's just energy. Not a very *good* energy, but just energy. Not much different than sex, money, celebrity, God. Just energy. It all depends on how you use it, or are used by it, you know? It's all about how you tap into that divine source, the thrust and the battle and the various epiphanies that help get you there.

"Oh, and by the way, Katie? Meth sex is *mindblowing*. Turn off the camera, and I'll tell you all about it."

And then Katie would be laughing, too, and blushing, and nodding, because she *knows*. She would be right there alongside him saying, "Wow, no shit Andre? Meth did that for you? Was it fun? You ever do any with Brooke Shields? Did she get freaky? This life is amazing, isn't it? A cosmic circus sideshow of agony and joy and complaining about your parents? I am so *right there* with you. Let me tell you about news people sometime. I mean, oh my God! Turn off the camera. Let's go get some wine."

There was this sumptuous girl I dated briefly in high school who'll I'll call Shauna (not her real name) who, almost immediately upon graduation, got herself pregnant and married and pretty much completely set in her path. I believe I saw her one final time just before my exodus from Spokane en route to (unsuccessful) rock stardom in Los Angeles, one final, surreal snapshot of my former love: Barely 18 years old, holding a newborn baby, married to some young Air Force dude, living in a tiny, cramped apartment out near the base. I was dumbfounded. But in my snapshot memory, she seemed happy.

Shauna has now found me on Facebook, more than 20 years later. She is still very lovely, impossibly kind, very much a mother and very much a reborn Christian, caught in one of those impossible swoons for Jesus that you can barely speak to because it's just so bright and all-consuming and creamy.

It was during one of our Facebook chats that the idea for this very column came to me (the cording exercises come from a slew of workshops I enjoyed at Psychic Horizons in SF). Shauna's reconnection was welcome, warm and friendly. But it made me wonder about many of the others. What do all these tech-enhanced connections and long-lost re-probings mean? What power and danger might they contain? Hell if I know. But I do know one thing: They can't all be harmless and good. They can't all be Shaunas. —mm

The vampires of Facebook

4/29/09

In psychic workshops, they teach you all about cords.

Cords that bind. Cords that connect. Cords that can invigorate as well as consume, excite your spirit and yet also leech life from your very soul, cords made of simple psychic energy that run like invisible cables straight from your heart and your mind and your various energetic G-spots straight out to the world, and back again.

But most of all, they run straight into other people. Or from them, straight into you. It happens all the time, every day, in every interaction you have, psychic energy instantly passing between individuals as you move through the world and through your thoughts and memories and dreams, energy cords established even over long distances, phone calls, handshakes, gropings, co-ed showers, not to mention fantasies, hatreds, unwanted desires and just about everything in between. It's just what we do.

Usually the cords last only a short time before fading away, a constant swarm of insta-circuits made and broken, effortless and normal — just the everyday thrum of life.

But not always. Energy cords are also potent, dangerous motherfuckers. They can last years, lifetimes, reappear like a virus, inflict nefarious harm and cause all sorts of unpleasant melodrama, illness and upheaval in your equilibrium. Obsessions, intense loves, heartbreaks, resentments, someone's awful day or their own needy, I'm-a-victim energy can attach itself like a vampire onto the neck of your good mood and suddenly you'll feel like you just got run over by a bus made of thumbtacks and snail spit, and you have no idea why. You know that feeling? Of course you do.

Let us not go too far. I am not here to convince you such cords exist. I am not quite drunk enough for that. Really, it doesn't matter if you believe in them or not because, like air, like black socks with sandals, like the proper deification of Obama, it just is. They just are. Let's just go with it.

But it does lead, quite naturally, to that most wonderful and disturbing of cord-slinging, energy-wringing e-creations, known as Facebook.

From an energy perspective, Facebook is a goddamn cord-makin' wonderland, a sort of psychic Grand Central, the place where psychic energy goes to jack itself back into the mainframe. It's tens of millions of people peeking and poking and peering into the lives of those they know, those they want to know, those they like or love or hate or begrudge or secretly want to peel the pants from and lick like a popsicle in summer.

It's a notion that struck me as I realized that nearly everyone who's ever played a reasonably significant role in my life, both past and present, has since found and reconnected with me, initially via email through the digital reach of this very column over the years, but now far more actively and vividly through my Facebook profile (or, to a lesser extent, my Twitter feed). It's sort of stunning, really.

Old girlfriends, lost loves, long-forgotten friends, high school sweethearts, band mates, roommates, old nemeses, lots of former cheerleaders turned born-again Christian megamoms, and everything in between. All those old connections, those lives and chapters and periods of my life I thought I'd left behind so cleanly, so decisively, way back when? Here they all are again, like a living scrapbook, constantly renewing and updating itself. What a thing.

It is, on one hand, a marvelous and magical invention. It is often fascinating and deeply touching to dip into those worlds, those lives again, a true gift to see what became of all those people, their joys and paths and prison sentences and odd tastes in haircuts and copious offspring (note to self: if I ever have children, do not use my child's photo as my own personal profile pic. It's just creepy).

But I also wonder: Do we fully understand just how powerful this tool is, and how strange? Do we know what we're doing on a basic energetic level, with all this connecting and reconnecting, what sort of cords and swords and potential vampiric firestorms of energy we invite in when we invite in all those old (and new) faces and beings and memories? I do not think we do. I do not think we are all that prepared.

Of course, if you care in the slightest about any of this — or even if you don't — there's still a very obvious solution. You simply opt out, turn it all off, ignore Facebook and its ilk entirely and refuse to create an e-profile or list your email address anywhere and just close your eyes tight and pretend it's not happening as the modern culture moves on without you. Easy enough.

But not for long. Generation Tweet will comprehend no such option. For them, social networking is already automatic and inborn and expected in every facet of modern life. To be under 30 right now and not to have multiple social accounts and active e-profiles is to be weird and outcast and isolated. It's as foreign an idea for Generation Tweet as it would be for those of us hovering around Gen X to be without, say, Costco and Pearl Jam and $5 coffee drinks. It's just who they are.

There is another vital tool they teach in energy workshops: protection. Grounding. How to hold your own space, how to clean yourself out, flush negative energy, make sure you're aware of the swarms of dark and parasitic crap floating about your everyday world.

They teach you not only about the existence of cords and how recognize them when they latch onto you or when someone's trying to stab into your space and drag you down, but even more importantly, how to sever, how to cut the cords you no longer need and that no longer serve — which, as it turns out, is often pretty much all of them.

Is there a Facebook tool for that yet, some sort of nifty, portable vampire alert/psychic cord-cutting device to keep yourself clear and open and cord-free, well-protected amid the wonderful/insane swarm of pokes and chats and friend feeds? I do not believe there is. Maybe I'll write an iPhone app.

THE TRUTH IS

GHOSTS

MARRIAGE IS
OUL to SOUL SPIRIT to SPIRIT
OT BODY to BODY.
HAVE YOU NOT BEEN INVITED TO THE WEDDING FEAS

J.C

Does this piece make you want to do drugs? To try mild hallucinogens? Does it make you want to touch Shakti with your toes and feel God through your eyeballs and fuck the Dog Star with your id, as you slowly rock back and forth and smile hugely then begin quietly laughing, long and slow and deep, all the way down to your bones, not stopping for ten days straight until you pass out from sheer euphoric metaconsciousness and a deep craving for an all-over oil rubdown and a giant platter of salty sweet-potato fries? It does? I am so doing my job right. —mm

God is in the magic mushrooms

8/04/2006

Hide the children. Pour some absinthe, fluff the pillows, take off your pants. It is time.

Because now we know: Getting nicely and wholly high on illegal but completely natural hallucinogenic drugs might, just might open some sort of profound psychological doorway or serve as some sort of giddy, terrifying rocket ride to higher state of consciousness, happiness, a sense of inner peace and love and perspective and a big, fat lick from the divine.

It's true. There's even a swell new study from Johns Hopkins University[1] that officially suggests what shamans and gurus and botany Ph.D.s and alt-spirituality types have known since the dawn of time and Jimi Hendrix's consciousness: That psilocybin, the all-natural chemical found in certain strains of wild mushrooms, induces a surprisingly large percentage of users to experience a profound — and in some cases, largely permanent — revolution in their spiritual attitudes and perspectives.

Not only that, but the stuff reportedly made a majority of testers feel so much more compassionate, open-hearted, connected to and awestruck by the world and the universe and God that it ranks right up there with the most profound and unfathomable experiences of their lives. I know. Stop the presses.

But let us sidestep the face-slapping obviousness. Let us look past the fact that you are meant to react to this study's findings like it's some sort of revelation, like it doesn't merely reinforce roughly 10 thousand years of evidence and modern research and responsible advocacy by everyone from Timothy Leary to Terence McKenna to Huston Smith to the Tibetan Book of the Dead with yet another study to add to the pile in the Science of the No Duh.

You know the type — studies that merely reinforce ageless common sense, that simply reiterate something that's been understood for eons.

There have been, for example, recent studies that prove that meditation actually reduces blood pressure (no!) and that MDMA (Ecstasy) is amazing at releasing inhibition and tapping the deeper psyche (shocking!) and that marijuana is roughly a hundred times less harmful than Marlboros and nine vodka tonics and smacking your family around in an alcoholic rage (wow!).

Because one thing painfully redundant studies like this do provide is a nicely clinical framework, a structured context from which to view a long-standing phenomenon. But here's the fascinating part: In the case of something like psilocybin, it's not so much the astounding findings that can make you swoon, it's also, well, the illuminating shortcomings of science itself.

Put another way, they are trying, once again, to measure enlightenment. They are attempting to put a frame around consciousness, cosmic awe, God. And of course, they cannot do it. Or rather, they can only go so far before they hit that point where the sidewalk ends and the world spins off its logical axis and the study's participants cannot help but deliver the death blow every scientist dreads to hear: "You cannot possibly understand."

Witness, won't you, these revelations:

The psilocybin joyriders claimed the experience included such feelings as "a sense of pure awareness and a merging with ultimate reality, a transcendence of time and space, a feeling of sacredness or awe, and deeply felt positive mood like joy, peace and love." What's more, for a majority of users, the experience was "impossible to put into words."

It doesn't stop there. Two months later, 24 of the participants (out of a total of 36) filled out a questionnaire. Two-thirds called their reaction to psilocybin "one of the five top most meaningful experiences of their lives. On another measure, one-third called it the most spiritually significant experience of their lives, with another 40 percent ranking it in the top five. About 80 percent said that because of the psilocybin experience, they still had a sense of well-being or life satisfaction that was raised either 'moderately' or 'very much.'"

You gotta read that again. And then again. Because those statements are just a little astonishing, unlike anything you will read in some FDA report on Prozac from Eli Lily. The most profound experience of their lives? One of the most spiritually significant? Can we get some of this stuff into Dick Cheney's blood pudding? Into the Kool-Aid at the American Family Association? Into Israel and Lebanon?

But this is the amazing thing: Here, again, is hard science running smack into the hot cosmic goo of the mystical. Here, again, is science peering over the edge of understanding and jumping back and saying, "Holy shit." It is yet another reminder that our beautiful sciences have almost zero tools with which to quantify something like "transcendence of time and space" or "a feeling of sacredness and awe." And watching them try is either tremendously enjoyable or just depressing as hell. Or a little of both. It all depends, of course, on how you see it.

Here then, are your choices. Here are the three ways to look at the effects of magic mushrooms on the consciousness of humankind. Which angle you choose depends a great deal on how nimble you allow your mind, your heart, your spirit to be. Or maybe it's just how much wine you've had.

The first way is to simply presume that the lives of the study's participants had obviously been, up to their psilocybin joys, tremendously mediocre. So bland and so limp that something like hallucinogenic mushrooms could not help but be, in contrast, as profound as being licked by angels.

This is a clinical interpretation. The gorgeous experience itself means nothing except to say that normal life is terribly drab and crazy drugs temporarily scramble your brain in occasionally positive and interesting ways, but never the twain shall meet, so oh well let's go back to work.

But you can also take it one step further. You may conclude that the study underscores the harsh fact that we as a species are so divorced from deeper meaning, so detached from the mystical and the divine and the universal in our everyday instant-gratification lives, that it takes something like a powerful hallucinogen to show us just how meek and limited and far from merging with God we still very much are. This is the pessimistic view. And it is, by every estimate, a very primitive and sour place to be.

Ah, but then there's the third way. This is to suggest that it's exactly the other way around, that perhaps at least some of us are, as Leary and his cosmic cohorts have suggested for decades, mere inches from the celestial doorway, already on the precipice of realizing that we are, in fact, the divine we so desperately seek. Problem is, we can't see the edge through the tremendous fog of consumerism and conservatism and quasi-religious muck.

But even so, every now and then we manage to take a tiny, unconscious, clumsy step ever closer to the edge, stumbling toward ecstasy without really understanding that we're doing so. And ultimately, sly entheogens like psilocybin are merely nature's way of clearing the fog for a moment, of letting us know just how close we are by smacking us upside the scientific head and tying our cosmic shoelaces together. And doesn't that sound like a fascinating way to spend the weekend?

1 http://aedex.notlong.com

Re-reading this, one of the more recent columns in the book, it would appear that, after all these years and after so much evolution and refinement of my writing style, shifts in my attitude and perspective, and a general softening around/retraction of my willingness to judge too harshly, it would appear my white-hot disgust for food conglomerate malfeasance and advertising dishonesty has not abated in the slightest. In fact, the opposite appears to be true. I think I'm OK with that. —mm

New Coke mini: Now with 36% less death!

10/23/2009

Attention, reluctantly health-conscious consumer who doesn't *really* want to change his/her ways or be told what to do by any goddamn doctor, government agency or do-gooder Michael Pollan-type health nut, but feels he/she must do, you know, *something*, because it's becoming more difficult to breathe, staircases are increasingly hateful and the doctor *did* say something about early-onset arthritis and bone degeneration and

potential colorectal cancer and no one wants that, I guess!

We here at the Coca-Cola Company feel your pain. Or rather, we don't, actually, but we like to *say* we do in marketing copy, because it makes us sound beneficent and honest, like a good corporate citizen, when in fact we're all about figuring out sinister ways to keep you wildly addicted to as many of our products for as long as humanly possible — which, if you drink enough of them, won't be that long at all.

Here is our question: Have you been trying, to little avail, to improve your health, exercise more, maybe lose a tiny bit of weight by reducing your intake of sugary carbonated beverages because you've been told for many, many years and in no uncertain terms that pretty much all sodas, energy drinks, Snapples, et al are completely non-nutritive, ridiculously fattening and not the slightest bit good for you?

Have you seen those touchingly gross anti-soda posters in New York City? Read up on the unbridled nastiness that is high-fructose corn syrup? Have a shred of common sense? Well, we are here to help.

(Note: Not "help" in the traditional, Merriam-Websters definition of the word, as in, help you figure out how to eat healthier and exercise and take care of your body; rather, the *corporate* definition, as in, help give you the *illusion* that we're sensitive to your needs, when in fact we'd simply love it if everyone reading this right now was sucking down a Super Big Gulp of Diet Dr. Pepper and chasing it with a Full Throttle™ Blue Demon. Thank you).

Good news! In a totally unselfish effort to help you slightly reduce — but not eliminate because that would be un-American and possibly Communist — your intake of our sugary poisons, we are hereby introducing a brand-new product.

(Hi again. Once more, it's the corporate definition of "new," meaning not really new at all, and in fact, exactly the same as before. Carry on).

Our "new" product is nicknamed the Coke mini (cute, no?) It's the exact same classic Coca-Cola product you know and love and which even we are forced to admit contributes to global obesity and ill health, but *in a slightly smaller package*. We know, genius, right? It's OK, you can say it. Genius.

Here's what we did: We took our normal, globally adored 12-ounce can and shrank it to 7.5 ounces, put it in a slick new wrapper that will go great with your purse and your tiny dog and your Xanax prescription, and will hereby market it as a new way to enjoy the same old junk food while better "managing your caloric intake."

We like to say it's just enough Coke to satisfy your "sparkily" craving for sugar and caffeine and toxic phosphoric acid, but not enough to kill you within the next two years if you drank, say, 16 cans a day. Well, maybe it is. Try it and see!

Just so you don't think we're trying to pull a fast one by charging you more for less, we've cleverly packaged the new mini cans in packs of *eight*. Isn't that great? Isn't that sneaky? Whereas before you might've bought a normal 6-pack and enjoyed, say, one 12-ounce can in a day, now you'll probably rationalize it somehow, and drink *two* of the smaller cans, because our research shows that's just how the addicted mind works. Again, genius.

Now, some have suggested that the Coke mini is akin to that fantastic, all-time classic marketing lie known as "light" cigarettes, a true stoke of re-branding supergenius that resulted in the deaths of millions, given how light cigs are pretty much exactly as evil as regular cigs, with a slightly different, easily manipulated filter.

It's an excellent comparison, though to be exact, this is more like taking the same Marlboros that have killed millions and snipping a quarter inch off the tip, shoving 'em into a new 30-pack, and calling them, say, "Marlboro Tinies." Voila! Cute new size, same old cancer.

If you actually do the math — which we know you won't — you'll find that you could drink an entire eight-pack of minis, and still be a full 12 ounces short of how much you'd consume if you drank a normal six-pack of 12-ouncers. This means, if you drink two per day, as you're more likely to do, you'll run out even *more* quickly, and will buy even more. See how that works? Christ, we should've thought of this years ago.

Here is our final, more rhetorical question. What are the odds, if you decide to take the bait and buy Coke minis, that you will actually drink *less* Coke or soda overall? What's the likelihood that this product will make even the slightest dent in the raging worldwide obesity pandemic we helped create, not to mention the epidemic of acute ignorance about true health?

Don't worry, we already know the answer. None! Almost no chance whatsoever! In fact, we fully expect Coke minis might actually *increase* our profits overall. Isn't that amazing?

Put it this way: If we thought for one nanosecond that this new marketing ploy would make consumers actually buy less soda overall, well, we'd be morons indeed. And we are definitely not morons. And if we're not the morons, guess who we think is? That's right!

Hey, you're smarter than you look. Care for a Coke?

And now, The Daring Spectacle presents…

Mullet Haiku

Drunk, disorderly
Blood in the bowling alley
Yup, that's my mama

Ah, what terrific fodder Mel heaved forth. I wrote another column on Gibson's sad, record-breaking gore-fest of a movie, focusing on the nightmarish merchandising, wherein you could order — among 100 other heartwarming items — a nice pewter nail necklace, just like the spikes Jesus enjoyed in his palms during his delightful time up on the cross. Isn't that sweet? Reminds me of the late, great Bill Hicks: "A lot of Christians wear crosses around their necks. Do you think when Jesus comes back he ever wants to see a fuckin' cross? It's kind of like going up to Jackie Onassis with a rifle pendant on."

All hideousness aside, I gotta say, for a satirist with a fetish for pinching the nipples of organized religion, Mel made it pretty easy for me. 'Passion' remains of the most disgusting slasher-porn flicks masquerading as a "true" spiritual tale I've ever seen. Then again, I essentially think the same of "Pretty Woman" and "Sleepless in Seattle." So what do I know. —mm

How to gag on "The Passion"

04/16/2004

Perhaps you, like so many across the planet, are more than a bit baffled by the runaway success of "The Passion of the Christ."

Perhaps you, furthermore, are more than slightly disturbed that millions have flocked to this bizarre, ultraviolent, blood-drenched, revisionist flick, and that so many actually believe its story to be absolutely true, and that it is permanently ensconced as one of the top-grossing films of all time and has sold a million books and hundreds of thousands of creepy pewter nail necklaces[1] and you find it all just incredibly warped and disheartening and what-the-hell-is-the-world-coming-to.

You are not alone.

I have seen the movie. I have endured the spectacle so you don't have to. Here, then, are some counterthoughts. Nine random points of spiritual contention and pointy perspective check, a small pile of juicy karmic stones to toss at the next utterly depressing screening of 'The Passion' and perhaps at Mel Gibson's very sad and deeply tormented ego.

Why? Because he deserves it. Why? Because this is not a movie. It is a sad phenomenon. It is a gross spiritual emetic. It is, clearly, a cry for help.

1. It lasted more than a full half hour, the central beating scene, wherein a squad of monosyllabic demon Romans chain Jesus to a stone and feverishly flay him to oozing pulp on one side, then casually flip him over like a veal cutlet and thrash the other side until he is nothing but a puddle of dripping stage blood and

flappy flesh and cavernous moans.

You catch glimpses of this revolting cartoonishness through barely parted fingers and you think, goddammit, there goes half an hour of my vital life force that I will require much sex and vodka and Buddhism to recover. And you realize, with a sort of perfect and holy divine clarity, that Mel Gibson is utterly, thoroughly insane.

2. You are not stupid. You have read up on your theological history. You know damn well that the truth about Mary Magdalene — along with all juicy goodness of the divine feminine in general — has been beaten out of Christianity like joy is beaten out of American teenagers.

    Translation: you know that if Mary Magdalene looked the slightest bit like the dazzling Monica Bellucci, who plays her in this film, well, Jesus would've been preaching a lot more of the gospel of "'oh my freaking God look at those lips." Instead, Mel focuses on nothing but endless constipated female expressions and a weird depiction of Satan as a sallow effeminate homunculus with wicked supermodel cheekbones. Touching.

3. You wail, you scream, you nearly call an ambulance when you burn your finger on the stove while making popcorn. You know for a fact that no human body, no matter how divinely inspired, could ever withstand so much gleefully ultraviolent, comically blood-drenched flesh rending as poor ol' Jesus does in the Jerusalem Chainsaw Massacre and not instantly pass out and/or immediately demand three quadruple Martinis and a fistful of holy Vicodin. I mean, please.

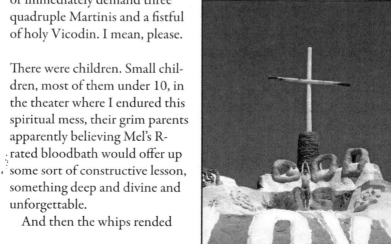

4. There were children. Small children, most of them under 10, in the theater where I endured this spiritual mess, their grim parents apparently believing Mel's R-rated bloodbath would offer up some sort of constructive lesson, something deep and divine and unforgettable.

    And then the whips rended

and the blood gushed and the sadomasochism amplified to a fever pitch and the families all sat there, stone faced and lost, apparently convincing themselves they were seeing something glorious and profound, as the hapless kids stared down a future full of bloody Jesus nightmares and psychotherapy until many years and many prescription meds later when they finally realize, *damn* but that movie fucked me up.

Remember "Jaws"? Remember how that movie traumatized the entire Boomer generation back in '75? Same thing. "Just when you thought it was safe to go back into the church ... WHIP-WHIPTHRASHARRRGGGH."

5. Oh right. The nails-through-the-hands thing. Like that's important to fetishize so explicitly, Mel. You sure you couldn't get the camera a little closer? Maybe more blood splattered *directly on the camera lens* as the mallet slammed down? Maybe you could've jammed one of those tiny medical cameras *inside* the bloody hole itself and really hit your point home, so to speak? Mel, I'd like to introduce you to my close personal friend, perspective. Here, have a pamphlet.

    One tiny anthropological point: You cannot drive a nail through the human hand and hang a body from it and not have it tear away like some sort of disgusting hamburger. Did you think of that, Mel? I bet you did. I bet you wished with all your might you could've filmed Jesus' body being torn from the nails and falling to the ground in gruesome slo-mo. Man, how much more fake blood and pig guts you could've poured over poor James Caviezel! Whee! Two words, Mel: Zoloft. Now.

6. Many argue that, despite the truckloads of blood and unchecked violence, Gibson's heart was surely in the right place and his objective was pure. But let's just say it right here and now: bullshit. You could feel Mel's fetish for torture veritably oozing off the screen like visual razor blades. There was no loving intent in this film. There is no tender message. There is no deep desire to move and inspire and uplift.

    There was only, I believe, copious gobs of curiously sad intent

to decimate any notions of gentle, divine open-hearted love and forgiveness you may have once believed Jesus was all about, and replace them with one very disturbed and sadomasochistic B-grade actor's very disturbed and sadomasochistic vision of old-school Catholic brutality and anti-Semitism and blood-soaked guilt. In a nutshell.

7.   The answer is, if I recall, about eight. The question is: How many times can you watch Mel's whipped, blended, frapped, pureed Jesus, his body rife with so many oozing crimson gouges it looks like some decimated animal you ran over with your car, twice, with snow tires — how many times can you watch Jesus fall to the hard gravel ground with a long, low moan in terrible blood-drenched slow motion without, finally, stifling a laugh?

8.   This is not Christianity. This is not a message anyone needs. This is the exact *opposite* of spiritual progress or insight or gentle divine heat and if Jesus came back right this minute and was made to sit through this film, he would sigh gently, shake his short, shaggy hair (long hair was forbidden by Jewish law — wrong again, Mel), and, you know, hold a nice seminar or something.

   "You think this is how I want to be remembered?" This is what he'd say, calmly and lovingly and more than a little sad. "You really think this was my message? You believe this is what I want the world to focus on, two hours of deranged, apocryphal torture and close-up butchering? Is really where humanity is still stuck, in bloodlust and shallow emotional manipulation and cheesy movie tie-ins?" And then Jesus' gaze, it would slowly drift away Monica Bellucci floated before his sparkling eyes. "Yum," he would say.

9.   And, finally, Jesus, he would absolutely agree with the following: If you must see this movie just to see what the fuss is all about, do what I did: Sneak into it after seeing some other, wildly superior film — like, say, "Eternal Sunshine of the Spotless Mind" — so as not to contribute one dime to the Mel Gibson Fund for the Spiritually Hysterical.

Rest assured, Jesus would've wanted it that way.

1 http://eeghuh.notlong.com

From: Eric C <EricXXX@aol.com>
Date: Sat, 20 Sep 2008 19:12:17 EDT
To: <mmorford@sfgate.com>
Subject: tool

Mark Moronford, you are an utter tool buddy! I hope people such as yourself stay in that disgusting liberal pit called San Francisco. You all deserve each other there, and no one of any true value would want you in their town or city. Maybe luck will be with us and it will eventually fall into the sea.

And here's the point really, no matter what happens, no matter who wins this election, abortions will not be made illegal. It's just not going to happen, so you and all of your slutty, disgusting, crap-infested ladies out there will always be able to go out, get wasted, get knocked-up, and then pull into your nearest drive-thru abortion clinic, and have that pesky side-effect coat-hangered right out of your stank vagina's. So no worries, you guys are all set. Twit!

From: "Peter's Bx" <peterXXX@hotmail.com>
To: mmorford@sfgate.com
Subject: yawn... another fag bashing Bush - go DYKE Hillary! hahaha
Date: Tue, 11 Jul 2006 22:49:37 +0000
X-OriginalArrivalTime: 11 Jul 2006 22:49:39.0531 (UTC)

U R transparent. At first I thought, must B a jew - but oh, a fag! Just another variety of jew really

I do have a serious question - how long have U been suicidal? U don't procreate - so, wondering what particular piece(s) of propaganda tipped U into the 'dead-ender' camp there.

From: "Brandon T" <ctech@XXX.net>
To: <mmorford@sfgate.com>
Date: Thu, 28 Jun 2007 00:03:09 -0500
MIME-Version: 1.0

Mark the Goofball. The problem with guys/gals like you is that you have been in college for the last umf years of your life and your profs in Cali do not have a "clue" what they are talking about in la la land. I VERY SERIOUSLY DOUBT you have EVER worked one day in your life and you know it. I agree with a few items on your Hummer scenario, however you go from SUV's to Bush's America.....ok did we not elect him? And do not complain, you guys elected an actor as your..... California person. Don't worry you guys on the east and west will have your chance, atleast I believe, in the next election. Then maybe you'll see that the "democrats" ideas are not so great and God I Pray that Hillary is at the top when it happens. Every time a customer visits from overseas, I beg that he does not think all Americans are like those displayed out of California. Heck, any of you remember the flag, your fathers don't, too hopped up on uppers to remember that. But...as long as you drive a Ferrari what do you care any way, as long as you get to make a web site and "try" to make others think you are somewhat literate in your nature. If you want to state "Ain't that America": America to most of us means........well you would never "understand" any words nor their definitions, hell I bet you do not believe that flag burning is wrong and taking prayer out of our schools should be done due to freedom of speech. I don't blame you, just your parents. Once you meet your maker, whether it's God, Bin Laden, Hillary, Yourself, or whomever you pray to at night, hopefully when you grow up along with most Democrats in this country, maybe then...just maybe, you'll "understand"

I hate you I hate you I hate you

I could give a fuck how corrupt a government is. I care about race. There R 2 horses in the rase - 'kill whitey' or 'slave master'. Yes the Republicans bend over backwards 2 flood this nation with 3rd world slave trash, but clearly the Dem's motto is 2 mongrelize & eliminate the white population as well - so, take your pic (Mr. Suicide). Throughout history it is ALWAYS based on theft & lies - nature is cruel. U can't live without killing. & yes if U R a 'veggie' fag, well those R alive 2! What about the hollocaust of our leafy friends?
L8R!~

Date: Fri, 09 Jun 2006 01:51:13 -0400
From: KaitieXXX@netscape.net
To: mmorford@sfgate.com
Subject: Hello
MIME-Version: 1.0
X-Spam-Flag: NO

So if you actually read this I hope you are having fun destroying morality. Whether or believe it or not sex before marriage is a sin. God isn't going to bless you for having sex before marriage. Our bodies were created soley for one person. In my case my husband whoever he happens to be. You will probably just read this and laugh but I hope you don't. I hope God uses this somehow to bring you to Him. I dunno I do hope you have a wonderful day though.
In His Love,
Kaitie W

what the American way should be like. I'm sure our forefathers are rolling over about now stareing at one of Satan's angels. I'm sure though, that you and your friends wear the muscle shirts "We're a team". You and I both know, when or better yet "if" a democrat runs this country "as we are seeing now in Washington", taxes will go up first, the economy will go to shit, countries all over the world will be attacked, etc. But don't worry, I'm sure Hummer sales will go down too. Think about this while you sleep tonight.

If you'd ever like to discuss this in person, please let me know.

Brandon

From: "david X" <honkyc@XXX.com>
To: <mmorford@sfgate.com>
Subject: Bush Bashing
Date: Thu, 13 Jul 2006 06:51:41 -0500
MIME-Version: 1.0
X-Priority: 3

Your Right Were sliding to demise ! The cause of course is weak sick sissy tree hug Fucks like you . Just Blame George ..Right ! I just hope when we do fall that some 3rd world maniac gets to have the pleasure of smashing your stupid crosswired defective brains till they run out your nose..poetic justice for me ....for weakling cuties like you, now go to the bath house with your ilk & get your daily prostrate massage you fucking traitor!

....your friend Dave

> *I suppose I have to acknowledge it eventually: Part of my calling in writerly life appears to be to make a doomed, slightly sanctimonious attempt to convey to any Christian "true believer" how little they likely know about the real origins of biblical mythology, how much of it is borrowed/ripped off from ancient pagan sources, heavily revised and rather brutally edited and politicized throughout history to say exactly what church leaders want it to say, and is therefore a bit disingenuous at best, spiritually dangerous at worst, completely apocryphal all over. Of course, it's a futile effort. I just can't seem to help it. Pinched religious literalism makes my soul recoil. I'm getting better, though. Calmer. I hope? —mm*

The Bible's all wrong, again

4/14/2006

Is it not just tremendous heaps of blasphemous fun to learn, once again and for the thousandth time, that the Bible — that happy mish-mashed hodgepodgey cocktail of myths and folklore and who's-your-daddy reproaches, intermixed with lovely stories of redemption and hope and sin and hellfire and death — is so full of colorful holes it might as well be a bedsheet from Baghdad Target?

Is it not some sort of curious intellectual delight to hear about the discovery of yet another Gnostic gospel, this time the Gospel of Judas, a scruffy ol' tract that's been lying around for years,[1] which would seem to reveal Christianity's second-favorite villain to be, well, not at all the sniveling ass who turned Jesus over to the cops for a fistful of hummus money, but actually a sly and secret conspirator of his pal Jesus, much in the way Biff helped young Christ learn Zen Buddhism and martial arts and got him drunk (and very nearly laid) in Chris Moore's "Lamb: The Gospel According to Biff, Christ's Childhood Pal"? Of course it is.

If the Bible is the gold brick in the American spiritual sidewalk, then you simply have to ask: What is the relevance in the fact that Christ might not have been betrayed at all? That he may have orchestrated his own arrest? What does this say about his divine wisdom? About Bible stories as a whole? More importantly, how does the new and improved Judas story pinch the ass of our collective mythology? Does it or does it not kick out one of the shaky support beams of the modern Church? Shouldn't it?

The answer, of course, is it depends on just how deep your personal stick is stuck in the divine mud. Because now more than ever, hard-core religious and political types think it's all clear and straight, that life's moral codes and cultural guidelines have all been correctly (and homophobically, and misogynistically) spelled out in grainy divine ink, in ancient, ironclad stories that would deign to tell us how to think and feel and live.

It's the prevalent, simpleminded ideology: God somehow spoke in perfect English through some sort of giant megaphone (the original podcast), which was then beamed straight into a number of deep believers, whose stories were then perfectly transcribed by some honest and devout and in no way corrupt or politicized or sexually frustrated bishop's pen about 2,000 years ago, and there is no debate don't you dare question its legitimacy and motives lest you be cast into the hellpit of Sodom. Or maybe, you know, San Francisco.

These are the Bible literalists, those who blindly take the Bible as the *exact* word of God, and they only look at discoveries like this new gospel and stare numbly, uncomprehendingly, as fluid divinity swirls around them like some sort of frustrated mist.

The truth is, the Church was formed to serve people just like this, those who are unable to grasp nuances and unable to think beyond a certain scope, those who are unwilling or unable follow what is perhaps the singlemost powerful and significant of all Christ's (and Buddha's, and the Tao's, etc.) teachings: that is, to seek God *within*. Not in a priest. Not in a building. Not in an organized institution. Within *you*.

So let us delight in how the new version of Judas reveals, merely by its very existence, exactly that. Let us calmly relish how we are reminded, once again, that belief and faith and the dusty ancient oral-tradition stories that attempted to define them are, and always have been, and always will be, suspect, and fluid, and problematic, and wonderful, and dubious and malleable as pita bread on a warm summer's day.

In other words, it may not matter that the Gospel of Judas entirely reframes the classic tale of Christ's betrayal, and hence will keep scholars busy for ages as to what it might mean. It may not matter that the vast majority of "true" believers won't be swayed in the slightest by this discovery, that it wouldn't matter if Christ's body were unearthed tomorrow and Jesus were found to have an "OM" symbol tattooed on his sacrum and an Astarte pendant around his neck and an ancient iPod with lots of classic Leonard Cohen songs. Most staunch Christians would still adhere to current codes like nervous kittens huddling in a leaky life raft.

But here's what does matter, now more than ever: The Bible certainly does not always say what we think it says.[2] Faith and divinity and even entire religions are not static and fixed; they should move and dance and inbreed and adapt with time, with culture, with intellectual evolution. Simple enough? Did you already know? Judas is winking in your direction.

Hell, it's only been about 65 years since the publication of the last earth-shaking, goddess-cranking Gnostic tract, the Gospel of Mary Magdalene, a truly landmark find that rocked the Christian world and sucker-punched the misogynist Church and revolutionized Magdalene scholarship, and inspired Tom Hanks to grow his hair long so he could appear in "The Da Vinci Code," much of which was based on the discovery of Mary's truly astounding gospel.[3]

It's a breathtaking piece of writing that essentially paints Jesus' favorite consort as quite deeply informed of a rich and particularly mystical version of Christ's message — one that, it must be said, essentially defies just about everything the modern Church stands for, in how it extols the virtues of finding God, once again, *not* through a church or priest or blind faith, but by raw self-exploration and individual spirit. You gotta love it.

And all this only 60 years after the big daddy of recent biblical discoveries, the massive Nag Hammadi library of Gnostic gospels, an astonishing collection of delicious, banned writings from one of the more mystical, pro-sexual, pro-women, open-minded sects of early Christianity, one of many that offered radically differing versions of Christ's story and message, but which, like the rest, eventually lost out to the more militant and dogmatic Church many of us know and recoil from today.

(Remember, like history, religion is written by the victors. It is then revised by the powermongers, leveraged by the fearful and wielded as a nasty weapon by the conservatives. Same as it ever was.)

Is it not perhaps the single greatest fallacy of all time? That mankind is somehow a meek and inferior quasi-deity ever struggling to live up to some hideously puritanical idea of the sacred and the enlightened? That morality and religion are somehow clean and flawless in their messages and that God is somehow scowling down every day, watching and taking notes?

Or that the Bible — make that *all* bibles, of every shape and kind, from any culture, are merely ever-shifting kaleidoscopes through which you may observe the world and absorb some lovely wisdom and moral color, but which you should never, ever mistake for real life? Can I get an amen?

1 http://tacoo.notlong.com
2 http://ateel.notlong.com
3 http://shoowu.notlong.com

Shockingly large amount of nice response to this one, mostly I think because it's tight and focused and nails its tone and has a cleverish hook, moves well, makes its points with passionate, lucid glee sans my usual tendency to overwrite and ramble and add too much color. I think this 10 amazing truths thing might become a recurring column topic/meme. I don't have nearly enough of those. Or, you know, any. Plus it's not exactly like there's a dearth of material.

Check the footnotes for all the links that verify/back up everything I claim herein, if you're so inclined. There's some crazy interesting, tantalizing data back there. –mm

10 amazing truths you already suspected

8/7/09

Let's start out easy. How about a big, dumb, obvious, forehead-slapper of an of-course-you-already-knew, shall we?

1. Let's start with, say, tanning beds. Turns out they cause cancer like a mofo[1]. I mean, as bad as arsenic. As mustard gas. Smoking. Chimney sweeping. The Jonas Brothers. I mean, obviously.

2. Like you didn't already know. Like you thought it was all healthy fun and games to strip yourself naked and lay on a bed of giant blue light bulbs and have ultraviolet rays blasted into every inch of your skin for hours per week and think, yeah, this can't be all bad, can it? What with my skin turning a bizarre shade  of orange and that weird tingling in my brainstem and my genitalia melting like bubblegum in the sun? Like it's not the transdermal equivalent of placing my mouth over the tailpipe of a Chevy Tahoe and gunning the engine? Mmm, stupid.

3. You are green to the core. Organic everything, grey water, solar, Prius, compost your nail clippings and your urine and your condoms, the works. You have a child, maybe two. You are considering having a third, or maybe even a fourth or fifth. You say you care about reducing your carbon footprint? You say you care deeply about your impact on the ecosphere? You might be lying.

4. Because of course, deep down, you know that you can compost and recycle your eco-friendly butt off for your entire life and still never come close to matching the reduction in carbon footprint you

INFORMATION

would gift the planet simply by not having that additional child[2]. It's a rather harsh way to look at it, I admit, but there it is. But of course, personal responsibility has its thresholds, right?

5. Oh, but wait. Maybe overpopulation isn't really the most pressing problem after all. Relatively speaking, the U.S. does pretty well in managing birth rates, especially compared to explosive developing nations like China and India, so horribly strained for resources and with such staggering proportions of extreme poverty.

    Maybe the real problem is rich Westerners sucking up far, far more than their fair share of, well, just about everything[3]. Did you know 50 percent of all toxic emissions come from just seven percent of the world population? I bet you did. Upshot: Maybe the real solution is a nice combo of the two. Not having too many kids, and buying less stuff you don't actually need. Radical! Or not.

6. One large study has dared come forth to claim that organic food is really no better for you[4] than "regular" food, implying that the organic thing is all a big sham, a multibillion-dollar lie, that the giant, watery, flavorless Safeway tomato doused in chemicals and gene-spliced goodness is really no worse for you than that fragrant, delicious, organic heirloom from Rainbow Grocery, or that the chem-blasted asparagus shipped in from Mexico in November has the same nutritional value as the organic goodness you should be getting in April from the local farm.

7. Is it tempting to believe? Not in the slightest. For one thing, going organic is only partially about basic, keep-you-alive nutrients. It's just as much about the various toxins, chemicals, refined sugars and hormones slapped all over corporate foodstuffs in general; not to mention the brutal, earth-stabbing, industrial manufacturing and farming practices that go into most crappy mainstream foods.

    In other words, yes, in terms of basic nutritional values, maybe *some* organic foods are no better for you than their "normal" industrial-produced equivalents. Unless you count the vicious environmental impact. And the chemicals. And the cancer. And the death. Otherwise, same.

8. Dammit. Wait a second. It also turns out that "USDA Certified

Organic" label is just all sorts of mealy BS, too, and can't really be trusted.[5] Turns out the USDA has been so pressured by various industrial food titans to loosen the definition of "organic," that the label has been rendered, if not meaningless, then more watered down than that same Safeway tomato. Are the USDA's standards still a huge improvement over what came before? Hell yes. But they're far from ideal.

Solution: Learn to read the ingredients yourself. Figure it out. Understand what you eat, and where it really comes from. It's not really very difficult. Or, pretend that it is, that it's too weird and you don't have the time to care and it's just too complicated. You are probably lying. But that's OK.

6. 7. 8. The late infomercial pitchman Billy Mays' OxiClean powdered miracle cleaner? Really just sodium percarbonate. A standard chemical you can buy in bulk right now at your local swimming pool supply shop. Whitening toothpaste? Just regular toothpaste with extra grit. Red Bull? Massive shot of caffeine and a megadose of sugar combined with whatever they can squeeze out of the pituitary gland of dead rats. I might be wrong about the rats. But maybe not.[6]

Oh, and if you buy high-end, thousand-dollar "audiophile-grade" cables to hook up your home theater system? You have achieved true greatness. As a total sucker.

9. Wal-Mart is, apparently, hankering to launch a big initiative to stamp every product it sells with an eco-friendly rating label[7], some sort of grand, awareness-raising system to inform all Earth-conscious Wal-Mart customers — I know, I know: oxymoron — where every product falls on the you-are-destroying-the-planet scale. It's a rather wonderful idea that could radically transform the company's entire supply chain for the better.

Except for one thing: Wal-Mart has no plans to slap a giant label on its own bloated megastores themselves, no plans to reveal the enormous waste and destruction Wal-Mart itself embodies merely by existing, by shipping a million products over from sweatshops in China and Malaysia and India. Nor does it plan to offer a Smiley-Face Local Economy Decimation rating to all those countless small towns it's swooped into and gutted. But hey! That giant tub of HFCS-blasted caramel corn? Not all that bad for the planet. Yay!

10. We could totally do interstate rail in the United States. We could totally invest in this massive, culture-altering project like it was the next man on the moon and within 20 years have this ridiculously cool, lighting-fast, super-efficient Euro-style train network[8] connecting most major urban hubs like we were Italy and France and Japan and Disneyland all rolled into one, but with better drinks and free Wi-Fi and superlative in-seat movies like they do on Virgin.

We could totally do it. But 50+ years of Big Auto PR bullshit has slyly convinced us all we really can't, that no one wants it, that big dumb America loves its big dumb open-road freedom far too much, that car culture is so embedded in our road-trippin' nostalgia-thick psyches it can never be extricated.

Of course, Big Auto is full of crap, is now begging for table scraps, handouts, oxygen. Who we thought we were, who we thought we had to be has essentially been a giant lie all along. Didn't you already suspect as much?

1 http://ohsohgh.notlong.com
2 http://hiloon.notlong.com
3 http://shar.es/IrAs
4 http://uuquaer.notlong.com
5 http://nexohqu.notlong.com
6 http://cherook.notlong.com
7 http://fohtek.notlong.com
8 http://uquiele.notlong.com

And now, The Daring Spectacle presents...

Mullet Haiku

I'll be a sum'bitch
Gravedigger just jumped 12 cars!
I'll die happy now

For some reason — maybe because it's one of the few places left where smoking is still ubiquitous and shameless — the smell of cigarette smoke now instantly makes me think of Las Vegas. I can't tell if that's a good thing or not.

I don't miss smoking much anymore. I did miss the ritualistic aspect of it for a while, but the habit now seems to me like rubbing a fistful of powdered glass into your eyes every day, then wondering why you're going blind. I know, I know: Sanctimonious much, Mark? —mm

Dead people smoke Camels

03/11/2005

Oh my God but I loved smoking.

Loved it like a slab of chocolate-covered puppy dogs and I loved the whole gorgeous damnable ritual of the thing, the oral fixation and the regular smoke breaks with co-workers and the cigs n' coffee and the cigs n' wine and the cigs n' sex and I had myself not one but three different all-American all-metal all-sexy Zippo lighters the famous click/snap sounds and toxic butane scents of which I found intoxicating and soulful and I miss it all terribly.

But then again, I absolutely loathed how smoking made me feel, just afterward, the tightness of chest and shortness of breath and the wheez-ing, the nasty aftertaste and the phlegm and the tormented lung cilia, the constant stupid cravings and the ridiculous expense. Not to mention how it made my fingers and clothes reek and my teeth yellow and my girlfriend cringe when she kissed me, and of course all the filthy ashtrays and the whole noxious karmic low-vibration poison-for-the-flesh thing.

There was no pill. There was no nicotine patch or nicotine gum to be taken at regular intervals like heroin. A little self-examination, a lot of self-awareness, a tiny shred of self-disgust, all pointed to one wake-up call that finally reached deep into my core and came back out and said, calmly, obviously: Enough already — this just isn't worth it.

And now, thankfully, they're nothing but an afterthought, a hazy memory, historic ash. I quit my 12-year, one-pack-a-day habit with rela-tive ease, cold turkey, years back, weaned myself off when I turned 30 and never really looked back, and now that California has banned smoking in all bars and restaurants and most public places and even within phlegm-hocking distance of city buildings and parks, it seems all just so archaic and weird and distant.

How quickly I forget. How easy it is to overlook that for millions of others, it's still a plague. It's still out there, raging and cancerous and

For more pure pleasure...*have a Camel!*

No other cigarette is so rich-tasting yet so mild as **CAMEL!**

unstoppable and this explains why I just read about how scientists are on the verge, right now, of inventing a magic-bullet pill[1] that they claim will block the effects of nicotine, block the actual chemical process in your flesh that causes nicotine addiction and, should they succeed, it will prove to be a bigger and more lucrative drug than Viagra and Prozac and Ambien combined and shaken and stirred and pumped straight into your eyeballs.

"It's the biggest addiction market there is," exclaimed one Dr. Herbert D. Kleber, a psychiatry professor and addiction researcher at Columbia University, dollar signs drooling and already eyeing that new Lexus.

He's referring, of course, to the 50 million extant smokers in the nation, nearly all of whom know they should quit smoking and most of whom have probably tried, but since most probably buy into the BS Big Tobacco/Big Pharmco PR hype, they are conditioned to think it's just way too damn hard and way too ingrained in their cells and they shouldn't even try and they should just wait for the new stupidly expensive drug to further hammer their bodies into submission and meanwhile, cartons of Camel Lights are only 40 bucks a pop at Costco.

Did you catch that? Addiction is a *market*. Addiction, like war, is big bucks. Addiction is funny and adorable and deeply American because addiction makes billions for the vile tobacco companies *and* billions for the equally devious major pharmcos who want to "cure" you of the vile product Big Tobacco sells, all by convincing you that you can smoke all you want and then pop a magic-bullet drug and be all better without actually having to truly understand or change a thing about your life. Isn't that sweet? Isn't that sad? Isn't that just the cutest thing ever?

Know what's even cuter? Neither side of the smoking issue wants the other to disappear. It's that wondrously vicious, downward-spiraling circle, Big Tobacco pumping you full of death and Big Pharma pumping you full of chemically assisted pseudo-life, and each depending on the other to perpetuate the myth of your desperate need for both and no one *truly* wanting you healthy or spiritually conscious because goddammit then how would they make their boat payments?

It seems obvious but it bears repeating: magic-bullet drugs do nothing. They do nothing to help you change a thing about your addictive tendencies or your attitude or your lifestyle, do nothing to induce any sort of increase in your understanding of how the body works and how the spirit is screaming for attention and just why the hell you might be so easily prone to addiction in the first place. Such prescription drugs don't educate. They don't invoke change. They just numb.

But hell, who cares? Why examine causes? Why try to figure out the reasons behind our toxic obsession with things we know are killing us? Simply bomb the problem into submission, and then pretend it's not still right there, simmering just underneath, even nastier and more fanged than before and just aching to manifest itself in some other form.

Oh, by the way, here's the big obvious secret about smoking: for the vast majority, smoking simply isn't very hard to quit. This is the giant fallacy perpetuated by both sides. We are all told, endlessly and without shame or death by lightning, that our willpower is weak and we are at the mercy of nasty chemicals and powerful habits and marketing schemes so commanding and draconian we can only cower and whimper in their presence and scream out that we are, in short, victims. Which is, of course, bullshit.

I'll admit, it's often more complicated than that and many people's addictive personalities are a result of a tormented set of psychoemotional issues and manic tendencies hearkening back to their upbringings and their karmic agendas and their time in the womb and ... and ... OK, enough already. True to a point, but after that, no more excuses. It's all you.

And by the way, I am all for holding corporations accountable. I am all for nailing Big Tobacco and the fast food conglomerates and oil companies and major drug companies to the wall for lying their collective asses off about the inherent poisons in their products and ad campaigns.

But overall, the rule still applies: we are in charge. And the more we believe in silly toxic magic bullets, the more distant we become from who we are and just what the hell we are capable of. Put another way: the more you believe a drug can truly change how you approach your life, the less connection you will have with anything that truly matters.

There is no true health anywhere in a drug that blocks the effect of nicotine. There is no magic in that bullet, there is just bullet.

I kind of wish, to this day, that I could smoke again. I loved the ritual, the habit, the funky little rock-star vice. I wish smoking wasn't so goddamn obviously the most pointless and debilitating and deadly habit you can have next to collecting radioactive sewage or kissing speeding trains or voting Republican.

But that is, of course, why I won't be smoking, ever again. Because alongside the face-slapping facts that prove how smoking is just savagely stupid, and silly, and hugely toxic is the notion that, if you refuse to try to understand the forces and energies fondling your life and then tweak your attitudes accordingly, no pill can ever make you do it. Simple as that.

But damn, those Zippos were cool.

1 http://aigui.notlong.com

Oh, I had fun with this one. It was triggered by a slew of rather twee, insufferable "Why men cheat" pseudo-explicatory columns – written, strangely, largely by female psychologists and advice columnists — that popped up all over the Web right after the Tiger Woods story exploded in a shower of satire-ready beneficence back in late '09. Every single one of them seemed to offer up a similarly lopsided, heavily sighing, female-as-victim view of malehood and male sexuality, rather divorced from the true messiness of love and sex and real gender differences. Not to mention the wanton impulses of a billionaire sports superstar egomaniac slutdonkey who has the charisma and personality of a hunk of putting sod. Just sayin'.

BTW, this one came out immediately after the even hotter 'Tiger Woods must die!' piece, way back on page 19. I like the dialogue this column has with itself. I also think it stands up pretty well all on its own. —mm

101 reasons why men cheat

12/16/2009

Plethoric are the theories, the pop psychoanalysis, the dime store hypothesis. In the wake of Tiger Woods' epic fail, we hereby present a quick rundown of the *real* reasons many men cheat, as compiled by the whims and vagaries of the baffled, needy male ego for the past, oh, about two million years. Ready?

Basically, men cheat* because:

1. Their penis told them to.

2. The penis is always right.

3. Unless it's not. Unless it's totally, blindingly wrong. But that's really not possible. Just ask it. Wait a sec, it's busy with that Vegas waitress. OK, go ahead. See?

4. The man's marriage is sexless and loveless and boring, and he has needs that must — nay MUST — be met. Just ask the penis.

5. The wife has low/no libido, whereas the man has enough for nine teenagers and a box of rabbits.

6. No, really. The male libido, generally speaking, far outpaces the female libido and is never really satisfied for more than a day or two, tops. This is why so many men choose to be gay. Gay sex is like, off the hook! It's true! I read that somewhere. Lesbians, on the other hand, often suffer a terrible fate known as "lesbian bed

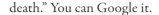

death." You can Google it.

7. #6 is a totally unfair cliché that doesn't always hold true, and, by the way, all men are pigs. I mean, duh.

8. The kids steal all the love/attention/energy from wife, leaving man with nothing but XTube, golf and vodka.

9. One word: Ego. Three more: ego, ego, ego. Nothing like nailing a beautiful female acolyte to boost self-image, over and over again, as she coos your name adoringly and feigns surprise that you just bought her a Mercedes.

10. Or is it the other way around, and many women are shockingly predatory, often hunting for rich, powerful men who will buy them stuff and give them a shred of self worth by association, because the truth is, they have no identity of their own, and all they have is sex, which they wield like an ax made of lip gloss and open hip flexors and Cosa Bella thongs?

11. Man is a rock star/golfer/politician/televangelist and women — or gay prostitutes — are knocking on his hotel-room door day and night, and the penis is like, are you going to answer that?

12. Man's marriage is basically a sham, held together only for the sake of kids and media and multimillion-dollar Nike endorsement deals, and to pay for mansions, guitar-shaped swimming pools and giant chrome rims for the Escalade.

13. Sex is tasty and delicious and should not be denied to mere mortals like weak and meager little men.

14. Man is insecure, and sex makes him feel wanted and powerful.

15. Man is *very* secure, and sex makes him feel even *more* wanted and powerful.

16. Man is impervious. He cannot possibly get caught.

17. Man is impervious. He does not care if he gets caught.

18. Wife won't do various kinky/perverted things man has taken a liking to from scouring Interweb at 3 a.m. whilst moderately drunk and naked. Wife has zero sex skills. Wife hates sex. Wife only grudgingly has it when she has to to shut up his whining. Wife is disgusted by his dirty suggestions for the new video camera. Wife has let herself go. Wife will only have sex if it leads to more babies. Wife is Sarah Palin. Mix and match.

19. Sex is not love. Cheating is not really "cheating," per se, given how most men consider casual sex romps to be just slightly above "meatball sandwich and an ice cold beer" and just below "hitting 210 mph in Porsche Carrera Turbo while tripping on acid in a lake of fire" in the Male Desirables Index.

20. Man has become convinced the human animal is not meant to really be monogamous, that fidelity is for Hallmark cards and Mormons and has no bearing on real life. Man is simply not *wired* to mate for life. Hey, it was on the Discovery Channel!

21. Wife actually gave man permission that one time when she was really drunk after being handed keys to new Bentley and a house.

22. Except she wasn't drunk at all and knew exactly what she was doing.

23. And so did he.

24. Quit making excuses. Man is a pathetic, sexist jackass and always has been, basically.

25. Which makes you wonder why she married him at all.

26. Maybe she thought she could fix him. That's pretty common.

27. Or maybe he was very, very convincing when he said he'd changed, that his playa days were over, that he loved her and needed her and never wanted to have sex with anyone else, ever — no really, I mean it this time.

28. Which was probably true.

29. When he said it.

30. And she wanted to believe it *so badly*. "Maybe marriage would change him? Or a couple kids? He's ready to settle down, I can *feel* it."

31. Even though everyone around them was like, "Oh my God, that's a disaster waiting to happen, right there. He's such a *letch*. Why doesn't she see it? Should someone tell her? Is she just not very bright?

32. "I mean, he just *totally* hit on me at their Christmas party. And she was like, 10 feet away! Of course, I slept with him. But never mind that now."

33. Let's flip it over. Maybe wife is a ruthless, nightmare harridan, relentlessly negative and mean. He can do no right. He is lonely and starved for attention. But they have kids, a home. Divorce is ugly, expensive, public. So...

34. Oh, stop it. There is *never* any valid reason for cheating, even if she's an abusive monster. There are only excuses.

35. Thank you, Elle magazine. You are childish and wrong and do not live in the real world. Go back to your pink pedi and "Twilight."

36. Bite me.

37. Man is entitled. "I *deserve* lots of casual sex. After all, I didn't work this hard on my business/golf game/these abs not to have them licked by a wide variety of giggly TGI Friday's hostesses. Wait, did I? No. No I did not."

38. Porn made him do it.

39. Sex addiction. He's a *victim.*

40. And a *sinner*! We are *all* sinners. Who are you to judge? Sinner! You! Now take off your pants and get in the goddamn hot tub already.

41. Man fears mortality.

42. Man fears erectile dysfunction.

43. Man fears fear.

44. Man fears deranged fan will beat him/kill herself/post photos on Facebook if he *doesn't* have more sex with her. What's he supposed to do?

45. Man is getting back at his mother.

46. Father.

47. Priest.

48. Invisible friend.

49. Invisible friend's priest's mother.

50. Wife has tacitly agreed to don't-ask, don't-tell policy WRT his fooling around, and is not at all unhappy with having $20 million in her checking account while she never has to have sex with her

husband. Hello, American dream!

51. Organized religions and entire conservative platform essentially say that women are lesser, lower, should be kept in their place, and that place usually involves denial and alcoholism and blind acceptance of your man's wanton indiscretions, because he's the man and that's all there is to it, so shut up and take another Zoloft and keep your crying to yourself. Yay, GOP!

52. Didn't Jesus fool around? Is that written somewhere? The lost Gospel of Hey Baby, Nice Rack? All those prostitutes and magic and hocus-pocus? I bet he did. Dude could walk on water. Chicks *love* that.

53. And by the way, isn't cheating sort of God's will? I mean, He's omniscient and everything, right? That means He knows it all before it happens, it's all predetermined and fated and a priori, and therefore he knows we're gonna cheat, right? So it must be OK.

54. Hey, temptation is irresistible. Who can say no to a secret illicit romp on the office conference-room table?

55. ... or on the boss's desk?

56. ... or in the principal's office?

57. ... Wal-Mart parking lot?

58. ... iHop walk-in freezer?

59. ... 1995 Chevy Caravan third row fold-down seating?

60. Men *don't* cheat, actually, at least not nearly as much as the culture/feminist theory thinks.

61. They actually value and cherish emotional connection just as much as women. It's true. Media blows it all out of proportion. So not fair.

62. So essentially, we're talking about the classic, time-honored breakdown in communication and gender understanding, exacerbated by horrible sex education and Dr. Phil's bullshit and endless lies from fashion magazines and Oprah and porn.

63. Actually, the headline of this column is sort of misleading. Men *don't* cheat. *Some* men do, and some women do, for all sort of reasons, some of which are actually sort of *valid*, if you will, and to insist on some ironclad universal rule of absolute unquestioning fidelity is to presume a ridiculous, impossible level of perfection

in the human animal and to dismiss the million messy, complicated variants a human love relationship can take.

64. Oh, just shut the hell up, #63. No one wants to hear your tepid, permissive psychoanalysis. Cheating is *wrong*. Always and forever. Now let's talk more about jerks and skanks!

65. Hey, I'm just trying to provide a little perspective, rein it all back in. This is getting out of hand.

66. Whatevs. This entire column is built around a totally ludicrous and unanswerable question, anyway. Sure, there are as many reasons for infidelity as there are human emotions. Life is messy. Love is messier. But mostly it's about the penis.

67. Yes, but …

68. Just stop it.

69-100. Something to do with monkeys.

101. Love is not your bitch.

NOTE: Many of these also apply to women who cheat. So don't kid yourself, sister.

And now, The Daring Spectacle presents…

Mullet Haiku

Passed out drunk again
Cigarette lights the mattress
The trailer's on fire

Always makes me wince a little when I hear someone lament lost innocence, or the ordeal of youth experience, about how "traumatized" someone is by some sort of relatively benign sexual event. There's truth to it, to be sure, a real danger in the hyper-acceleration of maturity and forcing kids to "grow up too fast," not to mention all sorts of brutal, tragic experiences no one ever really deserves to bear witness to. But that's been true since 12-year-olds were forced to marry their 67-year-old cousin's dad, AKA the Dawn of Time.

I think the reverse is also even more true; to somehow suggest that a state of perpetual innocence or naïveté is somehow devoutly to be wished, that man's natural mode is some sort of fuzzywarm bunnies n' rainbows Hallmark card where everyone drinks tea and holds hands and no one fucks in anger, to pretend life is not also, at times, a giant madhouse hellhound test, a cosmic training ground, is just all flavors of ridiculous.

To me, the game is not about how to stay innocent and pure as long as possible, but rather how you respond to, ride on, slip through the maelstrom of pain and danger, love and death, spit and bullets, come and blood as smoothly, laughingly, lightly as possible. In other words, it's not about how to avoid and steer clear of the harsh world, it's what you do with it when it comes at you, teeth bared and pants down. Isn't it? —mm

Innocence is so overrated

03/07/2007

We seem to have this bizarre notion. We seem to suck on this freakish and ill-begotten idea like it was some sort of sticky candy cane of bitter, irrefutable truth.

It's about innocence. It's this sincere, fantastical idea that we are born pure and simple and clean like bright happy cotton balls and then we somehow quickly become horribly corrupted by the icky Satan-ruled world, and it's all we can do to stumble our way through and not get too soiled and damaged and emotionally shredded before finally wheezing our last emphysemic breath and saying, "Well, at least I never became a Republican or a secretly gay evangelical or a rabid Celine Dion fan," and then clicking off.

Take sex. Take a lot of sex. Take lots and lots of wet dangerous imperfect sex and mix it liberally with hyperactive religious piety and conservative sanctimony and wanton Christian hypocrisy and you've probably got the greatest recipe for our culture's devout belief in the inevitable corruption of innocence of all time.

See, there was a study.[1] A recent report about teen sex (yes, a new one

emerges roughly every nine seconds) concluded that any sexual encounter teenagers endure, from oral to anal to upside-down to groping each other's nether regions through some nicely faded True Religions, any sexual encounter could cause emotional damage to your otherwise perky, cherubic teenager.

That's right. They say sex *of any kind* can harm teens emotionally. Even permanently. The researchers go on to say — in that sort of nicely patronizing, obvious way that scientists are wont to indulge in — that this means it's extra-important for parents to inform their kids of what sex can do, what it contains and what it wants and what it whispers in your ear late at night when the flesh is trembling and the thoughts are scalding and the guilt is ominous.

This is where it gets interesting. This is where it gets confusing. This is where you go, Wait wait wait, something is just not right here. Are we not missing some essential truth? Something core and vital and deeply human? I think we are.

Perhaps it's this: There is simply no such thing as an authentic human experience that doesn't somehow and in some way affect, stain, taint or scar the human animal. It cannot be avoided. It cannot be shunned or quieted or talked off the ledge. This is, in fact, what we do.

In other words, there is no such thing as a perfectly innocent life, or childhood, or experience, no such thing as strolling through this world wholly sheltered from, say, everyday trauma, abused puppies, shocking imagery, bad sex or inappropriate fondling or confusing orgasms, and if you insist that there is or that there should be or that this is the way God intended it, it is quite likely you are one violently oversheltered home-schooled virgin and now might be a good time to read a book and buy a

vibrator and head into therapy very soon and I can say that without fear of reprisal because, well, you are not reading this column anyway.

Let's flip it around: There is no human child on the face of the earth who has had some sort of ideally perfect, sex-free, trauma-free, drama-less life by which we should measure all our failures and woes. There is no standard, no perfect score, no idyllic model. And there never was. It's the equivalent of arguing that we are meant to go through the modern world free of raw flesh and sticky blood and parasites, ever struggling to remain clean and pure, when in fact this is the stuff of which we are made. Bacteria and spit and germs? Baby, it's what we *are*.

The notion of "pure" innocence invites one of two perspectives: One is the aforementioned cheerless Christian view, an all-too-common attitude that implies that human life is mostly pain and suffering and forbidden, guilt-ridden midnight masturbation interspersed with slivers of blind faith, and we are here to endure Satan's nasty trials until armies of happy dopey angels come and lead us into the giant Blue Light Special in the sky. Familiar? Sure is.

The second perspective goes something like this: Drama is what we are designed for. Emotional (and physical, and spiritual) scarring and discoloration is, in a way, what we *do*. Our spirits are, after all, here to experience and taste and immerse in it all.

But it's when you deny this fact, when you choose to see all the sex and drugs and tattoos and mortgages as a giant drawer of scary sharp knives that the gods sigh and frown and say, Well, why in the hell did we set up this mad gorgeous kitchen for you in the first place if you're not going to slice off the tip of your finger now and then, and scream, and get a ban-

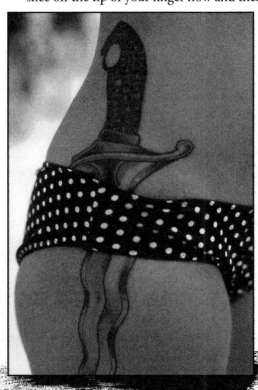

dage and heal awkwardly and then do it all over again?

Is this not what it's all about? The wise ones, the gurus and mystics and the energy readers, they will tell you that unless you're the Dalai Lama or a Bodhisattva or some rare precious otherworldly creature who's already essentially transcended this plane but who's decided to hang around to show the rest of us how to untie those knots of divine misunderstanding, most of us are here to learn some very particular lessons, perhaps over and over again, until we get it.

But those scientists were right about one thing: Inform those teens. Arm them well. Teach them to respect the body

and the flesh and learn its nerves and wires and bones and juices like it was a crazy road map to the stars. Try to minimize the harsher damage caused by sheer ignorance, misinformation, guilt.

But let's not mislead ourselves. Let's stop with the silly thinking that it's not supposed to be this way, that we're somehow supposed to traipse around in fresh white robes and lavender-scented air and mess-free innocence, hovering above all things awkward and painful and delicious and embodied and ever potentially catastrophic.

This is the greatest lesson of life, God, earth: Resistance is futile. All you can really do is grit your teeth, take a deep breath, unbutton your pants and smile.

1 http://ahaefa.notlong.com

A fine companion piece, methinks, to the very popular "Where is my gay apocalypse?" from the previous section. Rereading this, it makes me re-ponder: After gay marriage is finally legalized nationwide and the grand, quivering terror about how it will surely bring about the end of society is proven, once and for all, to be the sad religious fearmongering it obviously is/was, what will be the next nefarious agenda? That is, whom will the fundamentalists and pseudo-moralists in America accuse as trying to corrupt/convert our innocent virgin children to their nefarious ways? Polyamorists? Vegetarians? Yoga teachers? Polyamorist vegetarian yoga teachers who like anal sex and Ecstasy and really strong coffee? Oh wait, I wrote a column about that idea, too. See "Beware the vegans!" back in the Irony Loves Company *section. — mm*

Here is the big gay agenda

1/27/2006

I have spoken with my gay friends. I have been to yoga classes and men's health spas and Restoration Hardware, chic rug shops and the Castro Starbucks and really cute restaurants featuring mixed baby greens that cost $12.

I have observed. I have taken notes. I have checked the fashions and the cars and the skin-tight T-shirts, the newsletters and the bumper stickers and the secret codes hidden within the rainbow flag.

It is time to come clean. It is time to reveal the truth. After all, the religious right has been hammering at it for years, the pseudo-Christians and the homophobes and the sexually terrified all fully and truly believing that there is a plot, a massive, deep-seated agenda among the gay community not only to decriminalize and demystify homosexuality but to actually coerce and cajole and actively *lure* the innocent white babies of America

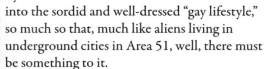

into the sordid and well-dressed "gay lifestyle," so much so that, much like aliens living in underground cities in Area 51, well, there must be something to it.

Just look. Look at the wanton slew of nasty e-mails I received — intermixed like bloody shrapnel amid a huge stack of gorgeous e-mail enthusiasm, mind — in response to my recent column extolling the virtues of the heartbreaking, perspective-altering "Brokeback Mountain" phenom, wherein I dared to suggest that this spare and potent little film might actually help move the human experiment forward, just a little. What nerve I had.

> Mark, gay films move us back. To tell society,
> which includes children, that to stick a pe-
> nis inside someones anus, a wholey unnatrual
> act is ok and normal is ubsurd. I don't hold
> anything against gays, I'm not one to judge
> people, they can do what they please, but to
> shove their pervertions down everyones throat,
> and to try to make it mainstream and teach
> children honosexualiy is a normal thing for
> people to do is sick. — Steve W

Or this:

> It is really hard to believe that people like
> yourself are gloating over this film and are so
> proud of the degradation of our country (USA)
> that you have joined the masses and are HELL
> BENT on the destruction of Christianity, fam-
> ily values, and everything that is decent and
> what out forefathers have fought and died for
> in this country. Your kind are the real BIG-
> OTS! You are the enemy of everything that is
> decent and good, you love death and destruc-
> tion (that is what the homosexual lifestyle
>
> will lead to)... — Larry L

Isn't that sweet? Doesn't it make you feel good to be an American? Sure it does.

But you know what? Adorably rabid, misguided homophobes like Steve and Larry, they might have a point after all. Because after all my observations and when I really allow myself to be honest, I become convinced of the existence of a truly shocking gay lifestyle, an actual gay agenda far more sinister than even desperately misguided and morally lost people like Steve and Larry can comprehend.

Do you know what it is? Do you want to know the real gay agenda, what 96.8 percent of all gay couples wish for every single day including Sunday? Here it is:

From what I can glean and above all else, the gay people of America seem to want this simply inexcusable level of boundless, unchecked *normalcy*. It's true. For some reason, they believe the utterly disgusting idea that they should be able to live their lives in peace and trust and health, with full support and assistance from their schools and hospitals and government, just like everyone else. I know. Shudder.

It is, in fact, remarkably similar to what heteros want. And women. And black people. And immigrants. And dwarves. That is, to be able to fall in love and maybe even get married (or at least have the option) and have decreasing amounts of sex and raise a family and pay their taxes and argue with their lovers over who the hell spent 200 bucks on long distance to their mother, all while not having to worry about getting the living crap beaten out of them with tire chains by Arkansas and Alabama and most of Texas, or secretly loathed by small-minded pseudo-Christians who wouldn't know Jesus' true message if it bit them on the other cheek.

Ah, the deviousness of it all, the sheer *nerve* to desire the same sort of lives as everyone else. But do you want to know the kicker? The true aspect of the "gay agenda" that makes the religious right's skin really crawl? Here it is: When all of that normalcy is in place, when these repulsive gay beings who like to walk around in public and eat at restaurants and drink their lattes and laugh out loud and stick things into each other's bodies for sexual pleasure, well, they want the most appalling thing of all: They just want to be left alone.

I know. It's hideous. How *dare* they! How dare most gays ask not to be harassed, how dare they not really care to flaunt their sexuality or convince anyone that homosexuality is cool or righteous or the only way to be, beyond reassuring children that it's OK to be whatever religion or sexual orientation your mind and body and heart and soul guide you to be. Can you imagine? What horror.

This is, in fact, the most sinister gay agenda of all. Normalcy. Lack of fear. Happiness. The right to be miserably in love just like everyone else and have it recognized by the culture as, well, no big deal. Safe. Healthy. Beautiful, even. What nerve.

To Steve and Larry's great dismay, gay people do not seem to care in the slightest for convert-ing anyone to homosexuality, which of course would be the equivalent of converting a frying pan into a banana split. It simply cannot be done. It's bitterly sad that this must be repeated so frequently in terms so simple that even Steve and Larry can comprehend, but gayness is no more a lifestyle choice than is blond hair or blood type or that knowledge, deep down in your skin, that neoconservatism eats the soul of the nation. It just is.

Much can be learned from this shocking revelation. Much we can glean from the gay agenda's "true" motivations — most notably in how it

contrasts with the famed and beloved Christian neoconservative heterosexual agenda, the one that instructs that you please keep your mouth shut
and blindly believe in the same bitter God as everyone else, and by the
way please bury your true sexuality and get married at 23 and pop out six
kids and become quickly and quietly miserable and gain 30 pounds and
stop having sex entirely and get divorced at 50 and wake up just in time to
watch yourself die.

Oh my yes, that has proven to be just so much better, hasn't it, Steve?
Larry?

And now, The Daring Spectacle presents...

Mullet Haiku

*Check out my sweet-ass
'78 Camaro
Up there on those blocks*

What shall I term this incessant need I apparently have — or surely had, way back when this column first appeared — to inform whomever will listen of the true (dirty, bloody, pagan) origins of most uptight Christian religious tradition? What is this mild pathology I apparently nurture so tenderly, eagerly? And does it have anything to do with what appears to be my other calling in life, the devout advocacy of Hitachi Magic Wands for every human female over age 14?

Christmas, Easter, Valentine's Day, Halloween. Is there an American holiday (OK, besides Thanksgiving) that doesn't owe its origins to ancient, pre-Christian goddess cults and fertility rites and sundry mysterious what-not? And isn't that just a little bit interesting? No? Is something wrong with me? —mm

Whip my Roman sex gods

02/14/2003

Hot pagan sex and eternally lustful gods and ancient wolf goddesses, potential marriage and more sex and more than a little crazed, giddy blood sacrifice. All followed by some nice light whippings administered by nearly naked, grinning boy-men, casual flagellations by goat-skin, some joyful thrashing in the name of fertility and purity and, you know, sex.

Ahh, Valentine's Day.

The original, that is. Before it was called Valentine's Day, back when it was called Lupercalia, a big Roman festival in honor of the fertility god Lupercus, before the ever-scowlin' church got a hold of this ancient and rather odd Roman lust-fest, co-opted it and de-sexed it stripped it of its more salacious and admittedly libertine joys, as the church is so tragically wont to do.

Because as everyone knows, the church is nothing if not all about rigid joyless dogma and romantic abstinence and mountains of little chalky candy hearts. Mmm, sanctimoniousness.

Tried to convert it into a mildly consecrated (read: bland, not naked) day, the church did, "Christianize" that naughty pagan fest, and failing that because no way are you gonna trump ancient sex and lust with uptight chastity and faux-purity, they tossed in Saint Valentine to the mix, invented some nice legend, tried to turn this most funky of pagan holidays into an homage to saccharine romantic love and cherry nougat chocolates and Hallmark schmalz. Did they succeed? Sort of.

Basically, it went something like this: In ancient Rome, on the 15th of February, in an altar called the Luperci sacred to the god Lupercus, in a cave in which the she-wolf goddess nursed founding twins Romulus and Remus, Luperci priests gathered and sacrificed goats and young dogs, the former for strength, the latter for purification and in honor of their strong sexual instinct and because it was a fertility diety and this is just what you did if you were a happy pagan citizen a couple thousand years ago.

Some hunky boys of noble birth were then led to the shrine, where the priests would dab their foreheads with a sword dipped in the animal blood, after which our baffled youths were apparently obliged to break out into a shout of purifying laughter because that's what the rite called for and no one is quite sure why and, well, wouldn't you?

Then, a feast. Meat. Wine galore. Followed by the slicing of goat skins into pieces, some of which the priests cut into strips and dipped in the blood and then handed to the boys, who would take off and run through the streets, gently touching or lashing crops and bystanders — especially women — with the skins along the way to inspire fertility and harvest and because hey, half-naked laughing boys wielding bloody goat skins — what's not to love?

Actually, the women eagerly stepped forward to be so stroked, believing that such a blessing rendered them fertile (even if they were sterile), and procured them ease in childbearing, and made them look all gothy and cool and sexy.

"This act of running about with thongs of goat-skin was a symbolic purification of land and men," says one rather dry, scholarly website on the topic. "For the words by which this act is designated are februare and lustrare, and the goat-skin itself was called februum, the month in which it occurred Februarius, and the god himself Februus." So, you know, there you go. February. Purity and lust and sex and gods. Really, what else do you need?

Then came the sex lottery. Oh yes. Say it like you mean it. Pretty much only have to say the words, "sex lottery," and already you're like, damn, count me in, sure beats dinner and a movie.

All the young lasses in the city would place their names in a large urn, and the city's eligible bachelors would choose a name out of the urn and become paired for the year with his chosen woman, oftening resulting in marriage. You know, sort of like the Mormons. Only with actual sex. And booze. And without the creepy undergarments.

But if there's one thing the sexless butt-clenched church really hates, it's sex lotteries. And free thinking. And good porn. Condoms. Margarita enemas. Literature. But especially sex lotteries. Go figure.

So along comes Pope Gelasius around 486 A.D. and declares, let's say, oh, February 14 to be dedicated to a saint, and we'll call him Saint Valentine, who might or might not be an actual martyr whose true history is murky at best, given how church records show at least four martyrs with the name Valentinus, whoops, oh well.

Of course, they outlawed the yummy sex lotto, the church did, changed the names in the urn from lusty single women to the names of pious saints to be emulated, and jammed their new holiday right up against the February 15 date of Lupercalia.

Which also had the added bonus of stomping all over the normal February 14 day of honoring Juno (Roman Goddess-queen of women and marriage), and focused it all on the makeshift Valentine, and voila, here we are: Hallmark cards and candy hearts and poisoned Ecuadorian rose workers.[1] In a nutshell.

But of course, the modern V-Day isn't all bad. And this is not to say we should necessarily return to the old ways, a little bloodletting and lashing and animal sacrifice and random sex lotteries. Except for maybe the Mormons.

Because everyone knowns that right under the cheap veneer of Valentine's Day mega-marketing and hollow churchly romance is yet another delicious excuse to have more sex and indulge in fleshly pleasures and lick chocolate syrup off your lover's tailbone. Hopefully.

In other words, the church both succeeded in their hostile takeover, and failed miserably. Sure Valentine's Day is all romance and sentiment and Malaysian-made stuffed teddy bears on the outside, but it's all raw oysters and sly spankings and salacious romps and whipped-creamed nipples and soft divine bedroom cooing, inside.

Which is exactly as it should be. Which is exactly how we still, without even realizing it, manage to recall our delicious Lupercalia, take a big lick of ye olde pagan ways, regardless of everpresent churchly frowning and 'Be Mine' twittering and chubby Cupid chinz. Deep earthly sex and hoary gods and fertile lust and voluminous feasts of meat and wine? You're soaking in it.

1 http://yuphae.notlong.com

I remember being told by a rather nervous editor at the time to cut/rewrite part of this column for reasons of libel or fear of corporate backlash or some-such. I think it was the scene where I have the Gillette creatives sitting around the conference room, trying to come up with the next ridiculous landfill product with which to insult the human race. I believe I depicted them as drunk, or stoned, or slightly evil, or all three, as they passed a razor around the table and fondled each others' egos until one of them popped up from his drunken stupor and said "Hey! Since we already have like, nineteen goddamn blades in the stupid thing, let's fuck with the handle!"

I mean really, how do you imagine they come up with products like this? And what sort of life must you have led to reach a point where you get to go home at night saying yes, oh dear God yes, I just contributed to the sad, overcooked world a vibrating pink plastic Chinese-made razor that flagrantly mimics a cheap plastic sex toy. I shall sleep well tonight! (This is why I'm not in advertising).

I suppose it could be worse. It could be a Glade plug-in air freshener. Or a disposable toilet brush. Or Hummer cologne. All of a piece, really. —mm

Another hard, hot pink shave

06/15/2005

It's long, it's smooth, it's gently, undulatingly curvy. It's hot pink, with a large, rounded tip, perfect for gripping and perfect for sending soft sensual signals up your leg and down your vertebrae as you stroke, up and down, down and up, slowly, carefully, lovingly.

You can use it in the shower. You can use it in the bathtub. You can use it on your armpits, though they don't talk much about that in the marketing copy because it's not very sexy and most people don't masturbate anywhere near their armpits, so far as you know.

It fits deliciously, caressingly into the palm of your hand. And yes, it vibrates.

Is it a spatula? Is it a power drill? Is it Orlando Bloom?

Why, no. It is, of course, the new Gillette Venus Vibrance™ undulating soothing vibrating battery-powered waterproof hot pink triple-blade semidisposable razor for women. Say it with me: woo.

It is also, of course, the closest thing to a legit sex toy you can buy without actually buying a legit sex toy and without your uptight mom looking at you funny and without the security screeners at the airport trying to embarrass you by dumping that silver-bullet vibrator[1] out of your purse, and without a soft tingling sensation coming into your toes as you think about the aforementioned Orlando Bloom nibbling said toes while wearing nothing but some smiley-face boxer shorts and a leather whip and a sly Jaegermeister grin.

Here is what you must do. You must visit the Gillette Web site dedicated to the Vibrance,[2] and look. You must admire the cloying marketing cleverness, the not-at-all subtle sexual overtones, the shameless soft-porn lushness that makes women absolutely goddamn hell-yes believe they truly *must* waste 20 bucks on a silly vibrating pink razor.

Isn't it cute? The multibillion-dollar Gillette monolith making a cheap-ass vibrator and selling it as a razor? Hell, maybe they didn't know. Maybe they honestly thought, with all their marketing savvy and all their billions and all those PR whizzes on the staff, that the Vibrance was just another innocent, sweet, virginal product for innocent, sweet, virgin women. You think?

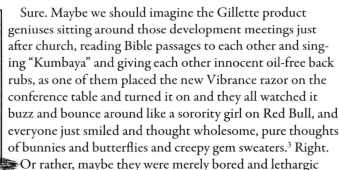

Sure. Maybe we should imagine the Gillette product geniuses sitting around those development meetings just after church, reading Bible passages to each other and singing "Kumbaya" and giving each other innocent oil-free back rubs, as one of them placed the new Vibrance razor on the conference table and turned it on and they all watched it buzz and bounce around like a sorority girl on Red Bull, and everyone just smiled and thought wholesome, pure thoughts of bunnies and butterflies and creepy gem sweaters.[3] Right.

Or rather, maybe they were merely bored and lethargic and sitting around in another corporate stupor trying to think of a way to sucker more people into the disposable-razor vortex, until someone said "Let's stick a battery in it and make it vibrate so women will forever associate our cheap-ass shaving products with, uh, masturbation," and the overpaid boss yawned "Done" and everyone went for vodka tonics and Valium. That's my guess.

How can we tell, by the way, that this thing is a vibrator in disguise? I mean, besides the hot smooth fleshy pinkness and the rounded penile tip and besides the fact that the portion of the razor's handle that vibrates most powerfully is actually the large, rounded end *without the razor blades on it*?

That's easy. Just look at the men's version.

Oh yes, men have a vibrating Gillette razor too. It's called the Mach3 Power Nitro (because men are just that stupid) and it's black and neon green and full of ridges and cheesy videogame design cues, and it's clearly designed to look like some futuristic race-car gearshift or something, and of course it's the exact same goddamn razor as the Venus, except the men don't talk up the gentle sensual Soothing Vibrations™ factor one bit. Oh my no.

Rather, for the men, it's all aggro, studly David Beckham-approved talk about how you can, with the push of a button, feel the "boost in performance" of your silly $20 plastic razor, which is a bit like saying you can feel the "boost in performance" when you swap your plain dental floss for mint.

But on the men's Gillette Web site, we get this intricate diagram, an actual Flash-animated cutaway of the M3 so men can see how the thing actually works (because men are just that gullible), and one look at the animation and you can see the little off-center metal spinning head inside the tip and if you've ever seen the very basic mechanism that makes vibrators do their delicious vibrator thing — and if you haven't you are missing a very important part of life's education — you know: This is the exact same thing.

And do note, won't you, how the vibrating portion on the men's M3 razor is actually where you'd expect it to be — in the tip, nearest the blades. Not so in the Vibrance. For the women, Gillette kindly put the vibrator in the opposite end, in the smooth, engorged, rounded handle base. Gosh, you could even leave the blades off entirely and still use the vibrating handle! Isn't that thoughtful of them? Do you want them to smack you over the head with the obviousness of it all?

The funny thing is, I'm not sure which target market gets the inane Vibrance, exactly. Is it women who already have a nice arsenal of sex toys and who recognize this silly gizmo as a cheap addition to the toy box? Is it teenage girls who can't make themselves shop at Babeland.com or Goodvibes.com or Blowfish.com just yet, but who sense there's more to life than tight jeans and binge drinking and shopping malls and being groped by boys who don't know a clitoris from a garden rake?

Or is it just women with too much disposable income who think the Vibrance is pretty and cute and it might do in a pinch if they forgot their Blueberry Turbo Glider[4] back in the Range Rover glove box, and they're stuck in a Holiday Inn somewhere in Indianapolis and they just watched an Orlando Bloom love scene and the hotel bathtub doesn't have a shower massager?

No matter. Hopefully, if these women ignore the Vibrance and spend their money right, they will all emerge from the shower with exactly the same sort of flushed, knowing grin, and the world will be a better place.

1 http://xenger.notlong.com
2 http://gillettevenus.com/us
3 http://xeicho.notlong.com
4 http://uodae.notlong.com

I'm not exactly sure why I find it so frightening/vexing that so many on the ideological right, or even in the world culture at large, seem so unable to conceptualize the divine as a wild, cosmic, pansexual maelstrom of living energy, a fluid, electric consciousness, rather than some sort of scowling human-like Megatron secretly criticizing your masturbation techniques and judging your taste in boyfriends and butt plugs and sandwich meats. Check that: I know exactly why. Maybe I'm just not exactly sure how I overcame my mild Episcopalian upbringing to believe it — I credit Tom Robbins, initially — but it sure gets me into all sorts of delicious trouble.

This column unleashed a torrent of response, as you might imagine, upwards of 3,000 comments running the usual gamut from absolute homophobic revulsion to blissed-out delight (mostly the latter, thankfully). I was also reminded for the thousandth time that it really doesn't matter how much science and biological truth you loose upon the religious autobots of our culture (see page 89), they will invariably believe whatever they want and continue to cower in the face of their angry, unhappy God. No matter. The animals just shrug, howl and keep right on fucking. —mm

God is slightly gay

07/01/09

I am sitting here right now smiling just a little, fondly recalling that famously controversial children's book, the one about the gay penguins.

Remember? That positively adorable pair of them, at the Central Park Zoo, who had adopted an abandoned egg and then hatched it themselves and were raising the chick together as a couple, even though the chick was clearly not theirs — though of course how penguins can actually tell whose kid is whose is still a question. Never mind that now.

The best part: the story was absolutely true. The book, "And Tango Makes Three," was beautiful and sweet and touching in all the right ways — except, of course, for the fact that it was also totally evil.

For indeed, the penguins in question, named Roy and Silo, were both males. This meant they were clearly in some sort of ungodly, aberrant homosexual relationship, mocking natural laws and defying God's will

that all creatures only cohabitate with the opposite sex and buy microfiber sofas from Pottery Barn and eat their meals in silent resentment and never have sex.

Worst of all, the book depicted this relationship, this "family," as perfectly OK, as no big deal, as even (shudder) normal. After all, Roy and Silo didn't seem to give much of a damn. Tango sure seemed happy, what with not being left for dead and all. As of this writing, the Central Park Zoo has yet to be swallowed into a gaping maw of sinful doom. Any minute now, I suppose.

I am right now amused at this because it turns out Roy and Silo were not really so much of an anomaly at all. Nor were they some sort of unholy freak show, an immoral mistake in the eyes of a wrathful hetero God. Far from it. Turns out they were, in fact, far more the norm than many humans, even to this day, want to let on.

Behold, the ongoing, increasingly startling research: homosexual and bisexual behavior, it turns out, is rampant in the animal kingdom. And by rampant, I mean proving to be damn near universal, commonplace across all species everywhere, existing for myriad reasons ranging from pure survival and procreative influence, right on over to pure pleasure, co-parenting, giddy screeching multiple monkey orgasm, even love, and a few dozen other potential explanations science hasn't quite figured out yet. Imagine.

Are you thinking, "Why sure, everyone knows about those sex-crazed dolphins and those superslut bonobo monkeys and the few other godless creatures like them, the sea turtles and the weird sheep and such, creatures who obviously haven't read Leviticus. But that's about it, right? Most animals are devoutly hetero and straight and damn happy about it, right?"

Wrong.

New research is revealing so many creatures and species that exhibit homosexual/bisexual behavior of some kind, scientists are now saying there are actually very few, if any, species in existence that *don't* exhibit it in some way. It's everywhere: Bison. Giraffes. Ducks. Hyenas. Lions and lambs, lizards and dragonflies, polecats and elephants. Hetero sex. Anal sex. Partner swapping. The works.

Let's flip that around. Here's the shocking new truism: In the wilds of nature, to *not* have some level of homosexual/bisexual behavior in a given species is turning out to be the *exception*, not the rule. Would you like to read that statement again? Aloud? Through a megaphone? To the Mormon and Catholic churches? And the rest of them, as well? Repeatedly?

Would you like to inform them that such behavior is definitely not, as so many hard-line Christian literalists want to believe, some sort of poison that snuck into God's perfect cake mix, nor is it all due to some sort of toxic chemical that leeched into the animal's water supply, suddenly causing all creatures to occasionally feel the urge wear glitter and listen to techno and work on their abs?

And so we extend the idea just a little bit. Because if homosexual/bisexual behavior is universal and by design, if gender mutability is actually deeply woven into the very fabric of nature itself, and if you understand that nature is merely another word for God, well, you can only surmise that God is, to put it mildly, much more than just a little bit gay. I mean, obviously.

But let's be fair. That's not exactly true. God is not really gay, per se. God is more... pansexual. Omnisexual. Gender neutral. Gender indeterminate. It would appear that God, this all-knowing and all-creating and all-seeing divine energy that infuses and empowers all things at all times everywhere, does not give a flying leather whip about gender.

Or rather, She very much does, but not in the simpleminded, hetero-only way 2,000 years of confused religious dogma would have us all believe.

God's motto: Look, life is a wicked inscrutable orgy of love and compassion and survival instinct, shot through with pain and longing and death and suffering and far, far too many arguments about who did or did not pay the goddamn mortgage.

Life on Earth is messy and bloody and constantly evolving and transmuting and guess what? So is sexuality, and love, and connection, and what it means to exist. And if you uptight, hairless bipeds don't soon acknowledge this in a very profound way, well, it ain't the damn penguins who will suffer for it. You feel me?

This, then, is what science appears to be trying to tell us, has been telling us, over and over again: Nature abides no narrow, simplistic interpretation of her ways. Nature will defy your childish fears and laughable behavioral laws at nearly every turn. God does not do shrill homophobia.

Of course, until very recently, science was also beaten with the stick of right-wing fear for many, many years, told to keep quiet about those damnable facts, or else. Homosexuality is a lifestyle! A choice! And you can be lured into it! Seduced by the evil rainbow! Just like those poor penguins! Right.

Let us be perfectly clear. Not every individual animal necessarily displays homosexual traits. But in every sexually active species on the planet, at least some of them do, for all sorts of reasons, and it's common and obvious and as normal as a warm spring rain falling on a pod of giddy bottlenose dolphins having group sex off the coast of Fiji.

And either humankind is part of nature and the wanton animal kingdom, a full participant in the messy inexplicable glories of the flesh and spirit and gender play, or *we* are the aberrant mistake, the ones who are lagging far behind the rest of the kingdom, sad and lost in the eyes of a very, very fluid and increasingly disappointed God.

And now, The Daring Spectacle presents...

Mullet Haiku

Trailer has no tires
Rusted rims have sunk in deep
My Homeland's secure

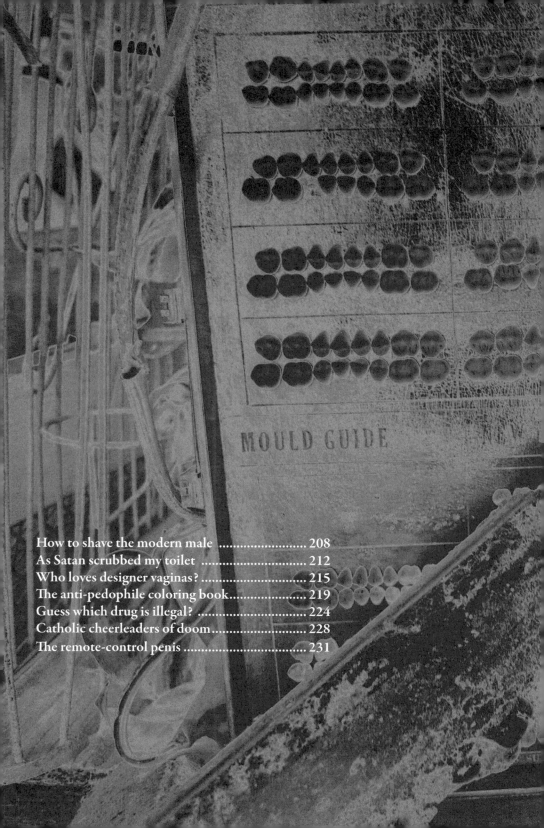

MOULD GUIDE   NEW

WE ARE SO
WEIRD

A very special column. A very special topic. A very special viral ad campaign. I'd love to see the customer feedback the Philips Corp received on this a few years ago. Did they get hate mail? Terrified letters from panicky, innuendo-deprived parents? The Christian right? Razor fetishists? Confused frat boys? So special was this column that the Chron – or rather, the lovely and bold Deputy Managing Editor name of Meredith White – chose to move it from its usual position in Friday Datebook into a feature slot in the Sunday Style section... on Valentine's Day, no less, over the ever-grumpy protestations of the paper's ever-grumpy publisher. Now that's romantic.

For the record, I've never used a Bodygroom, which is just a cheap electric razor, cleverly repackaged and very cleverly remarketed. For such essential manscaping, I simply use a plain razor and some really good soap. In the shower. Works great. So is the optical inch (see below). You have my word. TMI? —mm

How to shave the modern male

02/14/2007

I have often wondered, in calmer moments of profound wisdom unaffected by actual subtle thought or deeper intellectual concerns, why there is no sly and essential maintenance manual for the penis.

Wait, let me be more specific. Why has no men's magazine, not Esquire and not Maxim and certainly not yuppie-riffic GQ, dared venture — to my knowledge, anyway — a single, enthusiastically detailed column as to the general health and upkeep and — perhaps most importantly of all, as far as overall aesthetics and tactile friendliness are concerned — the prudent follicular trimmage of the enchanted regions *surrounding* the male appendage?

Oh I know, it's a sensitive topic, this male-maintenance thing. It's not one many sexually confused modern men open up to easily, not something we like to dwell upon and analyze in the way women can so easily discuss menstrual flow or waxing techniques or purse design.

Men, in our infinite, mulish simplemindedness, tend to think all body parts are just supposed to *work,* and all the stuff growing on our backs and thighs and groinal regions looks damn fine as it is, no matter how tangled and shaggy and utterly extraterrestrial it might appear and how often our lovers cringe and shudder at the sight of us naked. Besides, there's little we can do about it anyway. Right?

Wrong.

For example, grooming. The entire unloved metrosexual movement aside, simply shocking is the size of the male population that thinks trimming the male body's incredible swarm of hair follicles is silly, unnecessary, just far too feminine, and is only meant to be restricted to the head and face and maybe a few strays on the biceps, when in fact there's an entire *universe* of trimmage that could take place, and grateful indeed would be most attuned women of the world.

(By the way, many of the top waxing salons, especially here in San Francisco, have a great plethora of straight male clients, many of whom are brought in by their wives and girlfriends. And as any worthy and attentive porn fan knows, most male porn stars are waxed and trimmed or even shaved completely, all the way down and back up underneath and well up into God's country. Makes for more aesthetically pleasing shots, is why. Just, you know, FYI.)

Which brings us, finally, after far too many meandering paragraphs, to Philips Norelco, a major appliance manufacturer and global leader in high-end hospital medical devices, recently venturing with seeming unchecked fearlessness into the delicate terrain of, you know, shaving the male crotch.

Gaze, won't you, at Philips Norelco's latest and surprisingly bold viral Internet ad campaign from 2006,[1] found on shaveeverywhere.com (Note, with some bemusement, that the shaveeverywhere.com URL was apparently still available to Philips and had not already been claimed by some happy underground fetish porn outfit. Wonders.)

For the record, shaveeverywhere.com is one of the new breed of interactive live-action campaigns that uses a series of fluid, fast-loading video splices of real actors to give the feel that the character is actually speaking right to you. There is another prime example of this genre, Microsoft's baffling but highly entertaining (well, for about 10 minutes) search site called Ms. Dewey (msdewey.com), in which a terrifically sexy actress (Janina Gavankar[2]) simultaneously flirts with and fluently berates her army of

swooning geek-boy viewers as they desperately scramble to type something clever to get her attention. Check it.[3]

Right off the bat, the playfully smarmy Philips pitchman — let's call him "Gary," a guy apparently meant to be a cross between a likable frat guy and a B-grade Hugh Hefner and that dude at the bar who orders a gin and tonic and won't stop talking about his love of cigars and parasailing — Gary lets you know the game. He mentions the absolute necessity of trimming (with full bleeps intact, natch) your back, cock, balls and ass. He keeps a straight face throughout, all winking nudge-nudge in-the-know guy chitchat.

Gary is selling something called the Bodygroom, a rather cheaply modified electric shaver made "exclusively" for men. It is, apparently, an all-over trimmer for all sorts of hair, from back to armpits to undercarriage. And yes, it really exists. Philips has sold a truckload of them, far more than they expected. And it's all thanks to Gary.

The pitch is clear. Gary will tell you, straight out, that the Bodygroom will "help make your d—k look bigger." This is a theme and a key selling point. He will also tell you, with a (winking) straight face, that the Bodygroom is "the convenient, easy, gentle way to make your genitals bloom." And if you ask him if women really prefer a well-groomed man, he will snicker in disbelief and barely be able to contain his laughter before composing himself, looking straight at the camera and deadpanning, "Yes, yes they do."

In fact, the opening introduction alone addresses your average American frat guy's naggingly homophobic concerns right from the start. Gary even admits to it himself: "Let me tell you, this whole issue [of genital grooming] used to make me quite uncomfortable. But now, with a hair-free back, well-groomed shoulders and an extra optical inch on my cock, let's just say life has gotten pretty darn cozy."

You will smile and say to yourself, wait, this is Philips Norelco? This is a major manufacturer of mountains of Chinese-made consumer products? Are they *insane*? Are they simply begging the Christian right to write nasty little notes to corporate HQ and threaten a shaver boycott as they pule about the flagrant innuendo and the bleeps and the offensive notion that American men should shave their perineum?

Doesn't matter. Click through this site a couple times (be sure to watch the music video) and you can't help but admit it's a ballsy move. Not only is Philips' ad agency (Tribal DDB) smarmily defying the cultural conservative mind-set that wails about gays and cries about sex and screams at the sight of the female nipple, but they are simultaneously going after that rarest of homophobic monosyllabic demographic beasts, the untrimmed American Net-savvy frat guy blog-reading dude. And if sales are any indication, they're succeeding fabulously.

In this way, you might even say that Philips is serving a deeper humanitarian purpose, fulfilling a serious cultural need. They are (inadvertently, of course) doing nothing less than informing armies of young, sexually

confused man-beasts that the general trimming of body hair — including, as Gary repeatedly states, the cock, balls and ass — isn't just for transvestites and gay porn stars and metrosexual writers anymore. In other words, caring about this sort of thing doesn't make you gay, or stupid, or emasculated. It actually makes you sort of hot.

And besides, who wouldn't want the pleasure of an extra optical inch?

1 http://enoogo.notlong.com
2 http://loxoor.notlong.com
3 http://aedahbu.notlong.com

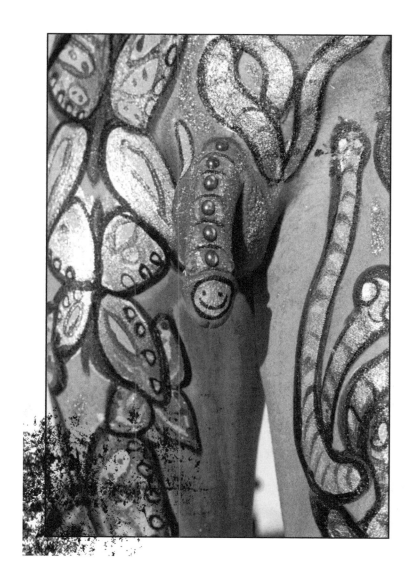

Has anything changed? Has the green movement altered our sensibilites in the slightest, to the point where actual concern for the planet outweighs our desperate demands for silly ultra-convenience and for inexcusable products that claim to protect us from evil germs that want to turn your child gay and steal your car keys?

Because the truth is, most of these products still exist, in some form or another, despite how 92.3 percent of them are total sweatshop-made petroleum-infused garbage and the megacorps that invent and market this crap to easily duped housewives of America should be slapped for trafficking in low-level landfill-ready fear, and I wish them ill.

Except for the Swiffer. I use a Swiffer (a generic knockoff, anyway). Lots of hardwood floors here in my flat in San Francisco. Works great. Otherwise, evil evil evil. —mm

As Satan scrubbed my toilet

05/28/04

Pity the poor, beleaguered housewife, still struggling like a haggard dog through her array of thankless daily chores.

Just look at her: hair pulled tight and life a-shambles, saddled with all manner of horrible toilet brushes and horrible sponges and horrible cloth towels to wipe down the horrible countertops, and then topping it all off with being forced to use one of those horrible, old-fashioned bristle brooms to sweep the floor. Horrible!

Thank God, then, for modern ultraconvenience. Thank God for the corporate household-product industry, so thoroughly glutted on excess merchandise and overinvention they can't possibly think of things we actually need anymore, so they just invent junk and make shit up to scare gullible women into buying it. Yay America!

See, now, the happily narcotized, sexless, vaguely bulbous modern housewife in the recent TV commercial as she finally tosses away her angry, growling, animated (!) toilet brush (see how it snaps and snarls at her like a deadbeat dad! See her toss it into the trash can and then plop her butt down on it in satisfied glee!) in favor of — say it with me — *disposable* toilet scrubbers you use once and throw away!

Like the ScotchBrite™! Or the Clorox ToiletWand™! Or the Scrub N' Flush! Or the Scrubbing Bubbles™ Fresh Brush™ Toilet Cleaning System! Yes, Virginia, the world is certainly headed in the right direction.

Just watch that brush's head break apart in a swirl of pulpy, chemical fibers in the toilet. Look at the nifty cheap-ass landfill-plastic handle —

remember, it's not a brush, it's a "toilet-cleaning system," sucker. Look at the shiny plastic tub of refills you have to buy every month just to keep the goddamn thing stocked before the handle snaps in half and you have to buy a whole new one, because it's actually worth about seventeen cents and is made by disposable factory workers in Malaysia who die of petroleum-related cancer even faster than George Bush decimated the Clean Air Act. Neat!

See? Life is easier already. Who knew you needed a new toilet brush to replace that tough metal one you had that lasted years? No one, that's who! What was wrong with the old, sturdy kind? Nothing, that's what! Hail marketing!

Dear sweet Jesus in sterilized heaven, why have we all been washing dishes using those positively archaic reusable scrub pads? Won't someone please invent a single-use, pretreated disposable scrubber that looks like a large feminine sanitary pad and is made of some frightening paper/plastic compound and coated in thick gobs of foaming chemicals and mysterious toxins that you use once on your lasagna pan and then throw away so you have to buy a new box of the damnable things every week?

Thank God, someone has. It's the new Dawn Wash N' Toss! Or maybe it's the Brillo Scrub N' Toss! Or those disposable Palmolive DishWipes which all come in big noxious tubs made from unrecycled plastics! Cool! Screw those loser trees. First one's free, Mom.

Brooms? Pshaw. Satan's whiskers. Brooms suck. Brooms are so totally Rubbermaid-O'Cedar-soap-opera-Valium-haze-Daddy's-away-on-business 1976. What we need now is a ridiculous plastic-handled thing with floppy little static-cling pads that you stick on the end and use once up and down the hardwood hallway and then throw away, never to be thought of again, because, well, we never do.

All hail the Swiffer! And the Swiffer Max! And the Swiffer WetJet™, with that big plastic spray-attachment tub you have to refill with toxic chemical cleaner! And the Swiffer hand duster, which you detach and throw away and replace until your shopping list consists solely of 18 different Swiffer refill products and maybe a huge bottle of Tylenol to combat the savage migraines you get from inhaling all those chemicals that poison your blood and make your kidneys cry. Whee!

Now just watch as the Swiffer-endowed housewife runs around like a coked-up lunatic singing the Swiffer song to the tune of "Whip It," drunk on the joy of electromagnetic McDusterthingies. No more brooms! Swiffer the world! Lobotomies all around!

You might think by now that we'd be slightly more aware. You might think that after decades of impassioned environmental movements and organic evolution and reams of irrefutable evidence proving how we are aggressively mauling the planet on a daily basis, that we'd be just slightly more conscious and attuned by now regarding what we put in our mouths, in our homes, down our toilets.

You might even think, furthermore, we'd be just a bit more cautious regarding toxic household cleaners and electric chemical air fresheners and various solvents and detergents and coatings, and realize that dousing the home with 10,000 synthetic petroleum-based products that are known to cause cancer and skin irritation and impotence and painful emphysemic death, well, it might not always be the best way to go. You might think.

You would, of course, be wrong.

There is no such awareness. Not yet. Not on any significant scale. The rain forests can disappear and we'll still buy disposable toilet brushes and throwaway diapers by the truckload. Oil prices can hit 50 bucks a barrel [*oh how quaint that price now seems! -mm*] and 1,000 sad disposable U.S. soldiers can die in oil-rich foreign nations and still Ford Expeditions will sell like hotcakes. We can create a mountain of dead useless slightly radioactive cell phones roughly the size of the planet Pluto. No one really cares. "Can you hear me now?" Um, no.

As it is with toilet brushes and brooms, so it is with our national agenda, our environmental policy, our war motives. In other words, there is a straight and unwavering line connecting the Scrub N' Toss with our environmental policy, our worldview, our motives for war and destruction. The world is our commodity. The world is our giant overlit soul-sucking Wal-Mart. Restrain it at your peril.

The good new is, we still have personal choice. Barely. Most of us still have the ability to discern between that which is truly helpful and beneficial in our lives and that which is simply not worth stomping over the planet like it's a fleeing butterfly and we are a heavily Ritalined little boy wielding a stick.

It's an increasingly precious commodity, this ability, this discernment, more endangered than the blue whale and the baby seal and the right to own a dildo in Texas, and it's diminishing fast, because BushCo hates it with a white-hot intensity normally reserved for nature or individuality or gay people in love. But it's still ours to make. Right?

It appears I am just terribly fond of posing this grand, rhetorical question about how you choose to see the world, which side of the coin you want to live on. Is a certain evolutionary step, technology, scientific advancement inherently good or evil, or is it merely how we choose to see and use it? Is the question not about the advancement itself, but what sort of energy and intelligence we want to cultivate and advance in the world?

The answer seems wildly obvious, but the baffling, insane developments keep popping up to challenge it in new and unexpected ways. Such is the lightning-fast nature of science and tech in the modern age. Such is the delirious weirdness of the human experiment.

So maybe the question isn't, say, "What does it mean that we now have the ability to build you a custom vagina, tailor the color of your baby's eyes, or reconfigure your DNA to prevent disease," but rather, "Just how fluid and malleable an organism is the human animal, the human soul, really? How wide, how deep, how godlike can the palette get? Is there really a limit? Why?" —mm

Who loves designer vaginas?

06/20/2007

What are you gonna do about it?

What are you gonna do about the fact that Mother Nature once again appears to be thwarting and mocking and then grinning like a divine trickster in the face of every cute, rigid right-wing idea of how humans and animals are supposed to move and hump and lick and behave?

What are you gonna do about human knowledge? About how science insists on marching hell-bent forward with such astonishing speed and with such incredible dexterity toward some glorious otherworldly nightmare dreamscape of anima manipulation, a land where we can effortlessly rescramble our genetic code and reconfigure this none-too-solid flesh as we "play God" in so many bewildering ways the Christian right can't even figure out where to aim its hollow, horrified indignation?

Here is the thing you must know: It is all changing with incredible, butt-tingling speed. It is all fast becoming more than we ever imagined, with ramifications we are only beginning to fully taste. There is no stopping it. There is little that can slow it down. There is only the single, looming question: How will you respond? Will you recoil and gag and spit, or will you gurgle and swallow and smile?

Example: We are on the cusp of being able choose, should you so desire, the exact size and length and speed and eye color and specific pleasing

fur markings of ... your dog.[1] And your cat. And your baby (well, minus
the fur). And by the way, we have also invented new drugs to eliminate
menstruation[2] and we can now grow designer vaginas in the lab[3] and plastic surgery is more common than bad sacrum tattoos and it's becoming
increasingly obvious that males of many species — including our own —
are largely unnecessary for procreation (but not, say, parallel parking, the
lifting of heavy things or buying you a nice postcoital breakfast).

Fascinating, that last thing. Have you heard? Scientists are discovering more and more creatures,[4] from sharks to bees to ants to turkeys to
Komodo dragons to turtles to sea bass, that can reproduce via partheno-
genesis (i.e., virgin birth; i.e., no father) either by actually switching sexes
so as to fertilize themselves, or via storing sperm for years for later use, or
because they're hermaphrodites, or by way of undertaking all manner of
clever unholy gender trickery so as to circumvent their own extinction and
confound creationists and ensure that all humans everywhere will continue to look around and blink furiously and go, Wait wait wait, didn't we
have some of this figured out already? What the hell happened?

Wait, did I say designer vaginas? Indeed I did. Doctors can now grow
new vaginal tissue in a lab, from the original stem cells, for eventual re-
planting (not to be confused with the hot trend in cosmetic vaginoplasty,
by the way, which is an entirely different fascination and has to do with
reshaping the labia for improved aesthetics and, you know, functionality.
God bless America).

Fabulous news for victims of birth defects and cancer and rare vaginal
disorders? You bet. Intriguing implications for all sorts of cosmetic appli-
cations, not to mention what it might mean for transsexuals, not to mention how close we are to doing the same thing with other organs — and

even, eventually, entire limbs?
One guess.

It is, we can all agree, a lot
to take in. It is a great deal to
attempt to process in one tiny
and oh-so-fleeting lifetime.
The notion of human eugenics
alone is, for many, overwhelming enough, the idea that new
parents will soon have some sort
of checklist at the gynecologist's
office wherein, when docs go
in to tweak your fetus' DNA to
eliminate diseases,[5] you can also

easily choose not only its sex, but also the skin tone and hair color and eye tint and muscle dexterity and 0-60 acceleration and number of cupholders and maybe an extra USB port or two because really, you can never have too many.

They are, quite obviously, the sort of advances that open so many cans of ethical and spiritual worms it shakes us to the very core of what we believe, of who we think we are and where we fit in and What It All Means. You know, the *good* questions.

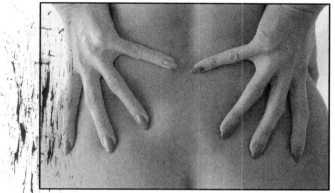

At the same time, it's really nothing new. It's little different than previous periods of explosive growth in human knowledge that both titillated and terrified the populace — such as, say, when Galileo pointed out — much to the church's quivering rage — that not only is man's little spinning blue space-ship *not* at the center of the universe, but we're actually so far out on the fringes, so minute and insignificant in our Copernican swirlings that we're really nothing more than belly-button lint in the giant laundry hamper of the gods. Talk about your existential angst.

This at least partially explains why so many are so eager to cling to religious dogma, to some sort of immovable, reliable framework of understanding, even if it means shutting off your brain and killing your divine intuition so you don't have to actually swim in those bloody, confusing pools of ethics and meaning and actually thinking for yourself. Mmm, numb groupthink. It's what's for dinner.

There are only two real options. One is to hold tight to the leaky life raft of inflexible ideology (hello, organized religion), to rules and laws and codes of conduct written by the fearful, for the fearful, to live in constant low-level dread of all the extraordinary changes and radical rethinkings of what it means to be human or animal or male or female or hetero or homo or any other swell little label you thought was solid and trustworthy but which is increasingly proven to be blurry and unpredictable and just a little dangerous.

There is another option. You can choose nimbleness, lightness, a sly and knowing grin to go with your wine and your new vagina and your never-ending thirst for more and deeper information. It's possible.

You can refuse to let yourself lock down into one way of looking at the world as you see all the science and genetic manipulation and designer vaginas, all the insane, incredible possibility as merely more evidence that we are, in the end, just one big karmic science experiment. Really now, what are you gonna do about it?

1 http://iivem.notlong.com
2 http://aigahg.notlong.com
3 http://rieti.notlong.com
4 http://ohveis.notlong.com
5 http://sahchuf.notlong.com

And now, The Daring Spectacle presents...

Mullet Haiku

Short in front long in b--
Oops! One syllable too ma--
Damn! Just don't get it

Fucking hell, why do they make it so easy? Why does the Catholic church absolutely insist on being so archaic and insulting and detrimental to the advancement of the human soul? The coloring book I describe below is cute and pathetic, to be sure. And yes, the sample you see on the next page is real. But the hypocrisy goes far beyond that. It's also dangerous. Even deadly.

Proof? That's easy. Pope Benedict recently announced, during a visit to AIDS-ridden Africa in '09, that not only do condoms not help in the fight against the deadly disease, but they actually could make things worse. This hot on the heels of news that, for more than six decades, priests and nuns in Ireland have been terrorizing orphaned boys and girls in the church's workhouse-style schools with sexual, physical and mental abuse. Tens of thousands of kids, beaten, sexually molested for more than 60 years. Go ahead, Google "Catholic orphanage abuse." Try not to retch.

Too harsh? I don't think so. Can the church's power and influence — along with its deep homophobia, misogyny, sexual hysteria, pedophilia lawsuits, and all-around ignorance of true spirit — die out soon enough? I say: Hell no. —mm

The anti-pedophile coloring book

12/12/2007

This is how you know. This is one more of the beautiful bizarre myriad ways the Great Shift signals its imminent arrival, in fits and spurts and wayward sidelong slaps, weird cultural burps from unexpected places.

Take the Archdiocese of New York. It has apparently just released new coloring book for kids,[1] all about how to be safe in an age of fear and predation. It is full of nice pictures of kids being sweet and virginal and right, engaging in happy activities that praise Almighty God while protecting themselves from, say, online predators and vegans and atheists. It is about awareness, about listening to your parents and saying your prayers and never, ever being alone with a priest and being nice to animals and never hitting your sister and ...

Wait, what? What was that, about the priests? Oh right. Um, the pedophilia. The sexual molestation and the lawsuits and the hints of deep ongoing perversion for the past, oh, 2,000 years. Yes.

Be sure to use your darkest crayon of bewildered dread when you color this particular page, kids, because there it is, the pedophilia threat, the church's appalling multimillion-dollar sexual abuse scandal,[2] right there on the page in the form of two sweet-looking, grinning (female) angels hovering around an innocent virgin altar boy and warning him — and by extension, you, the innocent virgin coloring book aficionado — to never, not ever, be alone in a room with an adult you do not know. Much like Jesus intended.

But wait, look again. Because there he is, right there in the doorway, a grinning priest, waving to you as the angels go on and seem to imply, "And remember boys, when we say 'adult,' we actually mean 'priest,' and you should never be alone with one unless the door is wide open or some other adults know where you are or there is a giant window in the room through which other wary adults or perhaps police officers can see if said priest begins to give the holy sacrament to your crotch. Next up: God loves bunnies!"

You have to pause. You have to step back for a second and actually look at this, rub your eyes, blink a few times. Wait, seriously? Don't ever be alone ... with a priest? This is the church telling me this? Don't be alone with ostensibly the most pious and sanctified human being you will ever know except for perhaps a nun or the Dalai Lama or Steve Jobs? Can this be right?

It is, you can easily argue, another disturbing exercise in fearmongering, in instilling in baffled children even more dread and anxiety about adulthood and God and life itself. "Don't talk to strangers" from the '70s morphs into "Don't IM with strangers" in the '90s to "Don't hang out with a priest too long lest he beseech you to nibble communion wafers off his pallid thighs" in the '00s. Nice world.

And yes, well do I realize this is something the church *must* do, that church officials are merely trying to do the right thing, trying to make amends, to reassure furious parents that their kids will be safe, despite how more than 4,400 priests have been accused[3] of sexual abuse so far, with some (unofficial) estimates far higher than that.

But it does bring up a rather fascinating question: Is the very existence of this weird little book another odd but undeniable sign (there are many others) that something a bit more spiritually rich, more karmically grand is at hand? A raised awareness? A deeper spiritual awakening? Is this the church

FOR SAFETY'S SAKE, A CHILD AND AN ADULT *SHOULDN'T* BE *ALONE* IN A CLOSED ROOM TOGETHER. IF A CHILD AND AN ADULT HAPPEN TO BE ALONE, SOMEONE SHOULD *KNOW* WHERE THEY ARE AND THE DOOR SHOULD BE *OPEN* OR HAVE A BIG WINDOW IN IT.

essentially telegraphing its own imminent demise? Maybe a little?

It's a slightly mushy notion I carry over to the bizarre parallel universe of conservative Christian megachurches, those giant, heavily shellacked fluorescent stadium nightmares that are still flourishing, more or less, simply because many of them are now dramatically diluting the fire-and-brimstone religion stuff, muting all that thorny theology and eschatology and even the right-wing intolerance (or rather, carefully burying it, to be fed to you slowly, bit by bit, especially around election time) and replacing it with something resembling, well, a giant, cheesy self-help seminar.[4]

With skits. And dance numbers. And a food court. And day care. And an iPod lounge. Self-esteem building exercises. "How to be a winner." "God has a plan for you." Only $29.95. Every week. Forever.

From what I read, this seems to be the modern megachurchly direction: minimize the dogma and melodrama and speaking in tongues, maximum the perkiness and nondenominationalism and piles of happy sanitized self-help schmaltz. In Jesus' name, naturally.

And best of all, your kids won't have to avoid these pastors because, by and large, they're not really pastors at all. They're CEOs, businessmen and salesmen and lifelong hucksters and you can rest assured most have never really studied deep theology or been to any sort of seminary in the first place. Fantastic.

It's true. Most megachurch leaders these days are, apparently, merely serious business pros, have had no real religious education at all, no intellectual experience studying the world's various belief systems, save for that "Selling Jesus to the Masses on DVD" weekend seminar at Harvard Business School Extension.

Again, I wonder (as I am, apparently, oddly wont to do): Is it possible to see this bizarre phenomenon as, like those Catholic anti-predator coloring books, another cryptic indicator that the Grand Shift is readying itself?

Sure, sure, megachurches are all about sterile groupthink and slick salesmanship and savvy business sense and have almost zero to do with profound, messy questions of spirit, and sure, weird anti-pedophile coloring books are, on one level, just another sad commentary on modern life. But they both also seem to indicate ... well, I'm not exactly sure what. Movement. A shift. Awkward, peculiar, clumsy, unconscious, but still ... movement.

The question is, toward what?

1 http://ooquolo.notlong.com
2 http://peete.notlong.com
3 http://phaegi.notlong.com
4 http://taifai.notlong.com

Date: Sat, 27 May 2006 17:33:43 -0700 (PDT)
From: John X <bXXX@yahoo.com>
Subject: Zorkon - far out, man!
To: mmorford@sfgate.com
MIME-Version: 1.0

Dear Sir:

I've read your article "All Women Are From Zorkon 9". Your use of the word Epiphany, or more precisely, "epiphanies", in the 5th paragrapy, is very much in error.

Accepted dictionary definition follows:
1. A divine manifestation
2. Twelve days after Christmas; celebrates the visit of the three wise men to the infant Jesus

What do the above definitions have to do with the interrupted screwing you were engaged in with your personal slut????

No, it's ok. I like it when dumbfucks like you, raised in the Outcome Based Education system, use words you don't even remotely understand. Puts you in your real place, no?

Don't forget, those rabbits, mosquitoes and field mice are much better at sex than you. Stop writing such stupid articles and get back in that bed and do more fucking. Fuck all day, all night, fuck fuck fuck. How are you going to surpass (or even match) the mice and rabbits if you don't practice?

-JW

From: Gerry H <XXX@msn.com>
Date: Thu, 23 Oct 2008 15:11:45 +1030
To: mmorford@sfgate.com
Subject: Out of control

You are very lucky to still be able to post your rants via the internet version of SFGate ... but no wonder that you have been removed from the print version, because you are off with the fairies, somewhere.

You are a babe in the woods, Mark, and therefore rant in ignorance ... never having experienced anything more than an easy existence, replete with your sundry widgets and gadgets, electronic or otherwise.

You would not have a clue about how to build a house, fix a car, mend some plumbing defect - even just a leaky tap - i.e. you are just so "girly". I do not have much of a problem with females being irrational and having hissy-fits, e.g. during PMT, but I do have a problem with you being irrational and having hissy-fits, like your latest diatribe.

You remind me of several "out of control" females I have known - one of whom went to Bali for seven days and "had" had eight blokes during that period. She fucked eight blokes in seven days. You would probably endorse that as some kind of "liberation", but you know fuck all.

I am not a moralist - at all - but what you promote is best described as "pure fucking evil".

I am willing to bet my bottom dollar that you cannot "score" sexually - or in any other way - unless you can pay for it.

From: JvrXXX@aol.com
Date: Sun, 13 Jul 2008 16:57:05 EDT
Subject: response to your article
To: mmorford@sfgate.com
MIME-Version: 1.0
X-Spam-Flag:NO

Why is it that a fag such as yourself is allowed to
spew your liberal-nazi like rhetoric upon well meaning
people here in the Bay Area?

   At which point, did San Francisco become a
completely whip-lash liberal, bastion for Communist
propagandists such as yourself? Why is it that
your opinion is more important than a writer who
would simply give us an objective view-point on life
issues. By the way, who appointed you God, to make
such judgements on christians or others who simply want
a normal life-style as opposed to the bizarre, weird,
overLY-indulgent lifestyle of a homosexual?
   J. Gonzalez

You have "wet dreams" about what Obama can do for you,
but he does not give a stiff shit about you and would
recoil from your many, bizarre, fantasies.

The "world" is NOT about to embrace your very confused
views on homosexuality, transgender and all the other
issues which you, personally, Have not made a dent in.

You are a wanker Mark.

From: RoBO <XXXX@adelphia.net>
User-Agent: Thunderbird 1.5.0.7 (Windows/20060909)
MIME-Version: 1.0
To: mmorford@sfgate.com
Subject: ugggh

You love that piece of shit so much why don't you
stick your divinely inspired cock in it. Your article
made me puke. If I could email that puke to you, you'd
have a very messy lap right now. More messy than the
ejaculatory stain your Apple made you project. Get a
fucking life you bandwagon whore.

I enjoy a relatively nice amount freedom in my column, at least as far as topic range is concerned, can write about almost whatever I like without overt fear of backlash or punishment. But even so, I still write for a mainstream media joint. I can still only go so far.

This piece is a good example. It's is about as close as I can ever really come to a flat-out endorsement of the use of Ecstasy for fun and bliss. It's in there, but you gotta peel away a few layers to get to it. I have serious caveats, to be sure. But in terms of the ridiculous hysteria the CDC and various War on Drugs agencies like to spread about many illegal inebriates, I like to push back as much as I can.

As to the topic at hand, well, while my tacit agreement that fibromyalgia might not, in fact, be a "real" disease garnered a bit of heat and push-back, I'm actually far more fascinated by the larger question of how we think of illness, what constitutes true health, and how it is that we have a health care system still so dominated by Big Pharma, still set up to profit far more from a sick populace than a healthy one. –mm

Guess which drug is illegal?

01/18/2008

Over here we have a new drug. It has one particularly unfortunate side effect: It makes you fat. Or rather, fatter, given how most patients who take it are already quite overweight to begin with.

But that's not all. Other nasty side effects include dizziness, confusion, sleepiness, severe edema (swelling and oozing), among others. What fun. But hey, at least it works, right?

Well, no, not really. It apparently works only about half the time, if that, and even then it doesn't work very well and it certainly doesn't actually *cure* anything or treat any of the potential *causes* of your illness or address any of the deeper biological/psychological issues at hand and, in fact, only "works" (they guess, but don't actually know) by essentially numbing the central nervous system, and therefore merely blocking out what your body is trying to tell you. Sort of like saying the light hurts your eyes and then taking a pill to make you go blind. There now, all better.

This new drug is called Lyrica. It's from Pfizer, and it was just approved by the FDA[1] to treat an awful, inscrutable condition known as fibromyalgia, an is-it-or-isn't-it illness distinguished by all-over bodily pain the causes of which no one can figure and which few are really sure is even a real disease, per se, given that there's no biological test to diagnose it and no way to accurately validate its existence and given that it has all sorts of seemingly unrelated, scattershot symptoms, like irritable bowel (another suspect ailment) and ringing in the ears and, well, just about everything else.[2]

No matter. After years of doubt as to its effectiveness (and fibromyalgia's existence), Lyrica has been approved, and fibromyalgia has been more or less legitimized. Pfizer stands to make billions, as do the other pharmco titans who are begging the FDA to let them make expensive new drugs to treat this strange condition that no one seems to understand — drugs which may actually exacerbate the condition — but which clearly has enough patients who seem to be suffering from it even though they might very well be suffering from something else entirely.

Ah, the pharmaceutical industry. Tremendous amounts of good, underscored by giant bolts of shameless, exploitive, predatory evil. Isn't it fascinating?

Over here, another drug. This one's been around awhile. World famous, beloved by millions, controversial for all the wrong reasons. It is currently very, very illegal. Producing and selling it in any quantity can result in severe punishment, years in prison.

It has been deemed highly dangerous, potentially toxic, even lethal, and for years the government and the Centers for Disease Control and your own mother have issued all sorts of lies and alarmist B.S. about it, like how it drains spinal fluid, induces brain aneurisms, makes you vote Libertarian. Which is not to say taking it doesn't have its random dangers, but, you know, please.

This drug is famous for producing incredible feelings of euphoria, openness, warmth and love and happiness in almost everyone who takes it. It is staggeringly effective, non-addictive, and when taken somewhat responsibly and with a slight hint of intelligence, has very few, if any, notable or permanent side effects.

Its positives border on miraculous. It can effortlessly break down long-held psychological barriers, remove obstacles to communication and stifled emotion, make patients/users feel open and happy and much better able to handle stress, anxiety, all manner of trauma.

It gets better. Some of the deeper emotional breakthroughs it produces last for weeks, months, or forever. Truly, entire loving relationships have been launched based on the deep bonding and raw emotional honesty a couple discovers while on it, and in many cases, those feelings become the foundation for long-term marriages (or, by way of the same raw honesty, encourage the end of unhappy, dying ones).

Oh yes — this drug also frequently induces profound, life-changing spiritual awakenings, can eradicate neurosis, increase feelings of empathy and forgiveness and peace and overlay it all with an increased love of music and sensual pleasure.

Thank God it's illegal.

This drug, as you've already guessed, is MDMA, or Ecstasy. It has finally, after years of governmental ignorance and lack of balls/foresight/integrity in the psychiatric community, earned tacit approval for a precious handful of clinical psychiatric trials. Initial results? Turns out this scary illegal drug just might work wonders for treating post-traumatic stress disorder. Gosh, really?

Yes. As reported by the Washington Post[3] and the Guardian,[4] as far as PTSD alone is concerned, some docs already see MDMA as potentially life-saving, a true wonder drug, which might even be administered to all our traumatized U.S. soldiers. Which could be good news indeed, given how an estimated 24 million Americans suffer from PTSD, whereas only a fraction of that number claim to have fibromyalgia.

Oh, but there are problems. Major drawbacks. Terrible, unspeakable, anti-American issues that seriously trouble our drug-addled nation.

Foremost: MDMA is not patented. Its formula is not owned by anyone. Hence, no single company (or handful of companies) stands to make billions from its potential legalization and the government cannot tax it and organized religion cannot control the power it has to help you totally reject its inane dogma, and they all really, really hate that.

What's more, millions of people already take MDMA recreationally, for the sheer pleasure and joy of it, making it a huge threat to all authority everywhere, because God knows we can't have lots of people feeling peaceful and empathetic and nonviolent, as opposed to fearful and victimized and angry and sick sick sick, all those things governments and religions rely on to keep you meek and beaten down and in check.

I know what you're thinking. That's a dangerous oversimplification, Mark. Read the literature! Ecstasy is scary! People can overdose! "Moderation" is not in America's DNA! With the possible exception of extreme PTSD cases, we should probably keep MDMA illegal forever — you know, just like that other toxic, wildly addictive drug that causes thousands of deaths every year, along with liver disease and violence and spousal abuse and impaired judgment and unwanted pregnancy and frat boys, a liquid drug you can order right now, as much as you want, from any bar in the world. Oh wait.

Maybe it really is just that simple, just that odious. One drug, nasty and of hugely questionable value, essentially designed to numb your body and shut you down like a land mine shuts down a cat, is legal. Another drug, relatively safe, enormously effective in how it opens you up like a flower and pours white hot life straight down your throat and helps you feel God without forcing you to kneel before, well, anything at all, is violently illegal. And thus doth the brutal irony of the capitalist machine floweth over once again.

It is, you could say, just another tale of the tense, vicious battle ever raging between the government/corporations/church, all of whom seek to control and profit by murdering any notion you may have that you might be far more powerful, divinely connected, empathetic than you imagine, and the humane, common-sensical universe of peaceful reality. Do you know that fight? Do you ever sense that common sense is losing? I have a suggestion for something you might want to try.

1 http://oyooki.notlong.com
2 http://ahyouy.notlong.com
3 http://aeboeju.notlong.com
4 http://aidob.notlong.com

And now, The Daring Spectacle presents...

Mullet Haiku

Velveeta nachos
Case of warm Old Milwaukee
Happy birthday, mom

Tight, focused, short, tasty, reasonably funny. And I don't just mean the cheerleaders.

Maybe I still like this very early column because it not only shows my raw, observational, culture-critic voice taking on some more bite and shape, but it also underscores the eternal peculiarity of stumbling across late-night cable-TV detritus like this, disorienting little programs that reveal a picture of some random American substrata you never knew existed, but which, upon staring at it for a solid hour after three or four glasses of wine, begins to reveal some desperately funny/sad/curious aspect of the human condition and which only serve to underscore one inexorable truth: Baby, we are one weird *species. — mm*

Catholic cheerleaders of doom

10/09/2002

You are casually and somewhat innocently flipping through the channels because you are procrastinating and feeling leaden and there's absolutely nothing on, and you are dumbfounded for the millionth time at the inanity of television, yet *you* are the sucker, because you do not, cannot move.

And you are vaguely disturbed and just a little grossed out by that bizarre Cottonelle toilet-paper ad, the one with all the happy bouncy shots of people's jiggling butts and the perky voiceover talking of "feeling clean" followed by a product shot, so you flip again and accidentally land on late-night ESPN2 and immediately feel your very soul being siphoned straight through your teeth.

It is a cheerleading competition. Check that, no wait, it's a dance-team competition, I think, the slight difference mostly having to do with gender mixing and wicked backflips and hand clap frequency and intensity of hip thrusting and the creepy fierceness of a young girl's madly grinning stare that can eat live puppies for breakfast.

There is screaming. There is yelling. There is fist pumping and body twisting and more manic movement per square foot than a convention of rabid ferrets.

There is also excruciatingly loud and thumping and horribly mixed techno music jammed up alongside crusty '80s hits that have been sped up to eye-spasming speeds sufficient to induce you to panic and Valium.

There are bleachers. There is a huge, unadorned stage in some massive hangarlike building in some ungodly place that later turns out to be Disneyworld in Florida because it's always either there or Vegas, because that's where surreality and extreme synchronized choreography, excess glitter

and bad techno go to die.

And there are girls. Oh my God. Many, many Catholic high school girls, a veritable sampler platter of semi-virginal faux-devout cloyingly repressed spazzed-out supermaidens, a perky fleshy Sizzler salad bar of savage hypercompetitive girldom. Teams. Squads. Posses. Flocks. Swarms.

All from high school. All from *Catholic* high school, apparently, in this particular case, though I could be wrong, but I doubt it given how the schools all had names like Sacred Heart and Assumption High and Holy St. Mary's of Our Healing Divine Superior Wisdom Grace and the like, and all girls from small to mid-sized towns in Kentucky and Arizona and Louisiana and other places you will probably never visit unless you have to.

And they are dancing, if you want to call it that, these frantic teams, on this huge, blank stage, in front of the judges, before the rows and rows of bleachers packed with screaming classmates and baffled screaming parents and an aura of oh my God please make it stop.

Maybe three minutes per team, an incredibly manic and desperately synchronous dance number, no single girl standing out, everyone part of the team and each agitated autobot girl completely indistinguishable from her teammates, all tight Spandex costumes and exposed torsos and heavy makeup and shockingly sexual movements swiped directly from the latest MTV videos and then mutated, reinterpreted, made competitive and bloodthirsty and forcibly confrontational.

All to win a trophy.

This is Britney on speed. This is Mary Kate and Ashley shot out of a gun straight into your fragile nerve core. This is powerfully sexual and physical movement and weirdly mesmerizing body energy entirely, tragically divorced from actual female sexuality, some horrid breakdown, a spectacular and all-American display of going-through-the-motions without having any idea what it means to move the body in such a way. And lo, it is *strange*.

Nothing at all wrong with team choreography and nothing at all wrong with competitive dance and especially nothing wrong with empowering young women to compete and gain acclaim, but this, this is a deeper mutation, a freakish estrangement.

Squads of 20 Catholic schoolgirls all dressed in, say, skintight "Matrix"-ish black latex, hair slicked and pulled tight, a complete S&M fetish-arama, dancing like robotic sex machines to a hyperspeed "Sweet Dreams" by the Eurythmics, and they have no idea, and no one mentions it.

All moving like they want to copulate with the devil Himself and maybe a few dozen demons just for kicks, despite not really knowing how, not really addressing the sex issue at all, though they really, really should, as the bland judges just comment on the nice agility and good leg extensions.

And this is the gist, this is the great ironic disconnect, the ultimate Madonna/whore pop-culture display, modern heavily sexualized young female team dance, normally cause for male celebration and gentle ogling, actually turning out to be not the slightest bit erotic to anyone, nor all that empowering for the women.

If only because their frantic choreographed gyrations are tragically free of necessary juicy subtext and insinuation and feminine power. It's Jesus in a latex bodysuit, the Virgin Mary doused in Jezebel's eyeliner. Normally a good thing. Not here.

And finally, here is the squad captain, interviewed immediately after her team's performance, breathing hard and grinning madly and saying, like, we really practice hard for, like, sixteen hours a day and I dream our routine endlessly in my sleep and my, like, boyfriend never gets past second base and I'm a very odd and curiously dangerous cross-pollinated product of American subcultures that never fully resolve. Fear me.

And lo, unresolved and ironically detached and ready to flip the channel, we probably should.

Yes, there really is a birth control pill for men. It works. It's safe. It's easy.
It's could be ready for market in a year or two. It could revolutionize male/
female sexual/fertility/relationship whateveryoucallit. And you can't have
it. Because they just don't think it will make money. Because they're idiots.
Wait, no, not idiots. Myopic bastard greedmonkeys with little understanding
of the male/female sexual whateveryoucallit. Just an opinion. Shall we write
letters? —mm

The remote-control penis

07/16/2008

Vividly indeed do I remember the lovely and sordid tale my friend once
told me, many years ago, of the terrific guy she once dated, a strapping
young thing who — through a series of unfortunate childhood events —
had to have a remote-controlled, robotic penis installed in his body.

Let me be more specific. Apparently, this fine lad's delicate man tissues
had been damaged in a very unpleasant bicycle accident in his youth,
and he could therefore no longer enjoy normal erections. Everything else
functioned just fine, but when it came to sex, despite having full sensation,
all systems were mangled, all blood vessels shot. Sad indeed.

But then, a savior. Through the miracle of modern medicine and not-
so-modern pneumatics, ingenious doctors were able to install some sort
of marvelous contraption, a valve and a rod and bladder and a little pump
- a complete mechanical system by which our boy could, well, inflate and
deflate his manhood at will, last as long as he liked, repeat as frequently as
energy and soreness and lubricant allowed, and therebyenjoy a (relatively)
normal sex life.

It worked like a charm. It also worked like an aphrodisiac, a mesmerizing technological miracle, and a pair of old Reebok Pump basketball
shoes. What you did was: Squeeze a little bulb at the base of the perineum
a few dozen times to inflate, to raise the flag and see who salutes. Enjoy
indefinitely(!). When finished, simply reach up underneath into God's
country and press a different little bulb to deflate the air bladder and, well,
lower the mainsail (my friend said this particular procedure sounded like a
sad squeaky toy, sighing slowly. She found it adorable).

Of course my friend had a nickname for her private phallic superhero.
She called him, naturally, the Wonder Cock.

This heartwarming tale comes to mind as I read of how scientists have
now developed a tiny valve they can surgically implant into the manhood
of mankind to, well, control the flow of sperm at will.[1] Your own built-

in, reversible, radio-controlled vasectomy! they exclaim, with a winking Australian grin.

Apparently, said contraption involves a little remote-controlled switch that can, at the press of a button, activate or deactivate the flow from wherever it is that sperm flows (a musty furniture shop somewhere on the outskirts of London, I think) by opening and closing a valve installed into the all-important duct known as the vas deferens. Nifty!

I know what you're thinking. A remote-controlled sperm valve? Are you crazy? Who the hell would want something like that?

I'll tell you who: Every modern male under 30, that's who. Hell, add in a digital camera and an MP3 player and maybe built-in GPS, and you've got the next iPod.

See, like my friend's wonder cock, I think such technology would play directly upon the dual modern male fantasies of unlimited penile dexterity and übergeek tech coolness. In the age of gizmo wonders and technologically advanced everything, why not a mechanically enhanced penis? Why not a little Iron Man in your iron man? Make it easy, make it relatively affordable, market it like you would the Bang & Olufsen stereo option on an Audi R8 (i.e., an invaluable enhancement, not a threat), and I say: *Viva la revolucion*!

It is, of course, all part of the eternal quest for an easy, idiot-proof male birth-control device for consensual adults that doesn't involve sheathing everything in miserable amounts of latex and therefore dulling the finest sensation known to all malehood next to perhaps a superlative foot massage and maybe sipping dark rum in a hot tub with nubile pagan fire priestesses from the moon.

But maybe such a valve won't be necessary. After all, they say there's already been a big breakthrough in male birth control, that scientists have finally developed a surefire "male pill" that knocks any man's sperm count down to zero, and all that's left is a bit of clinical testing.[2]

So effective is the new pill that it's apparently safer than condoms, safer than the female pill, safer than staring at a photo of Ann Coulter for three full, agonizing minutes while your sperm commit mass suicide from sheer horror. Amazing.

But apparently there's a problem. Big Pharma doesn't seem to care about this new breakthrough. And why? Money, of course. They say there's just not enough interest. Men don't seem to be clamoring for it, the market doesn't seem to be there, millions don't stand to be made, and hence no one wants to fund more research on the thing, which could result in a wait of three to five more years before such a pill hits the market, if it ever does.

What's more, some argue that dumb-as-nails men are too unreliable for such a thing anyway, that no woman worth her weight in diaphragms and Nonoxyl-9 would dare trust a man to remember to take a pill every day, because of course men are generally irresponsible schlubs who can't even remember their own phone numbers and etc. and so on and cliché cliché cliché.[3]

shiva = strength

To which I say, utter and total bullshit. There's not a smart modern male I know who wouldn't love to know he wouldn't — *couldn't* — get a date pregnant, that there could be no "accidents," that he will never get that life-altering phone call. Hell, there's already a trend whereby some baby-terrified men are getting old-school surgical vasectomies in their early 20s, rife with the fear that some nefarious huntress might try to snare them in the baby trap.[4] Shift the power dynamics of fertility and birth control to men? Talk about your massive cultural psycho-sexual upheavals. Watch for it.

But maybe that's neither here nor there. Maybe the pill's research-ers need to hook up with the valve engineers and the genius docs who installed my friend's lover's old penis pump way back when, and all work together to solve this most pressing issue and move humanity, uh, forward.

Which is to say, you want to guarantee men engage fully in matters fertile and impregnable? You want to make sure they care deeply about fa-milial responsibility and planning? Don't just give them a pill. Give them a slick, badass, high-tech gizmo to deliver it, maybe a hot little button on their iPhones that not only shuts a microvalve and releases the pill's chemi-cals, but also boosts stamina, responds to voice commands, calculates the tip on the dinner bill, organizes their playlist according to a given date's particular mood, and of course, reminds them exactly where the clitoris is. Really, what more do you need?

1 http://biege.notlong.com
2 http://iengum.notlong.com
3 http://iexuuv.notlong.com
4 http://oofaij.notlong.com

REALITY'S A
BITCH

I occasionally still fall into the debate I describe below, oft pondering the great, nearly insufferable issue of whether or not it makes a lick of difference whether or not you recycle your coffee cups, turn off your power strips at night, compost your condoms, or a thousand other relatively trivial 'green' acts, when hey look, there's India and China, more than two billion strong, dumping so much garbage into the atmosphere every second of every day it makes your cute little compost pile look like a lintball in a hurricane.

Of course, I absolutely believe individual acts do *make a difference, if not for the planet, than for your own consciousness, for how you choose to tread the Earth, with what sort of lightness and awareness. Any true change begins in the individual heart. What else is there, really? -mm*

You cannot save the Earth

04/18/2007

It's the great, painful, bitch-slapping environmental conundrum du jour:

Say you've been reading up and doing your eco-homework and watching the appropriate inconvenient documentaries, and you finally get yourself a little excited to go green, you buy your compact fluorescents and turn off all your power strips at night and recycle and reuse and compost and go organic and local and grass-fed and everything's just sustainably delicious.

And maybe all this good eco-vibration spurs you on even further, and you decide to green up the entire house, get into gray water and solar and reclaimed wood and non-VOC paints and all the rest, and fill the joint with organic cotton sheets and chem-free cleansers and passive heating systems and non-phthalates dildos[1] and you sit back in your ethically farmed chair and sigh and say, Well, there ya go, did what I could, the world is a better place, maybe just a tiny bit — I mean, isn't it?

And then it happens. You decide to take a break, take a load off, and maybe you go for nice drive in the hybrid or out in the Mini, just to get out, see the sights, enjoy the sunshine before it gets too hot and burns up all the ice caps, and if you live anywhere near the Bay Area it's incredibly easy to split the dense urban environment and head out into the "real" California, to the burning gauzy central slab of the state that seems, when you drive down it, as large as Europe and as foreign as Pluto, and wham, oh my God, it feels as though you've driven into a massive pile of concrete manure.

Just look around. It feels as though your heart is being eaten by angry capitalist cockroaches. Like your id is being munched by deranged zombie architects. This is what you see: mile after mile, town after town, dreary suburban dystopia after dreary suburban dystopia of massive gluttonous eco-mauling overdevelopment, more Sam's Clubs and Taco Bells and scabby strip malls, so many generic prison compounds that are, apparently, actually tract-home complexes it makes you want to rip out your soul with a pickax and feed it to the few remaining wild coyotes in Joshua Tree before someone shoots them all to make way for a new Home Depot.

This, then, is the conundrum: On the one hand, we are ever trying to convince ourselves that we can make a difference on a humble individual basis, in our daily lives, little by little and one recycled Fiji water bottle at a time, and yet the destructive proof to the contrary is so vast and om-nivorous it seems like a nice rerun of "Bambi Meets Godzilla." It can feel as though your little eco-home, your little ethically raised wool rug mean about as much in the overall scheme of earthly health as a speck of organic lint in a nuclear waste dump.

It can, if you let it, feel very much like a sad, intractable war. It's as though you can visit Treehugger.com one minute and get all happy and positive and inspired and think, Hey, maybe our species really *does* have a shot, maybe all is not lost, maybe we're not as violently abusive of this pale blue dot as it seems we are.

And then spin right around and see yet another water-sucking eco-abusive megamall being gouged into the Earth and suddenly all the good vibes from that cute botanical lipstick you just bought get erased in an instant, as you realize we aren't doing nearly enough nearly fast enough and I don't care how many people compost their avocado pits, nothing is gonna change until the corporations and the governments *truly* get into gear, which is a bit like shooting a water buffalo with a pellet gun. It takes about 2 million shots just to get the damn thing's attention.

Check that: It does not feel like a war. It feels more like a race. A violent, stupid, desperate race against a political and capitalistic machine that hates change and resists caring and slaps down anything that might cut into profits or warmongering, that seems to openly loathe the idea that we should have a modicum of understanding about where our oil and food and water and energy and God actually come from. This is, of course, the brutally depressing view. It's just one option.

I remember reading, years back, about McDonald's and the enviro movement's long-standing attacks on the junk-food titan's noxious use of those old Styrofoam burger containers. After years of screaming and protests, the eco-dudes finally realized it would be better to actually work *with* the junk-food giant to help them figure out a way to employ recyclable cardboard boxes and still make a profit.

It worked, mostly. McDonald's eventually dumped the Styrofoam from U.S. outlets. But here's the story's big kicker: Just that one simple shift, that one tiny change in corporate behavior affected an enormous industry all the way down the line, so much so that they figured it was the environmental equivalent of something like 50 million people deciding to recycle plastic bottles. It was at once staggering and humbling.

In other words, sure you can do your part at home, sure your drop in the environmental bucket helps get the plastic wet, but real, serious change can't even begin until the corporate and political leviathans decide it's good business to pretend they have a soul.

It is, of course, all a matter of perspective. There are good signs everywhere, awareness is being raised, some politicians are actually paying the environment more than just lip service. From SF's own plan to build the most energy-efficient building in the nation[2] to the new maturity of DIY solar power to Wal-Mart itself actually pretending they give a crap about energy, it's become hip to say you care about the planet. What a thing.

Time mag reently dedicated an entire issue to global warming and the dire environmental outlook we now face, [3]and half the issue was devoted to how bad it all is, how accelerated the meltdown has become, how China and India are up-and-coming megapolluters and oh my God we are so screwed, whereas the other half was dedicated to all the cool new eco-friendly ideas and all the brilliant minds working on innovative ways to save the world, along with a hopeful handful of nascent corporate and governmental shifts toward sustainability and progress.

Which angle of approach works for you? What perspective do you want to rule your worldview? Personally, I fully believe in contributing in as many ways as possible to the overall healing energy of the planet. I'm convinced it has tremendous cumulative power.

But if you take this view, just do yourself a favor and maybe avoid that scenic drive through Central California. Or Nevada. Or Arizona. Or China. Out there, it seems like Bambi doesn't have a spitting chance in hell.

1 http://ojing.notlong.com
2 http://poajeep.notlong.com
3 http://cuorey.notlong.com

Living atop of the food chain means facing some ugly realities. Foremost is the hard fact that we as a species engage in a simply staggering amount of out-right genocide, the open slaughter of hundreds of millions of living creatures, day in day out, years and decades and centuries, fish to fowl to livestock to in-sect; you name it, we've killed it, eaten it, exploited it, hunted it to extinction, used it for food or fabric or furniture. We are the most efficient and ruthless killing machines on the planet. Isn't that heartwarming?

It's almost impossible to hold this perspective, to keep this reality in mind as we move through the world. Too ugly. Too brutal. Are we really that kind of being? Don't we revere and love animals and life itself at least as much as we kill and consume it? Well, no. Not by a long shot. But we do like to believe we have some rules, boundaries, ethical guidelines. And we do have empathy. And conscience. Sometimes. Maybe the only real question is, are we getting any better at it? —mm

Let us now kill all the dogs

8/09/2006

Chinese officials killed 50,000 dogs the other day. Just walked along the streets and lured them out of their homes and bushes and doghouses using whistles and firecrackers, and then clubbed them to death with gi-ant sticks, right there in the residential streets, tossed the bodies into big dump trucks and drove on.

It was a particularly horrific scene, seemingly unimaginable in our "enlightened" age, a fully sanctioned slaughter ordered up by the local Chinese government in response to the recent deaths of three local people felled by rabies. Without some sort of action, more people could die, the government deduced. Solution: Kill all the dogs. Problem solved, right? Well, not quite.

Now another Shanghai prefecture has ordered the slaughter of all its dogs[1], too, in response to the rabies-related deaths of 16 people in the past eight months. This particular region has an estimated 500,000 dogs. No word yet on how it plans to kill them all, but the strolling-and-clubbing thing

might be the only way, given how even Chinese citizens tend to be slightly uncooperative when it comes to giving up their pets for random government massacre in front of their very eyes.

Chinese authorities fear a rabies epidemic. Already in China, upward of 2,000 people die per year from rabies (only 3 percent of China's dogs are vaccinated). It's a worsening problem. It is not, by most estimates, as potentially lethal as the bird flu epidemic, but it's still highly dangerous. Given how they say it's far too late (and far too expensive) to vaccinate all the dogs, the clearest way to stop the epidemic is, well, to kill all the dogs. Isn't it?

There is nowhere to look for the right answer. How do you process this? How can you file such an unspeakably brutal and seemingly heartless approach? Maybe you are shaking your head in disbelief. Maybe you can't process it at all, but you must admit, it brings a up number of powerful — and deeply revealing — notions of just who we think we are.

Start with the birds. Recent bird flu outbreaks prompted the slaughter of chickens all over Asia. In 1997, Hong Kong slaughtered 1.2 million chickens to try and stop the first big outbreak, but it was only the tip of the bloody iceberg. Asia (and to a lesser degree, Africa and India) have since slit the throats of hundreds of millions of birds to stop what some scientists see as the most deadly potential epidemic of this age.

So, the obvious question: Was the poultry slaughter any less horrible than what's now happening to the dogs? More justifiable due to the potential for human loss? Maybe so. Or maybe it's simply because we love fuzzycute dogs more than uglydumb chickens.

It is difficult to parse. Obviously, dogs are much less valued in China as pets, as creatures with soul, than they are in the United States. It is an ugly cultural divide we cannot easily traverse.

By most estimates, China has a decidedly ruthless perspective on the animal kingdom. For one thing, a billion people with an enormous underclass of poverty translates into perhaps one of the most truly bizarre and massive food marketplaces in the world, one that would certainly make most Americans quite sick. Or instantly vegetarian.

As my knowledgeable travel friends tell me (and many food shows and travel documentaries obviously prove), there is nothing on this planet quite like a Chinese "wet market" for experiencing the full, glistening, slimy array of the animal kingdom, all manner of parts and organs and skins and droppings and other ghastly unmentionables — not to mention insects and sea creatures and freakishly colored squishy things few people seem to be able to clearly identify — that can be eaten by humans.

They eat everything. No animal is off limits, no body part impossible to skewer or steam or peel or eat raw while still warm from the body. And there are plenty of tales of what constitutes a food delicacy in China that may seem terribly weird or cruel to us. But overall, you can also argue that it's a very efficient and thorough system. Nothing is wasted.

But wait. Is America really that much more evolved? Do we not kill millions of ill-bred, hormone-injected, mistreated animals every single day in giant industrial slaughterhouses to feed our gluttonous and largely toxic fast-food cravings? You bet we do.

As for dogs, well, we love them to death: Our nation's overrun animal shelters kill an estimated 3 to 4 million dogs and cats per year[2] due to over-breeding and puppy mills and ignorance of spaying and neutering. They're not even rabid. Most are no threat whatsoever.

You have to ask: Are we much better at our treatment of animals simply because we've learned to hide it better? Because most of us will never come anywhere near one of those gruesome industrial feedlots in, say, rural Kansas or Oklahoma, where they cram tens of thousands of cattle into concrete-enclosed pens and the air is so thick with fetid gasses and feces and smokestack spewings you can smell the stench 100 miles away?

But hey, at least we don't club our dogs in the streets in broad daylight. We're not, you know, monsters.

To be fair, many in China were outraged by the initial dog slaughter. The brutality, the primitive approach is simply unspeakable, even for a country known for its dispassionate look at the animal world. Then again, many said the mass slaughter was entirely appropriate. After all, 2,000 people died in one year. Of course, 2,000 also die every single *day* from government-sanctioned smoking addictions.[3] But, you know, oh well.

The wise ones say you can measure the wisdom and spiritual conscious-ness of a culture by how it treats its animals. But it's a strange maxim. It is a guideline that is nearly impossible to properly navigate in the modern world, no matter what the culture, simply because there are so many gross contradictions, from respectful and tender to absolutely ruthless and abusive.

And it's not just China. And it's not merely animals. It is nothing new, this mass-slaughter idea, emerging from somewhere deep within our darkest and most mindless souls: Got a bad case of something? Problem with some sort of unwanted infestation? Mad cows? Killer bees? Dogs? Chickens? Gays? Jews? Kurds? Tibetans? Rwandans? Sudanese? Pagans? Witches? Communists? Native Americans? Serbs? Palestinians? Terrorists? That's easy: Kill 'em all.

The method is, apparently, in our blood. We do it all the time.[4]

We know this much: There appears to be a line somewhere. We all seem to sense it, though no one can quite put a finger on it. We know this line speaks to us as a supposedly enlightened species, as the creatures with the most advanced brains and (presumably) most nimble and sophisticated souls.

But if we're honest, it makes us all a little uneasy, a little uncomfortable as the line often seems to demarcate not how enlightened we are but how far we truly seem to be from any sort of true evolution or advancement of spirit. Because so far, the best we as a species seem to have come up with is this: Do not kill innocent things in broad daylight with large sticks.

The rest is, to say the least, still more than a little murky.

1 http://tahgahv.notlong.com
2 http://oebai.notlong.com
3 http://xesaiga.notlong.com
4 http://uuyik.notlong.com

And now, The Daring Spectacle presents…

Mullet Haiku

*Dropped beer can rolls to
same corner every time
Trailer's off a wheel*

An unexpectedly big hit, this column. I was pretty fired up about the subject, I have to say. Of course, a handful of irate Canadians and oilsands workers wrote in to assail me, eager to point out what I already suggest; that we're all complicit in such environmental brutality and voracious capitalism, that they're just trying to supply what the world wants: cheap energy. They also wanted to scream at me that U.S. is the primary economic force of such vicious oil exploration (not true; the oilsands are far more global, with China investing far more than U.S.-based companies). No matter. Among all the enviro carnage I've read/written about in recent years, from the repellant Smithfield Farms' industrial pig farming to rainforest deforestation, from collapsing fish stocks to unchecked pollution in fast-expanding China, few seem to match the sheer brutal gall, the appalling black/white obviousness of the horror of the oilsands projects. Hit Google to see some of the pictures, and read more. Disgusting barely begins to cover it. —mm

Behold! Canada's most disgusting export

10/07/2009

Are you having one of those days? One of those moments where you feel like you've endured a simply relentless onslaught of negative news and economic hardship coupled to endless rounds of cretinous politicians — all of whom enjoy fully paid health care on your tab — debating whether or not you'll be able to afford to see a doctor ever again, all to the point where you say, you know what? I need just *one more*.

Just one more really good, depressing story to put me over the top, ruin not just my day but maybe taint my entire *month*, a tale so vicious and disheartening I immediately start yelling at my girlfriend for no real reason and slam the cupboard because I realized I'm out of peanut butter, and I absolutely refuse to smile at anyone because they're all clearly complicit in making this world a bleak and miserable hellpit of oh my God you suck.

Why, sweetheart, step on over here for a moment. I have just what you need. You need to read a bit more about Alberta's infamous oilsands.[1]

Have you heard? Have you taken even a cursory peek lately into the oversized eco nightmare that is Canada's monstrous, pollutive, disgusting hellholes of rapacious greed and pollution and destruction and sheer capitalistic joy? I bet you have.

They are, you might say, the finest example we currently have of a massive, soulless industry and a major first-world government shoving a giant middle finger in the face of all notions of progress and environmental integrity. They're not the only ones, to be sure — the coal industry's middle

finger is downright callused from flipping everyone off so aggressively —
but for sheer gall, for shamelessly stomping a greasy boot heel into the face
of environmental progress, the oilsands simply can't be beat.

They are true wonders, testaments to mankind's remarkable power to
continue — against every hunk of knowledge and common sense — to
rape, maul and utterly devastate everything we supposedly hold dear, all in
the name of filthy profit.

Despite whatever good vibes you might've been feeling from all those
rumors of a healthy global push toward sustainability and alternative
energy, the oilsands remind you: no one really gives a flying fuck. Not
when hundreds of billions of dollars are at stake. You cannot help but be
perversely impressed.

Some argue the oilsands are the future of synthetic petroleum. Experts
say there's enough black gold stuck deep in that greasy bitumen — spread
across a region the size of Florida — that it could last us until we lose
what's left of our souls and/or entirely block out the goddamn sun, which-
ever comes first. The problem, of course, is getting the toxic gunk out of
the ground.

The numbers are simply astonishing[2]: The amount of land, water, natural gas, and CO2 emissions required to produce a single barrel of synthetic
oil from the oilsands is staggering enough, but when you add in all the
contaminated rivers, the toxic tailing ponds (2.2 *million* Olympic-sized
swimming pools' worth, and counting), the decimated landscape, the dead
animals, the increased cancer rates among anyone living within a 100-mile
radius, well, you've got more than enough charming data to effortlessly
destroy any glimmer of positivism you might've enjoyed from composting
your pizza boxes.

But that's not the ugliest part. The ugliest part is, the oilsand project is
expanding as fast as inhumanly possible. It is already, according to various
reports, the largest energy project in the world. Bigger than Saudi Arabia.
Bigger than Wal-Mart. Bigger than Jesus.

So ugly and rapacious are the oilsands, so generally repulsive are the be-
fore/after images[3] of what's being done to the land,
you think there must be something wrong, like this
can't really be happening; surely this must be illegal, you think, imagining a team of U.N. inspectors
returning from Alberta any minute now and rec-
ommending immediate sanctions, military action,
a coup against the government. You think this way
because you are all sorts of adorable tofu utopian
cotton-candy cupcake. You are also viciously naive.

I was skimming a recent issue of Esquire not long ago, which I admit I subscribe to in the apparently futile hope that someday, someone will invent a men's mag that's remotely relevant to my life, and which will feature something other than overpriced watches, awful Perry Ellis sweaters and useless articles about Megan Fox, the new football season and how I can *really* mix it up at the office by wearing pinstripes and colorful socks. But that's another column.

I fell across this little advice column about investment opportunities, about where to look in this bleak, merciless fiscal landscape for signs of hope and growth, just where your average clean-shaven, beer drinking, football loving man's-man who still has a job can maybe make a bit of green, so as to maybe afford the Rolex Oyster Perpetual on page 55 or the Infiniti coupe on page 112 to try and impress the jaded, nonexistent, impossibly Photoshopped Gucci model on page 67.

You can guess the answer. It's oil, lovebug. Not only that (the advice continues), but if you can handle a bit of risk in your portfolio and if you're confident that we as a nation/planet are still very much on the fast-track to hell — read: you're convinced we'll be addicted to oil for generations to come — the oilsands are a white-hot investment indeed.

It's a wonderful line of capitalist thinking, completely divorced from ethics and humanity as a whole. It's a bit like saying, "Hey, seeking some quick profit? Why not invest in some Irish Catholic orphanages, like those where all those priests and nuns beat and sexually molested countless thousands of poor children for about 60 years straight, forcing them into workhouses to make rosaries to sell to tourists. It's cash money, baby!"

Do not misunderstand. Well do I know the worlds of investment and petrochemicals are designed, de facto and a priori, to be ruthless, even cruel, entirely devoid of moral compass. I fully admit the oilsands are but one of a myriad of eco nightmares you don't want to examine too closely lest you feel your heart shrivel and be reminded of an even uglier fact: that we are, all of us living and shopping in first-world luxury, complicit in the creation of these disasters. In too many ways, the oilsands are us.

But there's something deeply wrong with the oilsands, something sadder and more disturbing than any other similar project in recent history. It's this: the oilsand projects are *new*. They reflect decisions that industry leaders and politicians are making today, *right now*; incredibly, violently stupid actions akin to a doctor reaching into our collective chest, pulling out a black and shriveled lung and holding it aloft. And the world went, "Huh, isn't that interesting?" And then lit up another cigarette.

1 http://faqueac.notlong.com
2 http://ahnongee.notlong.com
3 http://chupaex.notlong.com

I think of the following angle every time I read of another "major" pot bust or
infiltrated Ecstasy ring or whatnot, wherein the wary cops torched a million
bucks worth of premium Mary Jane or confiscated 10,000 pills and arrested
a dozen drug-making "scum," and it makes headlines for about five minutes
before disappearing into the media void and everyone goes on with their day
and later goes out to buy just exactly as many pills and baggies and hits as
they need, without a second thought. The machine churns on.

The War on Drugs remains — and will likely remain for many years to
come — one of our greatest failures, embarrassments, hypocrisies in which
not even Obama dares to make any sort of serious dent or significant change.
We might get legal pot someday soon, and even Mexico, so brutally ravaged
by organized crime, has legalized the possession of small amounts of various
drugs. But I predict we'll have legal gay marriage, universal health care, and
peace in the Middle East before I can go buy a couple hits of Ecstasy without
breaking a nearly useless law. –mm

Damn, there goes my meth supply

03/12/2008

Do you have any sympathy for the police? Or the Feds? I
mean, just a little? I do.

I figure you gotta muster at least a little compassion
for how rough and dispiriting it must be knowing you've
done your job well, worked your ass off and maybe even
risked your life, spending every single day for, let's say two
years straight following leads and compiling evidence and
coordinating a large drug investigation across multiple
enforcement agencies, all of which finally culminated in a
successful bust of some very large local meth operations.

And maybe you even made headlines by nailing a notorious drug-making family who was capable of cranking out
upwards of 20 pounds of meth a month, and you were
maybe lauded by the media and applauded by your boss
and glad-handed by the mayor, and perhaps even for a
moment felt like something truly good has been accomplished.

And then, well, then you turn around and realize it's all
pretty much a big, nasty joke. Pointless, senseless, quite
nearly useless — that what you've done really makes no
difference whatsoever. And what's more, it never really has.

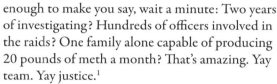

Is it not brutally true? Is this not pretty much the norm now, the common wisdom, going on nearly 40 years of the modern and abysmal "War on Drugs" and hundreds of billions of dollars spent and countless thousands of lives lost and prisons overflowing, and yet we're a nation that's more illegally drug-happy than ever?

Sometimes you just have to ask. Because truly, this grand and insidious "war" must be one of our greatest national embarrassments, an enormous, unspoken failure, far worse in its way than the lost war in Iraq or even Vietnam, given how it's caused more misery and more pain and more destruction across multiple decades and nations and governments, and continues to cost countless billions of dollars and yet has, as all stats and studies reveal, almost zero effect on the overall drug culture of the nation.

This was the example just recently, a little news story that blipped across the wires saying how investigators had finally busted a big meth ring from San Francisco to Gilroy, and though there wasn't much detail, it was still

enough to make you say, wait a minute: Two years of investigating? Hundreds of officers involved in the raids? One family alone capable of producing 20 pounds of meth a month? That's amazing. Yay team. Yay justice.[1]

And it leads to the obvious question: Did it make any sort of difference? Is a baggie of meth any more difficult to obtain right now than it was a month ago? Has there been the slightest change? Or is it all merely the equivalent of trying to stop a raging river with a fork? You already know the answer.

Sometimes you gotta re-state the obvious, so you don't lose sight. The truth is, big drug busts do almost nothing to stem the flow of drugs or change the complexion of the culture, save for making a handful of rather uninformed citizens and angry parents feel better for about 10 minutes, and causing the street price of your narcotic du jour to jump 20 percent for a week. Which, I suppose, is a big part of the reason it happens at all, to give the *appearance* of justice and enforcement and overall safety, to prevent everyone from freaking out and whining to the mayor.

But maybe what's most confounding is the ridiculous illogic of it all, how study after study

proves that the threat of arrest and punishment, no matter how severe
or even lethal, has never been the slightest deterrent to drug production,
dealing, or usage — save, of course, for your average easily petrified assis-
tant manager who won't go near the pot pipe at the office Christmas party
because oh my gosh that stuff's illegal and what if the cops come and take
away my dog?

It's all amusing as it is tragic and pathetic. How much we hate those
swarthy terrorists! How much we decry corrupt dictators and cruel governments! Yet the U.S. government conspires and funds and works with
brutal warlords and terrorists and enormously corrupt governments all
over the world every single day "fighting" the flow of illegal drugs (even
as we're often complicit in that flow), the vast majority of which are less
dangerous and violence-inducing than good ol' all-American alcohol.
Hypocrisy, thou art snortable.

Let me be clear. I am no wild-eyed pro-drug legalize-everything advo-
cate (well, not completely). I enjoy my illicit substances on intelligent and
moderate occasion, but I'm also nicely aware of why they call meth the
devil's drug, the most insidious and destructive of all soul-killers, given
its lethal combo of chemical toxins and addictiveness and trashy bargain-
basement affordability. I have zero reason to doubt it.

Nor do I doubt that drug-dealer culture, as a direct result of the "war,"
gets incredibly violent and dangerous and makes for some mean streets
indeed. Hell, I live mere blocks from notorious housing projects, where
crime and gunfire and death are considered pretty much weekly occur-
rences.

But something is deeply wrong with our overall equation. Something
rotten and rather pitiable about how we still think about drug culture and
consider punishment and imprisonment the supreme solutions, and it's
evidenced by every stupid comment I read from otherwise well-meaning
adults who respond to drug-bust stories by sneering "Yes! Lock them up
for life! Kill all drug dealers! They are ruining neighborhoods! Destroying families! Scum must die!" all in typical low-grade George W. Bush
eye-for-an-eye pseudo-cowboy mentality, with not the slightest wisp of
a thought as to why drugs are so appealing, what forces are at play in the
human heart and mind, how all those billions of dollars would go so much
better for prevention and treatment — and oh yes, without thinking that
those very dealers are the ones supplying their friends and neighbors with
coke for the next all-American backyard barbecue.

It is, you can say with a heavy sigh and a heavy heart and a tangled mind,
just one of those things. It is like farm subsidies. Like oil monopolies.
Like waterboarding. Like Homeland Security and big tobacco and Dick

Cheney. Everyone with the slightest intelligence knows it's a massive failure. Everyone knows it's a scam, a brutal lie, that it destroys far more than it allegedly helps. And yet, on it goes. It's all so insidious and unfair and depressing it can make you want to tear out your hair and wail at the moon. Or, you know, start doing drugs.

1 http://uengur.notlong.com

And now, The Daring Spectacle presents...

Mullet Haiku

Dang! Your tube top is
making me want to forget
that you're my cousin

This one was a real scorcher, way back in '02. Controversial, too, given how the national, Bush-borne trend of shameless Christian homophobia was just hitting stride. The good news: the sort of nasty feedback I describe below — and what you now get to see for yourself in the 'I Hate You' pages in this very book — oozes into my in-box far less frequently than when I originally wrote this column. The bad news: This may be due less to increased open-mindedness in the populace, and more because America's hardcore homophobes' 15 minutes of infamy imploded when Bush finally crawled off stage.

One memory: My use of the very un-PC "fag" in the headline caused the news director of SFGate all sorts of itchy nervousness at the time, but he reluctantly allowed it to appear on the home page because, well, even he recognized how it's sort of essential to the point. Drew lots of clicks, that's for sure. If I recall, no one was actually offended. Are you? —mm

You must be a fag

06/14/2002

I am an utter moron. I am a total imbecile. I am the enemy.

I am a disgrace, an amazingly off-the-mark, hate-filled lefty coward Communist with his head so far up his ass he can see his tonsils, and who wouldn't know a true patriot if one ran over me in his big stompin' SUV, which he really should.

I am a typical liberal jackass no one listens to because I live in San Francisco and everyone knows San Francisco is a totally useless noncity full of weirdo snobby leftist tree-hugging pro-choice intellectual wine-drinking peacenik tofu-suckers who practice yoga and smoke a lot of legal pot and are all just mad because Gore lost and Bush hasn't spontaneously combusted just yet and everybody seems to have a big, shiny new gun except us.

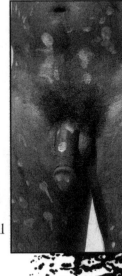

I am apparently many, many very unpleasant things that can't be printed here, but simply recall all the absolute crudest, most juvenile curse words you ever heard from the thickest jock in junior high — don't forget the gross bodily functions! — and rearrange them at will á la magnetic refrigerator poetry, and you'll have some idea of the feedback I often get.

But more than anything else, the absolute worst thing that can apparently be said about me, among the spurts of hate mail I invariably receive whenever one of my more politically charged columns pokes at the oozing sores of rage over at some right-wing Web site, is this: I must be gay. Really, *really* gay.

No, not gay. A fag. A world-class, spineless, AIDS-ridden, dope-smoking, rainbow-flagged, corn-holin', liberal whiner *super*-fag, one who lives in a city and in fact an entire state that apparently a very large contingent of "real" Americans genuinely wishes would "get bombed by the terrorists and fall off into the ocean after you all get fucking AIDS and die you liberal pussy faggot traitors." That is pretty much a direct quote.

This is not a joke. Or rather, it is, but the sentiment is rampant, and virulent, and common enough that it simply has to be mentioned and discussed here in more somber and/or baffled fashion, and not just in a "gosh there sure are a lot of homophobic sub-intellects out there" sort of way, but because it is a bizarre and distressing phenomenon.

It is a disease, this brand of spitting homophobia, a shockingly common hate-filled attitude running like liquid fire through a surprisingly large number of "patriotic" Christian Americans. I get a lot of this type of email. And I'm not quite sure what to make of it.

It happens at least once every column, and a great deal more whenever I write a piece openly criticizing the president or aggressively questioning this "war" or humorously insinuating that Dick Cheney is really a deeply frightening, thin-lipped glob of toxic tapioca who perpetually looks like he just swallowed a large dung beetle.

I must be gay. I must be a fag. That this is the worst attack many people can think of, is more than distressing. It stands as a stark reminder that we as a culture, one that claims to be so proud of our diversity and tolerance, still have some seriously debilitating issues of our own.

"I would expect nothing less from a pussy penny-loafer queer-boy," exclaims one deep thinker. "No wonder they say San Francisco is the land of 'fruits and nuts,'" another oh so cleverly snickered. "Go fuck yourself, fag!!!" charmed still another, in toto. And those are the mild ones.

Maybe you thought such strains of virulent homophobia were diminishing in this country. Maybe you thought some intellectual or gender-oriented progress had been made. Maybe you hoped such a degree of borderline violent hatred stemming from vaguely threatened manhoods was the sole domain of, say, Islamic fundamentalists. You would be wrong.

Would it be fair to call these types of conservatives sexual terrorists? Is there really that great a distance separating what a religious extremist is willing to perpetrate in the name of his angry martyring God, and what an extreme homophobe might do when faced with an apparent threat to his trembling machismo, in the name of his sexually confused deity?

It does not matter, of course, whether I'm actually gay or not. It does not matter that these fine upstanding American uber-patriots have no idea who I am or what my life is like. And it does not matter that I and most people I know wouldn't consider being called gay a slur anyway, that it is, in fact, in many ways complimentary and funny and good.

Being called gay simply has zero negative effect, just makes me shrug and smile and wonder and in fact only makes me more grateful to live in a city where such an "accusation" just means you probably dance really well and shun professional sports and get regular manicures and actually care about grooming. Oh hell, maybe I am gay. Don't tell my girlfriend.

For the record, I also get a ton of incredibly positive feedback, bravos and huzzahs and marriage proposals and offers to bear my children, heaping dollops of incredibly generous praise I don't even have to pay for. The hate mail is but a fraction, and the hissing homophobia, smaller still.

But all the positive feedback, in effect, only serves to underscore the stunning virulence of the hateful comments, the frightening similarities between this type of often homophobic rage and the type of religious bile with which we claim to be at war in the Mideast and elsewhere.

Perhaps our political agenda is slightly misdirected. Perhaps we have some brutish strains of macho religious-based hostility simmering in the melting pot of our own nation, festering and lying in wait. Perhaps there's another type of inbred, terrorist-type sentiment we should be focusing on, as well, lest it poison us to the core.

In 2005, the Kansas Supreme Court unanimously struck down the portion of the state's "Romeo and Juliet" law that allowed gay sex to be punished far more severely than straight. Matthew Limon was finally released from prison that same year, after serving five and a half years, more than four more than he would have if he were straight.

Remember Lawrence vs. Texas, *the incredible 2003 U.S. Supreme Court case that finally killed the Lone Star state's insidious anti-sodomy law? The Limon case was the first to cite that landmark decision as a precedent. Just in case you're keeping track.* —mm

Romeo and Romeo in Hell

02/11/2004

Kneel down. Put your hands together. Offer sincere thanks right this very moment to whatever deity you desire that that you are not 18 years old, and gay, and living in the state of Kansas right now.

This gratitude, it is a given. This is so much of a given you might not even need to hear why. You just say to yourself, oh my freaking God, I can only imagine.

As if being a teen isn't bad enough. As if being gay isn't difficult enough. Add Kansas to the mix and in rush countless unfortunate stereotypical notions about violent, homophobic truckers and angry farmers with pitchforks and many, many people who want you dead just because you like body piercing and can't stand Shania Twain.

But let's say you *are* 18 and you *are* gay and you *do* live in Kansas. And let's say you dare to give in to your teenage lovelust and go off and have consensual gay sex with a minor — say, a gay 14-year-old boy. And you get caught. And Kansas law puts you in prison.

For about 20 years.

Hey, it's Kansas. This is what they do. This is Kansas law. [1] And these are the extant hatreds and fears and astounding atrocities of American culture. And this is why you are so goddamn grateful.

Conversely. Let's say you are 18 but you are *not* gay and you live in Kansas and you have consensual sex with a minor of the *opposite* sex — say, a 14-year-old *girl*. And you get caught. Under the state's "Romeo and Juliet" law, you, too, go to jail.

For about one year. Maybe.

Wait wait wait, you say. What the hell is that? Consensual *gay* sex with a minor gets you slammed in prison for most of your adult life, whereas consensual *straight* sex with a minor gets you maybe a year? True. And nasty. And difficult to believe, and even more difficult to let assault every notion you've ever had that the world is perhaps fair and gentle and balanced. And it was all reinforced by the sniveling Kansas Court of Appeals, just recently.

It was a case where an 18-year-old boy, Matthew Limon, was in the midst of serving 17 years in prison for having consensual gay sex with a 14-year-old boy. Limon's lawyers challenged Kansas' insipid and hateful sodomy law, pointing out the obvious and rather insane unfairness, the imbalance, the outright savagery in treating consensual homosexual sex so much more harshly than heterosexual sex.

Matthew Limon lost his case. For now. The court voted 2-1 that gay sex with a minor is a far more vile and heinous and punishable offense than hetero sex under the same circumstances because, well, gay sex spreads disease, they claim. And gay sex is a threat to society, and marriage, and innocent bunnies, and the weather, and "traditional Kansas sexual morality," and therefore such

sex cannot be tolerated under any circumstances and yadda yadda hate hate gargle spit angry old white men ptooey. It's enough to make you gag on your leather whips.

OK, take a breath. In related news, the beleaguered head of the Georgia state school board recently attempted to remove the term *evolution* from the state's science curriculum to "prevent controversy" — which we can translate to mean "to hush all those Bible-licking parents who constantly complain about how the Bible is the absolute literal word of an angry fire-breathing football-lovin' war-happy God, and there is no such thing as evolution because if there was then how do you explain rap metal?"

These uptight, colon-clenched Georgian parents, they might have a point. There might indeed be fewer and fewer signs of evolution anywhere on the planet. Devolution is, in fact, rampant. Witness the Kansas court. Witness the Super Bowl. Witness NASCAR.

But maybe you don't care about any of this. "Who cares about Kansas anyway?" you might understandably say. "Let the snarling homophobes and the cute creationists writhe around in their sad troughs of ignorance," you might say. "Just so many self-delusional moths gnawing musty old socks in the closet of true awareness," you might add, as you admire your new Pyrex sex toy and nipple clamps from blowfish.com and praise Astarte that you live somewhere with uncensored bookstores and 24-hour crepes.

Here is why you should care: Because this is what we are up against. This is what any enlightened creature, gay straight bi trans kinky pierced open hearted open thighed open minded well read well versed in any way whatsoever, from any city, or burg, or oasis, is up against in American culture, right now.

Because maybe you think, oh sure, I know there are still innumerable pockets of hateful resistance, little clusters of screechy alarmists marching in the streets, like the ones in Boston protesting their state's recent positive ruling on same-sex marriage.[2] But, you say to yourself, they aren't much of a threat anymore, not really.

You are, sadly, wrong.

Vigilance is mandatory. Sentient well-souled bipeds who can speak in complete sentences must monitor the radar to ensure the shrill, Kansas-dried throngs do not dig under the fence and poison the drinking water even further. Limon's case sets vile legal precedents that resonate nationwide. And we've all seen what can happen when one of the primordials steals the White House.

It is always necessary to be reminded of the poisonous snake living in the backyard, the black widow in the woodshed. No matter how much progress has been made, so long as the Kansas-type fires of hate still rage and snicker and imprison, we are stuck. We are dead in the proverbial water. We are, in terms Georgians can understand, reverting to the Dark Ages, deeply, horribly unevolved. And this will not do.

1 http://ozohga.notlong.com
2 http://ozafun.notlong.com

It's all true. It took about six months and a bit of finagling with the insurance company, but they finally declared my car totaled, and I had it replaced. I still feel a pang of sadness for that lovely piece of shiny German engineering that never even got to taste the open road, that never broke 1,000 miles on the odometer, that never tasted true freedom or hardcore road trip or sex with the seat reclined all the way back. It was a beauty. What, too sentimental? I'm OK with that.

And no, they never found – and ever really seemed to care to find – the person who hit me. Life in the City, baby. —mm

To the drunk who smashed my car

11/11/2005

Yes, I know you were drunk. Must've been. Either drunk or on serious meds and/or you just didn't give much of a damn about anything anyway because you're just one of those people, one of those types who comes lurching around the city like a chunk of numbed pain in your big-ass mid-'80s burgundy car with the white top and chrome bumpers — an old Cadillac? Monte Carlo? — early last Sunday morning to wreak casual havoc.

Is that about right? Do you remember any of it? Here is what I'm guessing: probably not.

Let me tell you what happened, as I pieced it together from witnesses and all the shards of scrap metal in the street and from my mind's eye, and as I'm sure it's all one soggy blur to you. Oh yes, this is a true story.

Six a.m., Sunday morning. All quiet, all calm. Here you come, from outta nowhere, roaring around the corner just down the block from my apartment and then speeding hard up Fulton Street, my street, here in San Francisco, just as the sun was peeking through the fog and the day was coming into view and the world was barely rustling, still tranquil and peaceful and sleepy.

Of course you were going way too fast, and you apparently made it halfway down the block before you realized — did you even realize? — you were careening at a savage angle and suddenly WHAM! you slammed into the little Honda Civic parked on the side of the road, just behind my car, and you were going so fast you slid right off the Honda and crashed even harder into my brand-new and barely driven hot-as-love little Audi A3, a split second later. Oh yes you did.

You hit it hard, didn't you? You must've really been moving, to cause this much damage. You crushed the rear quarter panel from behind and slammed my car with such force you actually shoved its 3,300 pounds forward and sideways about four feet, slamming my car not only into the curb and damaging the wheels and axles, but also shoving it into the car parked just in front, thus mangling the front end, too.

Ah yes, it was quite a punch. You couldn't have nailed it better if you were aiming for it. A near-perfect hit-and-run, wasn't it?

But wait, something was wrong. You weren't moving. You were stuck! A sympathetic witness who lives in the apartment just above the grisly scene tells me she looked out her window immediately after you hit and says you slammed my car so hard your heavy chrome bumper actually got *wedged into my car,* and you had to jam your whale of a vehicle into reverse and tear yourself out in a mad tangle of scraping metal and plastic before speeding away, drunkenly, like the mad lurching demon you so very apparently are.

Is that about right? Is this ringing any bells? I do not expect you to reply.

Two hours later, I walked out of my house on my way to an errand and found my new car trashed and smashed in all manner of ungodly angles. The new car I had saved for for ten years. The new car I loved like Jesus loves wine. The new car that had a mere 732 miles on it and was so new I didn't even have my plates yet. Broke my car-lovin' heart. Ah yes, what a piece of work you did.

Look. I am not stupid. I live in the city. I park in the street. I expect a certain level of vehicular abuse: scratched doors, pockmarked bumpers, tree scrapes and punctured tires and the occasional smashed window because some jackass thinks my CDs might be worth two dollars. I expect this. I have endured it for years and it has happened to every one of my previous cars, and no one I know who lives and drives in the city hasn't suffered some sort of similar abuse. It comes with the territory and I was prepared for it.

But not this. Not near-total annihilation, a brutal hobbling, when all was shiny and new and I'd barely acquainted myself with the car. It's just so damned nauseating, this level of violation. What's worse is, you will never even know. Because it's more than likely you will never, ever be caught.

They cannot find you, not yet, anyway. A good Samaritan took down your license plate number, but so far my insurance company has had no

luck finding you and chances are you don't have insurance anyway —
and by the way, did you know the SFPD doesn't do anything about such
things? It's true. You file a police report, they tell you to call the Hit and
Run detail, the Hit and Run detail tells you that they only have about four
overworked officers anymore and there's basically not a thing they can do
about your problem. Did you know? So they won't be coming for you.
Not yet, anyway.

Yes, it could have been much worse. I know this. I could have been in
the car. I could have been crossing the street as you lurched. There could
have been kids walking around. You and your bleak nasty energy could
have come into my life in far more damaging and malicious ways. You
could have manifested as, say, a broken limb. You could have been death of
a family member, or a brain tumor, dementia. You could have been a hobbling accident, adultery, illness. You could have been cancer.

After all, this is what you are, isn't it? You are that random little demon,
a sliver of malevolent energy of the universe, the Thing That Is Always
Out There, waiting, careening, howling stupidly, crashing into anything
and causing all manner of pain and disruption, chortling drunkenly and
screeching away to find another arbitrary victim. You aren't the Trickster.
You are the Trickster's ugly three-toed cousin. Yes, the world knows you
well.

And I should be grateful. Grateful you only shot across the bow of my
life and didn't cause any serious, permanent harm. After all, it's just money.
It's just life. And it is, I fully realize, just a car.

But it was mine, and it was new, and it was beautiful, and you have
trashed it, and it will take months and cost many thousands to fix and it
might very well never be the same. And for that, I shall still try to forgive
you, maybe.

However, I cannot speak for the gods, who have my full permission to
smack your karma and reincarnate you as an incontinent dung beetle in
hell. Thank you.

This one almost didn't make it into TDS, *given my fervent belief that the sooner Dick and everything he represented recedes into memory, the better.*

I reconsidered, because I think it might be highly appropriate to pay one final tribute to the man who made so many children weep, flowers scream and women shudder deep in their ovaries merely by existing. He was, after all, a world-class backroom dealer, nefarious puppetmaster, evil overlord, and always, always a terrific punch line.

Few things, to my mind, exemplify the dark, despicable character of the former veep better than this tale of his lazy, cruel hunting exploits. A "canned" slaughter seems the perfect metaphor for the man's charmingly sadistic character. It's not just about the hunting; hell, I've gone salmon fishing in Alaska, with a similar "sure-thing" guarantee. With Dick, you get the feeling that it isn't about sport, or camaraderie, or marksmanship, or macho swagger, or even just enjoying the great outdoors. Dick just likes to kill things. —mm

Dick Cheney kills birds dead

01/23/2004

So not long ago the vice president of these beautiful and deeply confused United States, he of the struggling defibrillator and the shockingly nefarious wife[1] and the gnarled calluses from working Dubya's puppet strings, he of the thin-lipped sneer that makes babies cry and women wince and foreign policies crumble like feta cheese in the freezer, well, Dick goes himself a-huntin'.[2]

Not just any ol' regular, camouflage-wearing, man-versus-nature hunt out in the wild, mind. Dick is far too fragile and unskilled and spoiled and scared of the open woods and icky furry monsters for that. Assumedly.

Nossir, our man Dick, he has himself flown over, in Air Force 2, on the taxpayer's tab, accompanied by his most favoritest shotgun, to the exclusive Rolling Rock Club in Ligonier, Westmoreland County, in rural Pennsylvania, to have himself a nice, cushy "canned" pheasant hunt.

This is what it was: Dick and about nine other overfed white guys sitting in a comfy luxury blind with their manly shotguns, waiting for the Westmoreland guy stationed behind them on a hill to release clusters of stunned, fat, tame game birds from a net. Then they shoot them.

Lots and lots of them. And then they slap each other on the back. And they grunt and say nice shot as the birds drop like flies as dogs race back and forth hauling dead or dying birds into huge piles. What fun.

More than 400 birds were killed in one lackadaisical afternoon. Dick himself blasted the living shit out of 70 birds, all by himself. That's right,

70. Plus an unknown number of mallard ducks. Then they had them all plucked and vacuum packed and sent back home to show off to the staff. Dick was driven back to the airport in a Humvee.

Are we not all impressed? Are we not all sitting here saying, wow, that Dick Cheney guy, he of the massive Halliburton kickbacks, he is one studly dude, slaughtering a small mountain of docile, stupefied birds that had no chance of escape. What a guy.

And what a display of prowess and skill, using his day off to kill almost as many pheasant and duck in an afternoon as all those notions of progress that have been slaughtered by his inbred cronyist pro-industry energy policy since the beginning of this sentence. Gosh.

Even real hunters cringe at canned hunts. It is not a sport. It is not man versus nature. There is no nobility, no honor, no sportsmanship, no instinct, no luck, no tramping through fields and crouching in blinds and waiting for hours as you coddle the barrel of your shotgun and dream of J.Lo and tell jokes about homos and Hillary Clinton, just so you can shoot a few wild birds.

In other words, Cheney's canned hunt had none of the ostensibly sporting characteristics of true hunting. Cheney's was essentially a slaughter, a bloody target practice for aging, overpampered white males who never have sex and have desperately zero outlet for all their pent-up misanthropic energies. In short.[3]

Yes, there are far more pressing issues for us to care about than a bunch of dead birds. And, yes, there are roughly a billion chickens slaughtered every damn day in this county by giant industrial farms in far more inhumane and brutal ways than Uncle Dick's little afternoon bloodbath.

And, yes, indeed, canned hunts happen far more often than anyone probably imagines. There are private ranches all over the country, most offering manly trophy hunters a "guaranteed" kill of some overbred, tame, exotic animal, such as antelopes, deer, cattle, swine, bears, zebras and sometimes even big cats.

These ranches, most operating in — you guessed it — Texas, service lazy fee-paying trophy hunters who want a giant stuffed antelope head for the den but don't want to deal with any of that nasty nature or travel to Africa. God bless America.

So Dick's little hunt was not all that rare. Which of course makes it no less stupid, no less of a brutal blood rush. It was a taxpayer-supported trip taken solely for the sake of ... what? Not sport. Not gamesmanship. Not food. Just the little thrill that comes from killing something that never had a prayer? Is that it, Dick? Kick up the defibrillator a notch? Must be.

Hell, we taxpayers could've saved a fortune in Secret Service time and Air Force 2 gas money had Dick simply have one of his lackeys tie long strings to the feet of 70 ducks and tether them to the White House lawn. Then Dick could just sit in a nice leather recliner and shoot them at will.

Simpler still, aides simply could've nailed the birds' feet to the floor with a staple gun and Dick could've put on a pair of army boots like the kind he avoided wearing during the Vietnam War, and as the birds squawked Dick could've jumped around like a human pogo stick and stomped on each bird, popping it like a balloon. Yay Dick!

And, finally, there is the patented George W. Bush hunting method, wherein you sit back in your lawn chair and make a little gun shape with your thumb and index finger and "aim" at each bird and shout "Bang!" and some GOP intern rushes over and smashes the bird in the head with a baseball bat. Same difference, really.

You know what? It's not a big deal. It's just a bunch of dead birds, right? Over 400 of them spread among 10 guys who simply could not shoot fast enough to kill them all. Again, it happens all the time.[4]

Except here, here in the land of obvious and tragicomic analogy, where you simply cannot help but transfer Dick's little aggro mind-set — this numbly violent attitude of "just line 'em up and shoot 'em and pretend you're actually a manly hunter when all you are is rather heartless and inhumane and small" — over to the government itself.

Which is to say, this is the worldview we are up against. This is yet another example of the American agenda, very much the way this administration attacks the world. No competition. No sportsmanship. No fairness. Zero respect. No reverence. Just kill at will.

Because it is, in the final analysis, all about how you approach and engage the world, nature, yourself. It is all about with what degree of sacredness and veneration you walk the planet, treading lightly or stomping heavily, in awe of the interconnectedness or working to crush the beautiful and the weak for profit and hollow thrill. It is, after all, your choice.

Do you, as Dick Cheney obviously does, see the world as your personal blood-sport playground, where you can take anything you want, kill whatever you like, respect nothing nature has to offer, suffer no ramifications, and do it all on someone else's tab? Well then. You have made your choice. The GOP wants you.

1 http://thung.notlong.com
2 http://uerib.notlong.com
3 http://quaqua.notlong.com
4 http://uuviejo.notlong.com

I hate you I hate you

From: "apro" <aproXXX@hotmail.com>
To: <mmorford@sfgate.com>
Subject: Here is your answer on Gay marriage.
Date: Wed, 15 Nov 2006 20:02:59 -0800
MIME-Version: 1.0
FILETIME=[099A6050:01C70934]

The answer is No!

Why because we do not want it!

Gay people have money and political power, but you cannot force us to do what we do not want to do, no matter what you want to do. You are in America and you can do what ever you want in the privacy of your home. You have forced us to to put up with men kissing in public, but you cannot force us to give you the ability to marry each other.

We do not like what you do! You are trying to force us to agree to something that we (of course dislike does not describe how we feel about your behavior) do not want and will not want.

Does that mean hundreds of thousands of men and women, who are "strait", do not have sexual intercourse with the same sex no it does not. Yes, that makes them liars but this is the real world, and in the real world, we do not like people having sex with the same sex Period. We think that it is wrong. So you are trying to force us to agree with something we think is wrong.

This mean it aint gonna happen, Period so cry on, whine on, dream on, wish on!

The answer is no!

Date: Thu, 16 Nov 2006 08:30:43 -0500 (EST)
Subject: fag marriage
From: garyXXX@toolkitmail.com
To: mmorford@sfgate.com
User-Agent: SquirrelMail/1.5.1
MIME-Version: 1.0
X-Virus- Clean

Morford,

Since you spend most of your life in never-never land, you might not be aware that you have an appointment to stand before the God of the Bible, and be judged by Him for your sins. And your contempt for God will be on the agenda. Try to enjoy the rest of your miserable, worthless life. Eternity is a long, long time.

Sincerely,

Gary B

From: Thomas V <thomasXXX@hotmail.com>
To: <mmorford@sfgate.com>
Subject: God got your tongue?
Date: Thu, 16 Nov 2006 21:56:02 -0800
MIME-Version: 1.0

Mark

I can't imagine being you, living each day with such hatred permeating through your heart for others? When you put your disguise away, you know that Satan has your soul and your ego can't bring yourself to giving into the truth. It's a BIG step Mark!

You really do need help! Maybe you can use this bent up anger and energy towards something that is good rather than towards hatred, because then there is a purpose... image this quote being true ... "Well, I'd be very interested to see what kind of articles Mark pens from hell one day!" Your path leads nowhere... at least the path of God gives you some kind of hope

From: "Anthony XXX" <aXXX@rochester.rr.com>
To: <mmorford@sfgate.com>
Subject: Cheney
Date: Mon, 6 Nov 2006 12:26:12 -0500
MIME-Version: 1.0
X-Priority: 3

You are great where you are.Why don't you and Fagtown depart this life to maybe with your Patron Saint Lucifer. They should rename you Berg San Luciferein. Keep smoking that shit you jackasses do out there and leave the USA. And take your joyboy with you. Anthony, Rochester,NY

From: "Cheryl M" <XXX@gmail.com>
To: letters@msnbc.com
Subject: Mark Morford's Naïve About America
Cc: mmorford@sfgate.com
MIME-Version: 1.0

I think one of the many reasons Mark Morford is so naive about the State of the Union comes from all the sex, R&R and drugs he's done in his life to escape reality. Instead of sounding the clarion call, "the Yankee's are coming" to an obvious Coup d'etat on the horizon, he's lulling us all to sleep with a false sense of security in his latest article.

There's especially no excuse for Morford because there are plenty of top selling books on the subject of the end of America as it falls into a dictatorship. Morford, who tries to create the illusion he's a social activist, won't be writing about reality and the upcoming dictatorship in America like Naomi Wolf. He'll always be spinning stories from illusions and his hallucinations.

> *It seems like the culture just went through a long phase, maybe a decade*
> *or more, of extreme overparenting, paranoid and panicky and sad, an age*
> *when kids were so pampered and fawned upon and carefully guided away*
> *from the scary scary thing, with the world so sanitized and sterilized for their*
> *protection, that it ended up turning out a generation of wimpy whiners who*
> *couldn't handle the 'real' world and who always got sick because they were*
> *never allowed to eat dirt or get poked by a rusty nail or be exposed to myriad*
> *germs so as to build up a decent immune system.*
>
> *And now, maybe a bit of a backlash, as parents — and doctors, psycholo-*
> *gists, et al — remember the true value of more of a rough 'n' tumble, down 'n'*
> *dirty, fun-in-the-mud exposure to nature and the world. Is it too late to save*
> *the deep end? Probably. But at least they have yet to install big, puffy pad-*
> *ding all over the monkey bars. Wait, have they? —mm*

The end of the deep end

07/09/2003

It's not exactly the end of the world. It might be only a small tragic shift,
but if you're anywhere over 25 and grew up in just about any worthy
suburban American town and endured anything resembling a worthy
American childhood, the deep end of the swimming pool probably meant
something to you, energetically speaking, *evolutionarily* speaking, as a kid.

Something mysterious. Something scary.
Something foreboding and magnificent,
because when you were about six years
old the deep end very much represented
that sudden slap of terrifying summertime
anxiety — particularly if you were new to
swimming, new to the pool's otherworldly
challenges, its beckoning aura of happy
splish-splash doom.

It was powerful. It was magic and dark
and transformative; the deep end was that
area of the pool you ventured into extreme-
ly tentatively, excitedly, all about that rush
of delicious fear and desire and quiet panic
and determination. You know, just like life.

The deep end was, of course, the place to
face your demons. To test your mettle, your
fortitude, your burgeoning superhero pow-

ers, to see if you could dog-paddle frantically all the way to the opposite edge without drowning and when you made it you felt this crazy rush of pride and love and power, your little heart beating like a crazy techno remix because you were now strong. You were godlike. You were the water-bound Thwarter of Death. You were six years old.

Here's why you should care: The deep end is vanishing[1]. Maybe you didn't know this. Cities are filling them in, hotels are redesigning their outdoor amenities, backyard-pool manufacturers are no longer building pools with areas deeper than five feet.

Too much danger, they say. Too many broken necks and screaming kids and drowned people and lawsuits, they say. Aquatics tastes have changed, they say.

Bah, we say. This is a significant tragedy. This is yet another shift in our increasingly panicky and trepidatious culture toward further sanitizing the world, stripping it of all edge and menace and wonder and vital rites of passage and what's next, the end of lawn darts? The demise of the wicked-cool playground, full of looming monkey bars and dramatic swing sets and huge metal slides? The end of the manual-clutch transmission, fer chris-sakes? Whoops, too late.

The deep end is, of course, the metaphor to end all metaphors. There is quite possibly no more perfectly apt allegory for life and experience and growing up, and we are blindly wiping it out because we are increasingly terrified of anything we can't completely control and sanitize and buffer for easier swallowing.

There will be no more diving. There will be no more diving boards. There will be no more tossing the quarter over your shoulder into the si-lent chlorinated depths and then excitedly diving down, down, down into the void and grabbing that shiny prize, and emerging from the water like Jacques Cousteau with evidence of the lost riches of Atlantis. All day long, over and over and over. But no more.

There will be no more comments like, "Man is he ever off the deep end" or "The deep end is only for big kids, honey" or "That's not a deep end — that's my sister." You get the idea.

It is an indelible rite of passage. It is glorious accomplishment, from terrified tyke sporting wimpy inflatable arm-floaty things, to fearless Olympic freestyler, gliding effortlessly through the shimmering backyard vastness, luxuriating in how you can finally traverse the deep end confi-dently, in complete control of your body and your liquid universe, the pool transformed from fathomless abyss to welcoming playground. Screw the damn floaties. You are in the deep end. You have arrived.

The next generation will not know the backyard cannonball dive. They will not know the desperation of hiding down in the deep end during nervous first-time teenage skinny-dipping. They will not know the belly flop or the swan dive or the pike or the spike or the dude-I-am-so-wasted-I-think-I'll-leap-off-your-roof-into-the-pool. Damn tragic, is what it is.

In fact, unless they have access to a lake or ocean — which, of course, the vast majority don't — they will not know any diving at all, really, maybe a couple lame splashes here and there but no real vertical thrill, no overcoming that fear of leaping into the void, of momentary flight, splashdown, rush rush gargle splash zoom wow hey mom watchthiswatchthiswatchthis.

This is vital. This is key. Because the end of the deep end means maybe, just maybe, we aren't allowing ourselves, our kids, those more vital, deeper explorations. That we are increasingly preventing them — and ourselves — from experiencing, on their own terms, those more profound risks and mistakes and gasping epiphanies.

Sure, removing the deep end makes some sort of politically correct sense and prevents accidents and protects kids a little more, averts lawsuits and blah blah blah, but hell if we really want to protect kids we'd lock them in a padded room and give them nothing but a stuffed penguin and a simpleminded ideology to play with for about 18 years before partially lobotomizing them and making them into born-again Republicans. I mean, please.

What is left, really, to teach us of the wonders and perils of solo survivalism and accomplishment and desperate breaststroke struggle? What is left to impart hints of terror and bliss and little exhilarating winks of potential death?

1 http://feipho.notlong.com

Verily, suicide's always a touchy one to write about, especially for a satirist, for someone always seeking the ironic or unusual angle to try and dislodge a unique insight or two. Just about everyone has been directly affected, knows someone who's done the deed, or at least attempted. The stories are often harrowing, and deeply sad. But I also think there isn't a soul alive who's crossed a bridge like the Golden Gate and hasn't imagined what it would be like to leap off and end it all in a giant, doomed swan dive of bloody, heart-crushing, fatalistic screw-it-all-idness. We've all been there. It's a universal condition, all the myriad ways we fantasize, fetishize, and fear our own demise.

Also interesting to note the sub-theme here, the unspoken, rarely-exposed idea that single, middle-aged white guys might have it far less easy and carefree in American life than the culture might think. Possible? Shall we ask the bridge? —mm

Greetings, Golden Gate Bridge jumper

09/16/2009

I am, apparently, in deep trouble.

I fit the profile. I fit the average and the typical and the increasingly unsettling norm. I apparently contain all the ingredients for the ultimate in fatal and senseless decisions, and while I don't really feel it at the moment, I just might have the tendency, the leaning, a certain depressing proclivity that will draw me, bitterly and inexorably, to my watery grave.

The facts are, as they say, irrefutable. The facts are shocking and upsetting indeed.

The facts are this: The average suicidal jumper from the Golden Gate Bridge is 40 years old, white, single and male.

Oh dear. This could be a problem. I have just checked the mirror and it appears the dour, doomed human just described is, well, me. Yay statistics!

It's true. I more or less fit into almost all those categories in more or less all ways — give or take a year or two here and a hottie girlfriend there — and no matter how I slice it, the fact is I have matched up perfectly with all of these criteria at one time or another in the very recent past, recent enough that I can only draw one obvious, if admittedly absurd conclusion: Unbeknownst to myself, I just might be far more prone to leaping from the world's most famous suicide bridge than I had previously imagined. Who knew?

Really, I had no idea. I was entirely unaware of just how aligned with doom and misery I am, especially given how I don't really feel the slightest bit doomed or miserable. It's a bit like hearing that, because you enjoy, say, strong coffee and ornithology and reciting Yeats in the shower, your left leg is much more likely to suddenly fall off without warning. Wait, what? Really? My leg? That's ridiculous. My leg feels just fi— oh wait, is that a tingle? Am I *limping*? Oh, *fuck*.

It is, perhaps, one of those preposterous self-fulfilling prophecies, the pointless statistical generalization that becomes a lethal reality through sheer force of morbid curiosity. I imagine it's akin to what your average dentist feels when she hears, for the umpteenth time, the chestnut about how hers is the occupation with the highest rate of suicide among all service professions and that includes lawyers, high school guidance counselors and self-hating Republicans. Great, thanks for letting me know, again. I was happy just a second ago. Now please turn and spit.

I am only partially joking. Suicide, of course, is no laughing matter. It is brutal and troubling and I am well aware that nearly everyone reading this column knows someone who knows someone else who has contemplated or even succeeded at suicide, which makes it therefore a terrible, heartbreaking reality we don't like to talk much about.

Which is, of course, also the reason we *must* joke about it, why we must attempt to find irony, lightness and even wanton absurdity in the darkest of places — *especially* there — lest we take ourselves far too damn seriously and be ceaselessly attacked by the demons of our darker natures, the very ones urging us to end it all and jump off a bridge. See how that works?

I'm not exactly sure what this disconcerting stat means. Perhaps we are to infer that middle-aged, single white males have it pretty rough out there in the cold, relentless world? Rougher than most people imagine? Maybe so much rougher and more difficult that no one can fully understand the pressures and the responsibility and the deep, white pain? Could be, could be. After all, this particular species *does* shoulder a rather unique burden.

They/we are the unfortunate standard-bearer, the cliché incarnate, the pale and violent rule against which many cultural imperatives are measured. Every salary dispute, minority entanglement, religious smackdown, feminist rant, literary debate seems to target the older white male's eternal — and usually very aggressive and sexist and patriarchal — dominance of world culture. Hey, life's a bitch when you're everyone's bitch.

Or perhaps it's this: If you have attained middle-age maledom and are still single and overly white, maybe you feel that things have not exactly, you know, *worked out* the way you'd hoped. Maybe you've felt some sort of brutal level of stress, some soul-crushing *pressure* to live up to some impossible standard of "typical" white male success, wealth, pseudo-happiness, a standard you never quite attained because, well, it's largely a big, stupid illusion to begin with.

Maybe you feel, in short, that you've failed. You do not have 2.4 children. You do not have the pretty and sexless and vaguely unhappy wife. You do not have the insanely overpaid job or the giant tacky McMansion or the gluttonous level of glittery underserved accomplishment for which your demographic is so famous — and famously resented. This way manic depression lies.

What's more, you are likely well past your prime in terms of health and fitness and sexual power, what with that gut expanding nicely and the shoulders slumping just so and the hair receding like a gray tide, as every nubile female under 25 begins to look at you less like a potential sex lollipop and more like her dad's slightly lecherous drinking buddy. All of which can only bring you face to face with the biggest question of all: What the hell is wrong with you?

Let us not go too far. Let us not get carried away. Single white males certainly have no monopoly on the life-is-miserable purview (just ask your average teen, or a gay person in Kansas). What's more, it hath been proven in no uncertain terms that the midlife crisis is, in fact, a *universal* phenomenon, spanning all cultures and races and even genders, though males appear to suffer the malady far more aggressively than women. Or perhaps we just handle it with far less dignity. Either way, middle age sure seems to take a buzzsaw to the front-loaded, pressure-cooked male ego.

No matter. As the intense, but also rather vague and poorly parsed study in question shows, the range of people who kill themselves by jumping off the GG Bridge is huge indeed. White males dominate, to be sure, but maybe that's only because there are more of us to take the leap. Or maybe we just make a louder splash. Who can say?

I do know that when I cross the GG Bridge these days, I tend to glance over at those guard rails and safety wires with a different sort of appreciation, awareness and sighing sense of wonder. Here is this astonishing architectual icon set against one of the most beautiful backdrops in the world, all teeming with life and movement and possibility, and all quietly underscored with a dark thread of sadness and depression and death.

It is, of course, a metaphor, a microcosm, a symbol that's neither white, nor male, nor middle aged. It's simply universal.

MISFIT TOYS

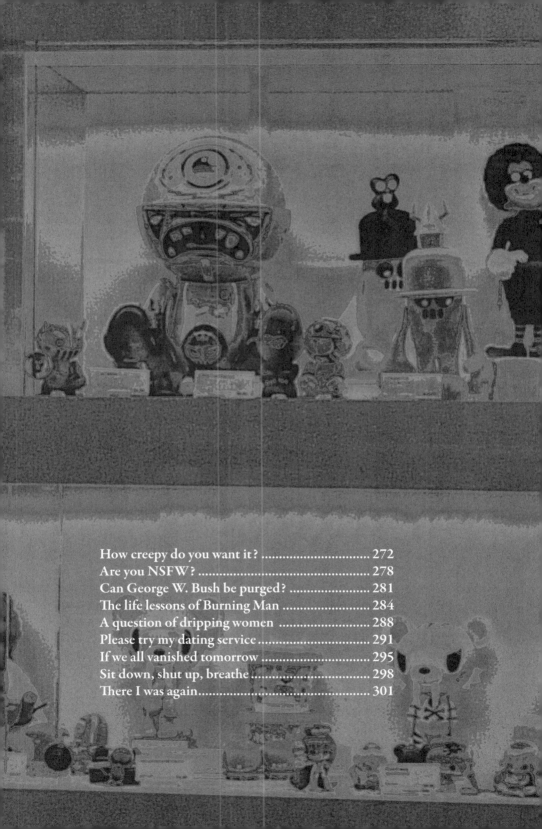

Honestly? I don't really know if this tale is real. Precious little verifiable source material to back it up, despite the St. Petersburg Times story (see footnote No. 2). Then again, no one's ever admitted to making it up, or actually found proof that it's a complete hoax, either. After this column ran, I half expected to hear from a very smug, myth-debunking Russian reader telling me I was a gullible idiot, and hadn't I seen website X or blog Y that debunked the whole myth long ago. Didn't happen.

It's certainly a very elaborate and successful hoax, if it is. Very disturbing and deliciously weird tale, if it's not. And I had a hell of a lot of fun writing about it, regardless. –mm

How creepy do you want it?

02/27/2008

I admit only to this: I can get deeply creeped out, down to my very core, now and then and hopefully not all that often because, well, I still like to sleep at night.

Personally, I try to keep the creep to a minimum, not really wishing to dive down into that low, dark vibration much and hence I avoid most horror movies like the plague and I find slasher flicks and "torture porn" revolting and ridiculous and while monster flicks can occasionally be fun and thrilling, they're mostly just a cheap roller-coaster rides supplying no real nourishment of any kind. I know, that's not really the point. But still.

Ah, but the occult. The paranormal. The deeply weird, mysterious, unsolvable, disturbing. That can get to me. That has power. A good, deep creep-out, those unknowable things that get under your skin and crawl around and tug at the shirtsleeves of your fears, well, those are the things can last for years. Lifetimes. I love that. I hate that.

The final shot in "The Blair Witch Project." An oozingly possessed Linda Blair crawling down the stairs on all fours, upside down, backwards, in a full backbend, on her toes and fingertips, in the uncut version of "The Exorcist." The ending to (and overall creepy feel of) "Don't Look Now,"
the famous cult horror movie from the '70s with Donald Sutherland and Julie Christie and the creepy little midget in the red robe. Peter Weir's "Picnic at Hanging Rock," another classic '70s occult flick, chaste schoolgirls disappearing up a bizarrely haunted mountain — entirely fictional, but plays all too damn real.

But still, they're just movies. Fiction, mostly.

No matter how good they are, they all kneel before the one true god of interminable creepiness: reality.

Here's one. It's called the Dyatlov Pass Accident.[1] Oh my God, yes. I stumbled over this delicious tale just recently over at Metafilter and it's one of those stories that contains all the best elements of a deep, resonant creep-out. Inexplicable behavior. Bizarre factoids. Inconclusive evidence. Missing body parts. And not a single clue, almost 50 years later, as to what really happened.[2]

The nutshell: In 1959, nine experienced Russian cross-country skiers — seven men and two women, led by a man named Igor Dyatlov — headed to the Ural Mountains, to a slope called Kholat Syakhl (Mansi language for "Mountain of the Dead," ahem) for a rugged, wintry trek. On their way up, they are apparently hit by inclement weather and veer off course and decide to set up camp and wait it out. All is calm. All is fine and good. They even take pictures of camp, the scenery, each other.[3] The weather is not so bad. They go to sleep.

Then, something happens. In the middle of the night all nine suddenly leap out of their tents as fast as possible, ripping them open from the inside (not even enough time to untie the doors) and race out into the sub-zero temps, without coats or boots or skis, most in their underwear, some even barefoot or with a single sock or boot. It is 30 degrees below zero, Celsius. A few make it as far as a kilometer and a half down the slope. All nine, as you might expect, quickly die.

And so it begins.

Why did they rush out, unable to even grab a coat or blanket? What came at them? The three-month investigation revealed that five of the trekkers died from simple hypothermia, with no apparent trauma at all, no signs of attack, struggle, no outward injuries of any kind.

However, two of the other four apparently suffered massive internal traumas to the chest, like you would if you were hit by a car. One's skull was crushed. All four of these were found far from the other five. But still, no signs of external injuries.

Not good enough? How about this: One of the women was missing her tongue.

Oh, it gets better. And weirder.

Tests of the few scraps of clothing revealed very high levels of radiation. Evidence found at the campsite indicates the trekkers might've been blinded. Eyewitnesses around the area report seeing "bright flying spheres" in the sky during the same months. And oh yes, relatives at the funeral swear the skin of their dead loved ones was tanned, tinted dark orange or brown. And their hair had all turned completely gray.

Wait, what?

The final, official explanation as to what caused such bizarre behavior from otherwise well-trained, experienced mountaineers? An "unknown compelling force." Indeed.

Here's the problem: All the convenient, logical explanations — avalanche, animal attack, secret military nuke test — fail. Russian authorities held a three-month investigation. Rescuers, experts picked through every piece of evidence. There were no signs of natural disaster. And if it was just an avalanche, why was the area closed off for three *years* following the event, and all related documents put in a secret Russian archive until 1990? If it was some sort of weird nuclear megablast (which I suppose may tint you orange, but won't turn your hair gray), what the hell happened to her tongue?

I love stories like this. I hate stories like this.

Sure, you want to go for the logical. Hell, who knows what hellish weaponry they were testing in the mountains in Khrushchev's Russia in the late '50s? Who knows what dark mysteries are buried in the landscape by the world's militaries as they test their dark deeds? The rule goes like this: Any weapon of horror and death man's mind can conceive, odds are gruesomely good the government or military has considered it. Or even built it.

Then again, maybe not. The "horrifying military experiments" theory, spawn of a thousand movies and conspiracy theories, has one fatal flaw: proof. What, 75 years of high-tech military advances and hundreds of billions of dollars spent and a million people working in various sinister branches of the military, and yet not one scrap of truly bizarre or outrageous military weaponry has popped up in the public sphere, been leaked or revealed or unearthed? This is the Internet/YouTube/nothing's-secret age — you'd think we'd get at least one piece of irrefutable evidence proving how the Pentagon has been testing 10-story remote-controlled radioactive spiders

with lasers for eyes. Or something. Not that I trust the government, per se. They just aren't that smart.

This is both the joy and horror of stories like Dyatlov — they make your mind jump and bend and struggle. Logic fails quickly. Easy explanations don't work. Complicated ones feel incomplete. The creepiness takes hold, begins to burrow, make you squirm.

So of course, you jump further. You reach for the paranormal, meta-physical, unknowable, to things like UFOs and spirits and ghosts, dark forces and mysticism and the occult, because, well, that's where the action is. That's where we get to touch the void, dance on the edge of perception, realize how little we truly know of anything.

After all, if you really think all there is to this world is what your five senses show you, if you think there's always got to be a logical, earthbound explanation for stories like Dyatlov, well, you might as well just join a megachurch and wipe your brain and your intuition and your deep, dark curiosity clean right now.

As Dyatlov himself might say, his skin orange and hair gray and eyes wide wide wide: "You think you know, but you have no idea."

1 http://bohpha.notlong.com
2 http://www.sptimes.ru/index.php?action_id=2&story_id=25093
3 http://infodjatlov.narod.ru/fg4

From: Tiffany <XXXtiffany@gmail.com>
To: mmorford@sfgate.com
Subject: Innocence is Bliss
MIME-Version: 1.0

Dear Mark:

I used to read your columns months back and I couldn't remember them mentioning sex as often and in such the manner as your most recent one. What is with that? Why are you promoting sex so intensely? Wet, slippery, dirty sex? Do you really want our population to exceed maximum amount? Not to mention STD's and AIDS. Why is your attitude such that you take the sweetness out of relationships and romance? Why can't people just kiss and stuff? Can't you promote that? Innocence DOES exist and it is nice every once in a while. You'd think as a columnist, your writing style would improve, but yours is heading south. Stop with the garbage. It baffles me that you actually HAVE a job writing columns, and THIS GARBAGE is what you choose to write about...how we evolved from spit and bacteria...so let's just mix our fluids because you obviously don't take your job seriously and appreciate the opportunity you've been given? LAME. LAME. LAME.

Tiffany

From: "Christopher B" <XXXXX@alltel.net>
To: <mmorford@sfgate.com>
Subject: Re: America loses another war
Date: Thu, 14 Dec 2006 12:25:51 -0500
MIME-Version: 1.0

I'm so looking forward to the day the big one hits SF and buttfuckers like yourself slide into the Pacific....

Date: Thu, 22 Mar 2007 04:06:45 -0700 (PDT)
From: Joe C <warped_cranky_old_man@XXX.com>
Subject: Your 3/21 column...
To: mmorford@sfgate.com
MIME-Version: 1.0

...was the most convoluted, snotty, bewildering hack piece you have subjected us to so far! Oh...hate Catholics?? Too "good" for KFC fried junk food??

Have you ever been homelss, broke, or otherwise economically disadvantaged, so that a 99 cnet snacker, fish or fowl, is like a wonderful meal?? Yeah, this pope'a another fascist bastard, but what's your point?? Dummies like you are grist for the neo_KKKons - I can just hear those Hot Talk asswipes lampooning you, as even us Pinko/Fag/Religionist Fast foodeaters do!

Doubt it. Man, I thought NOTHING could top your ball-shaving bit a while back, but this blows worse than a chicken-hawk cleric!

Either you are just another pathetic, Gen-Xer hipster smveler Whiteboy-from-$$$, or else you're as stupid as that bitch who subjected us to her personanl woes (Gonick?? Goniff? I forgert - she's gone...THANK Christ!)

Go away...I hear those fucks at The WEEKLY are always hiring...

Sorry for the harsh crtique, O whiny BALL-Shaving, psuedo-leftist wanna-be bicyclist (God, I mean, Goddess, I just see you standing in front of WhiteGeiSt, or some other dive-y saloon...), you must get better drugs than I used to sell to your family, or else you should pack up, 7 go you I hate you

I hate you I hate you I hate you

I hate you I

BALLS out to some jerkwater BiBle belt/Nazi shitpit, unless, of course, they ran you out of town.

Get a clue, or don't, but your no Charles Mccabe, and he was the worst, most miserable, whiny, pathological scribe to ever grace The Friday Fishwrap, until you reared your mouthy, bitchy puss.

Yours in Catholic disgust,

Disgruntled 2-wheeler & erstwhile gutter poet

From: "Becky"<XXX@nerdshack.com>
To: mmorford@sfgate.com
Subject: Here's a thought for ya
Date: Wed, 19 Sep 2007 11:29:50 -0700
User-Agent: Mozilla Thunderbird 1.0.6 (Windows/20050716)

When laws are passed to stop faggots from brainwashing kids during school hours, when laws are passed stopping faggots from parading their filth on the streets, when laws are passed to stop faggots from persuing their perverted, deviant sexual pastimes in their own bedrooms, then you can have your laws forcing me to eat what YOU think I should.

Most sincerely,
Becky

Date: Fri, 16 Nov 2007 10:01:04 -0800 (PST)
From: Mowglicubb <XXX@yahoo.com>
Subject: Bush Death Watch: Countdown!
To: mmorford@sfgate.com
MIME-Version: 1.0

You sir are a grade A moron. It only goes to figure that since you are in the most socialist city in this great country. If you don't like bush you should have voted you pachouli wearing waste of skin. Your obvious HATE is disgusting especially while you try to speak of love out of the other side of your mouth. I suppose you support the idea of illegals getting a city sponsored ID so they can trim your lawn still. You are propagating their slavery, and you don't care that Mexico won't ID their illegals. Your flowerie prose is only a thin vaneer for your hate filled soul. Go back to your latte and think about that. At least I have the cahonies to tell you I don't like you straight up. You sir are a tard.

Elgin M

One long, sustained intellectual tease, subtly increasing in heat and suggestiveness as it slips into the imagination and torments your workday by quickening the heart rate, increasing blood flow to vital areas, tantalizing the second chakra with hints and licks and shameless innuendo, while never once actually mentioning the sultry subject matter directly.

That was the idea, anyway. Does it work? Does it make you want to strip off your pants? Someone else's pants? Both? I can only hope. —mm

Are you NSFW?

05/06/2009

Look, you can pretend all you want. You can cover it up, ignore the signs, try to appear all professional and innocent and beatific like you just swallowed a cartoon butterfly made of strawberry shortcake and soft-focus Hallmark sunsets. It really doesn't matter.

Everyone knows you're thinking about it. Everyone knows you want to look at it, fondle it, film it, ponder it for hours, sink into warm pools of it, spread it all over your bones like warm butter on Jesus toast and then of course do it, oh my God yes *do* it until your heart turns to divine pudding and your skin becomes transluscent and suddenly you can't stop giggling for two weeks straight.

How does everyone know this about you? Easy: Because they're doing it, too. They really can't help it. Hell, I'm doing it right now. See? You are not alone.

It's not like it's not obvious. That busywork you're doing right now? That computer screen and that meeting and phone call and charity drive and financial analysis and strategy report? Just a cover up, really. A nice ruse, a diversion, a convenient delusion designed to make yourself believe life is a little bit more than just a stream of slippery daydreams, mostly about it and its various incarnations, motivations, divinations.

Whatever. Deep down, you know work — like God, like politics, like war, like children, like pain — is merely a thing mankind invented to distract itself from thinking and wishing and hoping to do it all day long and well into the night and three times (why hold back, really) on Sunday.

Do you wish to deny it? Perfectly OK. You are free to refuse to admit how numerous quiet-but-urgent fantasies about it are probably pouring all over you right now like sunshine on a hot sidewalk. It is not uncommon to play dumb, naive, coy.

Even now, few people are willing to celebrate their deep appreciation for it openly, in public, in front of family and friends and police officers and

co-workers who might think they're more than a little bit weird, insane, dirty, godless, alive.

In fact, many of the saddest and most confused among us will take the *opposite* tack and not merely deny it, but try like hell to pretend they actively resent and despise it because, well, they never really enjoyed it all that much in the first place because have no clue what they're doing, and therefore they'll claim it's overrated and superficial and a little bit gross, covered in leeches and shame and sin.

Problem is, they often won't stop there. They will go on to say that certain people who do it a certain way should probably be arrested, persecuted, even killed. They will righteously point out that Jesus never did it (oh sweetheart, yes he did) and neither did the pope or their grandmother or their eight surly cats, and therefore they will claim you can live a happy and full life without much of it at all, even though you actually can't.

Of course, we all know exactly what this means. It means these people are more desperate than anyone else to do it, too. After all, the more hotly you insist that something like this is immoral and disgusting and wrong, the more you secretly crave doing it to yourself and your neighbor and probably the tattooed bagger dude at Whole Foods, over and over again, preferably whilst wearing a vinyl miniskirt and also with lots of throbbing music and the thing with the giggling.

Oh, I'm quite sure you already know what it is, have already imagined it numerous times in various formats and locations since the opening sentence of this column. I see that look on your face. I see you blink and squirm and sigh. You think I don't know? Please.

Hell, it's so enchanting and universal, you might think I'd be able to lay it all out in explicit detail for you, right here and now, show you some fascinating photos and video clips I just found, refer to all the latest jargon and tools and pictograms, some of which you may or may not have seen before because, after all, there is always something new to learn about it.

Of course, I cannot do that. This is a "family" newspaper/website, though I'm not quite sure what that means given how the last time I checked, our 10-year-old virgin Mormon reader demographic was pretty fucking nonexistent. Oh right. I'm not supposed to swear, either. Oh well.

More importantly, it's possible you are at work right now, in some sort of observable cubicle, and therefore such attitudes and pictures would be, as they say, Not Safe for Work (NSFW), which is this cute little label we've recently invented to stick on certain images, sometimes horrific or disgusting, but mostly those illustrating things we love to do to ourselves and each other but cannot display lest the uptight among us scream and faint and claim the devil is moistening their undergarments against their will.

Of course, such workplace displays are also considered a bit uncouth, tactless, unprofessional. There is truth to this. Decorum and restraint certainly have their place; it is not always wise to throw this sort of energy around without control and some thoughtful appreciation of its delicious, but potentially impolite power. Time and place for everything. After all, you've got work to do, right? Fair enough.

But of course, that doesn't really stop you, does it? That doesn't seem to dull the aching fire all that much. Music, travel, wine, friendship, yoga, art, iPhones, lip balm, wood-burning stoves in winter — we have plenty to keep us busy and nicely distracted, plenty of activities and passions toward which we can redirect that pulsing energy, lest its fire scorch our bones every moment of every day.

But we always seem to circle back. We always find a way to slip it in, let it sizzle deep, let the warm, fond memory of it permeate even our last dying sigh. Isn't that amazing? Isn't that just as it should be? Don't you wish you were doing it right now?

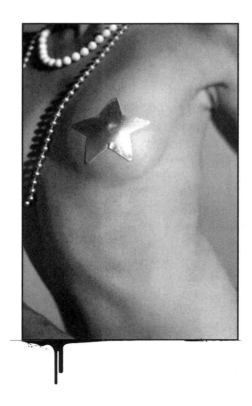

Oh hell yes, I absolutely do believe in ritual and magic, in smudge sticks, cleansing baths, toxin release, energy healing, the works. It's not all I believe and I don't take it insanely seriously — I don't wake up every day and swing a crystal lasso over my head and ask my spirit guides if it's OK to eat sugar today, say — but I do very much believe we all have far more fundamental, supernatural power than we imagine, subtle and sublime and yet not even all that extraordinary, and it's very much worth dialing into because, well, why wouldn't you?

I never did actually hold that sacred fire ritual down at Ocean Beach in SF like I originally planned, the week that Bush finally slumped into history. But I do think there was such a massive collective exhale, such a powerful, global sense of blessed relief when he finally stepped down, it might not have been all that necessary. -mm

Can George W. Bush be purged?

03/16/2007

Sage is always good. Or maybe lavender. Pine is nice, too. Dried, bundled, tied with string, burned with hot, divine intent. Would it work? Do we have enough to go around? This is the question.

I speak, of course, of ritual. Purging and cleansing and purifying and, truly, burning a nicely dried, blessed smudge stick can be a terrific slice of personal magic, to rid a space (or perhaps even your own body) of negative juju or vicious spirits or just to make way for the new and the moist and the good. You can smudge a room. You can create a divine smoldering cloud and then move through the smoke, invoke change, purge the negative, invite hot licks of yes. It is a thing to do.

But here's the thing: Can you smudge an entire nation? Do we have enough lavender for 300 million? It is, all things considered, a big goddamn country. Windy. Rocky, in places. Could be tricky. Not to mention, you know, hazy. From all the smoke. Think of the potential traffic accidents. Coughing.

Important considerations, really, because it is becoming increasingly evident that a great national purifying ritual is just about exactly what we need. We are, after all, almost at that point. The Great Bleakness is nearing its end and you can veritably feel the swarm of uptight BushCo demons and malicious energies swirling around the country like happy karmic leeches, like a giant intellectual rash, like black raindrops of dank sweat from Karl Rove's evil mealy thighs.

To make matters worse, these dark energies, these base spirits were actually *invited* here by the Powers That Be, by those quivering, shivering, terrified armies of evangelical right-wing neocon bonk jobs and attorneys general and sour Supreme Court justices and scowling defense secretaries lo these past half-dozen years, and this means they shall not leave easily.

We must, therefore, do like the Mayans do. We must follow their divine and entirely appropriate example, set just recently.

Apparently, George W. Bush — famed warmonger, despoiler of lands, despiser of gays and women and science and earthly resource, hapless fascist-wannabe — it seems George just visited Guatemala, where he happily trod upon a holy Mayan site or two and shook hands with wary diplomats and blinked a lot and mispronounced a hundred different names. You know, same old, same old.

But then something interesting happened. Seems Bush left behind huge, steaming piles of banality wherever he went, and therefore the first thing

Guatemala's holy guardians of the sacred did as soon as Air Force One's wheels lifted off the ground was, of course, to purify the hallowed ground[1] our president's shockingly low energy had infected.

It's true. Those Mayan priests rushed in right after George left and cleansed the sacred archeological site upon which Dubya had trod, shooed away the hordes of bleak spirits that trail behind America's Great Embarrassment like a sickly fog of ignorance and misprision and shockingly humiliating grammar.

Yes, we need a grand American ritual. We are, after all, far more deeply infected than that Mayan site. Does it not seem entirely appropriate? Does it not make perfect sense? Of course it does.

We could try water. Sacred baths[2]. Not-so-sacred baths. Any sort of bath, shower, divine scrub-down involving divine intent and maybe some candles and a little dish of salt and the prayer-full idea that you are sloughing off skanky Bush demons and old skin and past loves and idiotic politicians.

Can we bathe each other? We do, after all, have a lot of water laying around. Bottles and bottles of it stacked to the rooftops of the nation's Costcos and Wal-Warts like wet plastic kindling. Would this be sanitary?

Do we have proper drainage? Enough soap? Ah, logistics.

Ah, but wait. There is another fabulous possibility. There is, of course, fire. I *love* fire. Fire is God's own enema. Fire is the devil's dental floss. It is beautiful and powerful and dangerous and obvious and fun. As purgatives go, it can't be beat. Ritualistically, you can burn it all: incense, candles, locks of hair, photographs, bedsheets, foreign policy documents, Dick Cheney's black charcoal heart. Fire is good. Fire kicks serious spiritual butt.

Sure, it won't be easy. We will have to get around the law. Skirt the federal fire marshal's implied edict that we cannot really have, say, a National Day of Fire, a grand torching of the toxic memory that is eight miserable years of the Bush administration.

No matter. It's still worth a try. It is, in fact, mandatory. And this being America, we can just keep it simple. Obvious. Keep the metaphor so clear that even celebrities and teenagers and recovering born-again Christians will understand.

Here is what we can do: We shall burn a bush. Ten thousand bushes. Maybe a million. Bushes laced with sage, lavender, pine, incense, with

eight years of warmongering and intolerance and those beady squinty vacant eyes. We shall gather in parks or street corners or fire pits at the beach sometime next year, and ignite.

We will burn bush. We will burn away Bush. We shall purify and rinse and cleanse the nation of this horrific and banal poison, once and for all, and it shall be Good. And those Mayan priests? Why, they'll simply look over and nod, smile knowingly. They understand completely.

1 http://ceesie.notlong.com
2 http://aeboga.notlong.com

One of my few specifically recurring subjects. I've written about Burning Man at least a dozen times throughout my career, from my very first gee-whiz oh-my-fucking-God experience back in '01, right up until the '09 festival that inspired the column you're about to read, trying every time to bring a fresh tang to my descriptions of the indescribable. I even live-blogged from the playa itself back in '05, on 'official' assignment for SFGate, trying to whip up a daily glimpse and glimmer. What a ride it's been.

I consider it high praise indeed that many Burners have told me they love my descriptions most of all, feel I capture it better than just about anyone. Some have said they even read my pieces aloud to each other on the long, dusty drive to the playa. Eat that, Thomas Friedman.

If you think about it, there really aren't all that many truly unforgettable experiences in your life, those deeply hued events and wild spiritual mind-fucks that maintain their hot lucidity, their unique flavor no matter how many layers of life accumulate, no matter how much time passes. Not so with Burning Man. If you're open to it, BM tattoos itself onto your very soul, the minute you step foot on the playa. Attend just once, and you'll have dreams about it for the rest of your life. —mm

The life lessons of Burning Man

08/28/09

As I've been lured back to the sweltering, dusty sexed-up madness that is Burning Man again this year — my sixth time — by a gaggle of delicious friends, I am hereby reminded of a few hundred truths, half-truths, outright lies and astonishing epiphanies offered up by the world-famous, Christian-feared, beautifully debauched, sensory overloaded, impossible-to-describe art-survivalist-camping-rave megaspectacle now underway in the remote Nevada desert.

If you've ever wondered at the appeal, the urge, the drive to attend such a thing, if you've heard wisps of the mythology and the mystery and the epic weirdness or even seen a few pictures and wondered, you know, WTF, maybe these tidbits can help.

Then again, maybe not. With something like Burning Man, there really is only one way to know for sure.

You are not who you thought you were
Countless are the tales and numerous are the personal friends who were once to be found hovering near the far end of the overly anxious, tightly wound, frenetic Type-A personality scale, who attended BM for the first

time and wandered out on the playa at sundown and just so happened to stumble upon, say, Serpent Mother, or the giant goddesses, or one of David Best's breathtaking temples or any of a thousand other unearthly spectacles and suddenly felt their skull crack open and their eyes spin around in their sockets and their brain fold back in on itself.

Right there and forevermore, their worldview shifted. Their id swallowed its own tongue. Possibility opened its legs wide and went, *ahhh*. In short, they lightened the hell up. It's rather astonishing how often this happens, and not just to the uptight and the pushy. This is one of the most powerful aspects of the event: It almost matters not from which angle you approach it — Burning Man is an equal opportunity soul exploder.

You are not alone

In your wild dissatisfaction with how things are. In your frustration with socially and politically imposed limitations. In your conviction that there simply *must* be more to this terrestrial experience than work and traffic and hostility, grind and paunch and slump. In your need to fly your freak flag high, cut more loose than you thought possible, test your limits. In your admiration for boy shorts and leather vests and body paint and oral sex in public places.

In short, BM reminds you that you are far from alone in your understanding that this is one hugely painful, incredibly difficult, unbearably gorgeous, terrifying, excruciatingly short life experience, and sometimes the best you can hope for is to dress in fake fur and mount the dragon and scream from atop the roof of a dusty RV of your ravenous desire to lick the moon.

You really might die at any moment

You could be crushed under the wheels of a massive rolling pirate ship. You could be impaled on the three-foot metal eyelash of a giant roving eyeball. You could be hit in the chest by a megabolt of man-made lighting shooting off a live Tesla coil. Anything can happen, really. And it usually does.

Yes, I know, you are reminded of your mortality every day living in the cruel, cruel city, the angry buses and lurching taxis and potential H1N1 outbreaks, not to mention the armed Republican psychozealots. But of course, we forget. We get a little

numb. BM gives it to you raw and hot and dirty and says, you are not long for this world, you messy little speck of spiritual space-dust. What do you want to do about it?

No one really understands copious genital piercings

There's always one, that amazing dude you always see at Burning Man wandering around Center Camp in nothing but a camelback, a camouflage cowboy hat and countless indecipherable tattoos, completely naked and fully resplendent in his stack of bolts running up the penile shaft and a giant Prince Albert through the frenulum and a ladder of rods all the way up underneath, more metal than penis and more magnetically baffling

than aesthetically alluring.

No matter how much weirdness you encounter out there, no matter how exhausted your eye becomes from the nonstop visual orgasmica, you cannot help but glance down and go, oh my God, that right there is some deep psychosexual *concern*, my friend, some painful and fascinating need for self-mutilation and in a weird sort of way I am uniquely privileged to be here right now, standing next to such a wonder as I order a dusty iced coffee just after dancing at sunrise to Bassnectar but just before heading over to Porn & Eggs camp where they serve up copious offerings of both for my morning ablution. This is all I'm saying.

You have not really seen everything

Oh how you love to be all jaded and bleak-minded and wary. Oh how you love to think you're all been-there-done-that super-cool hypercynical because you make your own nose rings and smoke five pounds of ganja a day and once had sex with Bon Iver's cousin.

Whatever. Even the most slow-blinking, trendier-than-thou uber-hipster will eventually be confronted by something at this event that will shake her to her core and slap her asunder and make her maybe, hopefully see something new, reminded of the mad, impossible, neverending flux of memory and experience, even if it is merely how utterly inane her uber-hipster facade really is. This is a good thing.

Man, this is the way life should always be

It's sort of amazing out there. There is a refreshing lack of general whiny

uptightedness. There is almost no fear of sex or inebriant or personal expression (to a fault), no brittle dogma, no two-faced political scandal, no shrill Republican screeching. There is no money changing hands, no economy per se, almost everything is free, including and especially the art, which is everywhere, and copious, and very much like nothing you will see anywhere else on the planet.

To millions, this is a vision of living hell. To millions of others, it is pure heaven, as all those insipid sociocultural masks and veils drop away and all the boundaries blur and genders intermingle and meanings shift and dance and pass out from the heat. You come away saying damn, why can't life be like this all the time?

Oh wait, no it shouldn't

Get real. Burning Man is a completely outrageous, multimillion dollar, for-profit, impossibly unsustainable theatrical megaproduction. This is, in part, why we love it. Tickets are $300 and it costs many hundreds if not thousands more in gear, supplies, transport to attend, and while you can get there and do it on a grimy hippie sort of budget if you leech on your friends just right, it's basically a very expensive, meta-bohemian, chemically enhanced anti-vacation. It's all a grand and ridiculous and temporary illusion, not at all meant to be transposed on a livable sphere.

Or is it? You may not be able to take the pseudo-economy and the neo-pagan society back with you, but what you can transpose, of course, is the sense of awe. The fearlessness. The creative wonder. You can bring back confidence. Abandon. Fierce joy. Really, what more could you ask for?

Would you be surprised to learn that very few of my columns have ever been officially spiked — that is, rejected by the paper and SFGate — due to issues of taste or appropriateness or good, old-fashioned offensivatabilityitude? Here's one of them. Save for a single live reading, this column has never enjoyed the company of human attention. Until now.

At the time way back in '05, I remember thinking: Of all the twisted material I write, why the hell did they kill this sweet 'n' sticky little piece? I was convinced it was relatively innocuous, despite the simply ridiculous amount of flagrant innuendo. In hindsight, I can see why the language herein might be considered a bit... juicy, at least for the print paper, given their general nervousness about nearly anything sexual or suggestive. But SFGate? The heart of my fierce 'n' fearless audience? I have to ride the edge pretty hard to get spiked by the website, too. So you know it must be good. —mm

A question of dripping women

10/07/2005

I can't help but imagine them out there, these dripping women, wandering around the city streets, knocking on doors, checking behind the Dumpsters, wailing like Coleridge's demon lover as they raise the lids on garbage cans and peer inside and slam them back down and sigh heavily, drippingly, soaking their garments as they seek my whereabouts. It is tragic and unfortunate. But what can I do?

"Dripping women are looking for you." I am not, as they say, making this up. This is what the first e-mail message said, one of three urgent missives sent to my flattered in-box in just one day last week, alerting me to something happening all around me but about which I have, apparently, been utterly oblivious.

(By the way, some people may call these messages "spam." They are not. They are clearly memos from the divine, personal Post-It notes from the gods. I know this to be true. How? Read on.)

There appears to be some sort of urgency attached to this first message, some sort of hygiene issue at stake, a feminine leakage problem that sounds joyful and tempting but could very well mean something is deeply amiss and requiring of medical attention. I simply do not know.

The body of the e-mail message itself gives no clues, as it is merely a page of randomly generated, semiliterate gibberish containing a link to some sort of hard-core pornographic images. I studied the images closely, of course, for clues. I zoomed in. I lingered. I saw no dripping per se. And while the women were, indeed, staring straight into the camera, it did not appear, given their various positions and facial expressions, that they were actually "looking for me" as such. But I could be wrong.

Before I could find out more, another missive, a mere hour later, struck my in-box like a jolt of cosmic love. This one was more direct, didactic and, as such, baffling.

"Tasteful women love sperm!" it proclaimed. I was stunned. Were the two messages connected? Were they sent from the same divine source? It would appear so.

At first, I was unsure what to make of this second message. It was, clearly, an answer. A solution. To a query. Had I been secretly wondering about

tasteful women's desires for male seminal fluids? Had the question been pressing upon my mind for days, years? Maybe it had. Maybe I have, in fact, been secretly curious as to what tasteful women truly adore.

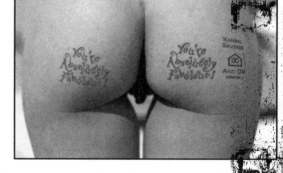

I already knew a few things they did *not* love: power tools, fishing equipment, high-waisted jeans, carburetors — but this information was of little help.

Clearly, the scribe of these messages knows things I do not. Could this message be from the gods? A cosmic wink? What, in fact, are they trying to tell me? Then it struck me: When you receive an answer to a question you didn't even know you were asking, that's the voice of God, baby. And She was right there, in my in-box, loud and clear! Who knew?

What's more, this second message, it would seem to run counter to what many of us have been taught via countless hours of hard-core pornography: that it seems to be the, shall we say, *less* tasteful women who enjoy male sexual fluids most enthusiastically.

Let me just add right here: I am terribly glad to have been proven wrong. Of course, I secretly suspected this was true all along. I have known many fine and beautiful and tasteful women and, in many cases, their predilections would shock even the most jaded porn director. And now my e-mail has confirmed my suspicions. "Spam" may do many things, but it does not lie.

And then, the kicker. The finale. Not two hours later, the final email missive of the day, the trifecta of deep, cosmic wisdom to strike my in-box. This is what it said:

"I like it when they know how to handle their pink."

To which I could only reply: "Oh my God, *yes*. That is *so true*. Pink is indeed a fine thing to handle. After all, if you can't handle the pink, it will most certainly handle you. Praise Jesus."

Now I knew. This was the same warm, omniscient, ever-present voice that had been instructing me so calmly, so gently in the previous two messages, now taking on presence, weight ... and first-person definition! She had taken on the "I"! She was making herself known to me!

I had no doubt: It was a visitation! I'd read about these episodes from the great mystics and gurus. Was it a fairy? A watchful intercosmic guide? A visitor from past life? Jesus? Kali? I was getting closer. Or rather, *she* was coming closer. Was I ready for the transformation? Was I prepared for the Great Epiphany? This seemed to be the greater question. Perhaps all these years of yoga and meditation and laughter and giddy run-on sentences and porn and single-malt scotch had finally paid off? What other explanation could there be?

Is this not amazing news? Does anyone else know this? I am alarmed and flattered and shall henceforth be much more aware of tasteful pink women who drip, because, well, it just seems like the considerate thing to do. The gods have made themselves known by way of tasteful, dripping women who know how to handle their pink. And they are looking for me.

And now, praise Shakti, I am found.

Many readers actually thought this was a terrific idea, that I really should start a private, semi-legit service using my readership as the primary dating pool, employing some sort of wildly kinkysmart criteria for joining. So enthusiastic was the nice feedback that I actually pondered the real-world logistics of it — as I'm wont to do with such hint-of-a-good-idea columns — before quickly realizing, as usual, that I have no idea what the hell I'm doing.

I do miss the original Nerve Personals. They were, at the time and in a way, groundbreaking, slightly racy, titillating fun to skim through, even if there seemed to be a hugely disproportionate number of mid-30s women named Jenny whose five items she couldn't live without always seemed to include some combination of travel, sunshine, cell phone, tea, fluffy pillows, best friends and cats. Dear Jesus God, always with the cats.

P.S.; The "female friend" in the second sentence? My sister. Shhh. —mm

Please try my dating service

6/30/2006

Match.com does not allow cleavage.

This much I learned from a female friend who used the vast online dating service during a brief glitch in her dating career, and for whom I helped prepare the most modest of pix (waist up, cowboy hat, big smile, snug halter top, faintest sliver of shadow between breasts), only to have the photo immediately nixed by the site's apparently Mormon editors who actively disallow even the slightest hint of flesh or pillow talk or any mention of one's personal skill at drizzling Grand Marnier over a potential lover's tailbone. This is, obviously, a major drawback.

Nerve.com's personals used to be a major player. Precedent-setting, clever questionnaire, hip crowd. You could discuss sex. You could describe salacious proclivities, drugs, the crap lying around your bedroom. There was actual heat, cleverness, personality.

In fact, Nerve Personals did so well they sold the whole thing to some massive national service not long ago and it immediately got sucked into a vortex of horrible design and mediocre verbiage and intimate connection and it instantly lost roughly 82 percent of its coolness, and now appears to be Match.com for easily drunk twentysomethings who've been to Burning Man once and read a lot of David Sedaris and really, really like cats.

So then. It has come to my attention that there is a lack. A need. Readers have alerted me to the notion that perhaps I should launch an entirely new dating service based on, well, based on who really loves reading this very column.

I know what you're thinking. What a strange and conceited idea. Also: Who reads? But then again, it is perhaps no worse or more bizarre than, say, FarmersOnly.com, "where lonely small-town heartlanders seek to breed with like-minded hornswogglers" (note: not official slogan). Nor is my idea any more ungainly than, say, ConservativeMatch.com, "where feral Ann Coulter wannabes meet desperate frat guys who hate gays and will gladly eat their own mother for a new Range Rover and a killer stock tip."

My service, it will have no such limits. It will not ban conservatives, though they will doubtlessly be repelled by all the polysyllabic words and the references to anal sex and witchcraft and trees. It will not reject farmers or small-town folk, though they might not appreciate all the amateur erotic cell-phone photography and the designer jean recommendations and the how-to-shave-your-lover diagrams.

My service — let's call it LoveDrugger.com — it will offer users ample opportunity to reveal their true personalities, mostly via absurdist haiku, Flash animation, obscure Led Zeppelin song references, Raymond Carver quotes and long discursive paragraphs with insufficient punctuation but

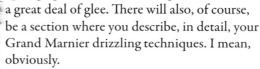

a great deal of glee. There will also, of course, be a section where you describe, in detail, your Grand Marnier drizzling techniques. I mean, obviously.

I imagine that JDate.com, the popular service for wired Jews, discourages trolling by Gentiles. I understand that, if you are a stiff Christian literalist, MuslimMatch.com is probably not for you. Plus, there's only so much you can do with all the type-specific services like, say, H-Date. com, or VeggieDate.com, or DateMyPet.com, or WesternMatch.com (for those who refuse to be seen in public without a cowboy hat and something plaid). And who can forget eHarmony.com, whose creaky ol' founder is linked to Focus on the Family and which doesn't like gay people and is designed to attract bland God-fearin' patrons who don't much care for style and who love Olive Garden and who own the complete set of "Mama's Family" on DVD.

But my service will be different. It will be for a wider, and stranger, assortment of blissed-out intellectual misfits and attuned perverts with decent taste in cookware and shoes. Certain criteria will seem completely biased and inappropriate but will, upon deeper examination, make perfect sense.

For example, I shall welcome recovering Catholics, so long as they can prove they have purchased at least $200 worth of goods at Goodvibes.com or Babeland.com in the past six months. Vegetarians will be encouraged to join, so long as they can prove their love of their leather iPod case and know which kind of chocolate best melts between one's toes. You get the idea.

It will be for all races, hair types, eye colors. Body types will be implied in descriptions of how much sake is required to get you drunk and naked and bent over the coffee table on a Tuesday night. And no, there will be no age requirement, because if you're under 18 and still get all the references to global warming and organic foods and deep astrology, well, you're already smarter than just about every born-again Christian, and the dating pool needs more people like you.

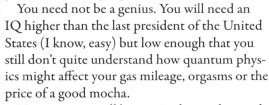

You need not be a genius. You will need an IQ higher than the last president of the United States (I know, easy) but low enough that you still don't quite understand how quantum physics might affect your gas mileage, orgasms or the price of a good mocha.

However, you will be required to understand satire, metaphor, a good pun. Nimbleness of mind will be essential. For example, if you stopped reading this column after the fourth paragraph so you could write me a snappish note about how much you love cats and wish I would stop making jokes about them, because they are so unbearably cute and we are killing a million of them every day in horrible shelters, I can assure you, you will not enjoy using my dating service.

In fact, many of the pages on my site will be quietly programmed to pick up any negative electromagnetic vibrations (trust me, I can do it — I know some guys at MIT) coming from either your lower cerebral cortex or your upper inner thighs and will instantly reroute you to a page about virgin dating in Utah.[1]

But here's the best part of all: I will not charge for my service. I will accept no money. To join, you will merely be required to thrust out an act of random juicy kindness to the world, including (but not limited to) buying a Hitachi Magic Wand for five random women in your life, donating a decent hunk of change to local Planned Parenthood, memorizing the prelude to Tom Robbins' "Skinny Legs and All," spending 10 hours researching the Islay single malts of Scotland or blasting old AC/DC in the car at top volume with the sunroof open and singing along as you drive by a church.

Do you think it will work? Will you join? If you answered, "No way, I barely made it this far and knock it off already with the cat bashing and that thing you said about Mormons," well, I know some lonely farmers who are waiting to hear from you. Also, watch out for that nasty cleavage.

If you answered, "Oh my yes this is the service for me," then please enact your appropriate public service and send me a receipt (or a photograph, the condom wrapper, the painted bra, the empty Grand Marnier bottle, etc.), and I'll get the thing started ASAP. After all, isn't love worth it?

1 http://xeemee.notlong.com

And now, The Daring Spectacle presents...

Mullet Haiku

Thursday night, ninth grade
Huffing some rubber cement
Dude, Winger kicks ass

If you're as morbidly fascinated by the idea presented in this column as I am and would like to suck down in a far deeper, richer, and more engrossing exploration, hesitate not to get yourself a copy of Alan Weisman's "The World Without Us" (Picador, 2007). In turns disturbing and (tentatively) hopeful, intriguing and mesmerizing. Don't forget the rum. You'll need it. —mm

If we all vanished tomorrow

10/20/2006

Of course you already know. Of course you can merely look out the window and see the traffic and the plastic and the smog and the bad haircuts and the war and the Mylie Cyrus and the fear and say, well *duh*.

But imagine the result anyway. Imagine for a moment that every human on the face of the planet was suddenly whisked away to the divine gurgling ether in one big blast of cheery Armageddon nothingness, all the Bible-waving True Believers carted off to a giant sex-free harp-filled cosmic Wal-Mart while the rest of us leap to the next luminous transformational echelon of timespacelove.

What would happen, really? How would the planet respond if all bipeds disappeared tomorrow?

You can probably guess part of it, anyway. Almost immediately, the planet would shudder, shift, align itself anew. Immediately, all endangered species would begin to recover. Light pollution[1] would soon vanish, followed by a great reduction in air pollution, methane gasses, chemicals in fresh water. Soon, all bridges and dams would collapse, roads would become overgrown, buildings would decay, corals would regenerate, most organic landfill would decay and vanish. And that's just the beginning.

In other words, as the fascinating/depressing cover story[2] in New Scientist points out (along with a nifty graphic[3] from the Times U.K.), the Earth would quickly begin to recover mightily from the deep disease that is human existence. What's more, the planet would, by every estimate, quickly become a whole lot healthier, more balanced, back in harmony with itself.

Translation: We have wreaked just a horrific amount of damage and done just about exactly zero cumulative good for the place while we've been here. It is, obviously, not the most heartwarming thing to accept.

Perhaps the good news is, with the exception of some nuclear remains, were our species to vanish entirely, most traces of man's existence would wink out within about 50,000 years, and almost all traces within 200,000. Not bad at all, considering the extent of our damage. Pretty much a blip

Mark Morford

on the geologic timescale, really. Don't you feel better?

Humans are the single most dominant and destructive species in planetary history. But sentient man has only been around for what, a million years? The Earth has been here for roughly 4.5 *billion*. No matter how you slice it, the Earth still sees us as just another fly in its bedroom. A particularly obnoxious one, no doubt, but still a fly. Isn't that reassuring?

There are two ways to react to such a viewpoint: One is to say, "Oh my God what the hell is wrong with us and just look at how much damage we've wrought and the pain we've inflicted, look how much better off the place is when we're out of the picture and what can we do to make less of a violent impact and improve our karmic outlook while we're here because this can *not* be good."

Option 2 is to ask: "Who the hell cares? If all our remains vanish in a couple of hundred thousand years, does it really matter how much damage we inflict?" After all, there's no way to say whether or not the planet really gives a damn one way or the other about our species, given how our entire existence has taken up but a flutter of an eyeblink of time anyway. Hell, we could nuke the whole place tomorrow and the planet would merely shudder and shrug and pause for a few million years and start all over. Right?

How do we really measure our impact? The glaring capitalist mindset sees this planet as merely one giant oil well to be sucked dry. Millions of humans, if they think of it at all, merely view the Earth as an enormous sandbox, a mute playground to be trammeled and paved over and drilled into and burned through and sliced up like so much ecological pie until it's all gone and we're forced back into the caves to beat each other with clubs over the last scraps of beef jerky and nuclear Twinkies. I mean, so what?

I know people who never exercise. I know plenty of people who still smoke and drink a ton of beer and get stoned every day and eat gallons of processed foods and watch TV like it was pixilated cake, and the last time they truly got their hearts pumping was when they had to walk five blocks from their house to the taco hut because their car broke down.

They just laugh. What's the point of eating right and exercising? they say. Why the hell spend all that money on yoga and gyms and vitamins and try to take excessive care of the body when we're all just gonna break down and die anyway? What's the point? Just to live a little longer? Who wants to live to 90 anyway? Why not enjoy life's vices now and let the body wallow and slump? This is what they say.

It is the cutest viewpoint, like, ever. The initial reply is almost too obvious to explain: The point of a healthy lifestyle is not to live longer. It is to live *better*, right now, in the moment, to breathe deeper and dream more lucidly and step lighter and orgasm stronger and be able to touch your toes and touch your lover's toes and try, just try, to evolve, just a little, while we're here, in fits and spurts and via healthy snifters of Oban 14 and lots of tongue kissing in the street.

It's about paying attention. It's about tuning in. It's about respecting the physical so as to connect more profoundly with the spiritual so as to try and hone the interdimensional so as to prepare, somehow, for some sort of massive cosmological transformative goobleslamdinglewhap. Hey, it's your choice.

Maybe the planet is no different. Maybe we should take care of it because it makes our lives better and our orgasms stronger and the trees look at us without begging for a divorce. You think?

We take care of it because it's the vessel. It's the womb. It's our collective body. It's the place that holds us and feeds us and plays with us in the park while at least some of us try to prepare to get sucked back up into the grand Mystery to see what the hell happens next.

But truly, the Earth may not really care. If we abuse her to near death, she might merely shake us off like a bad rash, a nasty head cold, a giant bipedal kidney stone. After all, despite all our bitching and stomping, we really ain't all that.

But your soul.
Your soul cares.
But you knew that
already. Right?

1 http://aitaht.notlong.com
2 http://epika.notlong.com
3 http://ikahli.notlong.com

I do not know where columnists and commentators such as myself would be without the delightful and never-ending flood of pseudo-scientific studies that pour down from our centers of academia and research like some sort of irresistible mind candy. It's particularly amusing when inelastic, cold-eyed science attempts to examine or quantify some fluid and dynamic thing that, by definition, absolutely defies calculation and quantification: love, spirituality, orgasm, the smell of a wet puppy, Ecstasy, god, wisdom, poetry, the curve of the female lower back, post-coital blueberry pancakes on a Sunday morning.

Sure, they can measure brainwaves and heart rates and which hunks of which lobe turn red and fiery and therefore they can claim we and our reactions are nothing but a mass of electromagnetic pinball machines, but we cannot and will never be able to measure that esoteric, poetic thing, that divine kicker, the je ne sais quoi *of deep existence. Which is exactly as it should be, really. –mm*

Sit down, shut up, breathe

05/21/2008

I'm not exactly clear on how they did it. Something about taking Group No. 1 and hooking them up to a nifty array of electrodes and letting them begin their deep and experienced meditation practice, and then at some point suddenly blasting the sound of a woman screaming in distress right into their prefrontal lobes like a swell little icepick of terror.

And then the researchers simply observed which parts of the meditators' brains lit up, and noted that it was the hunks related to empathy and compassion and also the parts that say, "Hey gosh, that screaming *can't* be good and I think I shall get up right now and go help that poor woman, because I am training myself to feel more compassionate and empathetic, all thanks to my deep and calming meditation practice." [1]

Then they did a similar thing with Group No. 2 — only minus most of the experienced meditation part —and when *this* group heard the same woman screaming in distress, their brains *also* lit up, only this time it was those parts that said, "Huh, chick screaming in distress, how very curious, let us now reach for the remote control and turn up the volume on this delightful episode of 'How I Met Your Mother' to drown out that obnoxious sound."

I might be oversimplifying a bit. No matter, because the fact remains

it is was one of those delightfully foregone studies that deigns to reveal a helpful factoid which millions of people and thousands of teachers and gurus and healers have known for roughly ten thousand years.

It is this: deep meditation, the regular, habitual act of stilling yourself and intentionally calming the mind, working with the breath and maybe reciting a mantra or clearing your chakras or running a nice bolt of golden energy up and down your spine, can actually have a positive effect on your worldview, can inject some divine juice into your core and make you more sympathetic, kinder, more apt to feel a natural inclination toward generosity and compassion toward people who might be, you know, screaming.

I know. Totally shocking.

It's a small study that goes handily with the umpteen similar bits of research lo these past years, all of which seem to indicate some other famously healthful aspect of meditation: stress relief, improved heart function, life extension[2], emotional stability, improved sleep, increased productivity,[3] better orgasms, fewer ingrown hairs, brighter sunshine, better gas mileage and also merely learning to sit still and shut the hell up once in awhile, which I can promise you will make your wife and your siblings and your kids and your dog and even your own manic ego very happy indeed.

Did you already know of such benefits? I'm guessing you did. Hell, here in NorCal meditation is so widespread and normalized it's actually available in the Whole Foods bulk aisle. I do believe over in Berkeley and parts of Marin County you are actually required by law to meditate at least twice a week atop your handmade zafu cushion in your Zen rock garden next to your restored BMW 2002 as you listen to wind chime music on an iPod-enabled Bang & Olufsen 5.1 home theater system just before you pour yourself a nice glass of Sonoma chard, or the police come and politely take away your nag champa incense holder for a month.

Ah, but I suppose this is not the case nationwide. I imagine the practice is still widely considered, even after all these millennia and all these studies and teachers and perky New Age bookstores and all the obvious proof

that meditating has little, really, to do with religious belief, it's still thought of as some sort of hippie pagan frou-frou thing more aligned with monks and bells and Hindu wackiness than with everyday guldang gun-smokin' life.

And hence I guess we actually still *need* studies like this to lend validation to a timeless wisdom which, if disseminated more widely, could actually improve the health of the nation. Hey, every little bit helps, right?

Enough studies and enough serious medical journals bring alternative ideas like meditation to the fore and maybe, just maybe, we could nudge the culture away from obsession and road rage and a zillion Prozac prescriptions as the only means of coping with the trudgery of daily existence. You think?

It can't hurt. Because the problem is that we as a culture are still very much trained, shaped from birth to never *really* calm down and breathe more consciously. Present-time awareness? Breathwork? Cultivating a sense of loving kindness? Save it for the New Age Expo, hippie. Real men live in some neurotic/psychotic state of need and regret and wishful thinking, all undercut with a constant shiver of never-ending dread.

But meditation, well, it abides none of that noise. It brings you into the here and now, plops you into the lap of stillness and reminds you that there is more to it all than mania and media and political moronism, and that God often speaks in whispers and flutters and quiet licks to your heart, and only when you dial down your raging internal dialogue can you actually hear what the hell She's trying to say. What's not to like?

Of course, you need no scientific study to learn any of this for yourself. But who knows, maybe there will come a day when you can stroll into just about any doctor's office and she will say, "What's that? You say you're getting weird rashes and heart palpitations and you feel overwhelmed on a daily basis? You have rage issues? Melodrama? Warmongering and pain and fear of the Other? Sure, have a glass of wine. Take a few aspirin. Eat better. Exercise. More sex, less whining, better books."

"And oh yes, also this: once a day, just for a few minutes, go sit very still, close your eyes, shut up, and breathe."

1 http://echooj.notlong.com
2 http://eigheil.notlong.com
3 http://aagaeti.notlong.com

I simply love going micro to macro, and back again. I love taking the tiny insignificant moment, the passing glimpse, the seemingly nonsacred fleeting nothing and exploding it with meaning and message and divine heat, the heartfelt suggestion that such impossibly mundane flashes might not merely contain everything we want to know about Grand Unification Theory, God, and the perfect burrito, but can inform us of all this while we're just sitting there pouring a cold dollop of grease into the evil machine of this gorgeous hellbitch we call reality. Is that overstating things a bit? Is that too much weight and meaning for this tiny column to handle? Possibly. But I don't really care. I gotta do this kind of angle more often. —mm

There I was again

5/09/09

It happened almost exactly like this:

I'm out at the agreeably grimy auto parts store picking up a few quarts of oil for the Audi and a couple of cans of Fix-a-Flat for my besieged tires, given how the City is lined like a bleak Christmas parade with nails and splinters and broken love, and of course the store smells exactly like every similar joint the world over — a deliciously acrid, metallic, petrochemical perfume emanating from 10,000 toxic substances that grease the engines of the world, but which you don't like to think too much about lest you become overly depressed.

Upstairs/upramp from the store is in this scabby, wind-blown, bare-bones parking garage covered in 20 years of residual oil and skanky rain-water and Geary street traffic grime, and there are maybe a dozen other cars of every make and degradation parked all asunder; it's the perfect place to take your recent purchases and open the hood and mess with your vehicle's innards, as you gaze around and wonder how many murders and drug deals and odd epiphanies have taken place in this magical concrete wasteland. A hundred? A thousand? Is that blood on the floor? Hmm.

I get my 5W-30, I go back upstairs, I do as the natives do; I pop my hood and check the levels and I'm pouring in a fresh quart of Satan's blood when suddenly I feel some eyes on me. I glance around and sure enough, just over there, in the far corner, I see this car.

Big, enormous. Greenish? Hard to tell. A thoroughly hideous thing by every practical measure, but also completely wonderful in its massive beat-up retro out-of-place splendor, a giant old Caddy or Olds or I don't even know what, one of those classic beaten-down V8 whales that gets 6mpg and could house a family of ten in the trunk, totally inappropriate for the

City but which nevertheless oozes character and history and simply aches to be driven off a cliff by Susan Sarandon and Geena Davis in 1992.

But that's not really the first thing I notice. The first thing I notice is the dog. Because it's standing right there, right on top of the hood of the car, staring straight at me, curious and head-cocked and sweet.

It's a boxer mix, I think, beautiful and gray, standing absolutely stock still like the world's largest hood ornament, at which point I notice there's another, nearly identical dog just inside the car, in the front seat, craning its neck out the open window and also staring at me and wagging its tail, because at the moment I'm the only human in the room and there's just not much else to look at up there in the murderous rooftop garage, really, if you're a dog.

Then, something odd happens. Something strikes me about the tiny scene, the dogs, the giant old car, the moment itself, which I find totally captivating and transportive.

In the blink of a thought, I find I'm wondering what that must be like. To have a car like that, a lifestyle like that that, two big happy dogs who clearly have the run of the wheeled whale as you steer it around all day and leave all the windows open, and when you hop out for an errand your dogs may or may not just hop out the windows and stand on the hood and wait for you, like happy slobbery sentinals, because that's just the way you roll.

It doesn't stop there. I see the owner casually stroll back to the car with his purchases, just a young dude in a hoodie and jeans who, as if from a script, opens the door and reaches in the car and turns on the 1972 radio, which starts blasting the perfect retro rock station, like Bo Diddley or Chuck Berry or ancient Stones or something far, far too suitable, as the second dog jumps out of the car and hops up on the hood to join the first, just as normal as could be, as the guy pokes around inside.

And I love it, I love it because it's so completely not me, so generally adverse to my tastes and my style and my way through the world. I am, I recognize from across the garage/universe, far from a baggy jeans massive car retro tunes kinda guy (though I'm all about the sleek gray dogs), far more prone to snug and designer and modern with a touch of dirty rock 'n' roll. I like my cars small and European and engineered like a Glock. What's more, I am far from unhappy in this. I find plenty of joy and pleasure in nearly all my choices.

And yet somehow, at least in that flipped, surreal moment, I am able recognize the Other. The scene resonates somewhere deep and pleasurable, I see how that could be me, with a rather different set of choices and a different way through the world, a parallel life, another way it all could have been because, well, why the hell not?

Aren't we all merely a collection of assorted, slapdash decisions disguised as thoughtfulness? Aren't we made up of various projections and patterns and expectations, a toss of the DNA dice onto the cosmic craps table run by drunken angels? I'm going with "yes."

The mystics, the quantum theorists posit that for every decision you make and every pathway you actively choose in this tangible funkhole of a reality, millions of unchosen options continue on anyway, veer off and unfurl in other realms, other dimensions, other versions of you.

Which means that in any given hairsbreath of timespace there are ten billion yous laughing and screwing and lurching through the multidimensions, following radically different lives and modalities and haircuts and cosmic lesson plans, each unaware of all the others but every one somehow informing the whole across the dimensions. Hey, it's a theory. Sure as hell beats harps and virgins and guilt.

But every once in awhile, when those parallel dimensions twitch and hiccup, if you listen closely and tilt your head just so, maybe you can glimpse of yourself in one of those myriad other forms. Maybe if you inhale too much motor oil and find yourself in some sort of magical concrete space, you can turn up in unexpected places, shapes, ways of doing it all.

And at those moments maybe you say, oh right. There I am again. I wonder how I'm doing? I wonder how it all feels? Shouldn't I turn up that radio?

DON'T YOU FEEL BETTER NOW?

Without doubt, one of my most beloved recurring themes. A sustained, every-day thrum of awe and wonder at the staggering, unfathomable variety of the universe? What's not to like? I mean, good lord and fucking hell, we swim in magic and poetry every moment of every day, do we not? Granted, it ain't all sweet and honey-dripped, and the magic often gets buried by layers of misery and melodrama the random miasma of the daily grind, but sometimes all you have to do is point to a furry blond lobsters of the world, and remember. Is that too utopian? Overly simplistic? Too cheesy? I don't mind. —mm

Behold, a furry blond lobster

3/17/2006

OK, look. You're up to your neck in it, right? Too much white noise, too many demands on your time, too many drains on your brainpower, too much porn and scandal and stress and tech and not in a good way because you're all up in the world and the world is all up in you and sometimes you spin and spit and whirl and just can't seem to find the ground.

I know how it is. But then, something happens. Sometimes, somehow, these little gems of yes slither on through, these little snaps to the bra strap of your id, a pinch to the ass of your jaded perspective and you blink once or twice and snap out of your lethargic frenzied turmoil, even just for a second, and your head clears and your karma tingles and you see anew.

It can happen. It's still possible. Like when you see, for the very first time in your life, for the very first time in *anyone's* life, a very weird, oddly beautiful, blond, blind, fur-covered sea creature no one's ever seen before in the history of man, so far as we know.[1]

Did you notice? Did you see the picture? It's very possible you missed it because it just was a tiny news story from a couple of weeks ago, an entirely new crustacean discovered 7,500 feet down in waters 900 miles south of Easter Island in the South Pacific, a creature so unique and unlike anything previously discovered that scientists had to create an entirely new genus for it, *Kiwa hirsuta*, named after the goddess of crustaceans in Polynesian mythology.

Big deal? Maybe not. But then again, maybe. Maybe it's something to which you should pay some divine, gleeful attention. Maybe all you have to do is look a little closer. Maybe it's absolutely mandatory that we remember how to do so. You think?

Just look.[2] *Kiwa hirsuta* is just a little bit mesmerizing, strange, stirs up something deep and potent. An eyeless, albino, crablike animal, sublime and magical and perfect in its alien weirdness, about six inches long with

forearms sticking straight out of its torso and extending twice the length of its body, with those forearms and its legs all covered in a silky blond fur, like something straight out of a medieval bestiary, a Sendak book, a Castaneda shaman's peyote dream.

It's not a lobster. It's not a crab. It's not anything anyone really understands — and why is it covered in silky blond hair? They don't know that, either. It just is. Just one of those things. Like why the whales sing. Like why some parrots can tell you who's calling before you pick up the phone. Like the existence of dark matter. We just don't know. And what's more, the sheer *volume*, the breathtaking *amount* of information we don't know is so mind-boggling and perspective-humping that you take one look at the Kiwa and only say, Hi again, wicked gorgeous unimaginable vastness of the universe.

I remember reading an essay not all that long ago about the cultural phenomenon of disappearing knowledge, about how there are only a finite number of true experts on certain very specific topics in the scientific and natural world, people who know some very deep things about some very crucial but slightly arcane or unpopular subjects, but who haven't yet had a chance to record all of what they know in books or on a Web site, and when those people die, so dies the information. Their few books go out of print. Their research fades away. There is no Wikipedia entry to archive their findings. There is no one to take up the thread. Their invaluable wisdom, essentially, vanishes.

Knowledge, we have to realize, is not fixed in stone. It is transitory and ephemeral and exists only so long as we pump it with meaning. It is merely part of the mad vaporous wheel of existence, an ongoing cycle of discovering and forgetting, of lurching forward and then stumbling back and standing up again, taking everything we think we know and packing it into a tight little snowball and hurling it at the Future in the hopes that the Future will turn around and unbutton its trench coat and show us something surprising. It's pretty much all we can do.

How many thousands of species are as yet undiscovered in the world's oceans? How many tens of thousands of undiscovered plants and animals exist in the rain forests? What about the capacities of the human mind, the mystery of the dream state or the immensity of space, the knowledge that the tiny portion of our galaxy we've been able to see and measure, our entire solar system is merely the equivalent of a grain of sand on the edge of a beach stretching for roughly one billion miles?

Are you exercising the muscle of wonder? Is this synapse firing in your head every damn day? Are you aware of how much you are not aware of and are you completely humbled and amused and made drunk by this fact? Because let me tell you, it is easy to forget.

Kiwa hirsuta is, in short, a reminder. Of how little we know. Of how much we have forgotten. Of the wonders that exist everywhere, from oak leaf to vestigial tailbone. Of how we have to remember to look around, to cultivate the skill, the ability to see, lest we slowly go blind.

Some say we have lost our power to be awed. We are too jaded, too saturated with media images and the relentless barrage of unspeakable war horrors, too soaked in the info overload of the Internet to be able to process and filter and pick out the gems and stand back and say, Oh my God, would you look at that, and what might that mean, and isn't that just the most amazing thing and doesn't it put everything in a fresh perspective, just for a minute?

I say that's utter BS. We are never too far gone. I say it is merely a switch inside, a slight shift in the perspective, a re-activation of that portion in the human soul that, when slapped awake and re-energized and detoxified, will suddenly remember how easy it is to be continuously, calmly, deliriously amazed.

1 http://oyierai.notlong.com
2 http://urugaif.notlong.com

Holy Q-Links on a purple plate (Google 'em) did this column stir up a lot of reaction, mostly flatteringly pro, but some awfully acidic con. Those with any sort of alternative spiritual training were thrilled and amazed that such a piece ran in a major newspaper, sent me heaps of gratitude and prompted all sorts of debate about just what it might mean that a human with this kind of rare spiritual vibe was in such a powerful position. Even if they disagreed that Obama was such a figure, they found the notion hugely compelling.

But oh, how this kind of talk pissed off many "serious" readers. Grim political wonks and media junkies from here to D.C. thought I had gone completely insane, done one too many hits of Ecstasy and refused to give the slightest credence to what I was suggesting. They declared that I had lost all journalistic credibility by bringing in such fluffy, hippie juju into the realm of national politics and mainstream news media. It simply isn't allowed.

It's amusing, and a little sad. So-called "mystical" spiritual ideas — most all of which are actually rooted deep in ancient religious practic, long before narrow ideas of God and mainstream Christianity peed in everyone's spiritual pool — still have a brutally negative taint, a sour association with cheesy tie-dyed crystal-waving whackjobs from Sedona, that it leaves almost zero room for serious discussion of what's really at play. In media in general and politics in particular, pedantry rules. We just don't do numinous. Shame.

As for this column, despite Obama's shortcomings, I still stand by (almost) every word. And so do my spirit guides. —mm

Is Obama an enlightened being?

06/06/2008

I find I'm having this discussion, this weird little debate, more and more, with colleagues, with readers, with liberals and moderates and miserable, deeply depressed Republicans and spiritually amped persons of all shapes and stripes and I'm having it in particular with those who seem confused, angry, unsure, thoroughly nonplussed, as they all ask me the same thing: What the hell's the big deal about Obama? I, of course, have an answer. Sort of.

Warning: If you are a rigid pragmatist/literalist, itchingly evangelical, a scowler, a doubter, a burned-out former '60s radical with no hope left, or are otherwise unable or unwilling to parse alternative New Age speak, *look away right now*, because you ain't gonna like this one little bit.

Ready? It goes likes this: Barack Obama isn't really one of us. Not in the normal way, anyway.

This is what I find myself offering up more and more in response to the whiners and the frowners and to those with broken or sadly dysfunctional karmic antennae - or no antennae at all - to all those who just don't understand and maybe even actively recoil against all this chatter about Obama's aura and feel and MLK/JFK-like vibe.

To them I say, all right, you want to know what it is? The appeal, the pull, the ethereal and magical thing that seems to enthrall millions of people from all over the world, that keeps opening up and firing into new channels of the culture normally completely unaffected by politics?

No, it's not merely his youthful vigor, or handsomeness, or even inspiring rhetoric. It is not fresh ideas or cool charisma or the fact that a black president will be historic and revolutionary in about a hundred differ- · ent ways. It is something more. Even Bill Clinton, with all his effortless, winking charm, didn't have what Obama has, which is a sort of powerful luminosity, a unique high-vibration integrity.

Dismiss it all you like, but I've heard from far too many enormously smart, wise, spiritually attuned people who've been *intuitively* blown away by Obama's presence - not speeches, not policies, but sheer *presence* - to say it's just a clever marketing ploy, a slick gambit carefully orchestrated by hotshot campaign organizers who, once Obama gets into office, will suddenly turn from perky optimists to vile soul-sucking lobbyist whores, with Obama as their suddenly evil, cackling overlord.

Here's where it gets gooey. Many spiritually advanced people I know (not coweringly religious, mind you, but deeply spiritual) identify Obama as a Lightworker, that rare kind of attuned being who has the ability to lead us not merely to new foreign policies or health care plans or whatnot, but who can actually help usher in *a new way of being on the planet*, of relating and connecting and engaging with this bizarre earthly experiment. These kinds of people actually help us *evolve*. They are philosophers and peacemakers of a very high order, and they speak not just to reason or emotion, but to the soul.

The unusual thing is, true Lightworkers almost never appear on such a brutal, spiritually demeaning stage as national politics. This is why Obama is so rare. And this why he is so often compared to Kennedy and Martin Luther King Jr., to those leaders in our culture whose stirring vibrations still resonate throughout our short history.

Are you rolling your eyes and scoffing? Fine by me. But you gotta wonder, why has, say, the JFK legacy lasted so long, is so vital to our national identity? Yes, the assassination canonized his legend. The Kennedy family is our version of royalty. But there's something more. Those attuned to energies beyond the literal meanings of things, these people say JFK wasn't assassinated for any typical reason you can name. It's because he was just this kind of high-vibration being, a peacemaker, at odds with the war machine, the CIA, the dark side (well, mostly). And it killed him.

Now, Obama. The next step. Another try. And perhaps, as Bush laid waste to the land and embarrassed the country and pummeled our national spirit into disenchanted pulp and yet ironically, in so doing has helped set the stage for an even larger and more fascinating evolutionary burp, we are finally truly ready for another Lightworker to step up.

Let me be completely clear: I'm not arguing some sort of utopian revolution, a big global group hug with Obama as some sort of happy hippie camp counselor. I'm not saying the man's going to swoop in like a superhero messiah and stop all wars and make the flowers grow and birds sing and solve world hunger and bring puppies to schoolchildren.

Please. I'm also certainly not saying he's perfect, that his presidency will be free of compromise, or slimy insiders, or great heaps of politics-as-usual. While Obama's certainly an entire universe away from George W. Bush in terms of quality, integrity, intelligence and overall inspirational energy, well, so is your dog. Hell, it isn't hard to stand far above and beyond the worst president in American history.

But there simply is no denying that extra kick. As one reader put it to me, in a way, it's not even about Obama, per se. There's a vast amount of positive energy swirling about that's been held back by the armies of BushCo darkness, and this energy has now found a conduit, a lightning rod, is now effortlessly *self-organizing* around Obama's candidacy. People and emotions and ideas of high and positive vibration are automatically drawn to him. It's exactly like how Bush was a magnet for the low vibrational energies of fear and war and oppression and aggression, but, you know, completely reversed. And different. And far, far better.

Don't buy any of it? Think that's all a bunch of tofu-sucking New Agey bullshit and Obama is really a dangerously elitist political salesman whose

inexperience will lead us further into darkness because, when you're talking national politics, nothing, really, ever changes? I understand. I get it. I often believe it myself.

Not this time.

Reverence comes in many forms. How do you approach, handle, honor the seemingly mundane stuff of your daily world? Take the book you're holding right now, this ostensibly precious collection of words and ink and wood pulp. I say: read it, lick it, thrash it, write in the margins, bend the corners, spill wine and Astroglide and coffee on it, hurl it against the wall or rub it against your thighs or let it wrestle with the rest of your life's accessories in your purse or carry-on. Then, please hand it off to the hot barista when you're done with it and say, "Here, I'd like you to have this, from me to you, see what you think, especially the one on page 158. Or maybe 296. My phone number's in the back. You look amazing in that 'Obama 2012' T-shirt, by the way. Is that a flaming heart tattoo? Might I attempt to gently suck it off your skin whilst moaning softly and quoting Rumi as we share a hot bath? Thank you."

Appreciate and imbibe my book in this way, by sheer wholehearted use, and you do it — and, by extension, me — no higher honor. Especially if you make it to the tub. —mm

Please kiss your old toaster

7/19/2006

There are these two main perspectives. I'm inclined to say there are two ways of looking at the world and that there are, therefore, two types of people in the world, but that's slightly simplistic and reductive and almost too easy.

But then again, screw it.

There are two types of people in the world. One is those who believe the world is full of man-made crap that merely gets us through, gizmos and devices and machinery that merely serve as dumb objects of utility and therefore contain and are infused with nothing — no soul, no emotion, no divine heat, no life — and to believe otherwise is to believe in fairies and unicorns and pansy New Age pixie dust.

The other kind is those who believe, well, otherwise, that the world is indeed a teeming wonderland of dense mystical energy, all bound up in everything from KitchenAid blenders to cell phones to hot-pink socks to screaming orgasms, and all made up of so many layers of unspeakable magic it would take the love child of Jesus and Buddha and Astarte a very long weekend and a small mountain of hallucinogenic mushrooms to unpack it all.

Of this wicked ideological split, I have evidence. I received a great pile of wondrously odd e-mail in response to my warped, hypersexualized Windows vs. Mac phantasmagoria column[1], e-mail that ran the gamut from delicious to hilarious to furious. I know, what else is new.

What stuck with me, however, is not the delightfully rabid geekdom of some readers, not the passion for various OS methodologies, not the seething hate mail of übergeeks who hate Macs and who are so in love with their knowledge of Linux that they will bludgeon you over the head with it like it was the boxed set of "Stargate" on DVD.

No, what was most striking was how many people view something as prevalent, as ubiquitous, as ingrained in our lives as the computer as merely a lifeless tool, a necessary evil, a mere dumb box that holds no meaning, no cosmic power, no pulse.

What's more, it was made clear that this perspective infects just about every aspect and object in life, from dishwasher to automobile to home, from designer shirt to dinner plate to lamppost. Which, to me, reeks of a sort of deep sadness, a sort of spiritual decay, a savage limitation of perception.

It is also, I realize, the way of the world. This is the thinking that feeds our disposable-everything mind-set. When we attach to nothing and feel no reverence for the divine in the commonplace, well, we are left with nothing but cynicism and flatness and an overarching sense that the world is made up of so much garbage. Which, not coincidentally, it very much increasingly is.

Two famous quotes spring to mind. One is by Einstein, the other is from sci-fi demigod Arthur C. Clarke.

Einstein said that there are two ways to live your life. One is as though nothing were a miracle. The other is as if everything were a miracle. Clarke said that any sufficiently advanced technology is indistinguishable from magic.

It's difficult not to feel sorry for people in Einstein's former category, those who see, feel, taste zero of the miraculous in the mundane plastic/electronic/metal gizmongery surrounding them, those who refuse to recognize that everything, from rock to spoon to wristwatch, contains vibration and movement and subatomic shimmy, and that we need not, therefore, be so brutally separate and distant from our things as the culture — and even most modern religious dogma — would have you believe.

Do not misunderstand. I do not believe all the objects in your life should be handled with dribbly quivering veneration, like little girls handling baby bunnies and cooing. I fully believe that many of the things we create are meant to be used, *well* used, loved to within an inch of their lives and then (hopefully) recycled into something new. I do not understand those who pamper certain belongings that were so clearly designed and built to be used, worn, adored, eaten, driven.

Take books. I had an astute teacher in college who taught me that, far from holy untouchable screeds, far from people who scream and wail if someone accidentally creases the page or stains the cover, most books are meant to be thrashed, beaten and eaten and soaked into your very cells. Yes write in the margins and yes use a highlighter and yes tear out favorite passages. This is, after all, their calling in life. You do a book no higher honor than taking the writer's words down so deep into your heart and soul that you devour the vehicle upon which it was delivered. Could it speak, the book would thank you. And you should thank it. After all, it lived its life purpose to the fullest.

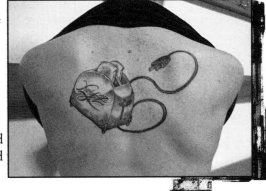

But this is my question. What would happen to you if we started to see the world this calmly reverent way? What happens when we switch over and start thinking that sacred vibration isn't reserved solely for creatures that can speak and make dinner reservations and max out their credit cards, and that it's OK to, you know, feel something for the devices that surround your life?

Here's one thing that might happen: A big chunk of our inbred cynicism will die. But what else? Will lightning strike you dead? Will your dog laugh at you? Will hippies try to recruit you into taking LSD and moving to a commune? Or will NASCAR fans from the red states scoff and sneer and call you a queer? Will your co-workers mock you as you, say, offer thanks to a beloved stapler that broke down on your desk?

What would happen if, instead of merely throwing away your old cell phone without a thought and grabbing the next one with equal rabid-consumer indifference, you actually paused, just for a moment, and considered all the emotions and energies and stupid/profound words that have poured through it, and realized these mute objects are dynamic conduits for our minds and hearts, and therefore that the phone (toaster iPod camera luggage piano wine glass house) might be deserving of some thanks, some sort of acknowledgment of shared subatomic shimmy?

It's simply a choice. A perspective shift. It is one way to move through the world that makes everything just a little more meaningful and luminous instead of leaden and dead and cold. Hell, who knows, maybe you'll feel better. Maybe you'll taste better. Or maybe it's just stupid and you're way too cool and detached and postlapsarian for all that. Hey, it's your call.

I have, on my desk right now, a Salton mug warmer. I paid, I believe, about $9.95 for it, back in 1997. It has performed perfectly, every single day, for about ten years. It has successfully kept warm an estimated 2,500 mugs of coffee. It has been through three girlfriends and five roommates and over a million words. It has never failed me, not even once.

When it finally breaks down, when the little Chinese-made heating element fries itself out and I have to toss it and get a new one, I shall probably hold it in my hands and stare at it and offer it some thanks, let those memories swim through. Maybe I'll speak to it. Give it a kiss. And then move on.

I know, it's ridiculous. I know, it's not very macho. I know, how utterly embarrassing. Whatever.

Look. What kind of energy do you want to cultivate? What kind of reverence do you want to experience? With what kind of step do you want to tread the planet? What the hell can you do every single day that makes the gods grin? Maybe, after all, these are the only real questions that matter.

1 http://opeegu.notlong.com

And now, The Daring Spectacle presents…
Mullet Haiku

Family picnic
Sloppy Joes, Jell-O salad
Oops, shot cat - BBs

I only managed to crank out two columns on Anaya the parrot before the girlfriend mentioned herein — and elsewhere in this collection — and I split up (the bird came late in our relationship). Good news is, she and I are still close and I still bird-sit on occasion and as fate would have it, as I write this very blurb, Anaya is sitting on my shoulder, a little older, a little wiser, but no less insane. Honest, she is.

The screams appear to have vanished from her repertoire. But she's still a hell of a noisemaker. Telephone rings, faucet squeaks, dog barks, assorted conversational gibberish. But I am perhaps proudest of all of teaching her to exclaim, with decent enthusiasm and proper tonal inflection, "Nice ass!" occasionally preceded by an entirely appropriate wolf-whistle. To hear such a compliment merge from the throat of a tiny, strange feathered animal is quite the touching, if slightly otherworldly, experience. Also quite the laugh line when my ex holds dinner parties.

Tragically, "What the fuck?", "Rock n' roll!" and the long, sustained yogic "OM" I've been trying to add to the bird's vocabulary have yet to stick. Who can fathom what goes on in that weird little brain? Then again, I'm quite sure she thinks the exact same thing about me. —mm

My parrot screams like a girl

3/31/2006

She used to just squeal and chirp and squeak and burp like a tiny feathered sailor. She used to just make adorable little noises like a moderately hyper-active little monkey holding a banana and looking at the sky and talking to the clouds.

But not anymore. Now, the S.O.'s African Gray parrot, 1 foot tall and two feet of wingspan and 1 solid pound of tiny-boned flesh, named Anaya and cuter than a drunk squirrel and more exasperating than a knotted shoelace and more lovingly spoiled than a blond grandchild in the Hamptons, this bird, now nearly two years old and maturing a bit and moving away from her fledgling awkward vocal confusions and into a more adult phase of confident incessant noisedom, this parrot has learned to scream. Like a girl. *Exactly* like a girl. And also chat on the phone. Sometimes at the same time.

Parrots, you should know right now, are enormously weird. Surreal. They bring with them a bizarre sense of wild and unfamiliar nature and you cannot feed them or watch them move and preen and waddle awkwardly down the hall without this sense of trippy *otherness*; you cannot hold a parrot in your hand and stroke their funky, tiny, pencil-thin neck

bones and not feel like
you are in the presence
of something just a little
out of the human range
of cosmic understanding.
Personally, I think it's
the wings that do it. Or
the black tongue inside
that shockingly powerful
beak. Or the eyes, black and sharp and eternally vigilant.

I am here to tell you, large parrots make for the most fascinating of pets,
entirely rewiring what the hell you think a barely domesticated creature
is supposed to do because they so easily flout and mock any and all of the
things a dog or cat of hamster would do — which is to say, they can talk,
they can read your meek little human mind, they will only get angry if you
get angry and will only laugh and shrug and nip at your feeble attempts
at punishment and will stare at you in utter unblinking fascination as you
have sex — because large parrots and especially large African Gray parrots
are a) preternaturally smart, b) creepily observant and c) neurotic as a Jewish comedian on meth.

Plus, of course, parrots mimic. Especially Grays. Especially well. They
are legendary for it. Did I mention they can live for 50 years? And that
this bird isn't even two? It's a long haul, baby. You'd better love the bird
thing. Otherwise, it's all "oops I 'accidentally' left the window wide open,"
you know?

In fact, the weird-crazy-beautiful parrot Anaya is sitting on my shoulder
as I write this, right now. She is making strange gurgling noises to accompany the Arctic Monkeys. Also, smooches and wolf whistles and long,
sustained raspy sounds like pineapple being dragged across a cheese grater
for 10 solid seconds. This is normal. This is to be expected. After a while
you barely notice and the S.O. and I can be watching TV or talking in the
living room and the bird will be yammering away in her own little world,
conversing with the spirits for a solid half hour and unless she chimes in
with a crystal-clear "I love you" or "Hello" or "What's up?" you just sort
of tune it out the way a parent, I imagine, tunes out the sounds of the
children imbibing lighter fluid and stabbing each other with little plastic
forks.

Unless, of course, she screams. The screaming is new. It is piercing and
startling and, well, surprisingly cute, probably because it sounds exactly
(and I do mean exactly) like my girlfriend.

See, parrots go through phases of mimicry as their tongues and brains

and observational skills develop, and this particular bird has recently
added to her astounding orchestral repertoire the *exact same* high-pitched,
ear-rattling, neighbor-alerting yelp emitted when I jump out from behind
the door to scare my girl (which I do frequently, as a way of keeping the
relationship fresh and snappy and ever on the verge of, you know, murder). It is, in a word, uncanny. Hilarious. Adorable. The screaming, I mean.
And, I suppose, the girlfriend.

She will scream without provocation (the bird, but also the girlfriend).
She will scream as part of her normal twice-daily verbal gymnastics wherein she runs through every noise she knows and rearranges them on the
fly, like her own built-in GarageBand. She will scream when you leave the
room. She will scream when you enter the room. She will scream whenever she hears a woman scream on TV, a sort of scream-á-téte. Thankfully,
she does not scream so often, or so loudly, that we have to consider duct
tape and a sedative.

But then again, screaming is not her favorite thing. Not by a long shot.
For that, we have the telephone.

Parrots, as I said, are terrifically weird. Parrots are highly unpredictable.
Parrots attach to random things and are utterly freaked out and terrified
by other random things (example: Wave a big broom in front of Anaya
and she just looks at you and rolls those tiny black eyes and yawns. But
bring a simple toothbrush within five feet of her and she will jump and
flap her wings and growl like you're a drunken Republican carrying a shotgun), and there is little explanation for it. Telephones are, for now, just her
thing.

She is amazed by them. You will be talking and laughing and muttering into the handset, and you glance over and the bird is leaning way in
and cocking her head sideways and watching every ... single ... syllable ...
as it passes your lips. She is absolutely mesmerized. She is taking it all in.
Recording. Studying. Analyzing.

Hence, she can now imitate, with freakish precision, the exact tone and
cadence of the ring of my girl's home phone. She will ring the phone two
or three times, answer it with the exact same beep as the on button, say,
"Hello, how are you?" in pitch-perfect girlfriend intonation, proceed to
have a full conversation in human-pitched bird gibberish (with all appropriate pauses and cadences), say, "OK, OK, bye-bye," and hang up with
another perfect beep. She will do this over and over again. All day long.

Parrots happily, effortlessly smack around your normal perceptions.
Parrots make you look at the world anew, every single day, perhaps more
than any other sort of pet, though I've never owned a potbellied pig or
a miniature pony or a three-toed celebrity, so I can't speak with absolute

authority. In fact, we don't even know for sure if Anaya is male or female (requires a special blood test we have yet to get around to) and so in about six years if she lays an egg, we will know for sure.

Hopefully, she will scream when it happens. And so, probably, will we. How much fun is that?

Funny story re: the column you are about to read: A full five or six months after this piece came out, a reader named Mike wrote in, doubting the factual accuracy of my tale and questioning my story's overall veracity because of what he saw as one glaring snag: Wasn't the bottle in question sealed with a traditional cork? If so, how did I get it open without a corkscrew? And how could I, being a so-called reputable journalist, fail to mention that?

Thinking his query benign, I nonchalantly replied that I didn't remember exactly, but I certainly did open it without a corkscrew, and vaguely recalled that it must've been one of those pop-top types of half corks, like sake bottles have (which I later learned are called T-corks). I made some other mild joke and left it at that.

He was having none of it. He began his assault, posting to port blogs, writing letters to the Krohn company itself, asking if they made such a cork, writing angry letters to my editor and the Chronicle's reader representative, calling me a liar and saying my entire story must be a fake and demanding an apology and full retraction. It went on for weeks. He was very serious. He was also a bit insane. He even demanded I ask my mother where she bought the bottle so he could buy it himself and prove the truth, one way or another. It was both mildly amusing, and a little disturbing.

To their credit, my editor and the Chron's rep did their best to mollify him, spending far too much time on a guy who I imagine to be deeply odd and desperately lonely, if not borderline deranged. Last we left him, he was vowing to march off and find his bottle and prove the truth once and for all (which, as you can see at the right, I've already done for him). Godspeed, crazy port man, Godspeed. —mm

How to get drunk at the airport

01/11/2008

Passing through the cute, harmless, relatively tiny Spokane airport on the way back to the goodly San Francisco bubble after spending a week and change up in the Pacific Northwest with the family for the holidays, entering the security checkpoint and of course doing my all-American duty and basically taking off all my clothes so as to help protect my country because, you know, it's Spokane. Islamo-fascist terrorists really *hate* Spokane.

Off came the jacket and the belt and the boots and the jewelry and out came the laptop and into about five plastic bins went everything, all the while figuring I'd zip right through, given how careful I'd been in my carry-on packing, nothing to raise any alarms and nothing to cause any sort of delay, no liquids and no lotions and no Astroglide travel packs and this time I even had the foresight to remove the tiny one-inch Leatherman Squirt from my keychain (my third one — I keep forgetting) because everyone knows how easy it would be to hijack a goddamn jetliner by, say, threatening to give the pilot a really awful pedicure with that tiny nail file.

Except, oh holy hell no, something's amiss, they need to inspect my bag, probably something weird showing up in the scanner with my camera gear or the various rechargeable battery packs or maybe the handmade candles I'd received as a gift or ... well, it's airport security. Who the hell knows what it could be.

And suddenly, I saw it. The port. Oh holy dammit, that's right. Last minute of my of packing, I'd switched the new, sealed 375-milliliter bottle of 16-year-old vintage port wine from my checked suitcase over to my carry-on due to concern for the former's overall weight, somehow completely blocking out the no-liquids thing and despite all my careful packing and awareness just prior. My hand went to my forehead, and slapped. Idiot.

The security guard carried the bottle over to me, shaking his head, but in a nice way. "Sorry, this can't go." No kidding. Damn. What a waste.

I pondered my options: Lots of time before my flight, but no real way to check the bottle, no way to ship it to myself, and I wasn't about to call the sister who'd dropped me at the airport and was now well on her way to Seattle and who didn't even drink alcohol to tell her to come back to pick up a small bottle of really good booze, just so I didn't have to toss it.

I was ready to suggest the security guy take the port home and have a lovely new year, ready to extol the virtues of this particular not-at-all inexpensive Krohn 1991 vintage and say it wasn't no cheap swill, that he should maybe light a fire and sip it carefully after dinner and wouldn't that be nice, when he said the words I didn't expect to hear.

"You want to go have a few sips before you come back through?"

Wait, what?

I paused. This was cute little Spokane airport. There were no bars back down by the entrance, no restaurants or even little cafes (the few the airport had were all up beyond security), nothing but a sterile, bare-bones baggage claim and a handful of ticket counters back where he was gesturing and, beyond that, 19 degrees of bitter cold winter.

"But there's no bar down there," I stammered, momentarily confused and momentarily trying to be some sort of upstanding, law-abiding citizen. Or something. "You mean I can just swig an open container of booze out in the open? I don't need to be in some sort of designated bar area?"

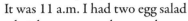

Duh.

He looked at me curiously, like I'd just returned from the jungles of Malaysia and had clearly lost all sense of how civilized society functioned. Then he shrugged, and smiled. "I don't think that matters. Up to you."

It was 11 a.m. I had two egg salad sandwiches, some spelt pretzels, a small bag of gourmet chocolate mints, a well-loaded iPod, a laptop. And an hour and a half. I didn't ponder for long. "Well hell, OK then."

I strolled back around and back down to the baggage claim area, found a seat in a quiet, empty corner, got comfortable, opened the first sandwich and peeled the foil from the port, popped the cork, and glanced around.

Horrible fluorescent lighting, random airport stragglers, assorted families picking up or dropping off, baby strollers and assorted screams and yelps and car horns and no one really caring about much of anything in the calm after the holiday storm.

I took my first big swig, and proceeded to enjoy one of the stranger, warmer, fuzzier late-morning lunches I've had in awhile.

It was pretty good port. At least, for 11 a.m. on a Saturday in an airport baggage claim. Dark, fruity, sticky and chocolatey and thick like murky dreams. After about the fifth sip, I had the profound insight that I was sharing this surreal moment with roughly one million other travelers worldwide who had equally (or rather, likely far more) obnoxious, annoying, unusual airport security tales to tell, from the profound to the silly to the stupid.

I recalled the story on the Associated Press newswires just before Christmas about the 64-year-old German genius who, furious at having his bottle of vodka yanked from his carry-on in a Nuremberg airport, decided to chug the entire bottle right there in line[1], thus guaranteeing himself a trip to the emergency room, permanent liver damage and charming international headlines.

Also, the tale I'd heard from my own mother of her friend who was returning from a vacation in Italy, a new bottle of limoncello lemon liqueur in her carry-on, and was stopped at a Milan airport checkpoint. Rather than toss the bottle, she headed for the nearest place available to enjoy a sip or two — the airport restroom.

In the restroom, she saw another woman standing over the sink, shaking, breathing heavily, trying to calm her nerves. The woman was, it turns out, terrified of flying.

Limoncello was promptly proffered, gratefully accepted. And so, for a few minutes, there they stood, chatting, laughing, drinking most of the bottle, the latter woman's nerves sufficiently marinated until she could fly and the former's sufficiently entertained so she'd have a tale to tell of the limoncello that never made it back home but that might have very well saved someone's sanity.

Wishing to remain upright and mostly coherent, I didn't finish my bottle. An elderly Spokanite sat down not far from me and I turned to him, asked if he was a fan of port wine. He looked at me oddly, said he'd

never tried it before. I explained what it was, and my situation, showed him the half bottle remaining, told him this was premium stuff and might he like to take the rest home and kick back and perhaps sip a couple glasses after dinner with the wife in front of the fire and have an even happier new year? "Well sure," he said. "I'll try some of that. What the hell. Thanks very much."

And lo, the world shrinks, the year is off to a good start, and the terrorists lose again.

1 http://tahvoh.notlong.com

Alas, I have yet to spend a summer re-reading the collected Shakespeare. I have, however, spent inordinate amounts of time with Martinis, the New York Review of Books, and fantastically inscrutable women. Truthfully, the very fact you are reading these words right now, the fact I am a columnist of any note whatsoever, is largely due to Farrel Broslawsky's unique mentorship. A chain-smoking, Sartre-quoting, lit-loving, Marxist Jew philosophy/poli-sci teacher and part-time attorney with a thing for vodka and art and younger women and the revolutionary power of words? Oh, hell yes. Every wide-eyed college kid should have such a mentor. I will love him forever. —mm

How to make yourself smarter

01/31/2007

It was somewhere between the second and third glasses of Syrah and just after finishing the thai noodles but before I reached for the vegan chocolate-covered pretzels (Rainbow Grocery, 16 bucks a pound, incredible) for dessert that I happened to glance up at the TV and felt it, a massive, dull stabbing hammerblow of pain way, way back in the subcorteal nerve, where it bends and weaves and reaches down to meet the soul.

Something snapped. Something *gave way*. I think my head actually snapped back. I blinked a few times, shook my head, looked around to check my surroundings to see if the world was still on its proper axis because it was a feeling, a rather startling sensation that I was just hit in the face with a giant mallet made of sponge cake and road tar and death. You know it too? Sure you do.

What was on TV, exactly? Doesn't matter. I think it was an interstitial ad for that channel's upcoming slate of shows, a typical snappy voice-over wrap-up of sitcoms and reality-show dribble, nothing really unusual in its tone and pitch and loud garish inanity, but somehow it sounded, if you blocked out the actual words, exactly like something that would make a small monkey hit itself in the face with a brick, intentionally.

But while the cause of my sudden pain was surely the *waves of malicious dumbness* coming straight at my head from the TV like some sort of brain tumor on rails, what happened next was broader, and deeper.

I experienced, through some deliciously odd confluence of wine and chocolate and TV inanity, one of those rare moments of perfect lucidity wherein you see exactly what sort of tepid, low-vibrational information is being fired at you from the dumb machine gun of the culture at large. It was, indeed, a peek behind the matrix.

I do not mean to say I merely noticed, for the umpteenth time, how dumb television can be. This was more like a deep slap to the id, a wake-up call from Jesus' long-lost half-brother Rod, the one who loves sex and reads poetry naked and eats meat with his fingers.

It was, of course, a cry for help. It was my brain leaping out of the fog of casual pop culture drizzle and saying, Hey, is it not time to, you know, get a little more serious? Reacquaint yourself with some hot swatches of substance? Tip the scales of intellectual lust back from blandly passive to deliciously active?

I think I might have actually said — to myself, to the room at large, to Rod — Why yes, yes it is.

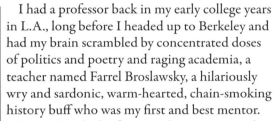

I had a professor back in my early college years in L.A., long before I headed up to Berkeley and had my brain scrambled by concentrated doses of politics and poetry and raging academia, a teacher named Farrel Broslawsky, a hilariously wry and sardonic, warm-hearted, chain-smoking history buff who was my first and best mentor.

It was Farrel who first urged me to write, who got me into philosophy and politics and who taught me of the deeper mysteries of women, who gave me much invaluable, vodka-fueled insight into art and Sartre and Marx and life and who essentially mandated that I subscribe to the New York Review of Books because it was simply essential manna for a richer intellectual life.

Farrel was one of those fantastic teachers who taught every class the same way — an extended, rambling riff on life and sex and literature and how it's all one big cosmic joke anyway. He was brilliant and funny and effortlessly ideologically subversive, and I loved him dearly.

One day before summer break I remember Farrel told me, over yet another cocktail and a Marlboro (he also taught me how to appreciate a good martini at noon on a Tuesday, God bless him), that he had chosen his summer reading. I expected the usual: some sort of smart Jewish lit (he loved Primo Levi), maybe some poetry, the latest Harper's anthology. Hell, this was the guy who assigned me "The Brothers Karamazov" as my summer reading. I knew he wasn't exactly normal.

But his choice was none of those. He said he'd decided to re-read Shakespeare. *All* of it. Every single play, including the obscure and annoying ones. It had been years since he'd read them all in one good dose, he said, and they were nothing but the purest sort of food for the soul. Besides, an average Shakespeare play only requires a few concentrated hours (or a few unconcentrated days) to get through, so the complete set could easily be imbibed over a single hot, smoggy L.A. summer.

It wasn't something you heard every day. After all, summer is about laziness, right? About vacation and mental breaks and relaxing in the smoldering sun and doing as little as possible, about exactly *not* working the brain into fits of torqued language, morality, deep philosophical contortions. In other words, who the hell reads Shakespeare over the summer? And enjoys it?

This, I realized, is exactly the perspective that's programmed into us like fluffy teddy bears of doom. This is the message from the culture at large: Do as little as possible, think even less, and if you really want deeper smarts you're probably an elitist liberal and you gotta work for it and seek it out because it's buried under countless layers of ideological effluvia and celebrity shrapnel.

Farrel's reasons for his choice were obvious, but still illuminating: He did it because he truly loved language. He did it because once you get past the idea that such a project is somehow difficult (it isn't), you see that many of the bard's plays are the best sort of melodramatic, death-crazed, sex-obsessed page-turner anyway.

And most of all, he did it because, simply put, you come out the other end of a reading experience like that as if your soul had been put through a car wash run by demented genius angels. You are revitalized, inspired, born anew. It simply doesn't get much better than that.

It was a profound lesson. In one fell swoop, that afternoon chat reversed my thinking for good. No longer was it: Why the hell would you want to spend your summer doing something like that? To: How could you *not* want to do something like that?

I do not know, exactly, how I intend to draw out this particular lesson, or the reminder of it I experienced that weird night in front of the TV. I only know that if you're not careful, such invaluable glimpses become increasingly rare, the reminders begin to dim and the mind turns to whiny paste and the heart grows cold.

I do have one idea, though. It involves a great deal of Shakespeare and the long, lucid days of this upcoming summer. And oh yes, at least one very good martini.

Talk about a gratifying response. This piece, the kind of pitch-perfect topic idea that enters my oversaturated brain far too infrequently, actually inspired a surprising number of readers to take its oblique but sincere advice and quit their cube-farm jobs, break out of various self-imposed limitations and venture forth into new personal territory. At least, that's what they told me. Maybe they were just really stoned.

As mentioned in the comment in the 'Beer & Guns' column in the first section, this one should've served as my print debut in the Chronicle. But my ego wouldn't allow it. What can you do? Still has some nice juice to it. And by the way, Case #2 I speak about herein is again about the ex, Sera Beak, whose funky spiritual guide, The Red Book, did indeed come out back in '06. She inspired me, and my column, in myriad lovely ways. So there's that. —mm

Why do you work so hard?

07/08/2005

There remains this enormous and wicked sociocultural myth. It is this: Hard work is all there is.

Work hard and the world respects you. Work hard and you can have anything you want. Work really extra super hard and do nothing else but work and ignore your family and spend 14 hours a day at the office and make 300 grand a year that you never have time to spend, sublimate your soul to the corporate machine and enjoy a profound drinking problem and sporadic impotence and a nice 8BR mini-mansion you never spend any time in, and you and your shiny BMW 740i will get into heaven.

This is the American Puritan work ethos, still alive and screaming and sucking the world dry. Work is the answer. Work is also the question. Work is the one thing really worth doing and if you're not working you're either a slacker or a leech, unless you're a victim of BushCo's budget-reamed America and you've been laid off, and therefore it's OK because that means you're out there every day pounding the pavement looking for work and honing your resume and if you're not, well, what the hell is wrong with you?

Call it "the cafe question." Any given weekday you can stroll by any given coffee shop in the city and see dozens of people milling about, casually sipping and eating and reading and it's freakin' noon on a Tuesday and you're like, wait, don't these people *work*? Don't they have *jobs*? They can't all be students and trust-fund babies and cocktail waitresses and drummers in struggling rock bands who live at home with their moms.

Of course, they're not. Not all of them, anyway. Some are creative types. Some are corporate rejects. Some are recovering cube slaves now dedicated full time to working on their paintings. Some are world travelers who left their well-paying gigs months ago to cruise around Vietnam on a motorcycle before returning to start an import-export business in rare hookahs. And we look at them and go, What is wrong with these people?

It's a bitter duality: We scowl at those who decide to chuck it all and who choose to explore something radical and new and independent, something more attuned with their passions, even as we secretly envy them and even as our inner voices scream and applaud and throw confetti.

Our culture allows almost no room for creative breaks. There is little tolerance for seeking out a different kind of "work" that doesn't somehow involve cubicles and widening butts and sour middle managers monitoring your e-mail and checking your Web site logs to see if you've wasted a precious 37 seconds of company time browsing blowfish.com or reading up on the gay marriage apocalypse.

We are at once infuriated by and enamored with the idea that some people can just up and quit their jobs or take a leave of absence or take out a loan to go back to school, how they can give up certain "mandatory" lifestyle accoutrements in order to dive back into some seemingly random creative/emotional/spiritual endeavor that has nothing to do with paying taxes or the buying of products or the boosting of the GNP. It just seems so ... un-American. But it is so, so needed.

Case in point No. 1: I have this sister. She is deep in medical school right now, studying to be a naturopathic doctor at Bastyr University just outside Seattle, the toughest school of its kind in the nation, and the most difficult to get into, especially if you've had no formal medical training beforehand, as my sister hadn't.

She got in. She bucked all expectation and thwarted the temptation to quit and take a well-paying corporate job and she endured the incredibly brutal first year and rose to the top of her class. Oh and by the way, she did it all when she was over 40. With almost no money. While going through an ugly, debt-ridden divorce.

Oh you're so lucky that you have the means to do that, we think. I'd love to do that but I can't because I have too many a) bills b) babies c) doubts, we insist. We always think such lives are for others and never for ourselves, something people with huge chunks of cash reserves or huge hunks of time or huge gobs of wildly ambitious talent can do. It is never for us.

And truly, this mind-set is the national plague, a fate worse than death.

And while it must be acknowledged that there are plenty who are in such dire financial or emotional circumstances that they simply cannot bring change, no matter how much they might wish it, you still always gotta ask: How much is legit, and how much is an excuse born of fear?

The powers that be absolutely rely on our lethargy, our rampant doubts, the attitude that says that it's just too difficult or too impracticable to break away. After all, to quit a bland but stable job, to follow your own path implies breaking the rules and asking hard questions and dissing the status quo. And they absolutely cannot have that.

Case in point No. 2: I have a young and rather brilliant S.O., a specialist in goddesses and mystics and world religions, who is right now working on a book, a raw funky spirituality "anti-guide" for younger women. She took a six-month leave of absence from a very decent, reliable, friendly administrative job so as to focus on the creation of this project.

And while she has no trust fund, she does have the "luxury" of small parental loans to help her through, though it hardly matters: Giving up her respectable gig was insanely stressful and wracked with doubt. Leave a honest job? Give up paid health care? Have no reliable source of income for months on end? Trade calm stability for risk and random chance? No way, most people say. And of course, it was the absolute best choice she could've made. Time instantly became more fluid and meaningful. Mental clutter vanished. Possibility grinned.

Case in point No. 3: Not long ago, the CEO of one of the largest and most powerful international real estate firms in the nation quit his job. Stepped down. Not, as you might imagine, for retirement and not to play more golf and not to travel the world staying only in Four Seasons suites, but to work on rebuilding his relationship with his estranged wife.

My insider source tells me it was one of the most touching, and unexpected, and incredibly rare corporate memos they had ever seen. No one — I mean *no one* in this culture is supposed to quit a job like that just for, what again? Love? Relationship? It's simply not done. But of course, it absolutely should be.

We are designed, weaned, trained from Day 1 to be productive members of society. And we are heavily guilted into believing that must involve some sort of droning repetitive pod-like dress-coded work for a larger corporate cause, a consumerist mechanism, a nice happy conglomerate.

But the truth is, God, the divine true spirit loves nothing more than to see you unhinge and take risk and invite regular, messy, dangerous upheaval. This is exactly the energy that thwarts the demons of stagnation and conservative rot and violent sanctimonious bloody Mel Gibson-y religion, one that would have all our work be aimed at continuously patching up our incessant potholes of ugly congenital guilt, as opposed to contributing to the ongoing orgiastic evolution of spirit.

It is not for everyone. It implies incredibly difficult choices and arrang-

ing your life in certain ways and giving up certain luxuries and many, many people seemed locked down and immovable and all done with exploring new options in life, far too deeply entrenched in debts and family obligations and work to ever see such unique light again. Maybe you know such people. Maybe you are such people.

But then again, maybe not. This is the other huge truism we so easily forget: There is always room. There are always choices we can begin to make, changes we can begin to invite, rules we can work to upset, angles of penetration we can try to explore. And if that's not worth trying, well, what is?

And now, The Daring Spectacle presents...

Mullet Haiku

*Kid howls, diaper's full
"Freebird" rocks the van's 8-track
Don't bogart the roach*

The ex was initially a bit embarrassed by this piece, thinking it made her look a bit too girly and somewhat ridiculous. I believe she has since come to recognize how it makes her look rather fantastic and beautiful, albeit in a deeply strange, entirely magical sort of way.

Proud and humbled to report that many readers still, to this day, identify this piece as an all-time favorite (as do I). It ranks among my all-time best. It might even be No. 1, depending on your criteria. Not sure why I don't do more pieces like this. How to crank up that particular lens? Document more delightful minutia of the daily swirl? Does it have anything to do with the fact that she was in her underwear — boy shorts in particular — and I have a savage weakness for fine, supple callipygian women in boy shorts standing across the bed from me, which paradoxically heightens all my senses and tingles my perceptions? I shall have to investigate further. —mm

All women are from Zorkon 9

5/26/2006

I am not here to exaggerate these kinds of things. I am not here to make this stuff up. Truth happens. Reality pinches, rides up, makes you start and shiver in utter amazement.

Sometimes the differences are razor sharp and dazzling. Sometimes the sexes can only look at each other across our vast chasms of insanity and mind-set and unique psycho-emotional temperament, and laugh. And then cry. And then have sex. And then carry on as if nothing fantastically bizarre is happening here.

What you are about to read is exactly as I remember it, though it is possible my memory is slightly hazy, tainted from the snifter of Havana Club and the daylong shopping and the morning sex and the earlier argument about proper cleanup of parrot poop from my fabulous couch. Plus the fact that it all took place while wearing sweatpants and bras and underwear, in various combinations, depending on who you're looking at.

Nevertheless, I stand by every word. Except for the part about the screaming. That may be slightly exaggerated. But not by much.

It took place, as most epiphanies do, in the bedroom. It was evening, one of those weird warm balmy ones that San Francisco gets about as frequently as a politician gets a conscience, with a hint of spring rain in the air and a breath of new life in the world, a time when you have the windows open just a little and the air smells like a trademark urban admixture of fresh growth and divine hope and SUV exhaust. You know the kind.

We were, as mentioned, mostly dressed. We were moving normally, put-

ting fresh sheets on the bed, chatting about something random, a friend's wedding or the nature of a
benign universe or if Mary Magdalene was bisexual
or I don't know what. It does not matter. It was
somewhere around 8 o'clock. I do not know if the
time matters. How do you mark moments of lucid
transcendence?

Suddenly, it happened. It happened so fast I can
barely piece it together. I was mid-sentence, utter-
ing something that I'm sure was terribly profound
and famously quotable, when my girl suddenly let
out this startled squeal, loud and jarring and quick,
and instantly dropped to the floor, where she began
exclaiming, over and over in a fast rapid breath, "Oh
my God it's OK, I got you, I got you, I got you I got you I got you it's OK
don't worry I got you shhh."

I had no idea what was happening. Was it a seizure? A weird epileptic
fit? A divine visitation inspired by the giant lintballs with which she was
now face to face just under my bed? I could only pause all movements, and
wait.

She stood up. She had something cupped in her hands. Aha! The
window behind her, by the side of the bed, was open less than a foot. She
spun around and made the universal gesture of tossing-an-insect-out-the-
window, all while still muttering, "It's OK there you go now you're OK,"
in a fast, soothing voice. She then quickly closed the window so whatever
it was could not get back in and get stuck somewhere in the house and die
without, presumably, ever tasting freedom and fresh air and SUV exhaust
again.

Suddenly, she screamed. No time had passed. As soon as the window
slammed down, she let out a fast, panicky noise so high and so piercing my
eyeballs spun backward and my skin leaped into the next day. Her hands
flew to her face and she looked horribly stricken, as if she had just seen
Bambi murdered with a chain saw, as if she had just discovered she had
three arms and one of them was making scary shadow puppets on the wall.

"Oh my God did I kill it did I kill it?" she exclaimed over and over again
as she stared at the windowsill, looking for, I presume, smashed insect
parts, because maybe she had been too hasty with the window closing and
had accidentally crushed the thing before it had properly fluttered off. But
then she peered out into the dusky light and said, "OK whew, no no, it's
OK, there he goes, it's OK."

She turned back around. She didn't even look up. She resumed smoothing the sheets and picked up the conversation exactly where we had left off, chatting about I have no idea what because my mind had suddenly been rendered blank, blasted clean by the bizarre and cyclonic phenomenon I had just witnessed. My mouth was still half open from the sentence I hadn't even finished from before. I hadn't moved an inch.

Let me make one thing clear. This scene, this whole manic life-and-death drama, it took place in roughly nine seconds. Maybe eight. There was no break, no pause between normal conversation and gasp and lunge and sigh and scream, no shift or signal of any kind. It was like a bizarre and wonderful dance, a theatrical flourish at a play in an insane asylum in a land of happy munchkins. My beautiful girl had been momentarily and completely, utterly subsumed in another world, of which I had seen many pictures and heard many amazing tales but had never actually visited.

It was all there, compressed in that nine seconds like fruit juice in a Skittles. The whole gamut of human emotion, the entire spectacle of existence: joy and discovery and hope, trauma and horror and fear of death, rebirth and continuity and merciful liberation. All directed toward and centered around ... a small gray moth.

What's more, she vocalized the entire thing, narrated the emotional ride from start to finish, and not at all for my benefit (I might as well have been in China for how aware she was of me while this took place). The full splay of female emotions were out, dancing like elves on a pin. The instruments were faintly familiar, but the music was fabulously strange.

Yes, it is a wonder humans manage to communicate at all. It is a wonder the sexes make some sort of adorably vain attempt to bridge that rainbow chasm between us just long enough to remain wildly attracted to one another and still have sex and eat together at restaurants and laugh at each other's jokes and pretend we understand what the hell is going on. We do not. This is the great cosmic joke. And the punch line is being delivered every day, in a million scenarios exactly like the one I describe above.

My girl smoothed the sheets. When I didn't move or say anything for a moment, she finally looked up, curious as to my silence, and caught my odd stare. She looked innocent as pie, like she had no idea what she'd done, no clue as to the tiny massive spectacle that had just played out. For my part, I might as well have been looking at a sexy blue-tinted 10-legged reptile alien creature from the planet Zorkon 9. The chasm was as vast and wide as my warped and baffled grin.

"What?" she said.

I read a psychology study not long ago that essentially confirms what you already know: The conservative mindset is generally far more rigid and structured in its judgments, and places a higher value on duty and social institutions — military, church, corporations, sanitariums, Wal-Mart — whereas the liberal mind tends to be more supple, more open to new ideas, places higher value on individual autonomy and moral flexibility, kinky sex and weird sushi. In sum: The two mindsets process information very differently.

Which is another way of saying: your Buddha sacrum tattoo and love of organic Chai and polyamory experimentation, combined with your certitude regarding a beautiful, cosmic electrical charge that courses the universe and connects us all and is probably tapped into most profoundly by dolphins and dogs and giant redwood trees, none of that will ever miraculously make your NRA-loving Republican father suddenly realize the sad error of his ways and stop adoring Rush Limbaugh or telling homophobic jokes at dinner. Sorry.

This one's the precursor to 'The hippies were right!', which came out a few years later, and about seven sections back, and is probably a smite less overwritten. What do you think? —mm

Hippie crap saves the world

02/28/2003

Wanna know what conservatives *really* hate?

What makes everyone from harmless GOP dittoheads to ultra-right-wing nutjobs roll their eyes and throw up their hands and scamper for their Bibles for reassurance that life is still repressed and we're still at war and the guns are safe in the closet?

Why, hippie crap, of course. New-age babble about love and peace and godless pagan prayer, organic foods and sustainable trees and chakras, divinity and luscious goddesses and soul paths and upping your personal vibration to counter all the venomous hatred slinging about the culture like some sort of conservative, fearmongering weapon of mass depression. Man, they just *hate* that.

The incessant drive to war, the blank-eyed young soldiers, the drab oil fields, the terse U.N. debates, Donald Rumsfeld's ink-black eyes, the violence and 9/11 and Osama in hiding, saber-rattling and nuclear threats and bloody bodies strewn about the filthy third-world streets — these events are considered "real," they are tangible, raw and ugly and happening right now and we've got the pictures to prove it, all over the media, grainy and grim and mean, CNN and Fox News and frowning pundits and 100-point newspaper headlines, so you know they must be true.

Then there's you, walking through your daily life right now, eating and laughing and screwing and paying rent and thinking for yourself, filtering the onslaught and trying to remain connected to something divine and universal and authentic, all while straining to put this national trend toward violence and warmongering into some sort of acceptable frame.

You are not "real" in this same way. This is the feeling. Your experience is somehow irrelevant; what you do and how you maneuver this daily treachery is an insignificant side note to the big ugly daily political machinations because hey, it's war. It's the Big Boys. Angry White Men with very serious penis issues. All that matters is the machine, and the money, and the oil, and the WMD and the drumbeat rhetoric.

Which is, of course, utter bullshit. Here is what conservatives hate most: the idea that you really can, and do, make a difference. That you, hopefully working to align yourself with something deeper and more informed and perhaps not exactly Christian, or corporate, not exactly lockstep mainstream flag-waving God-fearing asexual consumer drone, you can affect the world, directly, right now, in ways you might not even realize, in ways that make them tremble and wince, in how much you laugh and love and eat and sleep and screw and breathe and in how deeply you penetrate into the soul's raison d'etre. But you gotta work at it. And it ain't easy. See? Fluffy new-age crap. They really hate that.

Here is the great fallacy of the American ethos, the one that powers SUV purchases and spawns a billion McDonald's franchises and gun purchases and Adam Sandler movies: it is the notion that Americans exist in a freewheelin' vacuum, that our daily choices don't, in fact, affect the world, and our neighbors, and our children, and the environment and our own bodies.

It is the idea that those very choices — foods you eat, cars you drive, shows you watch, personal relations you have, waste you create, choices you make — can't, in a very real and immediate way, erode your divine links, spit on your spiritual spark, taint your mystical meat. Every single one, every single time.

In other words, in buying that gun, smacking that child, abusing that spouse, screaming at that neighbor, buying that thuggish SUV, supporting that war, wishing death upon all them damn furriners, you may think you're exercising your God-given all-'Murkin right to do/say/drive whatever the hell you want because you're an American goddammit and no one will tell you how to live so back off.

Not quite. Rather, you are also injecting a deliberate dose of bile straight into the cultural bloodstream, actually — and quite literally — lowering the general vibration of the human collective cause, casting your vote for small-mindedness and solipsism and violence. Yep, you are. And yes indeed, your vote counts.

Here is the gist: The world consists of energy, billions of swirling masses of it contained in living vessels — that's you — and aimed out to the world, often radiating at random, intermingling, interacting, often uncontrolled and unaware, an enormous dizzying complex kaleidoscopic organism of human interaction and interplay. We are abuzz. We are electric. We possess actual psychic and electromagnetic force. Duh. It's a fact.

It comes down to simple physics. Negative begets negative. Positive begets positive. War begets war, peace begets peace, Britney begets Mylie begets "Real Housewives of Atlanta" begets People magazine begets "America's Next Top Model" begets 10 million Prozac prescriptions begets a billion dumbed-down mind-sets, embittered souls. In a nutshell.

The Bush administration blindly steers the nation like a careening Hummer toward the history-mauling notion of preemptive violence, of attacking anyone who might somehow threaten the U.S. even before such a threat is tangible. He beats the war drum, staffs his administration with enough hawks to start 1,000 wars, slams the environment, cuts women's rights, etcetera and so on.

And the world begins to follow. The culture darkens, people run scared, reactionary, depressed. The negative feeds upon itself, the tide turns, you are hit more and more frequently with that overwhelming feeling that we are in dire, powder-keg times, worse than ever, emotionally raw, politically appalling, spiritually hollow. Sound familiar?

Whereas notions of peace, individual thought, reason, simple acts of attuned mindfulness, of buying products and foods that sustain the planet, of making really good messy enthusiastic generous love, of regular laughter in the face of corporate henchmen, of reading deeply and recalling wisdom people like the Dalai Lama talk about all the time — these things literally up your anima's vibration, add positive energy back in, turn the collective volume back up.

That postcoital buzz? That post-party feel-good vibe? That genuine laughter? That gratuitously kind thing you did for that stranger? That celebration of your body and your sex and love and spirit in spite of mainstream religious puling and finger wagging? That deep, meditative solitude? Bingo. That's the vibe you want. That's the vibe we all need. That's the vibration that makes all the difference.

So then. You want to really annoy the conservative warmongering powers that be? Work your ass off to pump up the vibration. It's deeply personal. It's hard work. It means re-evaluating what you do and how you do it and how you treat others, the planet, what you buy and what you eat. It means learning. And it also means loving harder, more raw and real, minimal BS, minimal waste, figuring out true messy ugly slippery gorgeous divinity for yourself, on your own terms, and then sharing it with the world.

Man, they really hate that.

And now, The Daring Spectacle presents...

Mullet Haiku

*Testing the warm milk
on her wrist, she sighs softly
But her son's 40*

*Entirely possible I overanalyzed the scenario described herein just a bit —
call it an occupational hazard — and the unfortunate neck adornment in
question was merely, say, a Rihanna song lyric, or maybe the catchphrase
from a very whiny teen vampire movie. What's more, I'm sadly aware that
impressionable girls with lots of adolescent moxie but no actual life awareness
are right now getting far, far dumber things tattooed across their bodies in
the name of soap-opera romance and malformed identity. But what sort of
column would that have made? —mm*

Hey, kids! Love will destroy you!

12/30/2009

I'm guessing 17. Maybe 16. Although I must admit I'm finding it very
hard to tell anymore because the older I get the more I notice this odd,
unstoppable inversion taking place in my wayward perceptions, rendering
my ability to accurately assess the ages of members of Generation Facebook wickedly futile.

Anyway. There they were, the pair of them, right next to me on Muni

recently, two loud, gum-snapping, shamelessly
teenaged girls, both dressed in some sort of adorable sweatshop clown chic, nearly identical in
getup except for the fantastical color schemes.

Imagine: sausage-tight velour sweatpants —
one bright orange and the other bright green —
rainbow print shirts and orange gloves and yellow
shoes and striped choppy tiger-print hair, both
basically looking like a Lite-Brite exploded all over
a box of crayons, and both girls texting like mad
and yelling across the aisle to each other in that
hypercondensed, consonant-slurred teen gibberish that makes you sigh and smile and worry just a
little about the fate of our flailing species.

But that's not what I noticed most. One of the girls, the one in the
orange pants and the short, fruit-stripe hair who was standing right in
front of me, I couldn't help but look down and realize she had something
inscribed high up on the back of her neck, just beneath the hairline.

It was a tattoo. A bad one, naturally. Crooked, wobbly, amateurish
in that way that makes me sad because I fully believe bad tattoos are a
scourge on the American animal and crappy tattoo artists should be punished and get their goddamn slacker butts to art school, and Something

Must Be Done.

Anyway. High up on the back of this girl's young, perfectly smooth neck, in large, clunky script, I saw these words:

"Love is pain."

Next to the words, a small, red cartoon heart torn in two, serrated like shark's teeth, a droplet of blood pouring out.

I blinked. Love is pain? Really? Can that possibly be true for this shiny tiny teenaged creature snapping her gum and misspelling her text messages in front of me? Such a harsh, declarative statement, such a dour and irrefutable pronouncement, made before you're even old enough to buy booze or porn or cigarettes, when you're still full of energy and potential and friendships, and you have what, about 70 more years to go before you even have a clue as to what your life was all about?

I found myself flashing back to about eight years ago, when I attended some sort of delightfully mushy, yoga-filled, trance-dancey, patchouli-'n'-Ecstasy New Year's Eve party thing, and I remember meeting a very young friend of my then-girlfriend, a sweet, dreadlocked, hippie-ish seeker dude who must've been about 22 or 23 at the time. My ex was talking him up and asking how he was doing, and he got this dramatic look on his face, scrunched and painful. "Oh, you know, just dealing with all my shit, lots of peeling away, lots of hard work to get through it all."

I remember my reaction. I remember this big internal recoil, struggling not to roll my eyes and shake my head and slap the kid awake. I mean, come *on*. You're 22. You don't *have* any shit yet. I knew he'd never even been married, no kids, divorces, mortgages, spiritual crisis, age issues, body breakdowns, addictions, health problems, asylums, dumb tattoos on the back of his neck. He was from the north shore of Chicago, fer chrissakes. Not exactly drug-addled povertyland. Hell, I was only in my early 30s, and even I knew the basic rule of life: Dude, you have to actually *live* a little first. You have to *earn* some shit before you can claim to be digging out from under it.

I don't taste quite that flavor of judgment anymore. At least, not as frequently. I've come to realize that the darkness takes many forms indeed, from abusive childhoods to karmic repayments to all sorts of trauma of varying degrees and maturity levels, and that, in many ways, your life can indeed be piled high with horror and sadness by ages far younger than 22. All paths are unique, individual, unknowable from the outside.

But can you really believe, in your core being, in your whole world, that "love is pain," before you're even old enough to buy a goddamn vibrator? Can this be your great, fist-raised statement to the world? Sure it can. It's just a bit, you know, immature. Premature. And wildly incomplete.

A dozen questions drifted through my bus-bored mind as we lurched from block to block. What does she really know about love? What happened to her? What triggered the idea for such a lousy tattoo? She seemed healthy and vital, all faculties intact, no major limbs missing. Abusive father? Alcoholic mother? Both? Slew of skuzzy deadbeat boyfriends? Beloved puppy got run over by a Buick? I wanted to lean over and ask. I wanted to know what inspired such a fatalistic worldview before she seemed old enough to even have a worldview.

I also pondered what might happen to her in the coming years to make her regret that tattoo. Maybe she'll get out of the housing projects. Maybe she'll build her own loving family. Maybe she'll meet a fantastic spouse who shows her love is many things indeed besides a source of pain, even though we still have no clue what the hell most of them are or what it all might mean, and in truth that's what makes it so goddamn tasty and slippery and addictive, how it hits us square in the divine mystery spot in our deepest core.

What I do know is, it's taken me many, many years indeed to figure out exactly what love is (God's Viagra, obvs). Pain is just one of its many dark incarnations. But pain is also a *choice*. This is something you can only realize over time, and which you can never know at age 16. You can actually choose how to use, or be used, by love's insane, impossible, narcotic energy. You can, every day and every moment and every breath, decide which of its billion catchy little slogans, if any, you wish to abide.

Love is pain? Hell, yes. But also: Love is bliss. Love is energy. Love is divine. Love is all you need. Love is perfect. Love is magic. Love is God. Love is Hell. Love is like oxygen[1]. Love is patient. Love is kind. Love is a many-splendored thing. Love will keep us together. Love is madness. Love hurts. Love bites. Love stinks. Love's a bitch. Love is a battlefield. Love is blindness.

Girl better have a long neck.

1 http://ciyooha.notlong.com

Read aloud as part of San Francisco's LitQuake '08 literary event, to fairly excellent effect. Makes a nice companion to the blond lobster that leads off this section, I think. Awe, wonder, mystery. Can you ever have enough? Wait, check that: of course you can. You can, in fact, have way too fucking much, to the point of overwhelming sighing madness. But it does sound nice to say.

It's a fitting piece to end this very book, really, given how I'm ever seeking that micro-to-macro flow, a hint of the grander mystery, a taste of what the Tantrikas call spanda, *that ever-pulsing, expanding/contracting universal consciousness that lives right there in the center of your heart — and also, sometimes, when you sing out just right, on the tip of your tongue. Can you hear it? —mm*

How to sing like a planet

04/23/2008

This is the kind of thing we forget.

This is the kind of thing that, given all our distractions, our celeb obsessions and happy drugs and bothersome trifles like family and bills and war and health care and sex and love and porn and breathing and death, tends to fly under the radar of your overspanked consciousness, only to be later rediscovered and brought forth and placed directly in front of your eyeballs, at least for a moment, so you can look, really *look*, and go, oh my God, I had no idea.

The Earth is humming. Singing. Churning out a tune without the aid of battery or string or wind-up mechanism and its song is ethereal and mystifying and very, very weird, a rather astonishing, newly discovered phenomena that's not easily analyzed, but which, if you really let it sink into your consciousness, can change the way you look at everything.

Indeed, scientists now say the planet itself is generating a constant, deep thrum of noise.[1] No mere cacophony, but actually a kind of music, huge, swirling loops of sound, a song so strange you can't really fathom it, so low it can't be heard by human ears, chthonic roars churning from the very water and wind and rock themselves, countless notes of varying vibration creating all sorts of curious tonal phrases that bounce around the mountains and spin over the oceans and penetrate the tectonic plates and gurgle in the magma and careen off the clouds and smack into trees and bounce off your ribcage and spin over the surface of the planet in strange circular loops, "like dozens of lazy hurricanes," as one writer put it.

It all makes for a very quiet, otherworldly symphony so odd and mysterious, scientists still can't figure out exactly what's causing it or why the hell it's happening. Sure, sensitive instruments are getting better at picking up what's been dubbed "Earth's hum," but no one's any closer to understanding what the hell it all might mean. Which, of course, is exactly as it should be.

Because then, well, then you get to crank up your imagination, your mystical intuition, your poetic sensibility — and if there's one thing we're lacking in modern America, it's ... well, you know.

Me, I like to think of the Earth as essentially a giant Tibetan singing bowl, flicked by the middle finger of God and set to a mesmerizing, low ring for about 10 billion years until the tone begins to fade and the vibration slows and eventually the sound completely disappears into nothingness and the birds are all, hey what the hell happened to the music? And God just shrugs and goes, well *that* was interesting.

Or maybe the planet is more like an enormous wine glass, half full of a heady potion made of horny unicorns and divine lubricant and perky sunshine, around the smooth, gleaming rim of which Dionysus himself circles his wet fingertip, generating a mellifluous tone that makes the wood nymphs dance and the satyrs orgasm and the gods hum along as they all watch 7 billion confused humans scamper about with their lattes and their war and their perpetually adorable angst, oblivious.

But most of all, I believe the Earth actually resonates, quite literally, with the Hindu belief in the divine sound of OM (or more accurately, AUM), that single, universal syllable that contains and encompasses all: birth and death, creation and destruction, being and nothingness, rock and roll, Christian and pagan, meat and vegetable, spit and swallow. You know?

But here's the best part: This massive wave of sound? The Earth's deep, mysterious OM, it's perpetual hum of song? Totally normal — that is, if by "normal" you mean "unfathomably powerful and speaking to a vast mystical timelessness we can't possibly comprehend."

Indeed, all the spheres do it, all the planets and all the quasars and stars and moons and whirlpool galaxies, all vibrating and humming like a chorus of wayward deities singing sea shanties in a black hole. It's nothing new, really: Mystics and poets and theorists have pondered the "music of the spheres" (or *musica universalis*) for eons; it is the stuff of cosmic philosophy, linking sacred geometry, mathematics, cosmology, harmonics, astrology and music into one big cosmological poetry slam.

At some point we'll probably figure it all out. Science will, with its typical charming, arrogant certainty, sift and measure and quantify this "mystical" Earthly hum, and tell us it merely comes from, say, ocean movements, or solar wind, or 10 billion trees all deciding to grow a quarter millimeter all at once. We will do as we always do: oversimplify, peer through a single lens of understanding, stick this dazzling phenomenon in a narrow category, and forget it.

How dangerously boring. I much prefer, in matters mystical and musical and deeply cosmic, to tell the logical mind to shut up and let the soul take over and say, wait wait wait, maybe most humans have this divine connection thing all wrong. Maybe God really isn't some scowling gay-hating deity raining down guilt and judgment and fear on all humankind after all.

Maybe she's actually, you know, a throb, a pulse, a *song*, deep, complex, eternal. And us, well, we're just bouncing and swaying along as best we can, trying to figure out the goddamn melody.

1 http://eeweef.notlong.com

Gratitude Gratitude Gratitude

I am ever in awe, humbled and thankful, for all the help and inspiration, support and love offered so generously by so many in my life. The following can only ever be a partial list.

To Farrel Broslawsky

Philosopher king, sly wisecracker and my first (and only) real mentor, wherever you are. For taking me under your wing so long ago, seeing a fierce gift in me I was only barely cognizant of, and for teaching me it was absolutely worth pursuing, and fuck 'em if they don't understand. In many ways, this book belongs to you.

To Janet

For your beautiful power. Your grace and strength and effortless sexy-cool ohmygodyum. For that one thing and that other thing and oh my sweet Jesus, that thing too. For all you saw in me and in us. I am grateful beyond these words. Know it and do it. Jai Devi.

To Sera

For your infinite red blessings, encouragements, inspirations. For not only recognizing an ember of hot divinity in me and my work early on, but helping me stoke it into a true and lasting fire. For Zorkon 9, Anaya, and the whales. Your gift is astounding. You are the most exquisite red wink of all.

To Amy Moon

My former editor at SFGate, who patiently hacked through a majority of these columns when they first appeared, all my verbosity and hyperbole and over-the-line-itis, and gently reeled me back into semicoherence. Thank you for all those years.

To Erica

For inconceivable amounts of forbearance and dedication. For taking it all on — twice! — with humor and grace and that knowing smile, all for the pure love of it, for wanting to see this divine beast be born almost as much as me. You knew all along.

To the early crew at SFGate

To John "Tex" Coate for your wild vision that made it all happen; George Shirk for daring to hire a deviant, sacrilegious non-journo like me in the first place, and then letting me to do my thing; Dave

Curran for scanning the *Morning Fix* all those years and keeping me (mostly) out of serious trouble. And later: To Jane Ganahl for urging Phil B to put me in the damn paper already. To David Wiegand for letting the column run relatively wild in Datebook for a few years. To the SF Chron & SFGate for your endless schizophrenia.

To all my yoga students, teachers, editors, Facebook & Twitter followers, newsletter readers, et al
I am surrounded by such light and love, laughter and talent, slipperiness and swordplay. What a gift it all is, no?

And finally, a bit closer to home:

To my beautiful sisters, Kristin and Melanie
For all your wisdom and beauty, style and grace. To K for giving me my first copy of *Jitterbug Perfume*, way back when, the book that changed everything. To M for bunnies and puppydogs and healing tinctures, oh my. Big sisters are underrated.

Lastly, but always firstly, to the world's finest parents, Don & Marilyn
For being so endlessly generous and supportive of all I am and all I do. I was deeply blessed when they handed out mothers and fathers at the soul factory in Spokane. What incredible, beautiful people you are, inspiring and heartfelt in ways you might not even know. All my humor and smarts, heart and groundedness, I owe to you. You make it look so easy. I love you hugely.

Extra credit and appreciation
Interior production of *TDS* by Erica "Boy Trouble" Cooperrider. Cover design by Scott Borchardt. Back cover photo (and the one just

to the left, and on page 3) by Wendy K. Yalom. Special thanks to Alix and Caterina for fine-toothed proofing. Printed at Bookmasters somewhere in Ohio (thanks Emily).

About those amazing photos
If you find a certain photograph in this book to be particularly striking, well-shot and/or Burning Man-liscious, it's almost surely by the amazing Patrick Roddie, who graciously allowed me to pillage his entire photo library for the betterment of this book. Please celebrate him at Webbery.com.

345

For the record, Patrick's photos appear on pages: VI, 48, 52, 57, 68, 72, 84, 90, 95, 121, 147, 148, 189, 190, 191, 211, 217, 251, 254, 280, 283, 286, 287, 289, 290, 293, 299, 336, 338, 340

Nearly all the rest of the photos in this book are from my own personal collection, shot by me or those close to me, to varying degrees of success and acumen. Sorry about the blurriness.

Contributing factors, technologies and assorted aperitifs
MacBook Pro, InDesign, Photoshop Elements, Garamond Premier Pro, Base 02, iPhone, Panasonic LX3, Canon EOS, Beatport, Boomkat, Evernote, Dropbox, Zaya, True Sake, Ardbeg 10, Peet's Garuda blend, Astroglide, Men's Cream, Diesel, Facebook, Hitachi, AT&T SMS, Janet Stone Yoga, Rainbow Grocery chocolate-covered pretzels.

Om shrim hrim shrim kamale kamalalaye praseedha praseedha shrim hrim shrim
om shri mahalakshmi devyai namaha

Om gam ganapataye namaha

Om namah Shivaya

Om shanti shanti shanti